Web Site Desi Made Easy

2nd Edition

Dennis Gaskill

Morton Publishing Company
925 W. Kenyon Avenue, Unit 12
Englewood, CO 80110
http://www.morton-pub.com

Book Team

Publisher	Doug Morton
Project Manager	Dona Mendoza
Copy Editor	Kelly Kordes Anton
Cover & Design	Bob Schram, Bookends
Composition	Ash Street Typecrafters, Inc.

Printed in the United States of America

10   9   8   7   6   5   4   3   2   1

ISBN: 0-89582-639-9

THIS BOOK TEACHES YOU THE BASICS of web site design. While it does assume that you've spent at least some time viewing web pages on the Internet, it assumes no other knowledge on your part. Not only will you learn to plan and create a simple web site, but you will also discover how to add many of the tricks that take a site from basic to cool. Skills and concepts you will learn include:

- Coding pages to display the information you wish to present
- Adding links and other files such as images and sounds
- Formatting text and tables, using frames, and creating forms
- Netiquette (etiquette standards on the Internet)
- Basic copyright information
- Tried-and-true design principles
- Search engine optimization
- Web site promotion
- Online resources
- Uploading web pages to a server
- Other topics that are necessary or useful to know as a webmaster (the person who creates and maintains a web site)

With its basic focus, this book does not teach graphic design, JavaScript (although some JavaScript code is included in various sections), or other complicated programming languages. These topics are better taught separately.

New to this Edition

New to this edition is a chapter on search engine optimization, a server error chart, a deprecated and forbidden HTML tag chart, and a Cascading Style Sheets chart. Cascading style sheet coding is introduced earlier in the design lessons, with older formatting codes replaced with newer and more flexible style options. With a marked improvement in browser support for cascading style sheets, the chapter on this topic has been expanded from the previous edition. Still, this edition does teach many widely used older coding methods so you'll understand them when you encounter them. Since both methods are still accepted options, you'll be able to use whichever methods you prefer.

Also new to this edition is a tutorial on installing CGI scripts and setting file permissions, writing good page copy, new code bits and pieces, plus a few nice surprises along the way. Back by popular demand is my off-the-wall sense of humor. Lucky you.

Congratulations, you're about to learn an exciting and rewarding new set of skills.

A Brief Overview of the WWW

What is the WWW, you brilliantly ask?

The World Wide Web, the web, or just www for short, is the most visually appealing part of the Internet. The Internet, as a whole, is comprised of the World Wide Web, Usenet, Email, Gopher, Archie, FTP, and many lesser-known communication and file-exchanging entities. While email is the most often used arm of the Internet, the World Wide Web is the arm of the Internet that is the most exciting and fun to explore because of its colorful graphical nature and the contributions of millions of web authors. It is also the commercial arm of the Internet where fortunes can be made . . . or lost.

Until the 1990s, Internet access was limited to the technically elite, and it was extremely difficult to access information located on other computers connected to the Internet. In 1990, Tim Berners-Lee, a physicist, invented a way to interconnect information between computers using a programming language called HyperText Markup Language (HTML). These interconnected documents became known as the World Wide Web—or more simply, the web.

As recently as 1993, only about 100 computers were able to serve web pages. By then, browsers were available to retrieve and view the information stored on other computers. This was a marked improvement over the old information retrieval process, but it was still all text-based information. Along came Marc Andreessen, the inventor of Netscape. Netscape was the first browser to be able to view graphic images along with the text on a web page.

With easy to access information and colorful graphics, the web exploded in usage and popularity. Now, HTML designed web sites —full of graphics, sound, video, animations, and yes, good old plain text—are the standard. You can download whole computer applications, interact with web sites, and do hundreds of things that were not available a decade ago, including instant communications with friends and family anywhere in the world that has Internet access.

It's a brave, new world—another final frontier. It's funny how the final frontiers keep popping up.

About the Author

 Dennis Gaskill is the creator and owner of Boogie Jack's Web Depot, a popular webmaster resource site that provides professional graphics, web design tutorials, and other resources, mostly free of charge to the general public. The web site has received numerous awards and Gaskill's monthly ezine, *Almost A Newsletter,* was named one of the Top 3 on the Internet in *Writer's Digest Magazine* and the Best Ezine of the Year by ibizNewsletters, an independent newsletter review service. He also writes a weekly ezine called the *Internet Tutor*. Gaskill's ezines boast nearly 100,000 subscribers. His propensity for off-the-wall humor is a highlight for many of his readers and helps make learning fun. For more information about Gaskill's free ezines, logon to:

www.boogiejack.com

Words from the Author

Greetings! I hope you enjoy this book and find that learning to build web sites is fun and rewarding. The Internet has been very rewarding for me—not just monetarily—and it can be for you, too. Just be original, and remember that you have to give to get. You'll receive help and advice along the way, so give back when others need your help and advice. I live by this principle: the good you do comes back to you, sometimes when you least expect it, sometimes when you need it most. It's true that good deeds travel in a circle, eventually returning to you.

Dedication and Acknowledgments

The first version of this book was dedicated to my wife, Alison, to good friends Tom Dean and Shannon Taylor of www.sunset creations.com, and to various individuals who, in one way or another, helped me along the way or just make my days a little better by their presence in my life.

This, the second edition, is dedicated to all those wonderful folks who bought my first book and sent it into multiple printings. You've helped to make my family and my publisher very happy, which led directly to this updated edition.

Thank you one and all.

Note to Instructors

The Instructor's Manual, located at www.morton-pub.com, includes additional questions and answers and chapter exercises for use in the classroom. You'll also be given access to an instructors-only online bulletin board/forum where you can interact with other teachers.

Introduction

This book is written in an easy-to-follow, step-by-step progression. The first few chapters explain the basic coding that is at the heart of every web page. Each code snippet is explained and demonstrated, and often includes a graphic of how it actually looks on-screen. At times, I needed to jump ahead with an example to prepare you for the actual step. But don't worry, everything will be explained in due time. You will see that what seems perfect nonsense at first will soon make perfect sense.

The purpose of this book is to teach you the nuts and bolts of building your own web site. There is software that can assist you in web site creation, but it's wise to learn basic web page coding before using helper software. That way, when things go wrong, you'll be able to troubleshoot and solve the problem because you'll understand the code instead of just understanding how to use software.

Your first action is to decide on a practice topic. You will then combine the skills learned in the coming chapters with your subject matter and creativity to build a basic web site. Once you learn the basics, creating ever better web sites is largely a matter of learning a few new tricks and gaining experience.

Your site can be about anything you choose, from a personal site to a made-up business, as long as it's legal and within the bounds of good taste.

If you don't mind sharing your thoughts with others, you might make it a site of your poetry. If that's too personal, the site could be about your favorite hobby, volunteer work, gardening, or tips about anything. Your site could also be for a fictitious company with fictitious products and people behind it. Your practice site could be a dedication site to your family or a family member. You know they deserve it! It could be fan site for a television show, a band, a movie star, your favorite sport or team, or literally thousands of other things.

If I were you—and I used to be—I would choose a topic I am knowledgeable about. That way, you won't have to do a lot of extra research to complete these exercises.

Your web site needs to consist of at least five pages, more if you choose.

- The main page will describe your site's purpose and how visitors can benefit from exploring it. Plus, it should lead your visitors into your content. If you don't quickly show visitors the benefits of exploring your site, many of them won't. It's a little like training a kitten to use kitty litter— if you don't show your visitors to the nitty-gritty, they may never scratch around in your litter box. ☺

* A second page, a content page, will be about the topic you choose for your site. This is the section most people come to view, so you are encouraged to use more than one page here (one is just the minimum). If you're creating a personal poetry site, your poems would go here; if you have several poems, it could be a poetry index page with descriptions and links to separate pages, each containing a poem or three.

* For a business site, the content page might describe your products and/or services. Or, the content page might contain links to more detailed pages for each product or service. You get the idea, I'm sure.

* A third page, an "about" page, will be about the author or fictitious company that runs the web site. You might include a mission statement, qualifications, your photo or photos of the main staff with descriptions of their duties, personal or company accomplishments and accolades, etc.

* A fourth page will be used as a media kit. We'll assume your site is a flying success and people want to advertise with you. The media kit will describe how many visitors you have and include some demographics about them (we'll make these figures up) and list your advertising rates. It will also include a short and a long informational statement along with contact information for advertising buyers and media representatives.

* A fifth page, a resources page, will be a categorized page of links to other sites that complement your site's content. You might link your site to similar sites—although not to direct competitors. For example, if your site is about gardening tips, and you sell a book of tips but not actual flower seeds or bulbs, you might link to sites that do sell those products and request that those sites give you a reciprocal link. That's what you'd do in the real world of cyberspace—is that an oxymoron or what? For the exercises here, you'll just link to other sites without requesting reciprocal links. Naturally, if you include a link to my site on your links page, you'll probably receive a much higher grade! My site is at:

www.boogiejack.com.

Of course, you can expand on this sample site as much as you like. You may add as many pages and content areas as you please. What I've suggested is the bare minimum for learning to create a functional web site. Most likely, the more you put into it the more you will learn and the higher the grade you will receive.

Contents

Introduction to HTML

Chapter One

1.1 Chapter Introduction

B uilding a web page may seem difficult at first glance, but it can be easy and fun with just a basic understanding of how the HTML code works. I've broken it down into simple, progressive steps for you, so relax and enjoy a learning experience that is both fun and rewarding.

If you type exactly what you want to say and save it as a web page, the result will be single-spaced text, much like it looks if you type a letter on an old-fashioned typewriter. There would be no color, no adjustable text sizes, no images, and no links for access to other web pages. In other words, no fun!

To add the color, functionality, and layout control needed to display web pages, you need HTML. HTML is an acronym for HyperText Markup Language. How the language became so hyper is beyond me—too much caffeine maybe.

Excessive caffeine or not, web pages are made by using this coding language.

Simply put, HTML is various sets of instructions that tell a web browser how to display the information you want to present. These brief instructions are called HTML tags and are not visible on the web pages you see. The HTML tags are hidden in the source code for the page. The source code is essentially a plain text file that contains the information you want to present along with the HTML tags that control the page layout.

1.2 What is HTML?

H TML files are little more than glorified text files. If you can type, you can make a basic web page. Here is an example of an HTML tag:

```
<html>
```

Each tag consists of the containers, which are the lesser than (<) and greater than (>) arrows, and the HTML element within them.

1

Some webmasters call the HTML element an HTML command, and I tend to use both terms depending on the message I'm trying to convey. I hope you won't find that too confusing—just remember that when I refer to a command or an element, I'm basically referring to the same thing. The previous example tag is the beginning of an HTML document, otherwise known as a web page. It tells the browser it is a page written in HTML language so the browser knows how to render it.

There are two basic parts to most HTML elements. The first part turns the element on and the second part turns it off. For example, if you want to present the word "Popcorn" in bold text, you write it like this:

<b>Popcorn</b>

The first part, the <b> tag turns on the command for bold text. The second part, the </b> tag turns the command off. The command to turn off (cancel) a command is merely a repetition of the original command with a forward slash (/) in front of it. Remember, the HTML elements are instructions to the browser and are not visible to the user. Therefore, when viewed on an HTML page with a browser, the code would simply show up like this:

Popcorn

If it looks confusing, just play along. It really isn't that difficult once you become used to seeing HTML tags. These lessons will walk you through it one step at a time. When you finish the first exercise, you will have made your first web page.

1.3 Text Editor vs. HTML Editor

I choose to build web sites using a simple text editor such as Notepad (PC) or SimpleText (Mac OS) rather than an HTML editor. The wizards, one-click buttons that insert code, and other conveniences of HTML editors can make building a web page easier for beginners, but any plain text editor is all you really need.

Some HTML editors let you build a web site without ever having to look at a line of code. These WYSIWYG (what you see is what you get) editors make it so that you don't have to learn the codes at all. If you use an HTML editor, you're not really learning to build web sites—you're learning to use that particular piece of software. That's fine until you run into problems.

If you don't learn at least the fundamentals of coding, you will have a hard time trying to solve any code problems that arise. HTML editors also often add unnecessary code that slows your web site down, and they can make changes to code that you add by hand, thus breaking your hand-coded addition so it causes errors or doesn't work at all.

If you let an HTML editor do all the work for you, you're limiting what you can do to what the program can do. Plus, you will be forever tied to buying upgrades of the program to keep up with this ever-evolving medium. Been there, done that, don't recommend it.

Having said all that, some of you reading this will probably be happier using an HTML editor. The Resources page on my web site includes a list of popular HTML editors (but these are not my recommendations as I don't use them). Some are freeware and some are shareware—so shop carefully as the prices do vary greatly. Now . . . are you ready to build a web page?

1.4 Starting Notepad or SimpleText

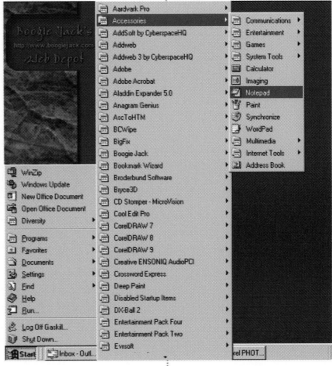

Y ou can use a different text editor if you prefer, but I will be referring to Notepad, which comes with Windows, and to SimpleText, which comes with Mac OS 9 and the Classic version of Mac OS X. One of the purposes of this book is to teach you how to build a web site inexpensively, and these text editors cost you nothing. If you have another text editor you prefer, feel free to use it as long as it lets you save the file you create in a plain text format.

To start Notepad:

1. Click the Start button.

2. Select Programs.

3. Select Accessories.

4. Click Notepad.

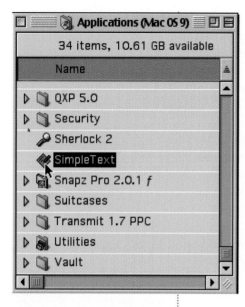

To start SimpleText:

1. From your Mac OS desktop, double-click your hard drive icon.

2. Double-click the Applications folder to open it. If you have Mac OS X, double-click the Applications (Mac OS 9) folder.

3. Double-click the SimpleText icon. In Mac OS X, you may see the message Classic Environment is Starting. If this takes a while, go get a cup of coffee—don't cancel it.

In Notepad, go to the Edit menu and make sure Word Wrap has a check by it, as shown below. If it is not checked, click the name Word Wrap to put one there. This keeps what you type from being one long line of text. You don't need to worry about this in SimpleText.

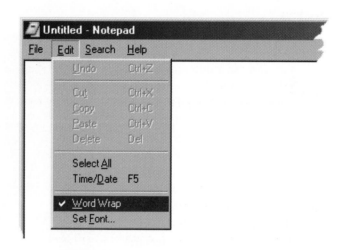

You are now ready to make a web page!

1.5 Basic Document Structure

Every web page has basic HTML elements that must be included for it to function properly. All web pages should have:

```
<html>
<head>
<title>. . . </title>
</head>
<body>
```

Your visible content goes here.

```
</body>
</head>
```

Each of these elements will be explained in the following sections.

1.6 The <html> Tag

Each web page starts with the HTML language identifier. At the top of the page in Notepad or SimpleText, type:

```
<html>
```

Remember, the left and right arrow brackets are the HTML containers, while the text in between them is the HTML element or command that conveys your instructions to the web browser. By typing the <html> command, we just turned on the HTML language. Because we have not finished our web page, we will not turn off the command until the very end of the page.

To keep web pages easy to edit in the future, I often start each new set of tags on the next line. That creates white space and makes it easier to locate the part you want to edit. You will appreciate getting into this habit as your skills grow and you create more complex pages.

Untitled - Notepad

File   Edit   Search   Help

```
<html>
<head>
<title>...</title>
</head>
<body>

Your visible content goes here.
This is the only part that will
show up in a browser.

</body>
</head>
```

NOTE

At one time it didn't matter if you typed HTML tags in UPPERCASE or lowercase. Technically, it still doesn't matter, but other programming languages require tags to be in lowercase, so it's a good practice to type all your HTML tags in lowercase as well. It may be a requirement at some point in the future. Learning good habits now can save you trouble later.

1.7 The <head> Tag

ress the Enter key to start on a new line. (Mac users, every time you see the "Enter key," use the Return key on your keyboard. You do not need to reach for the Enter key on your key-pad—although you can.) On the new line, type:

```
<head>
```

. . . under the <html> tag you already typed.

The <head> section of an HTML page is where you place the title of your web page. The text of the title tag is what shows up in the title bar at the very top of your browser when you view a web page. A search engine also uses the title text as the name of your page in a search result. You will add other items to the head section later, including meta tags and a site description, but only the title is visible to the viewer. Those additional tags, described in Chapter 2: The <HEAD> Section and in Chapter 12: Search Engine Optimization, are not necessary to make a web page, but as you will learn, there are good reasons to use them.

As with the opening HTML tag, the head section of our document needs to remain open, so we will not issue a cancel command yet.

1.8 The <title> Tag

ress the Enter key and type <title> under your <head> tag. Your document should now look like this:

CODE EXAMPLE

```
<html>
<head>
<title>
```

Now we will add the title. Since this is a practice page, I will not go into what makes a good title just yet. For now, we will call it "My First Page." Add the title beside your <title> tag like this:

<title> My First Page

Since this is the end of the title, add the code to turn off the <title> tag. Do you remember how to turn off a tag?

1.9 Issuing Cancel Commands

W ithin the containers, adding a forward slash before the HTML element tells the browser this is the end of the HTML element. With just a few exceptions, most tags require a cancel tag for the page to function properly.

We have not canceled (turned off) any other HTML elements yet because they are still active.

Finish your title tag now by typing </title> after the title. Your document should look like this:

```
CODE EXAMPLE

<html>
<head>
<title>My First Page</title>
```

Isn't this easy? I knew you could do it! This is going to be a piece of cake.

This is all we are going to put in the head section of our page, so now that you are an old hand at typing HTML commands, press the Enter key and cancel the head section of the page. Do you need a hint?

After canceling the head element, your page should look like this:

```
CODE EXAMPLE

<html>
<head>
<title>My First Page</title>
</head>
```

1.10 The <body> Tag

N ext, after the head, you place the body of the page.

The body area is where you put all the things you want people to see—text, graphics, animations, etc. So far, nothing we have typed will show up on the web page (with the exception of the title,

7

which shows only in the title bar at the top of the browser window, not on the page itself).

Press the Enter key now and type in the body element like this:

<body>

Noticing a pattern yet? The body tag is the word "body" enclosed by the arrow containers, just as the other tags are elements enclosed by containers. On a basic level, that is all HTML really is.

Your page should now read:

CODE EXAMPLE

```
<html>
<head>
<title>My First Page</title>
</head>
<body>
```

NOTE

Some webmasters do advocate having all your code run together without carriage returns and the white space that makes it easy to locate the parts you want to edit. They say it optimizes your code so your pages will load faster. In my opinion, the few milliseconds you gain aren't going to be noticeable to your visitor in most cases, and the difficulty in editing the source code isn't worth the bother.

As I said earlier, the body area is where we put the visible content of our web page. I usually add an extra line of white space between the tags and any of the visible content. Again, this is just to help make editing the pages easier at a later date. You will want to edit them repeatedly—trust me, it is addictive!

To add an extra line of white space, press the Enter key twice. That will not make any difference to the way your web page displays, it shows only in the source code for your editing convenience.

1.11 Adding Content

N ow it is time to finally add something you will be able to see on the page when viewed with a web browser. Type the following content into your document:

Gee, this really is easy.

Your document should now look like this:

CODE EXAMPLE

```
<html>
<head>
<title>My First Page</title>
</head>
<body>
Gee, this really is easy.
```

Believe it or not, we are almost done making our first web page. Previously, I said most tags need a cancel tag for your page to function properly. If you look at the code we have written so far, which tags still need canceling?

1.12 Finishing the HTML Document

he only tags we have not yet canceled are the body tag and the opening HTML tag. Can you guess how you would finish this web page? If you said by adding:

```
</body>
</html>
```

. . . then you'd be 100 percent correct! If you have not yet added that to your code, do so now. Your document should look like the example below. You just learned the minimum HTML tags and the basic structure needed for a web page.

CODE EXAMPLE

```
<html>
<head>
<title>My First Page</title>
</head>
<body>
Gee, this really is easy.
</body>
</html>
```

Congratulations, you have just made your first web page. In a browser, the page would look like the graphic on the left. You'll be able to see that for yourself in just a few minutes.

Content aside for the moment, learning to create quality web pages that go beyond these basics is largely a matter of learning more HTML elements.

Most are just as easy to learn and use as those you just applied. Don't worry, though, you're not expected to memorize them! Many resources, including Appendix A: HTML Chart in this book, list HTML elements.

1.13 Saving a File

I know you're anxious to save and view your web page to see if it really works, but first, there are two things to know about saving HTML documents.

Your main page, that is, the first page you want people see when they come to your site, should be named "index" (without the quotes). That is the default name browsers look for. After that, you can name the rest of your pages as you like, as long as you don't use any spaces or illegal characters in the name. Illegal characters include colons, slashes, extended characters, or even just spaces. If you stick to letters and numbers, you'll always be safe.

Documents destined to be web pages can be saved with the extension of **.html** or **.htm**; I recommend **.html**. Some web hosts do not set up their servers to automatically look for the .htm extension. Say your web address is www.yoursite.com. If someone clicks that link, but you named your index page with the .htm extension instead of .html, the user's browser will return an error message if the server isn't set up to automatically default to index.htm when index.html isn't found.

Using my site as an example, my entry page is saved as **index.html**. My site can be found using:

www.boogiejack.com

Clicking a link to that web address or typing it into your browser's address bar will bring up my index page. However, on some servers, if I saved my page as index.htm, you would not get my site at all. You would get an error message or, in some cases, a directory listing. To get to my site under these circumstances, you would have to use this address:

www.boogiejack.com/index.htm

That may seem like a small point now, but it can be the difference between people finding your site and not finding your site. You should save all the files with the same file extension rather than mixing them. That consistency will make things easier as your site grows. You don't want to have to look up which extension you saved each page with every time you need to know.

The page you just made will serve as your index page for our exercises, so name it index.html.

To save the file in Notepad on Windows:

Step 1. Choose **File > Save As**; the **Save As** dialog box opens.

> **NOTE**
>
> As we continue with these lessons, you will learn to set up your web site on your disk or computer just as it will be on a web server, which will deliver it to the Internet. This allows you to make sure your links and images work before you upload them to your web site. For now, the floppy disk or folder you save the files in represents your server space.

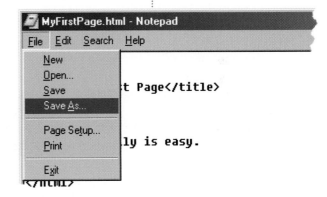

11

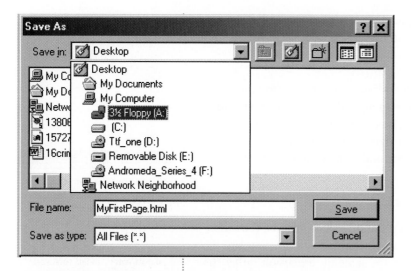

Step 2. In the **Save in** field, click the arrow to access the drop-down list, and then choose your floppy disk drive (usually A). Don't forget to insert a new floppy disk first.

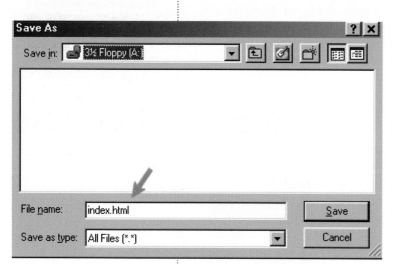

Step 3. Once the Save in field is set to the floppy disk drive, type index.html in the **File name** field.

12

Step 4. Click the arrow in the **Save as type** field, and then choose **All Files.**

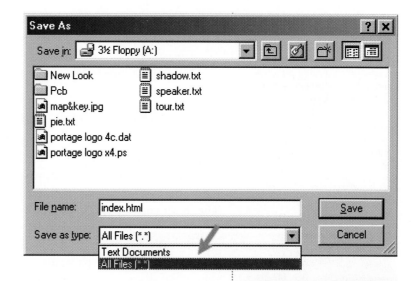

Step 5. Lastly, click the **Save** button located near the bottom right corner of the **Save As** dialog box.

To save the file in SimpleText on Mac OS:

Step 1. Choose **File > Save As;** the **Save As** dialog box opens.

Step 2. Click the **Desktop** button.

Step 3. Click the **New** button to create a new folder on the desktop.

Step 4. Type **My Web Site** in the **Name of new folder** field, then click **Create.**

Step 5. Type index.html in the **Save this document as** field.

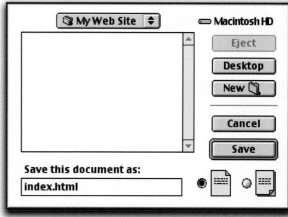

13

Step 6. Click the **Save** button to create the file inside the new folder.

You have completed your first web page.

1.14 Viewing Your Creation

$\boxed{C}$ an we see it now? No!

Just kidding. Open your browser and open the page you made. You will see a page with the text "Gee, this really is easy." That is all you will see, but don't worry—you'll be learning new tricks soon.

If you don't know how to open the page, just follow these handy-dandy instructions:

To open a page in Internet Explorer on Windows:

Step 1. With your browser open, choose **File > Open.** An even easier method is to press the Control key and the letter O on your keyboard.

Step 2. Click the **Browse** button.

Step 3. Navigate to the floppy disk drive or wherever you saved your index.html file. Click the index page in the main window so its name appears in the **File name** field, then click **Open.**

This returns you to the **Open** dialog box from Step 2. Click **OK** now and your web page should open in your browser window.

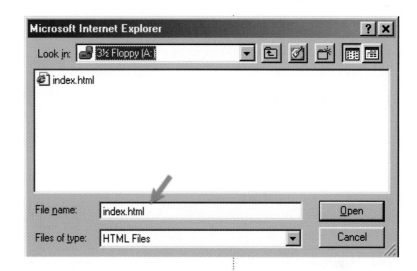

To open a page in Netscape on Windows:

Step 1. With your browser open, choose **File > Open Page.** An even easier method is to press the Control key and the letter O on your keyboard.

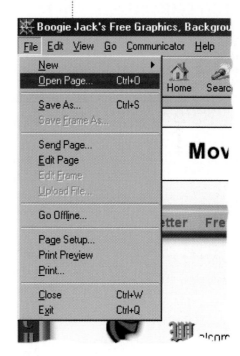

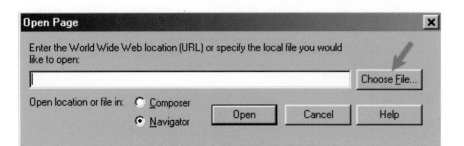

Step 2. Click the
Choose File button.

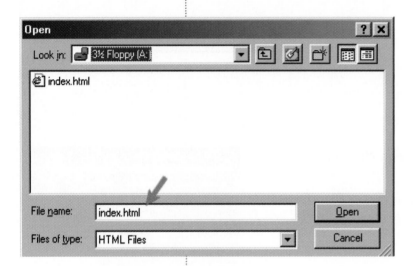

Step 3. Navigate to the
floppy disk drive. Click
the index page in the main
window so its name appears
in the **File name** field, then
click **Open.**

Step 4. This returns you to the **Open Page** dialog box from Step 2.
Click **Open** again and your page should appear in your browser
window.

To open a page in Internet Explorer on Mac OS:

Step 1. Choose **File > Open File.** An even easier method is to press
the Command key (aka the Apple key) and the letter O on your
keyboard.

Step 2. Navigate to the desktop: In Mac OS 9, click **Desktop;** in
Mac OS X, choose **Desktop** from the **From** pop-up menu.

Step 3. Scroll to the My Web Site folder and click on it to select it.
On Mac OS 9, click **Open.**

Step 4. Click on your index.html file to select it (if necessary,
choose **All** from the **Show** menu). Click **Open.**

16

To open a page in Netscape on Mac OS:

Step 1. Choose **File > Open File**. An even easier method is to press the Command key (aka the Apple key) and the letter O on your keyboard.

Step 2. Navigate to the desktop: In Mac OS 9, click **Desktop**; in Mac OS X, choose **Desktop** from the **From** pop-up menu.

Step 3. Scroll to the My Web Site folder and click on it to select it. On Mac OS 9, click **Open**.

Step 4. Click on your index.html file to select it, then click **Open.**

17

1.15 Attributes and Values

In HTML, pages are not displayed as you type them. For example, while you are typing on a computer, hitting the Enter key allows you to start a new paragraph. Hitting the Enter key twice places an extra line of space between paragraphs. If you type extra paragraph returns this way in your HTML code, it will look like that in your text editor. But in a browser, the words and sentences will be displayed as one long paragraph with no line breaks. In HTML, a browser does not recognize paragraph breaks in your code unless you add an HTML tag telling the browser it should start a new paragraph. Your text will go on and on until it runs out of screen space, at which time the line will wrap to the next line and the next and the next.

To make a single line break, you use the **break** tag:

```
<br>
```

This tells the browser to start the content that follows the break tag on the next line. The code for typing a **paragraph** break is this:

```
<p>
```

This tells the browser to start the content that follows the paragraph tag after two lines (a double space). In HTML, you have to tell the browser everything you want it to do with your content or it all just runs together.

To recap, a break tag starts the content that follows on a new line, while a paragraph tag starts the content that follows after two new lines.

CODE EXAMPLE	
Code written as: This is line 1. This is line 2.	Appears on a web page like this: This is line 1. This is line 2.

I also could have written the code like this:

This is line 1.
 This is line 2.

. . . and it would display the same on a web page as in the first example. The break tag controls the layout, forcing "This is line 2." to the next line.

CODE EXAMPLE	
Code written as: This is line 1. <p> This is line 2.	Appears on a web page like this: This is line 1. This is line 2.

See the difference? There is an extra line break with the paragraph tag.

Without any HTML tags at all:

CODE EXAMPLE	
Code written as: This is line 1. This is line 2.	Appears on a web page like this: This is line 1. This is line 2.

Remember, unless you specify how the page is to be laid out, it all runs together. Lines of text wrap to the next line in a browser rather than being one continuous string that goes forever horizontally. The text will not break until it reaches the edge of the browser window unless you tell it to break through your coding.

Many HTML tags can have attributes—tag modifiers—and these attributes have values. An attribute causes a basic HTML tag do a little something extra or different from the default values normally assigned to the tag. The attribute's value tells the browser exactly what the attribute is calling for. At the end of the book, you will find a listing of HTML tags and their possible attributes and value options.

Now let's add an attribute and value to the division tag.

```
<div align="center">
```

The <div> tag, which is short for division, doesn't do anything by itself, although it's very useful for assigning attributes and values to sections of an HTML document. It must have an attribute and value associated with it for it to affect the document. In the above example, I added the attribute of **align** to the tag, and added a value of **center**. With this attribute and value added to the division tag, all the content that follows will be centered on the page until you cancel the division element. Other alignment values are "left," "right," and "justify." The left, right, and center values will apply to all content within the opening and closing division tags. The value of "justify" will apply only to text, leaving other content at the default value of left.

Aligning the text to the left is the default value, so you don't have to add a division tag to have text aligned to the left. **Align left** makes each line of text line up on an imaginary vertical line on the left side of the page, with the right side left ragged (uneven vertically). **Align right** aligns the text on a straight vertical line on the right side of the page with the left side being ragged. **Align center** centers each line of text on the page and both the right and left edges are ragged. Justified text is when the text on both sides lines up evenly on imaginary vertical lines with no ragged edges. The browser accomplishes this by adding extra space between words, so you need to be careful where you use it or it can look a little funky. It works best when there is plenty of horizontal space. Justifying text is my preference when the necessary space is available. Depending on the content, justification can tidy up a page rather nicely, but is more of an authoritative formatting option that sets a less personal tone. Left justified text is the norm on the web, and is a fine choice as well.

Study the graphic to the left to see how the entire HTML tag breaks down into its individual components.

With this tag in place, everything on the page from that point down will be aligned left until the browser encounters a cancel division tag.

The equal sign between the attribute and the value represents the relationship between them. It simply means the attribute equals this value.

The quotation marks around the value are the official way to write code. In truth, with many tags you can get away with not using them. I recommend strongly that you always use them. Some oddball browsers may have trouble without them, and some tags do require them. Plus, there is something to be said for being consistent in your coding approach. It also may be that one day no tag will work without the quotation marks, so again, you will avoid future problems by developing good habits now.

1.16 Other Value Types

n the previous example, the division tag had an attribute and value used for layout control. Other tags have other types of

> **NOTE**
>
> Centering text is considered amateurish and should not be used on a site striving for a professional appearance. Centering images and headlines is sometimes desirable, but centering body text is not.

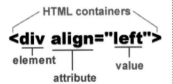

HTML containers
\<div align="left"\>
element · attribute · value

attributes and values that control formatting such as color, size, and other tweaks.

In HTML, there are often many ways to accomplish the same thing. The division tag shown in Section 1.15 isn't the only way to center things on a page. These multiple options were deliberately programmed into HTML to confuse people. How else would guys like me make the big bucks designing web sites and teaching HTML? OK, I was just kidding. They are really there to help make it a flexible language that meets many needs.

1.17 Chapter Quiz

1. What does the acronym HTML mean?

2. Every HTML document starts with the HTML language identifier <html>. What is the next tag of an HTML document?

3. Suppose the title for our web page is "Clever Things to Do." How would you write the title in the code using both the opening and closing command?

4. The actual content of your page goes between what two HTML tags?

5. Why is it risky to use .htm for a file extension instead of .html?

6. HTML tags can have modifiers that help control elements of a web page. What is the first part of the tag modifier called?

1.17 Chapter Quiz (continued)

7. What is the second part of the tag modifier called?

8. What symbol connects the two parts of the tag modifier?

9. What tag would you type to insert a single line break in a page?

10. What tag would you type to insert a double space between lines in a page?

11. HTML tags are enclosed between what two symbols?

12. How many babies were named "Boogie Jack" in honor of me in the last five years?

1.18 Chapter Exercises

Exercise Option 1 – Practice Site

U sing the index page you made as you followed along with this chapter, remove the "Gee this really is easy" comment and use the <br> tag, the <p> tag, the <div> tag, and the attributes and values discussed for the division tag to write the following as it appears in the layout below:

A Really Bad Poem

Once I sat down to think and ponder
On life's meaning and all its wonder

I sat and thought and sure enough
I couldn't think of anything but fluff

So I told myself, "harder, use all your might"
Moments later came a brilliant flash of light

My heart raced wildly, like a runaway horse
When a voice thundered with power and force

And spoke these words that I swear I heard
"I almost ran over you in the dark, you nerd,
Get out of the freaking road!"

I know, it's not a literary masterpiece, but what do you expect from a graphics and code guy? After you've added that to your index page, save it and make sure it turns out similar to the way it's laid out above. There should be a double spaced line break between the title and first stanza. There should be single line breaks within each stanza, and double-spaced breaks between each stanza. In addition, the title, first and fifth stanzas should be aligned left, the second and fourth stanzas are centered, and the third stanza aligned right.

Oh, and by the way, I didn't really make up that poem. My dog did. She's a real ham.

1.18 Chapter Exercises (continued)

Exercise Option 2 – Independent Exercise

 reate a new page using the following things you've learned from this chapter.

- Use all the basic HTML tags (<html>, <head>, <title>, etc.)
- Use the <div> at least four times, using each alignment value at least once.
- Use the <p> and <br> tags at least once.
- For content, explain why you want to learn web design.

The <HEAD> Section

Chapter Two

2.1 Chapter Introduction

I f you're wondering why we're skipping the opening HTML tag and going right to the HEAD tag, it's because no attributes or other tags are used with the HTML tag. Your document starts off with:

```
<html>
```

. . . and then goes right to the HEAD tag. Like the HTML tag, no attributes go with the HEAD tag, but many things can go into the HEAD section of an HTML page. They are placed in the HEAD section as nested tags, which simply means tags within tags. Most of what goes into the HEAD section of your document is used to help search engines index your site. Generally, it is information about the page content.

Programming functions can go into the HEAD section also, but they aren't necessary for your page to function (some will be covered in later chapters). This chapter covers the four tags most often used in the HEAD section.

2.2 Title Tag Uses

T he TITLE tag is the only thing in the HEAD section that is visible to someone viewing your page on the web. It usually shows up in the Title Bar at the very top of the browser window. I've seen many sites in which the webmaster wasn't paying attention when designing the pages. When you look at the title of the page and it says "put_title_here," you know the webmaster wasn't paying attention to details. A title like that is usually inserted by an HTML editor into a new file as part of the basic set of tags—and you're supposed to change it.

While that little mistake isn't critical to the functioning of a web page, it will not help others find your site. You must pay attention to details as you build web pages. While a browser can act only on correct code, search engines act on the code *and* the content you

25

give them. If that's not reason enough to pay attention to detail, then know that sometimes even making a small mistake can cause your page to become completely dysfunctional. Attention to detail is crucial!

The title of your page can help people find your web site. Aside from the title showing up in the browser's title bar, many search engines use the title as the name of your page in search results. A search engine is a web site that lets you search its huge database of other web sites to help you find the content you're seeking. When someone types a query into the search field, the search engine brings up a list of web sites that most closely match the search terms according to how that particular search engine evaluates and rates sites. This evaluation process is usually a set of rules that gives points for some things and takes away points for others. As in most sports, the one with the most points wins. Winning at the search engine game means your site is listed higher than other sites offering similar content. The set of rules a search engine uses is called an algorithm.

A well-crafted title intrigues users into clicking on your link and visiting your site. A title can also help you place higher in search engine relevancy ratings, so your site comes up before others in search results. Generally speaking, the higher you rank in search results, the more visitors your web site will receive.

2.3 A Little About Search Engines

Search engines use algorithms to determine the relevancy of a site against a search query. Algorithms are sets of rules that guide the search engine software in determining which sites best match the search being performed. The search engine programmers change these algorithms constantly as they try to perfect their search returns and thwart webmasters from manipulating the search results by trickery and artificial means. Even if the search engine programmers perfected the algorithms, they would still change them. They want to have different results come up from time to time so their database looks fresh.

Search engines also have sets of rules that must be obeyed by webmasters. The site administrators will penalize sites that break their search engine rules, either by lowering their placement or by banning domains from their database (in the case of extreme offenders).

To comply with each search engine's rules means visiting their sites and making note of all the rules. This can be time consuming and confusing. Rather than try to keep up with them all, I simply learn the lowest common denominators among them and code to that specification. Most people won't have the time or desire to build a site optimized for each search engine, so building a good solid cross-engine coded site is the next best choice. Happily, taking this approach has kept my site on top of many search engines month after month and year after year. Its position will go up and down from time to time, but it's always on top on a few, and often on top on many for my most important keywords. Search engines seem to reward your site for (1) offering quality content and (2) not attempting to manipulate them.

That said, I do attempt to manipulate search engines, but only with legal, cross-engine methods, which you will learn too. This chapter focuses only on the very basics of search engine optimization. Chapter 12: Search Engine Optimization delves into the real nitty-gritty of site optimization.

2.4 Crafting a Good Title

Keywords are the words someone might type into a search engine to locate sites with the kind of content your site offers. The secret to crafting a good title—one that will help your site's ranking with search engines—is to use your top keywords in the title.

Suppose we are building a page about a rock band named Cheap Dates. I think I made that name up—I hope there is no band going by that. If there is, hey you guys, send me an album for the free publicity I just gave you!

What do we know so far? We know the band is a rock band and that it is called Cheap Dates. From that, our title might read:

CODE EXAMPLE

```
<html>
<head>
<title>Cheap Dates—A Rock Band</title>
```

We have two keywords, or more precisely, two keyword phrases. One word makes a keyword; two or more keywords make a keyword phrase. When it comes to search engines, for the most part keyword phrases are more powerful than single keywords. So, we have the keyword phrases "Cheap Dates" and "Rock Band." Common words such as "a, and, the" are disregarded.

That's a good start, and it's as far as we'll go in this chapter. I don't want to weigh you down with too much search engine information before you learn more about basic web page coding.

One of these rules is the length of the title. The acceptable title length at the time of this writing ranges from 59 to 111 characters for various search engines. Each space between words also counts as a character.

This doesn't mean you should make your title between 59 and 111 characters. If you make your title 60 characters long, you're breaking the limit of the search engine that only allows 59 characters. As you can see, that means you should make your title a maximum of 59 characters for the best across-the-board results.

> **NOTE**
>
> Search engines each have their own set of rules. Unless you want to make a web site that is compliant with each specific search engine's own unique set of rules, you have to design your pages to be compliant with them all. That means coding to the lowest common denominator.

2.5 Keywords Meta Tag

T he keywords meta tag is used to help search engines index your site and assign relevancy. Not all search engines use keywords, but for those that do, they can help your site rank better. This tag isn't as important as it used to be, but it still should be treated as an asset.

As you might have guessed, the keywords meta tag is used to list keywords relevant to your site's content. In the early days of the web, the idea was to stuff as many keywords as you could think of into your keywords meta tag. That no longer works. Search engine algorithms now take "keyword weighting" into account.

Keyword weighting might be described as the ratio of relevant keywords to nonrelevant keywords listed as compared to the search query. In other words, the more useless keywords included as related to the search query, the less your useful keywords are worth.

It's the webmaster's job to determine how many keywords and keyword phrases to use. The more you use, the more each is watered down; but the less you use, the less chance there is you'll have the right keyword combination to match a search query. The best strategy is to keep your page tightly focused and use only relevant keywords. Chapter 12: Search Engine Optimization has much more to say about this.

2.6 Determining the Keywords

Y|ou can start by making up a list of keywords yourself. Next, ask your friends and family to make up a list of keywords they'd use if they were looking for a site like yours. You might also use a thesaurus to look up synonyms.

If you're really stuck in coming up with good keywords, go to a search engine that uses keyword meta tags such as www.altavista.com. Spend some time searching by typing what you think your top keyword or keyword phrase is, and then going to the first five to 10 sites listed. As you find sites that have similar content and would attract the same audience, then open the source code from the browser menu and look at their keyword meta tags. Make a list of what you find. To open the source code for a page in Windows, right-click a blank spot on the page and choose View Source from the pop-up menu. On a Mac, Control+click a blank spot on the page and choose Page Source (Netscape) or View Source (Internet Explorer).

Since you are looking at the top sites for your query terms, they may have a good list of keywords. They may be listed at the top by search engines for other reasons as well, but you should find enough this way to generate a good list of keywords and keyword phrases. It wouldn't be right to steal their terms—and you do want your site to be rated higher than their sites—so you should try to determine how you could refine their keywords and keyword phrases and make them better.

My favorite search engine for this technique is Alta Vista at: www.altavista.com.

As I stated earlier, search engines that use the keyword meta tag consider keyword phrases as more important than keywords. This is simply because most people surfing the web use search phrases rather than a single search word. Search engines place more relevancy on a phrase than on a word, because instead of just matching one word, you're matching two or more words. The search engine programmers have rightly determined that someone searching for "cast iron widgets" has a better chance of finding what he or she is looking for on a page with the exact keyword phrase rather than on a page that just has "widgets."

Returning to our Cheap Dates fictional web site, we already know from the title that we have the following keywords and keyword phrases:

> **NOTE**
>
> Before performing the Alta Vista routine, do make up your own keywords and keyword phrases. You may come up with something better on your own, before you get a head full of ideas from other places. If I come up with what I think is a great set of keywords and keyword phrases on my own, then I don't bother with this technique. I just use it if I'm stuck. Everyone needs a little help now and then—an idea generator or jump start to get things going—and that's when I use this technique.

Cheap Dates, Rock Band

Normally, commas separate keywords and keyword phrases, but we can combine the first two phrases to make one keyword phrase of "Cheap Dates Rock Band". Let's also add the following keyword phrases that would be very relevant to a band site:

Tour Info

Photos

Song Lyrics

Let's create the keywords meta tag now using the above keywords and keyword phrases.

CODE EXAMPLE

```
<meta name="keywords" content="cheap dates rock band, tour info, photos, song lyrics">
```

NOTE

As with the title tag, search engines have limits on the length of the keywords meta tag. As of this writing, the lowest common denominator is 105 keywords (762 characters). When you've reached either number, it is time to stop for search-engine compliance.

NOTE

Unlike most HTML tags, there is no closing tag for meta tags.

This meta tag is placed under your TITLE tag. There are other meta tags, so let's break this tag down just a bit so you understand it. The name="keywords" identify which meta tag this is. The content="..." is where you place your actual keywords and phrases, in other words, the content of the meta tag.

If you're anywhere near the 105-word limit, in my opinion you have way too many keywords. Your keywords and keyword phrases will be too watered down when you approach the upper limit of allowable words. The character count doesn't really matter when it comes to keyword weighting because relevant terms are relevant terms—long keywords are no more or less important than short keywords. It's how they match the query that matters. Again, there is more information about this in Chapter 12: Search Engine Optimization.

One final important point to remember is that you may not repeat any keyword more than three times.

2.7 Description Meta Tag

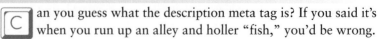 an you guess what the description meta tag is? If you said it's when you run up an alley and holler "fish," you'd be wrong.

The description meta tag is pretty much what it sounds like. It's a description of the web page content. On search engines that use meta tags, the description you place in this meta tag is what they show for the description of your site in the search results. Search engines that don't use the meta tags use the first few sentences of your page as the description.

Regarding the 22-word limit: I don't know of any search engines that penalize you for writing too long of a description. What happens is they simply cut off your description at their prescribed maximum length. I do use longer descriptions, but I work it so the first 22 words reads logically. If you don't, your description gets cut off in mid-sentence or in the middle of a word, which doesn't look as professional and inviting.

The next cut off point is 34 words or 246 characters. You can usually write a good description within those boundaries. I try to keep it to that. If you try to write as long of a description as you can, working within all the cut-off points, you end up with diminishing returns. The extra work isn't worth the extra time. The extra time is better spent in creating new content or promoting your web site by other means.

> **NOTE**
>
> Like the other "head section" tags we've covered so far, the description meta tag also has a length limit. The lowest common denominator is 22 words (154 characters). Twenty-two words isn't much to work with, so you'll need to write your description intelligently.

2.8 Determining the Description

A s with the title tag, you should weave some of your best keywords and keyword phrases into the description, keeping in mind that it should read like normal, properly constructed sentences. You want to convey what the page is about in a logical fashion, work in your keywords, and keep within the cut-off points.

Also, keep in mind that since this is the text people see, it needs to be a little like an advertisement without sounding like advertising. In other words, your description should make people want to click the link to see your site without using hype (because search engines don't like hype).

For the Cheap Dates site we might write:

Dedicated to the rock band Cheap Dates. Visit our photo gallery, view the band's current tour schedule, and read their song lyrics.

That description is exactly 22 words and remained under 154 characters—just perfect. This description will cut off at the low-end search engine at just the right place. Now we can safely add 12 more words to the description to reach the next cut-off point.

> **NOTE**
>
> One thing to remember is that, unlike the keywords meta tag, the description meta tag is viewed not on your web page, but as the description of your web page at some search engine sites. Therefore, it should be written in complete sentences.

31

Here's the added line:

Join our Cheap Dates Fan Club for free band news by email.

Now we have a perfect 22-word and 34-word description rolled into one, complete with keywords and keyword phrases. If needed, I'll add more to the description for the search engines that allow more, but I no longer worry about the cut-off points. Sometimes, you just have to let the chips fall where they may. To keep writing to cut-off points after this isn't practical—it involves fewer engines and more work, with fewer and fewer rewards for your efforts. Now let's put our description into code under the keywords meta tag.

CODE EXAMPLE

```
<meta name="description" content="Dedicated to the rock band Cheap Dates. Visit our photo gallery, view the band's current tour schedule, and read their song lyrics. Join our Cheap Dates Fan Club for free band news by email.">
```

NOTE

Remember, there is no closing tag for meta tags.

2.9 Author Meta Tag

This tag isn't required or even very useful, but some people like to sign their work. If someone is looking for you, for example, it may help a search engine locate you. You code the author meta tag like this:

```
<meta name="author" content="Dennis Gaskill">
```

I have seen others add other properties such as a web address, email address, or copyright information here. It's not official, but it doesn't hurt anything either.

Personally, I don't use the author meta tag. But if I did, I'd probably write it like this:

```
<meta name="author" content="Dennis Gaskill-Copyright 2004 (booj@boogiejack.com)">
```

2.10 The Completed Head Section

Now that you've learned the main components of the head section, here is the way the entire document would look from the opening HTML tag to the end of the head section.

Remember, since we are finished with the head section, we need to close or cancel it with a cancel tag:

CODE EXAMPLE

```
<html>
<head>
<title>Cheap Dates—A Rock Band</title>
<meta name="keywords" content="cheap dates rock band, tour info, photos, song lyrics">
<meta name="description" content="Dedicated to the rock band Cheap Dates. Visit our photo
    gallery, view the band's current tour schedule, and read their song lyrics. Join our Cheap
    Dates Fan Club for free band news by email.">
<meta name="author" content="Dennis Gaskill">
</head>
```

2.11 Online References

F or a character counter to help you determine the character count for keywords, keyword phrases, and descriptions, head to:

www.boogiejack.com/textcount.html

Meta tag tool for cheaters:

www.boogiejack.com/metamake.html

Note: On my site, the instructions differ slightly than the ones given here. I don't give away all my secrets online!

> **NOTE**
>
> In this code example, where the meta content is more than one line long, the subsequent lines needn't be indented. I indented the example to make it easier for you to read and understand.

2.12 Chapter Quiz

1. Name the four most commonly used tags within the HEAD section of an HTML document.

2. The title of your page shows up in the browser's title bar. Where else might it be found?

3. What is the secret to crafting a good page title?

4. What is a search engine algorithm?

5. To be compliant with all search engines, what is the maximum number of characters you can use in a web page title?

6. What is keyword weighting?

7. What is the maximum number of times you should repeat a keyword in your keywords meta tag?

8. Show the closing tag for the keywords meta tag.

9. What is the lowest common denominator for the length of the description meta tag?

2.12 Chapter Quiz (continued)

10. What's the next cutoff point for a description meta tag?

11. What are keywords?

12. How did the spice company send calendars to its customers?

2.13 Chapter Exercises

Exercise Option 1 – Practice Site

Y our exercise for this chapter is to decide on a topic for the mini-web site you're going to build, and then write the title tag and meta tags for it. Your site can be about anything you choose, from a personal web site to a made-up business, as long as it isn't illegal or defamatory. Choose a topic you're knowledgeable about, whether it's your family, your favorite TV show, or a hobby. The Introduction to this book fully explains the five pages (minimum) that you'll need to create, so take those into consideration while choosing a topic. Here is a reminder:

- The main page describes your site's purpose and benefits.

- The second page contains your content—or serves as a sub-index to pages that contain your content.

- The third page, an about page, describes you—the author or company creating the site. Fictionalizing is OK.

- The fourth page, a media kit, explains why businesses should advertise on your site along with your ad rates and contact information.

- The resources page, your final required page, contains links to complementary (but not competing) sites.

Once you've selected your site topic, write the title tag and meta tags for the index page (the main entrance to your site).

Exercise Option 2 – Independent Exercise

U sing the lessons from Chapter 1: Introduction to HTML, create a page using the title and meta tags learned in this chapter. Explain what makes a good title and description meta tag. Give examples.

Note: Because code will not show up on the page without special formatting, you may use the left and right parentheses symbols in place of the left and right arrow brackets: use (instead of < and use) instead of >.

You may also use special formatting that will allow the arrow brackets to show up on your page. To have a left arrow bracket show up on your page instead of having it interpreted as code, type: <

Those four characters will show up on your page as < (a left arrow).

To display the right arrow bracket use: >

The <BODY> Tag

Chapter Three

3.1 Chapter Introduction

W ith the body tag, we can finally begin to breathe a little color and life into our HTML documents. I can hear you sigh now, "ah . . . finally, something fun!" Yes, this is where the fun begins. You get to choose a background color or a background image, text color, and link colors. You can also remove the default page margins and set the background image so that it doesn't scroll with the page.

Links to various relevant pages on my web site are included at the end of the chapter. If you have Internet access where you're reading this, you'll be able to access a background color machine, color charts, free graphics, and other resources.

3.2 Understanding the Body Tag

T he body tag follows the cancel head </head> tag, which is where we left off in the last chapter. The minimum body tag is simply:

```
<body>
```

Using this code will leave every element of color on your web page at the default settings for each browser. Usually, this means black text with blue links on a white background color. The body tag turns on the content for the browser. That is, everything between the opening body tag and the cancel body tag, except for the actual code, is what is displayed in a browser's window.

The body tag uses attributes and values to control the background color and image, text color, link color, visited link color, and active link color. It can also be used to remove the default page margins and to set the background image so it doesn't scroll for those using the Internet Explorer browser.

3.3 Browser-safe Colors

S urprisingly, color can be a very complex issue. One color can look different on your computer than it does on another. Some colors can even look different in different browsers on the same computer. Browser-safe colors are supposed to look the same (or as close as possible) on all computers and operating systems and in all browsers. There is a color chart of browser-safe colors in Appendix D. This is all on top of the fact that actual monitor settings and lighting in the room affects color display—things, unfortunately, that you can't control.

Consider browser-safe colors as necessary when accessibility is an issue. Vision-impaired people use screen readers to access the Internet. Some screen readers have trouble with colors that are not browser-safe, and the program can crash when encountering pages using other colors. This is becoming less of an issue as screen-reading software improves, but should still be a concern for sites of primary interest to the visually impaired.

Cross-platform, cross-browser safe colors are made from combinations of the hexadecimal values: 00, 33, 66, 99, CC, and FF. These color combinations amount to 216 different colors you can use. Hexadecimal colors are explained in Section 3.5 in this chapter. Using these colors assures that your site displays in nearly the same colors on all computers. That's the theory anyway, and the theorists are sticking to it.

3.4 Setting the Background Color

L et's dive right into it while the watercolor is warm. You should set a background color for the body even if you're going to use a background image. The background image will take from a few seconds to perhaps a half-minute or more to download. (Download means to be transferred from the web server to a user's computer via the Internet.) Until the image downloads, your text is shown against the background color. Often, people don't set the background color when they use a background image, but they do change the default text color. If the text color doesn't have enough contrast with the default background color, it may be difficult to read or even invisible.

By setting the background color as close to the main color of the background image you've chosen, your visitors will be able to read your text while the background image is downloading. When the background image does appear, with the background color set to a similar color as your background image, the transition will be much smoother.

To set the background color, add the following attribute and value to the body tag:

```
<body bgcolor="blue">
```

In the example above, the background color of the web page would be blue. The value may be expressed in color names or hexadecimal color values. With color names, you can choose from 139 colors, which are listed in Appendix E of this book and on my web site.

Using hexadecimal color values, you can choose from millions of colors. It used to be everyone used the browser-safe colors. These were considered the safe colors to use since many computers couldn't display more than 256 colors, and the browser-safe colors fell within that color range. Nowadays, most computers display in at least 16-bit color, also called high color. Computers set to high color can display 65,536 unique colors. Most computers are set even higher, to 24-bit color or 32-bit color, also called true color, and are able to display 16.7 million or more unique colors.

Using statistics from visitors to my web site, which attracts a broad array of users and systems, less than 2 percent of those systems are in the low 256-color mode. Graphics are so much nicer when you go up to high color or true color that I don't bother with the browser-safe palette. I know I'm not alone in that thinking. Anytime the lowest common denominator falls below 10 percent usage, I consider it safe to upgrade to the next level. Your site will still be practical for all of your users, it will be optimized for most, and it may encourage those hanging on to old technology to upgrade.

Systems that display only 256 colors are truly dinosaurs now. To worry about the last few dinosaurs is counterproductive to progress. You have to move forward at some point, and in my personal and professional opinion, the time has come to move ahead to higher color levels for web site design.

I design in true color. Even if someone with a system set to high color visits, the high-color level offers enough similar colors that images degrade rather gracefully and shouldn't seem ugly to your visitor. As mentioned earlier, if accessibility is an issue for your site (or your instructor!), then choose browser-safe colors.

3.5 Hexadecimal Colors

H exadecimal codes are alphanumeric representations of red, green, and blue. That sounds a lot fancier than it really is. A hex code (abbreviated so I don't have to keep typing that really long, awkward word) is a six-digit number with each digit having a value from A–F or 0–9. The format is #rrggbb (red,red,green, green,blue,blue).

The graphic below explains what I mean.

The hash mark always precedes a hexadecimal value.

#FF8500

The first two digits are the red value.

The second two digits are the green value.

The last two digits are the blue value.

The hex code is always preceded by a hash mark, also known as a pound sign. The first two digits represent the red value, the next two digits the green value, and the last two digits the blue value. You can use any combination of letters and numbers in any order in the code. It doesn't have to be letters in the first two positions and then all numbers as I've shown in this example. The values represent a percentage. It works like this:

FF equals full intensity of the color.

B0 equals 75% intensity of the color.

80 equals 50% intensity of the color.

40 equals 25% intensity of the color.

00 equals 0% of the color.

A hex code of #FFFFFF is full intensity for all colors. The result is the color white. A hex code of #000000 is no intensity for all colors. The result is the color black. Everything in between is confusing!

If you don't get it, don't sweat it. You don't really have to know all that. You can make up numbers and see what color it turns out like, you can use software programs that let you pick a color and it will tell you the hex code, or you can use the color machine on my web site. In the appendices, you'll find a chart that lists several hex colors.

> **NOTE**
>
> If you know a color's RGB values, there's a formula for converting RGB color to hex color. The RGB values are usually available in any good graphics program. The resources page on my site also includes the web addresses of many helpful tools and utilities other than the ones I offer. The web address of the resources page is: www.boogiejack.com/book/resources.html

To set a hex color for the body background, you would code it like this:

```
<body bgcolor="#FF8500">
```

The hex code I chose here sets the red value at full intensity, the green value at slightly over 50 percent intensity, and the blue value at none. The whole thing comes out about the color of a carrot. Isn't that special?

3.6 Setting the Font Color

A dding a text color attribute and value to the body tag makes all the text on the page that color, unless you override the body tag with another font tag elsewhere on the page. Adding the text attribute and value is similar to adding the background color, only we reference text instead of bgcolor. Building on to our previous body tag, we add the text color and end up with this:

```
<body bgcolor="#FF8500" text="#400000">
```

To add a text color, you simply add the attribute "text" in the body tag and add the value for it. The text color of #400000 is a very dark brown, which would look about as good as anything on an ugly, bright orange background.

We've also just added a new wrinkle that you haven't seen before—a second attribute and value added to one tag. You can add as many attributes and values to a tag as you like, as long as they are legal attributes and values for that particular tag (and as long as they don't conflict with one another, such as setting two sets of the same attribute). Many webmasters code two or three tag repetitions to create a particular effect, when all they need to do is code all the attributes of each tag into the first one. That's a waste of your time and slightly increases display time.

For example, this set of tags . . .

NOTE

In Chapter 11: Cascading Style Sheets (CSS), you will learn other ways to code color into your pages. The World Wide Web Consortium, the regulating body for industry standards, recommends CSS for adding color to web page elements. The colorizing methods shown here are the original ways to add color, and are still valid coding methods. Because I believe it's still important to know this, I'm teaching the original methods in this chapter and the CSS methods in Chapter 11. That way, if you become responsible for a site using original color coding, or if you have to use an older web page editor, you'll have a firm understanding of the original method of coding color into a page.

CODE EXAMPLE

```
<font face="Arial"><font size="4"><font color="red">
```

41

. . . does the same as this tag:

CODE EXAMPLE

```
<font face="Arial" size="4" color="red">
```

The second version is a little shorter, and it's faster to code, download, and be interpreted by the browser. You also save time at the end of the tags. In the first example, you'd have to write </font> three times because you opened three font tags. The second example only opened one font tag so you only have to use one cancel tag. Besides being more optimized, it's easier for you to remember. The only time you might use more than one font tag as in the first example is when you want to cancel one effect but not the others.

Another example of old coding methods, this technique illustrates how to optimize code by using multiple attributes and values in one tag so you understand how that works. You'll learn the new way later, but it's still good to understand the old ways for previously mentioned reasons.

3.7 Setting the Link Color

The link color is the color of text that hyperlinks one page to another. The default color is a bright blue, and is often best left that way. People who are new to the Internet face a tidal wave of information all screaming for their attention. Changing the link colors can confuse users who haven't yet developed their web wings.

Having said that, let's change the link color! As you might imagine, changing the link colors works just like the other attributes and values we've added to our body tag. Let's see, what would be a good link color for an orange background? How about a navy blue?

```
<body bgcolor="#FF8500" text="#400000" link="#0000A0">
```

Now we have an orange background with brown text and navy blue links. I'm sure glad I don't have to visit a web site like that. Face it people, I'm not giving you good color combinations here and doing your work for you. When it comes time to pick your own color scheme, you have to do your own picking!

As you can see, adding the link is as simple as writing the attribute of "link" and adding the color value.

NOTE

When using hexadecimal colors, it doesn't matter if you type the letters in uppercase or lowercase. I use lowercase on web pages, but used uppercase here because it's easier to read.

3.8 Setting the Active Link Color

T he active link color makes a link blink! When someone clicks a link on a page that has an active link color programmed into the body tag, the link blinks another color ever so briefly. We want to get their attention with that, so let's make it flash a bright, fluorescent green color.

```
<body bgcolor="#FF8500" text="#400000" link="#0000A0"
alink="00FF00">
```

The only thing different from what we've been doing is that "active link" is shortened in HTML to "alink." In the next section, "visiting link" is also shortened to . . . you guessed it, "vlink." You're catching on so fast!

3.9 Setting the Visited Link Color

L azy webmasters skip attributes such as visited link colors, but they are doing their visitors a disservice. The visited link attribute changes the link color for a page you've already visited. The visited link color helps users keep track of previously visited pages so they can concentrate on looking at new pages. Visited link colors also help them find pages they've seen once and want to go back to.

For this orange beast, we'll set the visited link color to purple.

```
<body bgcolor="#FF8500" text="#400000" link="#0000A0"
alink="00FF00" vlink="800080">
```

As you can see, to add a visited link color we added the "vlink" attribute and a value. This color combination will definitely not win any design awards, but it sure will wake folks up.

3.10 Removing Page Margins

R emoving page margins is something you might want to do for aesthetic purposes. Browsers have a left side and top page margin of about one-quarter of an inch. If you want to place a graphic right next to the top or left side of a page, the only way to do it is to remove the page margins.

43

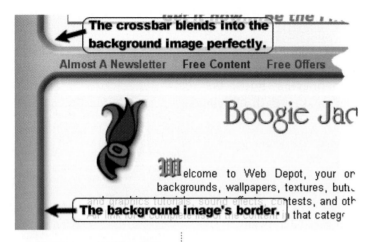

The crossbar blends into the background image perfectly.

Almost A Newsletter   Free Content   Free Offers

Boogie Jac

Welcome to Web Depot, your on backgrounds, wallpapers, textures, butt and graphics tutorials, sound effects, contests, and oth

The background image's border.

I've done this on my site in the past so a crossbar appears to blend seamlessly into the background image. Look at the partial screen capture of my old index page to see what I'm referring to.

The easiest way to bleed a graphic off the page is to remove the margins. Removing the margins is also useful if you design link buttons that work precisely with a background image to achieve a desired look.

If you have banner advertising on your site, removing the margins allows you to put the banner right next to the top so you keep as much of the first-view screen real estate for yourself as possible. The first-view screen—that is, the screen that people see when your page first loads before they scroll—is the most important real estate on your page. It's what convinces people to either continue checking out your site or causes them to leave for another destination.

In the case of removing the margins, the two browsers use different language to accomplish the task so you have to include instructions for both. IE ignores the code for Netscape, and Netscape ignores the code for IE.

Here's how to code it:

> **NOTE**
>
> The two major players in the browser market, Microsoft's Internet Explorer (IE) and Netscape, often do things differently. While it can be tiresome to continually check your pages in both browsers as you design them, and Netscape's market share is a fraction of that of Internet Explorer, it's still a good idea to design for both if you want them to look good in both.

CODE EXAMPLE

```
<body bgcolor="#FF8500" text="#400000" link="#0000A0" alink="#00FF00" vlink="#800080"
leftmargin="0" topmargin="0" marginwidth="0" marginheight="0">
```

You can see the code we added in blue type. Of course, you can also use the margin attributes to increase the margins, should you want them bigger. To make them larger, you'd just replace the zeros with another number. The numbers represent pixels. Most personal computer monitors display at a resolution of 72–96 dpi (dpi is dots per inch), with most falling into the lower end of the range. The display will vary slightly from computer to computer, but this gives you a good idea of how it will be rendered on most monitors.

The attributes of leftmargin and topmargin are for Internet Explorer, and the attributes of marginwidth and marginheight are for Netscape. Internet Explorer also has attributes of rightmargin and bottommargin, allowing you to set each margin separately. If you use all the attributes IE allows, start at the top and rotate clockwise as you code them into your body tag. Netscape sets both sides at once, and top and bottom at once.

3.11 Adding a Background Image

S electing or creating a background image is one of the fun parts of building a web site. The background image sets the ambience for the site. Take care in choosing a background image on several fronts:

1. As mentioned, the background sets the mood. Much of your choice depends on your site's content and focus, but in general, the color black sets an imposing and ominous tone, an evil tone, or a somber and serious, no-nonsense tone. White presents a no-nonsense business-like tone, an authoritative tone, or a clean and neat tone. Warm yellows, oranges, and reds present a variety of tones from happy and warm to angry and full of fury. Browns, blues, and purples set a trustworthy tone, conservative tone, or a royal and aloof tone. These are just a few of the moods color can create.

2. Background images can make or break your page—even if you start with a great or appropriate graphic. For example, a graphic with a busy background may make the text hard to read. And if the text is hard to read, most people won't bother reading it. Choose colors and patterns that offer the opportunity to choose a text color with sufficient contrast to make the text easy to read. Studies show that black text on a white background is the easiest to read. If your site will have a lot of text, you should strongly consider using a white background. You can use left border images for a nice splash of color to keep it interesting, as long as the main part of the page where your text goes is white. That's what I prefer to do. It's professional looking and optimal for readability.

3. Don't choose a background image that is either too large or too small. Too large means it will probably be a big file, and hence, slow to load. Too small and the image repeats too often, making your page look busy, something like a bad pattern on a dress.

> **NOTE**
>
> In Chapter 11: Cascading Style Sheets (CSS), you'll see other ways to accomplish many of the things you are learning here. While the margin attributes and values shown above are still valid at the time of this writing, I suspect they may eventually be deprecated in favor of CSS. A deprecated tag is one for which a newer method of coding is approved as the preferred method for coding the same effect. Deprecated tags may become obsolete at some point. At the end of the book you'll find a table of deprecated tags and the style sheet coding that is preferred. While deprecated tags still work and may always work, it's best to learn the preferred code so you don't have to make a lot of changes in the future if browsers stop supporting deprecated code.

45

4. Too much reliance on a background image and other graphics is also a design mistake. Most people's eyes go straight to text headlines, then they skim text messages, and finally they notice the graphics. Content is king. Graphics should be used to complement your content, not compete with it or dominate it.

5. Business sites almost always use a white background color or no background image at all. If your future plans are to have a business web site, I'd strongly urge you to stay very close to the tried-and-true traditional business design styles. A profitable Internet business is not easy to develop, despite what the get-rich-quick hucksters try to tell you. Deviating from the norm can make it harder for you to establish your business. However, if you are making a business web site for your assignment, feel free to use a background image for practice.

The two most common types of background images are left-border style images and full page style images. A left border background image has a strip of color, texture, or pattern down the left side of the page. The full page style background image has the same pattern or texture repeated from side to side and top to bottom on the page.

To add a background image, you must set the image path, file name, and file extension in the body tag. The image path, file name, and file extension are case sensitive. This means if you use capital letters where lowercase letters are used in the actual name of the file, it will not work. You must use the exact same capitalization pattern as the current file name.

For example, if you have an image saved as "**mygraphic.JPG**," then you reference it in your web page as "**mygraphic.jpg**," the file will not be found because you used lowercase for the file extension (jpg) in the code, but it is capitalized in the file name.

Coding a background image into our growing body tag might look like this:

CODE EXAMPLE

```
<body bgcolor="#FF8500" background="images/mygraphic.jpg" text="#400000"
link="#0000A0" alink="#00FF00" vlink="#800080" leftmargin="0" topmargin="0"
marginwidth="0" marginheight="0">
```

In the above example, the code to add the background image is in blue text. Notice the part that says "**images/**". This is the path to the image if you keep your images in a different directory from your HTML files (assuming you named the image directory "images"). I recommend doing it that way. As your web site grows, it becomes harder and harder to locate files if you have all the various file types mixed together in the same directory.

On my site, I keep my main site's images in a directory called "images," my free backgrounds in a separate directory called "bg," my sound files in a directory called "sounds," and so on. This makes it much easier to locate files since you don't have to sort through all the various file types.

Dividing up the files in this way also helps your pages download slightly faster. The more files you have, the more time you save. This is because the server doesn't have as many files to sift through to retrieve them. It doesn't make a noticeable difference for a very small site. But on a large site where you might have a combination of say, 500 HTML files, graphic files, and other assorted files, a server looking for the last file in a directory would have to go through the first 499 before locating the last file. If you keep them in smaller, more specifically focused directories, the server only has to sift through a handful of files to locate the file.

Conclusion: Do like I do and be happy about it!

3.12 Background Scrolling

W ith Internet Explorer, you can set an attribute in the body tag so that the background image remains fixed. In other words, it doesn't scroll with the page, it stays stationary.

To code your page so the background stays stationary:

CODE EXAMPLE

```
<body bgcolor="#FF8500" background="images/mygraphic.jpg" text="#400000"
link="#0000A0" alink="#00FF00" vlink="#800080" leftmargin="0" topmargin="0"
marginwidth="0" marginheight="0" bgproperties="fixed">
```

The code in blue text added to the body tag will keep your background from scrolling in Internet Explorer. It does not work in Netscape, but in the CSS chapter you'll see an alternate way to accomplish the same thing that should work in the latest version of Netscape.

3.13 Creating an Image Directory

B efore downloading images to use, create a directory or folder called "images" (without the quotes) inside the directory/ folder in which you're saving your web site.

To create a directory on a floppy disk using Windows, follow these instructions:

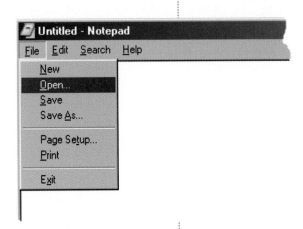

Step 1. With Notepad open, choose **File > Open.**

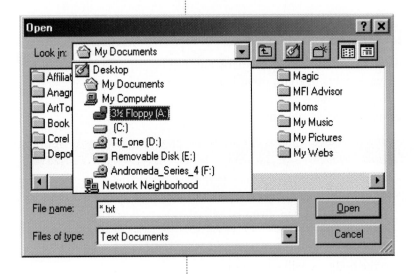

Step 2. Select the floppy drive.

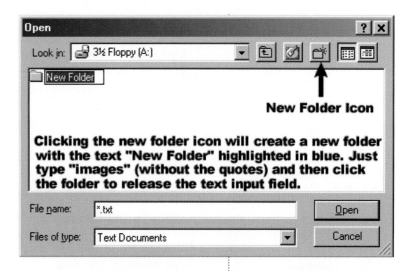

Step 3. Click the **New Folder** icon to create a new folder. It will create a new folder called "New Folder." Amazing, huh? It should be highlighted in blue. Just type "images" to rename it.

New Folder Icon

Clicking the new folder icon will create a new folder with the text "New Folder" highlighted in blue. Just type "images" (without the quotes) and then click the folder to release the text input field.

Step 4. Lastly, click on the folder icon to have the name take. Now you have a directory on your floppy disk called images. This is the folder you will place your background image and other images in.

On a Mac, create a new folder inside your My Web Site folder as follows:

Step 1. Click on the desktop, and then double-click the My Web Site folder to open it.

Step 2. With the My Web Site folder still selected, choose **File > New Folder**.

Step 3. The folder name is automatically highlighted, so you can change it. Type "images" and then click on the desktop again.

Incidentally, you can rename any folder or file by clicking the name of it, waiting one second, and clicking it again on most PCs. That will cause the name to be highlighted and allow you to type in a new name. Waiting another second and clicking again will place your cursor in the current name to allow you to edit a letter at a time.

49

3.14 Downloading Images

D ownloading images—the process of copying an image off a web site to your computer so you can use the file—is easy. Be sure, however, to abide by copyright notations when you download anything from the Internet. You do have permission to use the images in my image archive. You can read more about copyrights in Chapter 18: Good Things To Know. To download an image from a web site using a browser, first find an image you want (duh). On Windows, right-click on it; on a Mac, click and hold on it. A menu displays, giving you options to download the image.

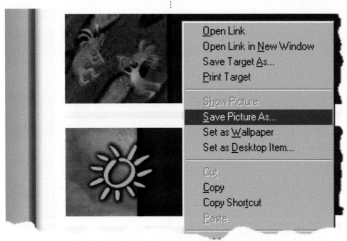

Step 1. The menu will include many options. In Internet Explorer, choose **Save Picture As** (Windows) or **Download Image to Disk** (Mac). In Netscape, choose **Save this Image As**.

Step 2. Open your floppy disk drive or click the **Desktop** button.

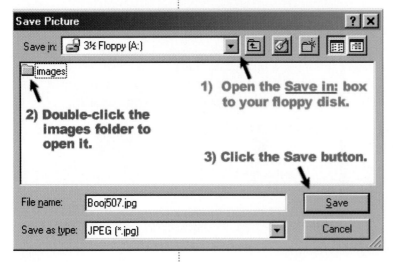

Step 3. Double-click the **images** folder icon to open the images folder.

Step 4. Click the **Save** button to save the image to the folder. The image file name will already display in the **File name** field and the correct file type should display in the **Save as type** field.

America Online (AOL) has a branded version of Internet Explorer, which may try to save images as .art images (a compressed proprietary format of theirs). This will result in a loss of quality. Plus, most browsers cannot see .art files, so you don't want to use them on your web site. To get around that, you'll need to change your default preferences in your browser. Changing the preferences will only take a minute, and you can stay online so there is no need to call the paramedics for withdrawal symptoms.

Step 1. Click **My AOL** at the top of the screen.

Step 2. Click **Preferences.**

Step 3. Click **WWW.**

Step 4. Click **Web graphics.**

Step 5. Uncheck **Use compressed graphics.**

Step 6. Click **Apply.**

That will take care of that, but . . .

If you return to a previously visited page, AOL will load the old compressed graphic, so let's clear out your temp files while you are still in **My AOL > Preferences:**

Step 1. Click **General.**

Step 2. Click **Delete files.**

Step 3. Click **Apply.**

You're done! Now explore the Internet as it was meant to be seen and enjoy the show.

> **NOTE**
>
> Odds are that new browser versions will be released during the lifetime of this book. The steps for modifying preferences in the AOL browser may change slightly—you may have to snoop around the preferences to find what you need.

3.15 Online References

|P| ages on my web site will help you find colors and images. If you don't have Internet access where you are studying this, most libraries have Internet access or you could go to a friend's house to access the Internet. From any of these locations, you can download free graphics onto a removable disk, such as a floppy or Zip disk, for use in building your web site.

For hundreds of free professional-grade graphics:

www.boogiejack.com/free_graphics.html

For a hex code color chart:

www.boogiejack.com/chart.html

For a chart with 139 color names with the resulting color display:

www.boogiejack.com/colornames.html

For a color machine that generates hex codes for you:

www.boogiejack.com/colormach.html

For a color schemer that chooses complementary colors for you:

www.boogiejack.com/colormach2.html

3.16 Chapter Quiz

1. What does the body tag use to control page colors?

2. True or False: If you're using a background image, you should not use a background color.

3. What do you need to specify in the attribute and value of the body tag to add a background image?

4. Write the code for a web page's body tag with the background color of #FF8080.

5. What is the format of a hex code?

3.16 Chapter Quiz (continued)

6. What happens when a user clicks a link with the following attribute and value in the body tag? alink="red"

7. True or False: The following attributes and values are all you need to remove the page margins from a web page: leftmargin="0" topmargin="0"

8. Choose the one true statement:
   a. You should keep your images in a separate folder from your HTML files so they don't corrupt each other.
   b. You should keep your images in a separate folder from your HTML files so they are easier to find and will load faster.
   c. You should keep your images in the same folder as your HTML files so they are easier to find and will load faster.
   d. You should keep your images in the same folder as your HTML files because the images won't show up on your page if they're not in the same folder.

9. True or False: Most people look at the headlines first, text second, and graphics last.

10. Why are large background images not recommended?

11. What attribute and value do you add to the body tag so the background image doesn't scroll with the page?

12. How old do you think my wife Alison is?

3.17 Chapter Exercises

Exercise Option 1 – Practice Site

N̲ ow you get to have some fun. You're going to pick out the background color and text colors for your site, and if you want to use a background image you will select that, too. Your assignment, should you choose to accept it—and you'd better—is to choose your color scheme and program it into your index page.

If you still have the bad poem on your page, you can use it to view the text color. If not, you'll have to add some text to be able to see the text color. The link colors won't show until we add links to the page. Hang on, that's coming soon—program the link colors anyway.

Remember, when you add a background image, you have to get the file name, path, and file extension coded in the correct uppercase/lowercase pattern. The path to the background image if you've followed instructions will be:

```
background="images/imagename.jpg"
```

The image extension could also be .gif. At this time, JPG and GIF images are the only file types viewable by most browsers.

You might want to download a few extra backgrounds in addition to your first choice. If you don't like the way your first choice background image looks when you see it on the web page, you'll want to have a few other background images to fall back on. Of course, if you are also taking a graphics course or are already proficient in creating graphics, you might want to make your own background image.

Well . . . what are you waiting for?

Exercise Option 2 – Independent Exercise

C̲ reate two pages, one using a background color only, and the other using a background color and a left border style background image. Use the body margin attributes to create a side margin so your page text doesn't display on the border for the page with the left-border style background.

For text content, type in the entire *American Heritage Dictionary*. Either that or just make something up. Hey, I'm easy to get along with. Be sure to use paragraph and break tags, and justify the text in at least one section of your page.

Formatting Text

Chapter Four

4.1 Chapter Introduction

his chapter introduces the many ways to format text with HTML. You can specify various font sizes, colors, and faces, and you can do so in a variety of ways. In web design, a font is just another name for a typeface. The default font web browsers' use is Times New Roman on a PC and Times on a Mac. If you don't specify another font, that is the typeface a browser will use, as long as the computer displaying the web page has that font installed. On most PCs, Times New Roman is installed and active, and on most Macs, Times is installed and active.

We'll be looking at the HTML ways of formatting text, and the Cascading Style Sheet (CSS) methods. The HTML way of formatting text has been deprecated in favor of CSS, but it's still advisable to know both ways.

4.2 Font Sizes

espite CSS, using the HTML font tag is still the most common way to format text. This is simply because there are more amateur and semiprofessional web pages in existence than professionally designed, up-to-standards web pages. Older web pages also fall into the former group.

The default font size is size 3. Unless you change the font size in your code, that is the size it is

> **NOTE**
>
> In web design, the term "deprecated" means that a coding method is no longer recommended by the World Wide Web Consortium (W3C), which is the governing body that writes the rules of coding. Deprecated tags are still legal code and are to be supported by browsers until they become obsolete, but the W3C encourages the use of CSS for formatting text instead. Only when a tag has been declared obsolete is browser support no longer assured. Browsers will likely support deprecated tags for years to come, but at some point the tags may become obsolete and browser support for them may end.

displayed at for most users. To change the font size using HTML, you'd use one of these two tags:

<font size="4"> or <font size="+1">

As you can see in the previous examples, you can change the size by specifying another value such as 4, or by using a plus or minus sign. I think it's easier to simply name the size, but some prefer using the plus or minus method. Since the default size is 3, naming the font size as plus 1 makes it size 4. A minus 1 would make it size 2. There are seven font sizes in HTML. They are:

COMPARISON CHART		
<font size="1">	is the same as . . .	<font size="−2">
<font size="2">	is the same as . . .	<font size="−1">
<font size="3">	the default size . . .	no need to code it
<font size="4">	is the same as . . .	<font size="+1">
<font size="5">	is the same as . . .	<font size="+2">
<font size="6">	is the same as . . .	<font size="+3">
<font size="7">	is the same as . . .	<font size="+4">

To give you an idea of how these sizes display on a web page, look at the graphic below.

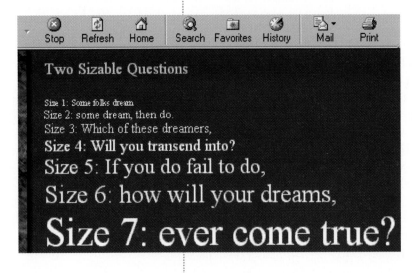

Corny text, huh? True though, your dreams will never come true if you don't act on them. The sizes shown are using the Times New Roman font— the default font most PC browsers use. Sizes shown here will vary slightly from what you see on your computer screen.

Using CSS to specify the font size requires an understanding of CSS, which is more thoroughly explained in Chapter 11: Cascading Style Sheets. To continue here and show both the HTML method and the CSS method for formatting text, a brief explanation of CSS is required.

CASCADING STYLE SHEETS OVERVIEW

In the early days of HTML, browser developers each had their own methods of implementing different code. This made developing web pages very difficult, as you perfected a page in one browser, checking the same page in another browser often returned a very different looking page. The response to this problem and other design problems was Cascading Style Sheets (CSS).

CSS is a hierarchical (thus the term, cascading) way of defining how each element (font, alignment, color, etc.) of a web page should display. CSS also added many new things that HTML didn't provide, such as colored scroll bars.

You can implement CSS in three ways: inline, embedded, and linked. All three options are covered in the CSS chapter, but to keep things simple as you start out, we'll only use the inline styles in this chapter.

CSS To change a font size using inline CSS, you code a font tag like this:

```
<font style="font-size: 12px;">
```

In the example above, the font size was set to 12 pixels high. There are actually several ways to measure size in CSS. You can reference the size using pixels, points, picas, ems, centimeters, millimeters, in relation to, and in percentages. We'll cover all that in Chapter 11: Cascading Style Sheets. For now, we'll use pixels because I think pixels are the best choice. Pixels offer more display consistency across the various computer systems and software in use.

4.3 Font Faces

Changing font faces is also quite easy, but there is one thing to keep in mind before choosing an alternate font face. Unless the system used to view your web page has the font you name available, it won't work. The default font, usually Times New Roman, is substituted if the named font isn't installed.

Arial
Arial Black
Book Antiqua
Bookman Old Style
Comic Sans MS
Courier New
Garamond
Impact
Times New Roman
Verdana

For this reason, you're really quite limited in the fonts you should name. You can—and may want to—specify alternate fonts in case the first one you name isn't active. That gives you a better chance of naming one that is active.

A short list of fonts that are commonly found on most PCs is shown at left. There's no guarantee that they will be on every computer, but they are on most, so the majority of your visitors will see your pages as you designed them if you stick to this list.

The graphic shows you all the typefaces in a 16-point font. (Traditionally, the size of text is measured in points, as you're probably accustomed to in a word processor or even your e-mail program.) The font size of 3 in HTML is roughly equivalent to 12-point type. This chart gives you an idea of how one font size in a particular font face relates to the same size font in another typeface.

On the Mac, for OS 9, you can always count on the presence of Charcoal, Chicago, Geneva, and Monaco—the fonts required by the system. Most users will also have Times and Helvetica, and possibly Arial, active as well. For Mac OS X, the system fonts you can count on include Geneva, Monaco, Lucida Grande, and Courier. Again, you can almost always figure that Times, Helvetica, and Arial will be active—especially Helvetica as many Mac OS X programs won't run without it. Although it's very likely that Mac users also have copies of all the PC fonts named on their computers, it's not as likely that the fonts will be active on their systems all the time. Mac users generally employ a font manager such as Suitcase or Font Reserve to carefully control which fonts are active at any given time.

To code your page to use a different font face add:

```
<font face="Arial">
```

To code an alternate font face along with your preferred font face:

```
<font face="Arial, Garamond">
```

In the previous example, Arial is the font used to display the text following the font tag. If Arial wasn't available on the viewer's computer, it would use Garamond.

If Garamond wasn't available it would revert to the default font of Times New Roman (unless the user has changed the default font in their browser's preferences). You can specify as many alternate typefaces as you like by separating each with a comma. HTML treats font names as case sensitive, so be sure to capitalize the first letter and follow the capitalization pattern within the font name.

To cancel a font tag, you simply type:

```
</font>
```

After the cancel font tag, the font used to display the page will revert to the default font.

CSS To code a font face using inline CSS:

```
<font style="font-family: Arial, Verdana;">
```

The same </font> tag is used in CSS. Using CSS also gives you new options. You can specify a generic family of fonts rather than a specific font. For example, if you wanted to use a handwriting style font such as Bergell, you can specify that font, and since it won't be found on most computers, you can also specify the generic "cursive" family as the alternate font. Doing this, a system without the Bergell font installed will substitute a cursive style font in its place. Although this assures that text will display in a cursive font, the results are not always the best when you let the visitors' systems choose fonts. To name a font this way, code it like this:

```
<font style="font-family: Bergell, cursive;">
```

Other font families you can use instead of cursive are: serif, sans-serif, fantasy, and monospace.

4.4 Font Colors

D rawing on your fine command of previous lessons, you can probably guess how to change font colors using HTML. However, I don't want you to say I left you guessing, so I'll show you how to change the font color:

```
<font color="red">
```

Can you guess what the font color would be with the above font tag in place? If you said red, you might be wrong! The fact is, it could be different shades of red in different browsers and on different operating systems and monitors. It could range from slightly pinkish to shades of brown or brick red. Using the hex code for red is a much better way to code if you want to ensure users are actually seeing red in a closer shade to what you had in mind.

The hex code for red is #FF0000, so you code your font color as:

<font color="#FF0000">

Remember, you must include the hash symbol before the hex code. Here's an example of using font colors:

CODE EXAMPLE

<font color="#ff0000">Sale!</font> Buy now for <font color="#0000ff">BIG</font> savings.

On a web page that would simply look like this:

Sale! **Buy now for BIG savings.**

You know, sometimes I think this stuff is just too easy.

CSS   The font color using inline CSS is:

<font style="color: red;">

Again, you can use hex colors instead of color names.

4.5 Headings

U sing headings is another way to increase font size. Headings, used for emphasis, are given more importance than regular text in most search engine algorithms. The search engine programmers have determined that if you code a text passage as a heading, it's probably more important than the regular text. This makes using headings combined with keywords an important part of your coding strategy.

Using this book as an example, the section headings (such as "4.5 Headings" at the beginning of this section) are the equivalent of using headings on a web page. This is proper design that will enhance the text's relevancy with search engines. Sticking to the rules and standard design concepts—rather than employing questionable practices and cheating—always pays better dividends in the long haul.

Headings come in six sizes. Unlike the font tags, in which the larger the number the larger the font display, headings are the opposite. The smaller the number used in the heading tag, the larger the font is rendered. This was another trick programmed into

---

NOTE

If you tried using a heading size to code a whole page—thinking it would help you with search engine rankings—it would probably have the opposite effect and cause a penalty in your ranking. Search engine programmers are aware that well-designed web pages don't use tricks such as that, and will not take kindly to your attempt to artificially enhance your ranking.

HTML intended to confuse the average person and give folks like me a chance to put a little jingle in our pockets explaining it all. Uh . . . you buying that reasoning? I might have made it up, but I'm not telling.

Coding a heading tag couldn't be simpler:

```
<h1>Your Heading Here</h1>
```

Simple! The heading sizes are from h1 through h6, but few people use h4, h5, or h6 as they are actually smaller than regular text. However, a heading is given slightly more importance by most search engines than a bold tag, so you might want to use an h4 rather than a bold tag for important phrases. This won't work if you want the bold text to flow within a sentence structure though. A heading tag automatically creates a paragraph break before and after the text inside the heading tag.

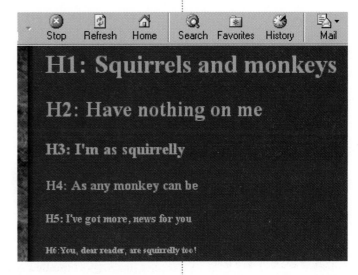

Look at the graphic to the right to get an idea of what different heading sizes look like.

This example shows the default font of Times New Roman. The actual size of the headings will vary a little with different fonts. Notice these are spaced farther apart than the font size samples. Headings automatically add a line of space above and below the line with the heading on it.

4.6 Alternatives to Headings

Headings are sometimes replaced with graphics to give more visual appeal to a page. This gives you the option of using any font you want, adding drop shadows and other effects, and creating a more stylized look. You can use one of the many free and commercial graphics programs to create images. While this book isn't going to teach you how to make graphics, creating headings is a fairly simple procedure that you can probably figure out on your own. If not, many tutorials on the Internet will help you learn how;

61

I've listed some of the better commercial and free programs in the book's resource page on my web site.

You'll learn how to add images such as heading graphics, buttons, photos, banners, and other images later. For now, I thought I'd show you a few examples of different heading graphics.

SUPER WIDGETS

1/2 Price Sale Now!

FREE - Lifetime Support!

Admittedly, I didn't take a lot of time to make the heading graphics. Having no real purpose on a web site, they're not much fun to do, but you can see how different font styles and effects can be an interesting alternative to standard headings.

One caveat though: a graphic may be more interesting for your visitor to view, but it is not as important as text headings as far as the search engines are concerned. However, by using the image "alt attribute and value" you can make up some of the difference. There will be more on the image alt attributes and values in Chapter 5: Adding Images, where you learn to add images to pages.

> **NOTE**
>
> Heading tags are not deprecated in HTML as font tags are, therefore I'll wait for the CSS chapter to show you ways to style your headings.

4.7 Other Font Formatting Tags

ther font formatting options are available as well. For example:

CODE EXAMPLE

This tag:	Does this:	Notes:
`<i>` . . . `</i>`	*sample*	Italics, creates italic text.
`<tt>` . . . `</tt>`	sample	Typewriter text, uses a monospace font.
`<big>` . . . `</big>`	sample	Creates slightly larger text.
`<small>` . . . `</small>`	sample	Creates slightly smaller text.
`<b>` . . . `</b>`	**sample**	Bold, creates bold text.
`<sub>` . . . `</sub>`	sample	Creates smaller text, positioned lower.
`<sup>` . . . `</sup>`	sample	Creates smaller text, positioned higher.
`<strike>` . . . `</strike>`	~~sample~~	Creates a strikethrough.
`<blink>` . . . `</blink>`	Um . . . yeah.	Close and open your eyes several times to simulate the blinking effect.

To see blinking text in this book, open and close your eyes several times real fast! Oops, blinking text doesn't work very well in a book does it? Just as well, most people find it highly annoying and its use is not recommended. It's also a Netscape specific tag—it doesn't work in any other browsers.

One note, the font formatting tags in this section are independent tags, and can't be used as attributes and values with the font tag. You can use them in addition to font tags, but not as an attribute and value for a font tag.

4.8 Combining Font Tags

f you want to make a font display more than one effect, such as a color change and size change, you don't need to create two font tags. Combine the two attributes and values into one font tag.

```
<font color="#00FF00" size="4">
```

63

Then, when you're ready to cancel the font tag, you only need to cancel the font tag once, because you've only opened one.

`</font>`

However, if you have two font effects and want to end one effect before the other, then you need to use two font tags. You should first code the tag you want to keep *open* the longest, and then code the one you want to *close* first. For example, if you wanted to have a size change and color change, but only want the color change for four words, you'd code as follows:

`<font size="4"><font color="#FF0000">`

I'm red and big.

`</font>`

I'm not red, but I am still big.

`</font>`

Your text would now return to normal, whatever normal happens to be.

The first cancel font tag closed the last font tag opened. The next cancel font tag closed the font tag opened just before that. Let's try another of my famous bad analogies here. When you're done groaning, consider this:

You're in your home office. You want to send me a check for $50 because I obviously need psychiatric help. Your checkbook is in the bedroom. As you leave your office, you open the office door to go down the hall. Because you're not finished in your office, you leave the door open. You come to your bedroom door and open it and grab the checkbook. With checkbook in hand, you leave the bedroom and close the door behind you; you're finished in there. You go back down the hall and enter your office and close the door.

Closing tags is like opening and closing the doors. You opened the bedroom door last; so on the way back to your office you closed it first. With tag sequences, you should close the last one opened first and work your way backward.

On second thought, though, send that $50 to my publisher. Many more bad analogies like this and he's going to need the psychiatric help.

For example, if you want a sentence in bold but want to italicize just one word, you use the same principal of opening the last tag to be closed first and the first tag to be closed, last.

WRONG WAY: <i> Don't </i> try this without adult supervision.

RIGHT WAY: <i> Don't </i> try this without adult supervision.

See the difference? The wrong example opened the italics tag and then the bold tag, but didn't close the tags in reverse order. Truth be known, it would still display correctly in most browsers, but would cause error messages in HTML validators and may not display right in some browsers. I also suspect some search engines treat your site better if it has properly coded pages. I haven't tested that theory—it's an observation based on known tendencies.

4.9 Creating Lists

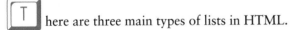here are three main types of lists in HTML.

- Ordered list: An ordered list is an indented list in which each list item begins with a number, a capital letter, a lowercase letter, an uppercase Roman numeral, or a lowercase Roman numeral. Ordered lists can also begin with any number or numeral. This is handy when you want to pick up where you left off from a previous list.

- Unordered list: An unordered list is an indented bulleted list. The bullet types available are the disk, the circle, and the square. The difference between a disk and a circle is that the disk is solid and the circle is an outline. This list you are reading is an example of an unordered list.

- Definition list: A definition list is an indented list without any numbers, letters, or bullets of any type.

With all list types, line breaks and indents occur automatically for each new list item. With an ordered list, the numbering or lettering is added automatically in sequential order.

Let's look at each type of list individually.

4.10 Ordered Lists

A n ordered list begins with the <ol> tag (that's OL, short for Ordered List) and ends with the </ol> tag. List items are added with an <li> tag (that's LI, short for List Item). There is no cancel tag for a list item, but there is for the list itself. If you do not specify a type of list, such as a lettered list, the default is a numeric list. To create a numeric list:

CODE EXAMPLE

```
<ol>
<li>First things first.
<li>Second things not first.
<li>Add an "LI" for each item.
</ol>
```

The code above would appear on a web page like this:

1. First things first.
2. Second things not first.
3. Add an "LI" for each item.

You might have situations in which you want to start a list, insert some text, then pick up the previous list from where you left off. To continue with the previous list, we'd add a start attribute and value to our opening list tag. See the example below:

CODE EXAMPLE

```
<ol start="4">
<li>Smiles...
<li>increase your face value.
</ol>
```

That would create a list that looked like this:

4. Smiles...
5. increase your face value!

Of course, you may not want to use numbers at all. You may want letters instead. Here is how to add an attribute and value to make a lettered list:

CODE EXAMPLE

```
<ol type="a">
<li>Friends are simply,
<li>family that we choose.
</ol>
```

That would appear on a web page like this:

a. Friends are simply,
b. family that we choose.

If you want to pick up a list like this from where the previous list left off, add both the attribute and value for the start and type (as shown in the previous two lists). To continue with this list, code the opening tag like this:

```
<ol type="a" start="c">
```

To code the various types of ordered lists:

CODE EXAMPLE

List type	Code	Results	Comments
1	<ol type="1"> . . . </ol>	1. 2. 3. 4.	Default list style.
A	<ol type="A"> . . . </ol>	A. B. C. D.	Are you having fun yet?
a	<ol type="a"> . . . </ol>	a. b. c. d.	I am.
I	<ol type="I"> . . . </ol>	I. II. III. IV.	I make my own fun.
i	<ol type="i"> . . . </ol>	i. ii. iii. iv.	Isn't that special?

4.11 Unordered Lists

An unordered list begins with the <ul> tag and ends with the </ul> tag. List items are added with an <li> tag. There is no cancel tag for a list item. If you do not specify a bullet type, such as a circle, the default is the disk. The bullet options are disk, square, and circle.

To create an unordered list with a disk:

CODE EXAMPLE

```
<ul>
<li>Everybody is somebody,
<li>be somebody nice.
</ul>
```

This would appear on a web page as:

- Everybody is somebody,
- be somebody nice.

To change that to a square bullet:

CODE EXAMPLE

```
<ul type="square">
<li>Everybody is somebody,
<li>be somebody nice.
</ul>
```

The other bullet option is a circle. Replace the word "square" with "circle" and your list would have hollow circles for bullets.

To code the various types of unordered lists:

CODE EXAMPLE

List type	Code	Comments
• Disk • Item • Item	`<ul type="disk"> . . . </ul>`	This is the default style.
▪ Square ▪ Item ▪ Item	`<ul type="square"> . . . </ul>`	Hi, how are you?
○ Circle ○ Item ○ Item	`<ul type="circle"> . . . </ul>`	Did you know you're special? You are, you know!

4.12 Definition Lists

A definition list begins with the <dl> tag and ends with the </dl> tag. After that, a definition list works a little differently from the other two list types. A <dt> tag goes in front of each term to be defined rather than an <li> tag, and a <dd> goes in front of each definition.

The <dt> stands for Definition Term. The <dd> stands for Definition of the Definition term. Silly isn't it? There are no cancel tags for <dt> or <dd> tags. The <dd> tag automatically causes a line break and indent. Bullets or numbers are not added.

Coding a definition list (also sometimes called a glossary list) looks like this:

CODE EXAMPLE

```
<dl>
<dt>This is the term to be defined.
<dd>This is the definition of the definition term.
<dt>What do long lines of text do within a list?
<dd>Long lines of text within a list—whether it's an ordered, unordered, or definition list—
wrap to the next line but remain indented.
</dl>
```

The sample definition list would appear on a web page like this:

This is the term to be defined.
This is the definition of the definition term.
What do long lines of text do within a list?
Long lines of text within a list—whether it's an ordered, unordered, or definition list—wrap to the next line but remain indented.

Definition lists, which are seldom used, are deprecated in HTML. You probably will never use one, but at least now you understand it. If you happen to take over as webmaster of a site that uses definition lists, you won't be confused by them.

4.13 Lists within Lists

By specifying different list types, you can create lists within lists. When coding this type of list, I always specify the type for each list, even for a numbered list in which nested numbers would be the default. It prevents any browser quirks from causing unexpected results when displaying the list. Unexpected results are not fun.

CODE EXAMPLE

```
<ol type="1">
<li>This is an item.
<ol type="a">
<li>This is a sub-item.
<li>This is another sub-item.
</ol>
<li>This is another item.
</ol>
```

This would create a list like this:

1. This is an item.
    a. This is a sub-item.
    b. This is another sub-item.
2. This is another item.

Of course, you can do this with any list types you want. If you create many lists within lists, it does get a little tricky. You have to make sure you close all the lists you open.

4.14 Paragraphs, Breaks, and Preformatted Text

W e covered paragraph and break tags in Chapter 1: Introduction to HTML, but we'll recap them here, go over a few other tips and tricks with them, then cover preformatted text.

<p align="center">   Centers every line of text or other content.

<p align="right">   Aligns content to the right side of the page.

<p align="left">   The default, aligns content to the left side of the page.

<p align="justify"> This aligns the text on a straight vertical line at both edges the page. Other content is unaffected.

NOTE

The paragraph tricks to the left are deprecated, but still work. It's better to use the <div align="..."> attribute and value, but I'm showing you these so you'll understand what they are if you run into a page you need to edit that uses them. This way you'll understand what it's all about... Alfie.

NOTE

Remember, the paragraph tag causes two line breaks. The break tag <br> causes one line break.

Sometimes, you might want a little more space then a paragraph tag offers. As with many other things in HTML, this can be accomplished in a variety of ways. You can alternate paragraph and break tags to create extra line breaks. That's really only practical for a few repetitions, after that you'd be better off using a `<pre>` tag. The <pre> tag is for preformatted text. The idea is that text is displayed more or less as you type it. In standard HTML, if you put three spaces between every word, only one space would be allotted on a web page. With the <pre> tag, all three spaces will be allotted. Line breaks work the same way. If you hit five carriage returns in HTML, it will not cause a break in text, the text will still break at the end of the line or where you place a paragraph or break tag. With a preformatted tag in place, the page will render it with all five line breaks (carriage returns). Because of this, you can code:

```
<pre>

</pre>
```

The number of line breaks you put between the <pre> tags is what you'll get on the web page—more or less. I say more or less because it does sometimes act a little quirky when you're formatting text along with spaces. Text used inside pre tags is rendered in a monospace font. A monospace font looks as if it was typed on an old-fashioned typewriter because each character takes up the same amount of space, whether it's as small as a period or as wide as a W.

4.15 The Division Tag

We covered this briefly in Chapter 1: Introduction to HTML, but let's recap and cover a little new ground with it. The division tag <div> by itself doesn't do a darn thing. When used with an align attribute and value, it is quite useful for layout control. Officially, the <center> tag is deprecated, but the majority of web site designers still use it.

There is a distinct advantage to using a division tag instead of a paragraph tag with an align attribute and value. If you use the following:

```
<p align="center">
```

. . . every time you start a new paragraph, you have to include the align attribute and value with the new paragraph tag. With a division tag, you only have to code the align attribute once. Every paragraph you add will have the same alignment—unless you over-ride the division align command by coding an align attribute into the paragraph tag.

To code a division tag:

```
<div align="center">
```

The other values are left, right, and justify. I prefer justified text—I believe it contributes greatly to a professional look. Justify affects only text, not images and other objects, which require other methods of alignment.

4.16 Transparent GIF Trick

W hen using left border backgrounds, you don't want your text and other content spilling over onto the border. Not only is it harder to read, but it also looks bad and is considered unprofessional. The transparent GIF trick is one way webmasters keep text off the border portion of left border backgrounds.

The idea is to place a transparent image on the left side of your page. The image forces the rest of the content over to the right and off the border. Because the image is transparent, your background shows through and no one is the wiser.

Another way to accomplish the same thing is to use a table, which you'll learn about in Chapter 7: Using Tables. Most new webmasters didn't understand tables, which is what made the transparent gif trick so popular. CSS offers a better way to create an empty border, while using tables is the way to go if you want to place content in the border area. We'll cover those methods later.

Regardless of all the new coding methods, a transparent GIF can be useful as a spacer for some layout problems, so I'll point you to the transparent GIF trick on my site. You can see how it's done and download a transparent GIF for your use. The URL is:

www.boogiejack.com/howx004.html

The transparent GIF is only a few pixels wide by a few pixels tall; the file size is minimal and will download as fast as text. You can specify the width and height of the image to the size you need, and the browser will stretch it to fit. Since it's transparent, no image quality is lost.

73

4.17 Chapter Quiz

1. The default font size is three. What are the two ways to change the font to size two using only HTML?

2. How would you change the font to 12 pixels tall using CSS?

3. You want to change the font on a page to Garamond. You also want it to be green. How do you code that using HTML?

4. You want one major heading and one smaller heading on a page. You want the first heading in the largest text possible, and the smaller heading two sizes smaller. The first heading should read "Music News." The second heading should read "Blues." How would you code the two headings?

5. Name the two main list types in HTML, not including the deprecated definition list?

6. Write the HTML code for an unordered list using circles for bullets. There are two list items, a dog and a cat.

7. You're in charge of your employer's web site. They want to mark down widgets from $29.95 to $19.95, and they want the old price to be crossed out. How would you code the price with a line through it?

8. What does "deprecated" mean in relation to HTML tags?

4.17 Chapter Quiz (continued)

9. You have several paragraphs of text to format. You want to justify the text, but don't want to include the align attribute and value with each paragraph tag. How would you do it?

10. Why would someone use the transparent GIF trick?

11. How would you use CSS to specify that the generic font family of cursive is used?

12. A year ago, a headline in our paper that lead to a story about why a permit hadn't been issued for a major construction project read: "Red Tape Holds Up Mall." Man, duct tape isn't even strong enough to hold up a mall, I wonder where I can get some of that red tape? Anyway, how many bricks are used in that mall, now that it's built?

4.18 Chapter Exercises

Exercise Option 1 – Practice Site

W ell now, time for another exercise already? Write the content for the index page and style it using the text formatting you learned in this chapter.

Remember, you should lead the users into your content by explaining the benefits of exploring your site further. That doesn't necessarily mean a detailed explanation. Often, just a teaser is more effective than a soliloquy. Depending on your site's topic(s), you might make it sound fun, interesting, educational, rewarding, profitable, humorous, enlightening, encouraging, heartwarming, or any of a thousand other things, just so a benefit to exploring your site is evident.

Be sure to use at least three text-formatting options. Five would be better.

Right. Let's get the show on the road.

Exercise Option 2 – Independent Exercise

C reate a new page. For content, write a brief explanation of what your page is about and what the benefit of viewing it would be. In the formatting use at least two different heading sizes. After your welcome message, write the text on your topic and create an ordered and unordered list. Be sure to use at least two font colors and two other text-formatting options.

Adding Images

5.1 Chapter Introduction

U ntil now, we've worked only with text, with the exception of adding a background image. Most web sites also use an assortment of images to add visual appeal. This chapter will teach you what kind of images you can use, provide guidelines on image use, and show you how to add images to pages.

Web images should be designed to load as fast as possible; therefore they are usually saved in a compressed format to make the file size as small as possible. A fully optimized image is compressed to the point that it will begin to lose noticeable quality if compressed any further.

5.2 JPG Image Type

T wo basic image types are used on web pages: JPG (or JPEG) and GIF images. The image type, derived from the compression method used to save it, is reflected in the file extension (such as image.jpg or image.gif). The image type JPG is an acronym for Joint Photographic Experts Group, the original name of the committee that wrote the standard.

JPG images use a "lossy" compression scheme, which means some image data is discarded in order to reduce the file size. The JPG compression scheme was designed to exploit known weaknesses in human vision. This weakness, that subtle color changes are not easily perceived, allows color subtleties to be discarded, resulting in smaller image files. The more the image is compressed, the more image information is discarded.

An optimized compression can reduce file size dramatically, with only minute visual differences. JPG images work best for real-world scenes such as photographs, textures, and similar material. JPG compression doesn't work as well on lettering, line drawings, large areas of one color, or images with color changes where there are sharp edges.

One of the nice things about JPG images is that when you save the image (in a graphics program, not as you download it from the web) you can set the compression level. By controlling the compression level, you can optimize the image to the point at which the file is as small as possible without sacrificing picture quality.

The other nice thing about JPG images is they are capable of displaying 16 million colors, far more than the human eye can distinguish. This means your images can be in full color and look as realistic as possible in a digital medium.

5.3 GIF Image Type

G IF, an acronym for Graphics Interchange Format, represents another type of image compression. GIF images work best for line art, cartoons, lettering, and similar images that have sharp edges and large areas of continuous color.

GIF images are limited to 256 colors. The fewer the number of colors in the image, the smaller the file size. A GIF image is an "interlaced image," which means that as data is downloaded, a fuzzy or poor-quality image begins to appear quickly, and as more data is downloaded, the image clears up. A newer form of JPG, called a progressive JPG, works the same way.

The GIF type features two unique options that sometimes give it an advantage over JPG. One advantage is that GIFs support transparency, so you can use a GIF as an invisible spacer on a web page or create images with a transparent background for special effects. For example, you might have the web page background or color show through part of the image, making whatever text or icon you placed on the graphic blend in with the page better. The other advantage of the format is that multiple, bundled GIF images can be animated.

> **NOTE**
>
> You may occasionally run into other image types on the Internet, but they are generally not recommended for use. Often, other image types cannot be viewed by all browsers. The exception is the PING format, which is generally viewable in most browsers, but for some reason has never caught on.

5.4 Design Principles and Image Use

I mages can be used to add clarity, navigation, color, interest, entertainment value, educational value, and many other benefits to your web site. In all cases images should complement your site and its content, rather than overwhelm it.

Too often, you find too many graphics on a web page. Too many graphics, and especially animated graphics, compete for the eye's attention and tend to distract and confuse the visitor rather than aid them in finding useful content.

Too many graphics will also considerably slow your web pages' download times. I've seen sites in which the total page size was larger than many software programs on my computer. That reflects an ignorance of how people use the web. Very few people will wait for a page like that to load. If you design like that, you might as well keep the page only on your computer, because you're the only one that's going to view it.

Generally speaking, the page's total file size is the size of the HTML file and all the graphics on the page added together. If you use any remote files on the page, such as Java applets or sound files, count those as part of the total file size because they have to download to make the page complete.

The general consensus is that a page shouldn't be more than 40K in size. You might consider making your index page even smaller. The faster it loads, the better the chance you have of the visitor staying around to sample your content. If users find something that interests them, they will usually wait longer for a page to load. But until your index page loads, they don't know for sure if anything interests them (unless they've been there before).

While much of the page-loading speed involves how well you manage the total page's file size, there are other factors. The speed of the visitor's Internet connection is one factor you can't control. But you can control the speed of your server to some degree. Pick a web host with fast servers and a good connection to the Internet backbone, and make sure they manage their systems well by not putting too many high-traffic sites on one server.

For every general rule, such as limiting total page size to 40K, there are always exceptions. Sites that offer an image archive (such as mine) are one of the exceptions. People expect a page full of graphics to take longer to load—and it's OK because they come there for the graphics. Of necessity, I make an exception for these types of pages. I do compensate for it by keeping my site with a reliable host that has fast servers and high-speed connections to the Internet backbone. Because I'm on a fast server, I can also allow my index page to be larger than 40K. I have a large variety of content to present, but because my site is very fast, my page loads as fast or faster than most sites, so the visitor does not become dismayed with the loading time.

Using Java applets also runs up page sizes. Java applets are small programs that create special effects or do other "tricks" that aren't possible with HTML only. Although sometimes this can't be helped, I always recommend against putting Java applets on your index page (with the exception of a small menu applet or other such small and well-behaved applet). Java runs off the user's system resources. Poorly written applets and applets that require a lot of memory can cause computers to crash. You'll discover that doesn't please people. I recommend that you place any Java applets on secondary pages, and that you warn visitors there is Java on the page. If a user's computer tends to crash when encountering Java, the user will at least have been warned and will enter the page at his or her own risk.

5.5 Adding an Image to a Page

A dding an image is easy, but you need to take care to use the correct path to the image and the correct capitalization pattern. Tags that do not reference a separate file, such as <div align= "right">, can be typed in either uppercase or lowercase and still work. But when a tag references an image file or other external file, the path and the name of the image must match exactly—and that includes using the exact same capitalization.

If you've followed along chapter by chapter, you already have a folder called "images" in the location where you're saving your web site. On a web server, the place where you keep HTML files is considered the root directory. On a floppy disk, your saved index page is in the root directory if you saved it to the disk without putting it in a folder. If you created a folder called My Web Site, or used another name, that folder is your root directory if that's where you saved your HTML pages. In the root directory of the floppy disk or folder, you also created a folder called images, so your path to the images folder is simply "images" in an image link (provided you were smart enough to put your images in the images folder!). If your HTML files are stored in a folder on a Mac desktop, that folder is the root directory. An image link for your web site then, would simply be:

<img src="images/me.jpg">

In the preceding tag, "img" is short for image; "src" is short for source. Therefore you're telling the browser that the image source is found in the directory called "images" and the image itself is called "me.jpg."

Suppose you had a lot of images and you created different folders within the image folder for different kinds of images. Let's assume one folder is of personal pictures of you and your family.

You created a folder inside the images folder and named the folder "Family." You then need to adjust the image path to reflect that additional folder. It would be:

```
<img src="images/Family/me.jpg">
```

Now you're telling the browser to go into the images folder, find a folder called Family, and then load the picture named me.jpg. Going back to the correct capitalization, if you named your directory Family as shown, but in your image path reference you type "family" in all lowercase, the result would be a broken image link. It wouldn't work because you didn't match the capitalization by using a capital F in Family.

The same rule holds true for the capitalization of the image name and the image extension. Additionally, if the image is a JPG and you reference it in your code as a GIF image, it wouldn't work either. Any reference to an external file has to be perfect or it's a no-go, Sluggo.

5.6 Basic Image Attributes and Values

Using the code shown in section 5.5 will add an image to a page, but it isn't optimized coding. Without adding the height and width attributes and values, a browser will start to display the page, then as the image data is downloaded it will have to start rearranging the page. By coding the height and width into the image tag, the browser reserves the space for the image and doesn't have to jerk the reader around by rearranging the page each time image data downloads.

You can probably guess how to add the height and width attributes by now, but I'll show you anyway. I have to fill up these pages with something.

```
<img src="images/me.jpg" width="320" height="240">
```

You can see in blue how to add the width and height attributes and values. The width and height don't have to be listed in that order. Most programs that tell you an image's width and height, however, do list width first so I find it easier to list them in this order.

The numeric values are the width and height as measured in pixels. If you don't have access to a graphics program that will tell you the image size in pixels, you can code the image into an HTML page, open the page in a browser, and find out the width and height in pixels. In Internet Explorer on Windows, you can right-click the image and choose Properties to display pixel dimensions. In Netscape on Windows, you can right-click the image and choose View Image. When the image opens in a new window, right-click it again and choose View Info. In Internet Explorer on a Mac, click and hold on the image to display a menu of options. Choose Open Image in New Window to see the pixel dimensions displayed in the window's title bar. In Netscape on a Mac, click and hold on the image to display a menu of options. Choose Open this Image. When the image opens in a new window, click and hold on it again. Choose Page Info from the menu to see the pixel dimensions. In this case it would read:

Dimensions: 320 x 240 pixels

In the image dimensions, width is listed first and height is listed second.

There is one other tag you should include with every image, and that is the image alt tag. Alt stands for alternative text. Some browsers do not display graphics at all, and some people have graphics capability turned off in their browsers. Although this is a minority of users, alt text is helpful for telling them what they can't see. This is especially important if you only use images for links to other pages. Without the alt text, anyone surfing with a graphically challenged browser will not know where the links take them—and probably won't be into guessing unless your site is extremely interesting without the visual appeal that graphics add.

An even more important reason to use alt text is for the physically challenged. Blind people and people with low vision use screen readers that read web pages to them. Without the alt text, the screen reader will have no information to pass on about the graphic, except perhaps that it is a link. For this reason, the alt tag for image links should be a descriptive and informative word or phrase describing what content the image links to.

The final reason to always use the image alt text is to improve search engine rankings. We will cover that in Chapter 12: Search Engine Optimization.

Let's add the alt text to our last image tag:

CODE EXAMPLE

```
<img src="images/me.jpg" width="320" height="240" alt="A picture of me at a New Year's Eve party with a lampshade on my head.">
```

As you can see in the blue text, you can write alt text to read as a sentence, phrase, or keyword. Whatever you put there is what a visitor will see until the image starts appearing. For Windows users, it is also what shows up in a little pop-up balloon when you rest a mouse on a downloaded image. Speaking of loaded images, I can just see you in that lampshade, you silly thing.

5.7 Image Borders

W hen you use an image as a link, HTML automatically creates a border around the image. Sometimes you might want it, sometimes not. I prefer not to have borders around image links. In the example below, you'll see how to add the border attribute and value. I've removed the other attributes and values (width, height, etc.) to simplify the tag in the example, but remember, you can and should use them all on your web site.

```
<img src="images/me.jpg" border="0">
```

Setting the border to zero removes the border from the image link. If you want a border around the link, you can either leave the border attribute and value off to accept the default value, or you can change the number from zero to the desired width in pixels.

If the image is not a link, you don't need to include the attribute and value unless you want a border (HTML only automatically adds a border to links). To add a border to an image that isn't a link, just include the border attribute and value, then set the border the number of pixels wide you want the border to be.

Unfortunately, you can't set the border color in HTML unless it is a link (and then it will be the link color). You can set the border color using CSS, which you'll learn later on if I don't forget to include it. If you find I did forget, don't tell me about it—I like to think I'm perfect. ☺

5.8 Image Alignment

R ather than coding separate align tags to help position an image, you can use an align attribute and value within the image tag. This allows the text surrounding the image to flow around the image rather than just above, below, or on the same baseline next to it.

```
<img src="images/me.jpg" align="left">
```

In the example above, I used the value of "left" for the align attribute. There is really no need to code that unless you're using other HTML commands that have changed the default alignment of the content, or unless you want text to flow around the image as discussed in the next section. The default alignment is always left.

The other possible alignment values are center and right. Center, of course, centers the image on the page or within a table cell, but text will not flow around a center-aligned image. Right aligns the image to the right side of the page or table cell. What's a table cell you ask? Patience Prudence, that lesson is coming.

5.9 Flowing Text Around an Image

I f you don't code the images for text to flow around them, the text before or after an image aligns to the bottom of the image for one line, then drops below the image. As you can see in the following examples, that doesn't exactly look good.

This is just a dumb bit of text to show how unprofessional it looks when you don't code your page so

that the text flows around an image. Rather unimpressive wouldn't you say?

This is another example of how the results can be rather unpredictable and downright ugly. Don't get caught making ugly web pages, it causes warts!

Isn't my wife cute! In the first example, there is an unsightly space on most of the right side of the picture. White space is good to plan into your design, but this is not a good use of it. In the second example, the picture was forced right by the short text that precedes it. Then it picks up with just one word before wrapping to the next line. This kind of coding will give you warts!

Now let's look at how much better it can look using an align command.

 In this example, the image has an align-left attribute and value so that the text will flow around the picture. When the text has reached the bottom of the image it will start flowing under the image as well.
Notice how the text flows along side the picture until it clears the bottom of the picture then wraps completely to the page edge.

This is much better, but wait . . .

Look at how close the text is to the right side and bottom of the picture. Wouldn't that look much nicer if there were a cushion around the image? We can add attributes and values to control the space around the image. Look at this last example.

 In this example, the image has an align-left attribute and value so that the text will flow around the picture. I've also included horizontal space and vertical space to the picture so that there is a cushion of white space around the image.
This creates a greater visual appeal and really makes you look like a pro. In addition, I've also justified the text to give this a tidy look.

Now this is really neatened up! Adding horizontal and vertical space to the image and justifying the text has given us a professional looking layout. If only I could get my lawn as neat looking.

Flowing text around the image uses the same image align attribute from section 5.8 of this chapter. An image can be aligned left, right, or to the center, although aligning to the center doesn't flow text around an image. It centers one line of text vertically and flows the rest below the image. So in practice, you really have two options for flowing text around an image, left or right. You can use tables to flow text in any way you choose, but we're not that far along yet. Discussed in Chapter 7: Using Tables, tables are a whole 'nother animal and represent new challenges.

So, the code for adding the align attribute to allow the text to flow around the image along with adding a cushion of space around the image looks like this:

CODE EXAMPLE

```
<img src="images/me.jpg" align="left" hspace="12" vspace="12">
```

The value of "12" for the hspace is measured in pixels. The hspace attribute is horizontal space, which creates a cushion on a horizontal plane between the picture and the text beside it. The vspace attribute is vertical space, and creates a cushion between the top and bottom of the picture and the text above and below it.

If we plugged in all the attributes and values we've learned in this section about flowing text around an image, our entire image tag would look like this:

CODE EXAMPLE

```
<img src="images/me.jpg" width="320" height="240" alt="My photo." align="left" border="0" hspace="12" vspace="12">
```

NOTE

Setting hspace and vspace in the image tag is deprecated in favor of CSS. You will learn how to set "padding" in the CSS chapter. As stated before, it's still wise to learn the HTML way of doing things because it's still much more prevalent on the web. Learning CSS also becomes much easier when you have a good understanding of HTML.

5.10 Clearing Image Alignment

With an image aligned to the left or right, text will flow around the image. At times, you may want to stop the text from continuing to flow around the picture and have it start below the picture. For example, a picture may have an explanatory note or caption, and you don't want the main body text mixed in with the picture's note or caption.

In this case, we need to use a break tag with a "clear" attribute and value. To do this:

```
<br clear="left">
```

This will stop the text from flowing around an image aligned to the left. If you align a picture to the right, then you'd change the clear value to right. If you have more than one picture and have used left and right align values, you can use the clear "all" value as well.

5.11 Low Source Option

[T]he low source option lets you add the URL or path of a low-quality image so it loads first, before a higher-quality image loads. The value of using a low source image is that it is usually a smaller file that loads faster. To create the smaller file, you can save a copy of the image using smaller dimensions, a lower-quality copy of the image (with more compression), a thumbnail of the regular image, or a combination of all the aforementioned.

The low source image gives the page the appearance of loading faster; after it loads, the real image will start loading. I don't use the low source option myself and I don't know many people who do, but you might want to. To add a low source image:

```
<img src="images/me.jpg" lowsrc="images/low_source_
image.jpg">
```

Where it says "images/" use the path to the image, and where it says "low_source_image.jpg" use the actual name of the low source image. You should also add all the other attributes and values to the original image tag as well as the low source image attribute and value.

5.12 Thumbnail Images

[T]humbnail images are small representations of bigger images. Rather than have several large images on a page, a webmaster makes miniature pictures of the larger images. The thumbnail images serve as previews of the full-size images, and usually link to the full-size images on separate pages. A visitor can examine the thumbnails and decide which full-size pictures they want to view. (You see this often on shopping sites.) This makes the page load faster and doesn't waste your visitors' time by downloading full-size images they don't want to see.

There are three basic ways to make thumbnails:

* The first method is to simply open the full size picture in a graphics editor, resize it to a smaller size, and save it. This is also called resampling. Some webmasters cheat—instead of

actually resizing and saving a second image to make a true thumbnail, they just use smaller dimensions for the width and height attributes of the image, giving it the appearance of a thumbnail. This isn't recommended because you don't gain any savings in download time. The full size images still have to download even though you coded it to a smaller size. All the data in the full size image is present unless you resize the image, no matter what size you code it to.

- A second method for creating thumbnails is to crop a small thumbnail-size section of the image. When you crop an image, you use a crop tool to trim away unwanted or un-needed sections. Rather than the thumbnail showing a miniature version of the full-size image, it shows an interesting section of the full-size image, with the rest of the image removed.

In most graphics applications, you'll find a resize or resample option in the Image menu or the Edit menu. For example, in Corel Photopaint, you'll find a Resample command in the Image menu. In Adobe Photoshop, one of the most popular graphics programs in the world, you'll find the Image Size command in the Edit menu. This screen shot shows you the Corel Photopaint menu.

- I like to call the third method logical thumbnails. It combines the first two methods. You crop out a larger section of the image than in the second method, and then reduce that to the desired thumbnail size. You get the best of both worlds this way. The thumbnail shows a greater section of the image than a simple crop, and more detail than a simple resizing. Logical and smart—if you get caught making logical thumbnails, you may be accused of being a brainiac!

It's beyond the scope of this book to also teach graphics, but there are recommendations for graphic programs on the Resource page found on my web site. I'll give you a quick look at how to resize an image in Corel Photopaint, one of my favorite graphics programs.

Look through the menus in your graphics program—you'll probably find a resize/resample command. When you find it, it's usually a matter of typing in the numbers for the new size or choosing a percentage. After resizing, choose:

File > Save As

. . . to save a thumbnail. Be sure to use a different name for the file or save it in a different location from the original file or you'll end up replacing the full-size picture with the new thumbnail.

A crop is a little more involved than that. Look for a tool like this on the toolbar. Clicking the tool icon selects that tool. Place the tool on one corner of the section you want to keep, and then drag it to the opposite corner of the section you want to keep.

You may need to play around a little to see how it works. In many programs, if you like the section you have selected, you just double-click inside the selected area. The rest of the image will be removed and the image size reduced accordingly. Then, if you're creating a simple crop thumbnail, you can save the image as explained before. If you're making a crop and resize, you just resize it and save it. Even with a simple crop, you'll probably want to resize it a little to make all the thumbnails a uniform size. Your thumbnail gallery will look a little neater and better planned that way.

5.13 Online References

Y ou'll find free web graphics on my site at:

www.boogiejack.com/free_graphics.html

Windows users can make their own graphics with my Background Magic software program. It makes a great graphic artist out of everyone, at least for making backgrounds and buttons. No talent is required, no difficult and highly technical paint programs to learn, no kidding. This program has won many rave reviews. You'll find the details at:

www.boogiejack.com/backgroundmagic.html

5.14 Chapter Quiz

1. What are the two main image file formats supported by most browsers?

2. Which image format is usually best for photographs?

3. The general consensus is that a page shouldn't be over _____ in size.

4. If you keep your photographs in a folder called "photos," which is in a folder in your root directory called "images," how would you write the code to put a picture called "Mom.jpg" on your web page?

5. Mom.jpg is 400 pixels high by 200 pixels wide and you want to align it to the right side of the page. What attributes and values would you add to the image to accomplish that?

6. The picture is of your mom in her army boots. Add an alt tag.

7. The text that flows around the picture of your mother in army boots is too close to the picture. Using HTML, how would you add a cushion of 12 pixels around the entire image?

8. Mom.jpg is a large file, and you want to add a low source image to it. How do you code a low source image into the Mom image tag using a low source image called "minimom.jpg," which is saved in a folder called "lowsource" in your root directory?

5.14 Chapter Quiz (continued)

9. What are logical thumbnails?

10. When using a browser to find image dimensions, which is listed first, width or height?

11. What is "cropping" an image?

12. If a group of slippery fish is called a "school" of fish, what is a group of slippery people called?

5.15 Chapter Exercises

Exercise Option 1 – Practice Site

The first part of this exercise is to create a welcome banner or business name banner. You can download blank banners from my web site or another web site and add text to them. Windows users can also download the free version of my software program, Background Magic, and make your own banners from scratch. You'll learn to use this intuitive program in minutes. For more information and the download link for Background Magic visit:

www.boogiejack.com/backgroundmagic.html

5.15 Chapter Exercises (continued)

You may use blank buttons and a blank banner for now if you like, because in Chapter 7: Using Tables you'll learn how to add text to blank buttons and banners using only HTML—no graphics editor required.

If you have a graphics program and can create your own buttons and banner, that's fine. Feel free to create your own. In addition to a welcome banner or business logo, you need either one blank button (that you will add text to during the lessons in Chapter 7: Using Tables and reuse for all the buttons) or one pre-made button for each of the following sections:

1. A Home, Index, Main, or similarly worded button indicating it's a link to your home page.

2. An About, About Us, About Me, Company, Mission, Mission Statement, Our Company, or similarly worded button indicating it's a link to learn more about the people or company behind the web site.

3. Media Kit, Advertise, Public Relations, Press, or other similarly worded button indicating it's a link to learn about advertising and media relations.

4. Resources, Links, Hot Links, References, or other similarly worded button indicating it's a link to other resources on the web.

5. A button to your content page indicating what the content is. It may be something like Software, Services, Poetry, Reviews, Photography, Art, Meet the Band, or whatever your site's focus is.

You already have text on your index page, and have added a banner or logo from option one. Option two of this chapter's exercise is to add the buttons. In the next chapter, the buttons will become links to your other pages, so place them in an appropriate place for site navigation. Buttons used for site navigation are usually placed in a vertical column on the left side of the page or the along the top under the company logo or welcome banner. Since we haven't covered tables yet, which you need to place buttons down the left side of the page, you will probably need to place the buttons under the banner/logo for now.

Exercise Option 2 – Independent Exercise

C reate a new page and place a banner or logo at the top. Under that, place at least four buttons to simulate site navigation. Next, use lessons from previous chapters to include a welcome message, a heading, an ordered or unordered list, and at least two text-formatting techniques.

Creating Links

6.1 Chapter Introduction

A s you may have picked up from previous chapters, a link is a small piece of HTML code that connects one file to another. Clicking on a link to another web page takes you from the page you're on to the other web page. If the link is connected to streaming audio, the link opens the default browser plug-in (if there is one) and starts playing the audio stream. A page can also be linked to software, fonts, or many other types of files that can be downloaded to your computer.

This chapter shows you how to link to other web pages on your site, and other sites on the Internet using hypertext links—those underlined words that take you from one place to another in cyberspace. It also shows you how to use images for links instead of words, and how to link to other types of files besides web pages.

6.2 External Links

Y ou know what a link does: it connects one web page to another web page or file so you can access it. The code to create a link contains the path to the other web page or file. Each file on the Internet has an address, called a URL, or Uniform Resource Locator. The link you create to the other file will include the web address of the page or file you're trying to connect to, and can be an internal or external link.

Generally speaking, an internal link is a link that goes to another web page or file on your web site. An external link is a link that goes to a page or file on another web site. An internal link may use a relative path or an absolute path. An external link must use the absolute path. That's fancy talk for saying an internal link doesn't need to use the full address, but an external link does need to use the full address. You should already be familiar with using a relative path. If you have followed along in the chapter exercises, you used a relative path to code the background image, banner, and buttons into your page. A relative path is the path to the file you

Chapter
at a Glance

6.1	Chapter Introduction
6.2	External Links
6.3	Internal Links
6.4	Opening Links in New Windows
6.5	Linking to Specific Points on Pages
6.6	Link Titles
6.7	Using Images as Links
6.8	Alternative Menu
6.9	Linking to Other File Types
6.10	Chapter Quiz
6.11	Chapter Exercises

want to link to in relation (relative) to the current location of the page you are coding.

An external link requires the full path because, without it, a browser simply looks in the directory on your web site for the file. You create links using the <a> (anchor) tag and the HREF attribute (HREF is an acronym for Hypertext Reference). The value for the HREF attribute is the URL of the file you're linking to. (If you remember, URL is an acronym for Uniform Resource Locator, a term often used to mean a web address.) It's the systematic way of keeping track of web site addresses used by the mighty keepers of such things. To create a link to my web site—and feel free to do just that!—you would add this code to your page:

```
<a href="http://www.boogiejack.com">Boogie Jack's Web Depot</a>
```

The "http://www.boogiejack.com" part is the value of the HREF attribute, and is the absolute path to my index page. The "http" portion is an acronym for Hypertext Transfer Protocol, the "www" is for World Wide Web, and "boogiejack.com" is my domain name. Web addresses also have a numerical address equivalent, but they are seldom used. Remembering "boogiejack.com" is much easier than remembering 209.15.70.105 or some other silly number.

Remember, in Chapter 1: Introduction to HTML you learned that the index page (index.html) is the default page name a browser looks for if a page isn't named. This link:

```
<a href="http://www.boogiejack.com/index.html">Boogie Jack's Web Depot</a>
```

. . . takes you to the same page as the first URL. The only part of the code that would show up on a web page is "Boogie Jack's Web Depot," and it would be underlined and in blue text, unless you coded the page to use another link color and/or to remove the underline.

To link to another page on my site, you merely replace "index. html" with the name and extension of the page you want to link to. For example, if you want to link to my newsletter sign-up page from another site, that page is named "**news.html**," you link to that page like this:

```
<a href="http://www.boogiejack.com/news.html">Almost a Newsletter</a>
```

That link would take you to a page on my site where you can sign up for my biweekly ezine that teaches webmaster tricks, computer tips, resources, and a little about life and how to succeed and be happy and make a difference in the world.

An ezine, by the way, is another name for newsletter on the Internet, which is short for electronic magazine. My ezine has received multiple awards, included being named the best ezine of the year and one of the top three ezines on the Internet, I'd be remiss if I didn't encourage you to sign up for it. You'll learn many things that aren't in this book. It's not that I'm holding the goodies back, but there will always be new developments that occur after this book is published. Plus, you simply can't put everything you know into a book. The old brain overheated the last time I tried that—you should have seen the smoke pouring from my ears. I had to go soak my head in water!

6.3 Internal Links

Internal links can use an absolute path the way external links do, but you shouldn't link to internal files that way. If you use an absolute path to files within your web site, the browser has to go back out onto the Internet, find your site all over again, then find the file you're linking to within your site. Since the browser is already on your site, using a relative link allows the pages to load much faster. The browser doesn't have to go out on the Internet and find your site because it's already there. It can simply look where you tell it to look within the confines of your web site.

The area your web host designates for your index page to be stored is commonly considered your root directory. If you keep your other web pages in that same root directory, simply include the page name and extension to link to them. For example, if you have a file named "music.html" and you keep it in the same directory as your other pages, to link to it you only need:

```
<a href="music.html">Music</a>
```

Not only is that easier to code, but it makes your web site work faster. This is relative linking. The file you named in the link is relative to your site only. There is no http address, so the browser doesn't go out onto the Internet—it stays within the directory it's already in to look for the file.

But what if you keep some HTML pages in other directories? Good question, Aunt Fred. You can still use relative linking. Look at the table below to see how some of the variables work.

CODE EXAMPLE	
Link Path & Page Name	**What It Means**
<href="page.html"> . . .	page.html is located in the current directory
<href="tips/page.html"> . . .	page.html is located in a folder (directory) called tips that is located in the current directory
<href="tips/other/page.html"> . . .	page.html is located in a folder called other that is located in a folder called tips that is located in the current directory
<href="../page.html"> . . .	page.html is located in a folder one level up from the current directory
<href="../../page.html"> . . .	page.html is located in a folder two levels up from the current directory

You probably didn't have too much trouble following along with the first three references in the table, but let me explain the last two. When you have a web page located in a subdirectory, and you're linking to a page in one of the higher-level directories, the relative path must indicate that. The two dots and forward slash (../) indicate to the browser that the file named in the link is one level up. For each level up, you add another set of two dots and a slash.

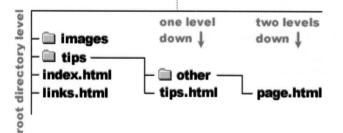

The graphic at left shows an imaginary root directory. When you're looking at it on your computer, it won't say root directory—you just see what's in the left column. In this imaginary directory, you have an images folder, a tips folder, an index page, and a links page in the root directory.

The images, tips, and other folders are actually subdirectories off of the root directory. You can see that to create a link on your index page to the tips.html file in the tips folder, you need to reference the tips folder in the path:

<a href="tips/tips.html">Tips</a>

To link to a file from the index page to page.html, which is two levels below the root directory, use:

`<a href="tips/other/page.html">Page</a>`

That should be clear by now; it's the same principle you used in linking to images. But suppose you want to place a link to the index page (located in the root directory) from page.html, which is located two levels below the root directory. You can't simply reverse the order used to get to the file—the browser will only look in folders within the current file's folder. That's where the ../ comes in. To get to a page on an upper level, like the index page from page.html, code the link as follows:

`<a href="../../index.html">Links</a>`

Since the index page is two levels up from the page.html, we coded in two sets of the two dots and a slash. For each level higher you need to go, add another set.

That's the tale of internal links. It's my story and I'm sticking with it.

> **NOTE**
>
> Note that the forward slash is always used to separate directory folders. Windows and DOS use a back slash, but that won't work for HTML. I have a friend who has a hard time remembering which is the forward slash and which is the back slash. Think of it as you type or read, which you do from left to right. If the top of the slash is leaning to the right (forward as you read or type), it's a forward slash. If it's leaning backward it's a back slash.

6.4 Opening Links in New Windows

Sometimes it's better to have linked content open in a new browser window. You shouldn't do it to keep people trapped on your site in one browser window, but there are instances when it's reasonable to open links in a new window. One example might be if you have an image gallery of some sort, and use thumbnails on the main gallery page. The link to the full picture can open in a new window. When your visitors are done viewing it, they can close the window, but still have the thumbnail index in front of them without having to use the back button and wait for the thumbnail page to reload.

I should warn you though: there will always be a percentage of people who don't like it when you open a new window, so make sure you have a good reason for doing so.

I use a strategy that works quite well and I've received many compliments on it. For links within my content that lead to external sites, such as with my product reviews, I code two sets of links. One link opens in a new window and one link opens in the current window. Folks like the choice I provide them. For links that are exclusive to my links pages, I code only the one link that loads in the

97

current window. They're ready to go somewhere else, so I let them go in peace.

Some people act like it's a tragedy if someone wants to leave their site, so they do everything they can to prevent it. That's a big mistake. Everyone goes elsewhere sooner or later. If you let them leave and give them good links to surf, there's a much greater chance they'll come back. After all, you've provided value to them. If you make it hard to leave, there's a good chance they'll never come back. If it happens to be a reviewer you trap, there's a good chance he or she will stop others from coming to your site with a bad review.

To create a link that opens in a new window, we add a target attribute:

`<a href="somelink.html" target="_blank">Some Link</a>`

This code will cause the link to open in a new window. Be sure to include the underscore preceding the word "blank" or it will open a named window. A named window is when you give the target a name, such as:

`target="chumbuddy"`

If you included the above target of "chumbuddy" with the link, the browser will open that link in the chumbuddy window. If a window named chumbuddy isn't already open, the link will open a new window. As long as the viewer has the window named chumbuddy open, all other links with chumbuddy as the target will open in that window. As you may have guessed, you can name the target to be most anything you want. Keep in mind though, target names are case sensitive.

6.5 Linking to Specific Points on Pages

So far, you've learned how to use the HREF attribute with the anchor tag. You can add the name attribute to link to the exact place on a page you want the browser to open the page to. This involves placing a special anchor on the page.

With the name anchor, among other things, you can create links from an index at the top of a page to a specific section lower on the page (and back to the top again). You can also link to specific sections on that page from other pages.

To begin, you need to know what section you want to be an anchor point. For this example, let's say you have a long page of

> **NOTE**
>
> The target attribute is also used in making pages that use frames. We'll cover that in depth when we get to Chapter 8: Using Frames, because we're so deep.

content and you want to make links at various points on the page to take visitors back to the top. At the top of the page, just under the body tag, write:

`<a name="top"></a>`

Notice you don't place any text between the anchor tag and the cancel tag. This allows the tag to remain hidden from visitors. The name can be anything you want (in this case, it's "top"). I use names that are relevant to the anchor point—usually. Sometimes I feel whimsical and might call an anchor point Snickerdoodle or something equally silly. The point is, you can use whatever name you like, just so you remember to call it by the same name in the link that takes the visitor back to the top (or wherever the link is supposed to lead to).

You can place anchor tags anywhere you want on a page, and you can use as many as you need. For the second part of the tag— the link part people see and click on—you place a tag like this at various strategic points on the page:

`<a href="#top">`Back to the Top`</a>`

The hash mark (#) means that the link is to a name anchor tag within the existing document. Next, you enter the name of the anchor you created, which was "top" in this case. Wherever you include this link, it will jump the visitor back to the top of the page. If you have a second anchor point that is named Digital Aroma, then you code the link that takes your visitor to Digital Aroma as follows:

`<a href="#Digital Aroma">`Digital Aroma`</a>`

This stuff is pretty easy when you start getting the hang of it. Now let's suppose you want to place a link to good ol' Digital Aroma on another page and you want the page to open right on the Digital Aroma spot.

To do that, you code the regular link, and then add the name anchor point:

`<a href="somepage.html#Digital Aroma">`Digital Aroma`</a>`

> **NOTE**
>
> Notice that there is a space between the two parts of the anchor name (Digital Aroma). You can do that with the anchor name, but not with the URL. You can't use spaces in web page names. Once the browser has found the page, however, it can find the anchor point even if it does have a silly name and a space in it.

6.6 Link Titles

A link can also include a title. These can be very useful for a number of reasons. When someone is using Internet Explorer (the most popular browser) and they rest the cursor on the link, the text of the link title will pop up in a little text balloon. You can use that to describe the content at the other end of the link without cluttering up a page. Link titles also give vision impaired people who are using screen readers a better idea of the content at the other end of the link. And finally, it gives you another chance to add legal keywords and keyword phrases to your web page without breaking search engine rules or looking like a redundant fool.

Add a link title like this:

```
<a href="photos.html" title="Check out my professional photographs.">
```

With that code, the words "Check out my professional photographs." will display in a pop-up balloon when a visitor rests the cursor on it. Search engines will feed on "professional photographs" as keywords (more about that in Chapter 12: Search Engine Optimization), and vision-impaired people will know they're going to have a hard time enjoying that page because they wouldn't be able to see the photographs. Mac users may not see the pop-up balloons, but the majority of your guests will. Screen readers for the Mac will pick up the title text for the user so it's still helpful to use link titles for them.

6.7 Using Images as Links

Using buttons or images such as thumbnails as links is popular on many web sites. This is very simple to do indeed. You already know how to add an image to a page. To use an image as a link, you simply replace the link text with an image:

```
<a href="somepage.html"><img src="images/linkbutton.jpg"></a>
```

The code in blue text shows where the link text goes creating a text link. By replacing the link text with a path to an image, the image becomes the link. In this case, the link goes to somepage.html, and the link itself is a button called linkbutton.jpg located in the images folder. The way this link is coded would create a blue border around the link's button graphic. The box would be the same color as the text links.

With buttons, the default border isn't very visually appealing, somewhat defeating the purpose of using a nice looking button. However, the border is helpful on thumbnails as it helps people realize the small picture is a thumbnail linked to a bigger picture. On graphic buttons though, most people remove the link border by including a border attribute and setting the value to zero:

```
<a href="somepage.html"><img src="images/linkbutton.jpg" border="0"></a>
```

This simple addition removes the border. Of course, if you're artistically indifferent or just a rebel, you can use the border attribute to make a larger border. Simply code a number greater than zero—and there are lots of numbers greater than zero, just in case you didn't know that. ☺

If you've been paying attention, you might be wondering what happens if you code a link title into the link tag for a link graphic along with an image alt tag into the link graphic. They both can't show up, can they? Nope. The image alt tag overrides the link title and shows up when a visitor's cursor is rested on a link graphic. Does that mean you should use only the image alt tag? Not necessarily. Using both will still give you extra keywords for search engines. Just code the image alt tag as the message you want to show your visitors, keeping in mind that the title may be read to people using screen readers.

6.8 Alternative Menu

A s a graphic artist, it is with great sorrow that I must tell you that some people just don't care about your pretty little link buttons and other graphics. They turn them off in their browsers because they want pages to load as quickly as possible.

This is just one reason you should always include alt text with graphic links. Without it, users won't have much of a clue where the graphic links lead. If you use graphics for links, it's always a good idea to include a text menu as well.

On my site, I have a text menu at the bottom of every page. It's the same on every page—each link leads to a major section of my site and it makes it easy to navigate even though there are more than 500 pages. By keeping the links consistent and in the same place on every page, you can quickly create familiarity for your

101

visitors. Before too long, they feel right at home. Of course, you can create familiarity with graphic links as well, but there are two other good reasons for using text links in addition to graphic links:

- Graphic links usually display on the first screen when a page opens. Pages are often longer than that, so as a visitor reaches the bottom of the page, the graphic links disappear. Rather than forcing your visitor to scroll back to the top of the page to regain access to links, text links at the bottom allow them to easily continue surfing your site.

- Text links show visitors the pages they have visited (if you have used the vlink attribute in the body tag). This makes it easier for them to continue surfing to new content instead of accidentally revisiting pages they've already visited.

Thoughtful little touches like these go a long way toward creating a positive experience for your visitors.

6.9 Linking to Other File Types

L inking to other file types—such as fonts, sounds, or zip files to download—is like coding any other link. For example, suppose you want to offer a zip file of your favorite quotes.

Say you save eight million quotes in a zip file called "quotes.zip." Then, you place the file in a folder called "zippies," which is in your root directory. To allow guests to download the zip file, you code it like this:

```
<a href="zippies/quotes.zip">Zip file of 8 Million Quotes</a>
```

When a visitor clicks that link, the browser asks if the user wants to save the file to disk or open it from its current location. You can offer fonts, sounds, and other files for download in the same way, although the response the browser makes will differ. With a sound file, your system will likely play the sound instead of downloading it. A visitor can still download and save the sound file. On Windows Internet Explorer, for example, just right-click sound files and choose Save Target to save it.

> **NOTE**
>
> A zip file is a file containing one or more files that are compressed to reduce the file size and download time. Zip files are comparable to Mac OS .sea or .sit files. StuffIt Deluxe 6.0 and greater, available from www.alladinsys.com for Windows and Mac OS, can handle zip files as well as .sea or .sit files.

6.10 Chapter Quiz

1. True or False: An external link is a link that goes to a file on your web site that is in a different folder from the current folder.

2. True or False: An internal link should always use an absolute path (the full address) to the file it's linking to.

3. In the code for a link, the "http" stands for what?
   a. HyperTerminal Transfer Path
   b. Hyper Transfer Target Protocol
   c. HyperText Transfer Protocol
   d. Hairy Tom-Tom Player

4. URL stands for:
   a. Uniform Resource Locator
   b. Unit Reference Locator
   c. Uniform Reference Location
   d. United Resources Lexicon

5. You have a page named "snerk.html" in a folder named "Other" that sits in your root directory. On snerk.html, you want to place a link back to your index page. Write the code.

6. You have a thumbnail image linked to a larger image and you want it to open in a new window. The image is on a page named "alien.html" and in a folder named "images." The thumbnail image is named "ALIEN.JPG" and is in the same images folder as the HTML file. You want to leave the border at the default setting. Write the code.

6.10 Chapter Quiz (continued)

7. You are as fickle as can be, and decide to remove the border from the alien image. Add the code to the tag from question 6 to remove the border.

8. You want to link to the top of your page from the bottom. What code would you place at:
   a. The top of the page?
   b. The bottom of the page?

9. Add "World Events" as a title for the following link:

   <a href="world_events.html">World Events</a>

10. You use graphic links on your site. Name one reason to also use text links.

11. Name another reason to use text links with graphic links.

12. When asked which block I live on, why did I forget where I live?

6.11 Chapter Exercises

Exercise Option 1 – Practice Site

This is a two-part exercise. The first part is to create the other four pages for your web site. Before you complain about what a taskmaster I am, take comfort in the fact that you don't have to create the pages with all the meta tags and content just yet. Simply create four pages using only the basic HTML tags needed to make them work. Include a simple text message on each one to identify which content page it will become. The idea is to practice creating workable links.

Part two of this exercise is to link the buttons on your index page to the individual pages you made. The text label on each individual page will help you determine if the link goes to the correct page.

Hint: If you include a link on each individual page back to the home page, you can easily click the link to go back so you can try them all.

Exercise Option 2 – Independent Exercise

Create a new page about a topic of your choice. Create a message selling your visitors on the idea of visiting a second page, which you will also create. The result will be a simulated index page about a topic of your choice and a content page dealing with that topic. On each page, create a link to the other page. Use at least two text-formatting options. On the content page, use at least one larger-size heading and two smaller headings as subheadings within the content. Be sure to use separate colors for the link, active link, and visited link.

Using Tables

7.1 Chapter Introduction

ables, a more advanced HTML layout mechanism, allow you to arrange a web page, or parts of the page, in a grid of rows and columns. Using tables allows you to better control spacing, draw borders around text or graphics, and set various background colors or images for each table cell. Using some spiffy tricks that I'll show you, you can even use tables to add text to blank buttons and banners without a graphics program. Tables may become deprecated one day in favor of CSS layout techniques or perhaps layers, but right now browser support is nowhere near what it needs to be to create universally compatible complex layouts in any way other than with tables.

7.2 Basic Table Facts

 hings to know about tables:

- A table is a design mechanism for arranging content into a grid of vertical columns and horizontal rows.

- Tables can be as large or as small as you need them to be, and you can gain further layout control by placing tables inside of tables.

- Each block of a table that holds data is called a table data cell.

- If you don't specify the size in the code, tables and table cells expand automatically to fit the content—but that may not produce the layout you expect or desire.

- Anything you can put on a web page you can put in a table. However, code instructions in one table data cell don't carry over to the next table cell. For example, if you code a font color in one table cell, that color won't carry over to the text in the other table cells—even if you leave the font tag open.

107

NOTE

For a table data cell to remain open, it needs content. If a table requires empty cells, they can be forced open by using a transparent GIF image as the content, or even more simply, with a no break space tag. (The no break space tag was originally created to prevent lines from breaking at inappropriate places. For example, you might use one to "glue" together text such as "2 1/2" miles, so the browser doesn't break the line after 2 and wrap 1/2 to the next line.)

Likewise, most of the code outside the table cell doesn't affect the contents inside the table.

- Tables can have backgrounds and background colors independent of the web page background image and background color. Table rows and even individual table data cells can have their own background image and background colors as well, giving you many design options.

- On tables with multiple columns, cell widths must add up correctly, or you may lose the control you're trying to gain. For example; if you code a table to be 500 pixels wide and have two columns that are 300 pixels wide, then something has to give, and it may not give the way you want.

- If you forget to close a table, Internet Explorer is smart enough to still display the page. Netscape will display an empty page from the beginning of the table to the end of the page. Whenever you have a page that doesn't show up in Netscape, the first thing to do is check to see if you left a table open.

This table shows you how table rows and columns read. On a web page, the border is often invisible, but it's included here for visual reference.

As you create tables, it's often useful to use a border as a reference, and then remove it when you're satisfied with the layout. Using a border as you design helps you visualize better and makes it much easier to troubleshoot problems.

As you'll soon see, table data cells do not have to be evenly sized. Table data cells can also span more than one row or column, giving you more layout control. You will learn how to do this later in the chapter.

	COLUMN 1	COLUMN 2	COLUMN 3
ROW 1	COLUMN 1 ROW 1 (table data cell)	COLUMN 2 ROW 1 (table data cell)	COLUMN 3 ROW 1 (table data cell)
ROW 2	COLUMN 1 ROW 2 (table data cell)	COLUMN 2 ROW 2 (table data cell)	COLUMN 3 ROW 2 (table data cell)
ROW 3	COLUMN 1 ROW 3 (table data cell)	COLUMN 2 ROW 3 (table data cell)	COLUMN 3 ROW 3 (table data cell)

7.3 Basic Table Tags

 or the simplest table, you need only these basic tags: a table tag, a table row tag, a table data tag, and the cancel tags.

CODE EXAMPLE

```
<table>
<tr>
<td>
The content always goes inside the table data cells.
</td>
</tr>
</table>
```

Of course, a simple table like that doesn't give you much more layout control than not using a table. Tables always start with a table tag and always end with a cancel table tag. The <tr> tag is for table row, which starts a row of one or more table data cells. The <td> is for table data, and all content goes within the table data cells.

Technically, you don't always have to close the <tr> and <td> tags, but I **strongly** recommend that you do. Not closing them will result in problems with some browsers. If you use an HTML validator, leaving out these closing tags will cause warnings. And there's always the chance that some search engines weigh valid HTML code, or lack thereof, as a criteria for relevancy.

Let's examine the basic table properties more closely.

<table>

The above is the opening tag for a table. Since we're making a table, that's a pretty reasonable way to start it!

<tr>

The above starts a table row. Every table must have at least one row.

<td>

The above starts a table data cell. Every table must have at least one table data cell. The actual content is placed inside the

109

table data cells. Table data cells can hold anything—graphics, text, links, green mugglewumpits . . . OK, *almost* anything. Green mugglewumpits usually escape because they're so good at tunneling.

The first table data cell must follow a table row tag, but each table data cell doesn't have to have to be on its own row. You can place several table data cells in one row, as you'll soon see.

</td>

The above closes a table data cell. If you have a table data cell open, you should first close it before opening a new one or before starting a new row.

</tr>

The above closes a table row. If you have a table row open, you should first close the previous table data cell and the previous table row before starting a new one.

</table>

The above closes the table. Go figure. That's the basic table format, although if you're using a table to display rows and columns of data, you should use table header tags <th> as well. They assist vision-impaired people who are using screen readers in matching table content to the correct heading. You'll learn more about table headers in section 7.19 of this chapter.

7.4 Simple Magazine-style Tables

A simple two-column table is popular for creating a magazine-style layout with two columns of text. As you'll see in the example, it is fairly simple and straightforward, which makes it a good place to start teaching.

This table could easily be expanded into three columns by adding one more table data cell after the second column and adjusting the column widths accordingly.

In the following example, I chose a 600-pixel width table. Later in this chapter, Section 7.20: Considerations, explains this and other design choices. Following is a miniature representation of a two-cell table with the code to create it.

```
<table width="600" height="1000">
<tr>
<td width="300">

This is a one row, two-column table. This is
column one.

</td>
<td width="300">

This is column two of the table.

</td>
</tr>
</table>
```

This is a one-row, two-column table. This is column one.	This is column two of the table. Smile ö It looks good on you!

The code on the left produces the table on the right. This type of table can be used to create web pages in a two-column magazine-style format. I set the width for each column at 300 pixels so they are nice and even. Notice that the two columns at 300 pixels each add up to the total table width of 600 pixels. You can also code the table and/or the cells in percentages. If you code the table as: width="80%", the table will fill 80 percent of the browser window on the computer viewing it. A cell coded to a percentage for width would be that percentage of the table, not the screen.

> **NOTE**
>
> The cell color isn't shown in the code, it was added for illustration purposes to make the graphic stand out. The "Smile …it looks good on you" line isn't in the code either. I really can ad lib sometimes. I should have been a professional ad libber. It would certainly look impressive on my résumé.

7.5 Cell Alignment

Cell alignment refers to how the content of each cell is aligned horizontally and vertically. The horizontal alignment attribute is simply referred to as "align," and the vertical alignment is referred to as "valign."

In the previous example, I set the table height to 1,000 pixels. You don't actually have to code height for this type of table, as the height will automatically adjust to the content. I included it here to demonstrate what happens to text (or other content) by

111

default when it's not vertically aligned. Without coding a vertical alignment, the text is centered vertically within the column, as shown in the graphic. Since two columns of text are often of unequal length, a vertical alignment attribute is used so the text in each column starts at the top.

```
<td width="300" valign="top">
```

Notice the valign attribute and value. This starts the text at the top of each column rather than centering it vertically within the column. The possible values for the valign attribute are: top, middle, bottom, and baseline.

By default, the horizontal alignment is to the left. The possible values are left, right, and center. To code the horizontal alignment, add this to the <td> tag:

```
<td width="300" align="left">
```

Since the default alignment is to the left, you only need to use an align attribute when you want to align the content of the cell to the center or right.

7.6 Cellpadding

Another concern with the example table is that the text extends to the edge of the table cells. Without white space between the columns of text, it will look sloppy and will be difficult to read. There are two common methods for adding white space within a table, each producing slightly different results.

The first method is to set the cellpadding attribute. Cellpadding creates a cushion of space between the table cell content and both the horizontal and vertical edges of the table cell. Cellpadding is set in the opening table tag:

```
<table width="600" height="1000" cellpadding="20">
```

This places 20 pixels of padding on the left and right edge of the table, and 40 pixels of padding between the two columns. This is because the left column will have a padding of 20 pixels on the right side, and the right column will have a padding of 20 pixels on the left side, resulting in a combined 40 pixels of padding between the columns. It will also give 40 pixels of padding between the bottom of one cell and the top of a cell in the next row (if the table has more than one row).

7.7 Cellspacing

$\boxed{T}$he second method for creating white space in a table is to set the cellspacing attribute. Cellspacing creates a cushion of space in between the table cells. This sounds very similar to cellpadding, and if you don't use a border or different background color or image in the table, the results are almost the same.

The cellspacing attribute specifies the space in between the cells, so text will still go right to the edge of each cell. Cellpadding creates the space within the cell, so the text does not go to the edge of the cell. It's a subtle difference—unless you use a border or different background colors or images that let the differences show. Look at the graphic to the right to see the difference visually.

In the graphic at the right, the black lines are the cell borders of a two-cell table. As you can see, the gray area within Cell A represents cellpadding. Text in Cell A would go to the edge of the gray area.

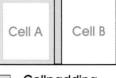

The yellow area in between Cell A and Cell B represents Cellspacing, or the amount of empty space in between table cells.

To add cellspacing to a table, add the attribute and value as follows:

```
<table width="600" cellspacing="20">
```

This will create 20 pixels of space between the table data cells, but unlike the cellpadding attribute, it only creates 20 pixels in between the columns. You can use both the cellpadding and cellspacing attributes in the same table. This is often the way to go if you use a background color or image. You can prevent the text from reaching the edge of the cell without doubling the space between columns with the cellpadding attribute. By coding it like this:

```
<table width="600" cellpadding="3" cellspacing="14">
```

. . . you will have 20 pixels of space between the columns (the cellpadding of 3 pixels times 2 two cells = 6 pixels, plus the cellspacing of 14 pixels), yet the text won't go right to the edge of each cell.

7.8 Left Border Table

The example table is the type of table commonly used on pages with a background image along the left side (commonly called a left border background). Typically, the left column of the table is set to a width that goes 20 to 40 pixels beyond the border color or pattern of the background image, with the second column filling the rest of the page with the main content.

Usually, the left column is either left blank to show off the border, or it has navigation buttons or links and perhaps advertising or other content. To set the table's border width correctly, you need to find out the horizontal pixel coordinates of where you want the column to end. You can do this by opening the background image in a graphics program such as Corel Photopaint. Or, you can just make a wild guess and then adjust as needed.

Most border backgrounds have from 100 pixels to 160 pixels of color or pattern. As a starting place, set the width of the first column to 120 pixels and save it. Open the page in a browser to see if you need to make any adjustments.

The following example shows how to code a border with an empty left column. It also introduces a new width value, a percentage of the page instead of a fixed pixel width. By setting the table to 100 percent of the page width, and setting the first column width to an absolute width, the first column will remain the width you set, while the second column will adjust to the remaining width of the browser window. The width remaining will vary from computer to computer because of different sizes and resolutions.

A typical page with a left border style table might look like this:

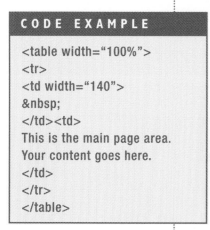

CODE EXAMPLE

```
<table width="100%">
<tr>
<td width="140">
 
</td><td>
This is the main page area.
Your content goes here.
</td>
</tr>
</table>
```

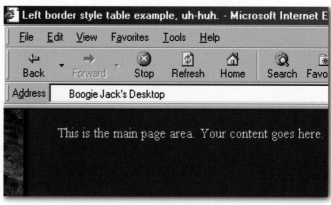

There are two things to note in the previous table code. First, notice the   tag (no break space tag) after the first table data cell column. This holds the cell open. Without something there, the browser views the cell as empty and collapses the column. The no break space tag is merely a space, but it's enough to hold the cell open. Typing a space on your keyboard into the cell will not hold it open—it has to be hard coded. Another commonly used trick is to place a transparent GIF image in the cell. The no break space tag is a slightly faster method of keeping the cell open because no image has to be downloaded.

The second thing to notice is that we did not include a width in the second table data cell column. With the table set to 100 percent and the first column set to 140 pixels, the browser will open the second cell to the space remaining on the screen. This method occasionally caused problems in older browsers, but so few of these are still in use that it's safe to code this way. Sooner or later, those folks hanging on to extremely old browsers have to upgrade. If you don't draw the line somewhere, all web pages would still be just plain text.

7.9 Left Border Table with Button Navigation

On the next page, the same table shown in Section 7.8 now has button links in the left column. You could probably guess how to accomplish this, but "allow me to show you because I need to feel needed," he needed to say.

A few things in the code need explaining. First, you may have noticed there is no URL (link) associated with the home button. This code was written for the index page. If you don't include a link with a button, it won't be active and visitors will know not to click on it. I wouldn't do it that way, but you might want to as it allows you to keep all your link buttons the same on every page. If I were setting up a small site using left border button navigation, I'd either remove the button for the page or use an indicator that the visitor is on that page. This indicator might be a second button that has a slightly different look such as a darker or lighter shade, different colored text, or perhaps an arrow or some other symbol to indicate the current page.

Second, notice the border on all the images is set to zero. Without doing that, there would be a blue link border (or whatever color you set the links to be) around the entire button. This defeats the purpose of using attractive buttons.

115

CODE EXAMPLE

```
<table width="100%">
<tr>
<td width="140">
<img src="home.jpg">
<br>
<a href="poetry.html">
<img src="images/poetry.jpg" border="0" width="120" height="30"></a>
<br>
<a href="about.html">
<img src="images/aboutme.jpg" border="0" width="120" height="30"></a>
<br>
<a href="advertise.html">
<img src="images/advertise.jpg" border="0" width="120" height="30"></a>
<br>
<a href="links.html">
<img src="images/links.jpg" border="0" width="120" height="30"></a>
</td><td>
This is the main page area. Your content goes here.
</td>
</tr>
</table>
```

The final thing to note is that a break tag is used after each image. With the borders set to zero, using a break tag makes the buttons touch each other on the horizontal edges, giving a nice menu-style appearance. Using a paragraph tag would have created too much space and resulted in an unorganized look.

With the table border set to 1 pixel, you can see how the table plays out. The graphic at left shows what the sample page from that code looks like.

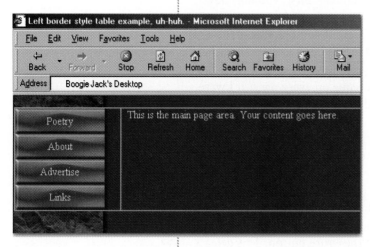

116

7.10 Adding a Background Color or Image

A table can have a background color or image that overrides the background image or color set in the page's body tag. Each table row or each table data cell can also have a separate background image or color. The background image or color set for the table, row, or data cell will override any other background tags set elsewhere. In other words, the most current command for the background is the one used.

First let's look at how to set a background color for the table:

```
<table width="600" bgcolor="#FF0080">
```

With the bgcolor attribute added to the table tag, the color value of #FF0080 will be used in all cells of the table unless a row or data cell is coded with another background color or image. The example uses a hex code, but you can use color names here as well.

Now let's look at how to add a background image to a table:

```
<table width="600" background="images/mybackground.
jpg">
```

Adding a background image uses the attribute of "background" with the value as the path to the image along with the image name and extension—just like you did for the page's body tag. In fact, coding a background image or background color into a table uses the exact same attributes and values as used in the body tag.

Pretty simple so far. But with all the other attributes available and the ability to nest tables within tables, they can become complicated and confusing in a hurry. That's why I recommend building tables with borders, even if you don't want borders in the final results. The ability to see the border is a tremendous layout aid—and it can always be removed when you're satisfied with the table.

To add a background to a table row, use the table row tag:

```
<tr bgcolor="blue">
```

or

```
<tr background="images/mybackground.jpg">
```

Depending on which tag you use, all the table data cells in that row would have either a blue background color or use the background image you name. Any table data *cell* within this table row

117

that is coded with its own color or image for the background would override the background set for the table row or the table.

Coding a background color or image for an individual table data cell is also done the same way, only in the table data cell tag:

```
<td bgcolor="#552144">
```

or

```
<td background="images/mybackground.jpg">
```

Any background coded for an individual table data cell will override a background coded in the table row or the table.

7.11 A Four-column Table

1	2	3	4
5	6	7	8
9	10	11	12

To present data in a more complicated setting, I've chosen a four-column table. You'll see how quickly the code can become confusing as the complexity grows.

In this example table, I used no align attribute in the first table row, therefore the content of cells 1–4 align to the left of each table data cell by default.

I used the align=center attribute and value for the second row, so in cells 5–8 the numbers are aligned horizontally in the center of each table cell.

For the third row, I used the align=right attribute for cells 9 through 12, so all the numbers are aligned to the right of each cell—except the last cell. In the last table data cell, I used an align=center value and attribute, which overrides the alignment coded for the table row.

This table is only three rows tall, so you can see how complicated things become if you have a few dozen rows worth of information to present in a table. The complexity multiplies in proportion to the number of attributes and values you use. As an example of a very complicated table—with tables within tables, different backgrounds, and different alignments—take a look at the source code for the ASCII chart on my web site:

www.boogiejack.com/ascii-chart.html

Notice how the page name is a relevant name for search engines. Chances are, someone searching for an ASCII chart would type "ascii chart" in a search field. I'm good to go with that page name.

Now, let's look at the actual code for the previous table:

CODE EXAMPLE

```
<table cellspacing="3" cellpadding="5" border="2">
<tr>
<td width="75"> 1 </td>
<td width="75"> 2 </td>
<td width="75"> 3 </td>
<td width="75"> 4 </td>
</tr><tr align="center">
<td> 5 </td>
<td> 6 </td>
<td> 7 </td>
<td> 8 </td>
</tr><tr align="right">
<td> 9 </td>
<td> 10 </td>
<td> 11 </td>
<td align="center"> 12 </td>
</tr></table>
```

If you study the code, you can see how the numbers and alignment in the table data cells correspond to each cell in the table shown.

You might have noticed that I only included the width for the table data cell in the cells on the first row. Since all the cells in the table are the same size, this is all that is necessary. The following rows follow suit. In fact, once you have the table data cells set in the first row, the following rows must be the same unless you specify a cell to span two or more columns, then you can set the cell to the combined width of those columns.

7.12 Spanning Columns and Rows

T able data cells can span one or more columns, allowing more flexibility in design. Look at the table on the next page, then check out the code that follows.

1 & 2		3	4
5	6	7 & 8	

NOTE

The table code below doesn't show the cell colors; I added that for better visualization because you're worth the extra work!

CODE EXAMPLE

```
<table cellspacing="3" cellpadding="5" border="2">
<tr>
<td width="150" colspan="2"> 1 & 2 </td>
<td width="75"> 3 </td>
<td width="75"> 4 </td>
</tr><tr>
<td width="75"> 5 </td>
<td width="75"> 6 </td>
<td width="150" colspan="2"> 7 & 8 </td>
</tr></table>
```

When looking at the actual table, there appears to be three columns in the first row and three columns in the second row. Actually, there are four columns in both rows.

The first cell in the table actually spans two cells, as does the last cell in the second row. Each time you span multiple columns, the columns must end where other columns are established. You couldn't, for example, specify that cells 7 and 8 are each 100 pixels wide because there is no true column established in the first row. Those widths would throw the table off and make it cry Uncle Goofy—and you wouldn't like that at all.

When creating a complicated table, it's often much easier if you draw the table on paper first. It's easier to visualize the table setup as you start coding if you have hard copy for reference.

As you can see, we made the cells span two columns by adding:

```
<td width="150" colspan="2">
```

In addition to adding the colspan attribute and value, we also adjusted the width to that of two columns. As the code shows, for a more complicated table like this it's better to code the table data cell widths for each cell. This helps prevent browser—and human brain—short circuits!

Table data cells can also span multiple rows. It works the same way as spanning multiple columns, only instead of the colspan attribute and value, use the rowspan attribute and value.

7.13 Spanning Multiple Columns and Rows

I f you start mixing different colspans and rowspans in a table, you really should plan it out on paper first because it gets very complicated in a hurry. Preparing ahead can save you hours of fooling around trying to do it all in your head. Look at the table at right:

The first table cell spans two columns.

The next table cell, in the third column spans all four rows of the table.

In the second row, we have two cells that span no other columns or rows, but since Column 3 spans all four rows, we no longer create a cell in the third column.

In the third row, we have a single cell again, then a cell that spans two rows.

Finally, in the fourth row, there is only one table cell left to code because the middle column in the third row spans two rows.

Columns 1 & 2 Row 1		Column 3 Rows 1, 2 3 & 4
Column 1 Row 2	Column 2 Row 2	
Column 1 Row 3	Column 2 Rows 3 & 4	
Column 1 Row 4		

The following code shows how this table was created. To help you see how it works, I've included the height and width of each table cell. Again, I left out the cell colors and other attributes to make the code easier to study.

CODE EXAMPLE

```
<table width="300" height="400">
<tr>
<td colspan="2" width="200" height="100"> Columns 1 & 2 <br> Row 1</td>
<td rowspan="4" width="100" height="400"> Column 3 <br> Rows 1, 2, 3, & 4</td>
</tr><tr>
<td width="100" height="100"> Column 1 <br> Row 2 </td>
<td width="100" height="100"> Column 2 <br> Row 2 </td>
</tr><tr>
<td width="100" height="100"> Column 1 <br> Row 3 </td>
<td rowspan="2" width="100" height="200"> Column 2 <br> Rows 3 & 4 </td>
</tr><tr>
<td width="100" height="100"> Column 1 <br> Row 4 </td>
</tr></table>
```

Does that look a bit confusing? Let's break it down the same way I set it up.

First, I started with a rough drawing of a three-column, four-row table, as shown here. Actually, I drew this example with a graphics program so it would be neater and easier to understand. If I showed you the drawing I did by hand, you would doubt my artistic abilities!

As shown here, all tables are grids of squares and rectangles. You can create a variety of layouts by combining different rows and columns with the rowspan and colspan tags.

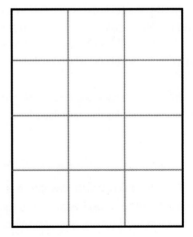

After drawing the basic grid, I then colored the columns and rows of cells to combine to achieve the layout used for this sample.

I wanted to combine the first two cells of the grid I drew (represented here by the red squares).

Next, I knew I wanted the last column to span all four rows (represented by the green squares).

Finally, I decided to combine the last two rows of the center column together (represented here by the yellow squares).

The rest of the cells are single column, single row cells (the white cells).

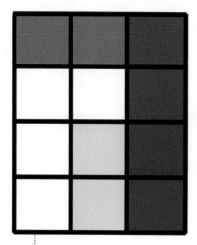

In my actual drawing, I just made the grid lines darker, but I thought the colors would be easier to understand here. You might use colored pencils or markers to color in the grid—at least while you're still green at making tables—and you'll probably find it much easier going.

With a handy drawing to refer to when making tables, there's a smaller chance you'll goof it up! Referring to my drawing, I started off with the table tag and added the width, height, cellspacing, cellpadding, and border. Often, you don't have to include the height, but it makes this example easier to understand because everything isn't scrunched together.

When coding a table, you work from left to right, just as you read. In looking at my diagram, the first thing I had to do was code the first cell to cover the first two columns of the table. You do this with the colspan attribute, so I typed:

```
<td width="200" colspan="2" height="100"> Columns 1 &
2<br> Row 1 </td>
```

Since I decided to compose my table of grids measuring 100×100 pixels, I knew the width of the colspan was equal to two grids, or 200 pixels. So I coded the width at 200, added the colspan tag and attribute, and finally the height. Then I added the words "Columns 1 & 2, Row 1" to the cell so you can see how the code relates to the actual table. I also put a break tag in between the columns and rows text to make it easier to understand.

Next, I closed the first table cell and started a new one. Looking at my drawing again, I see that the third column should span all four rows of the table. So I added the appropriate rowspan tag along with the height and width attributes and values as shown below:

```
<td width="100" rowspan="4" height="400"> Column 3<br>
Rows 1, 2, 3, & 4 </td>
```

Since this table data cell is now complete, I closed it. We've also reached the last column in this row, so I closed that table row. Remember, work from left to right just as you read. Having reached the end of the row, we must start a new row, just as when you reach the end of one line you're reading, you start the next line. So, we closed that row and started a new one:

```
</tr><tr>
```

Next, looking at my drawing tells me the next two cells are single column, single row cells. This part is easy, so we add them like this:

```
<td width="100" height="100" > Column 1<br> Row 2 </td>
<td width="100" height="100" > Column 2<br> Row 2 </td>
```

By now you may be thinking, "What about the third column?" Good thinking, Uncle Betty! Since the third column has a rowspan of four, and we've coded the second row up to the third column, we are at the end of this table row.

Technically, the third column was already coded into this table row, and all the table rows, when we added the rowspan tag to the third column in the first row.

So now we cancel this table row and start on row three:

```
</tr><tr>
```

Having canceled row two and started row three, we look back at our drawing and see the first cell is a single column, single row cell, so we add that:

```
<td width="100" height="100"> Column 1<br> Row 3 </td>
```

That was easy. Now, according to our drawing, the second cell in this row, the cell in the second column, has a rowspan of two, so it covers both rows 3 and 4 in the second column. To accomplish this, we add the rowspan tag to this cell and adjust the height to the combined height of two rows (or 200 pixels):

```
<td width="100" rowspan="2" height="200"> Column 2<br>
Rows 3 & 4</td>
```

Now we've coded this cell up to the third column, and can see that the third column covers all the table rows. So we cancel the third table row and start the fourth and final table row.

Looking at our drawing again, we can see only one cell is left. The third column covers all four rows. The cell in the second column, third row, also covers that column in row 4, so there is just the first column, fourth row cell remaining to code:

```
</tr><tr>
<td width="100" height="100">Column 1<br> Row 4</td>
</tr></table>
```

At the end of the table, we cleverly remembered to close out the table to prevent page errors. Now the table is finished and looks like we intended. Let's celebrate with some ice cream!

If you don't want a border on the table, now is the time to go back and remove it. If spacing isn't crucial, just remove the border attribute and value. If it is, set the border to zero. Why? Because if you remove the border attribute and value, the border doesn't show—but in some browsers the space it would occupy remains. If you set the border to zero, the space the border would occupy is removed. This is a small point unless you're trying to join two graphics together to look like one. If you don't set the border to zero, you'll never get them to connect. If you're joining two graphics together, you'll also need to add cellpadding and cellspacing tags and set them to zero. Some browsers leave a 1-pixel space in their place if they aren't set to zero.

Whew. That was a doozy, wasn't it!

7.14 Using Tables to Add Text to Blank Banners

A trick not widely known among webmasters is that you can add text to blank banners using tables. This is very useful if you don't have a graphics program or graphics skills. This technique is also useful on pages where you might want to change the banner often. One little change in the code and it's like having a new banner, saving you the time it takes to continually make new banners.

To accomplish this, use a blank banner as the background for the table cell. Here is the code from the sample on my site.

CODE EXAMPLE

```
<table width="305" height="81" cellpadding="0" cellspacing="0" border="0">
<tr>
<td background="images/blank.jpg" valign="middle" align="center",
<font size="7" color="#6a570d">Boogie Jack</font>
</td>
</tr>
</table>
```

As you can see, it is just a simple, single cell table. The table's dimensions are set to the width and height of the blank banner. The cellpadding, cellspacing, and border are all set to zero to make sure none of the banner is cut off. The banner is then coded as the background image for the table cell. The valign and align attributes and values are set to center the text on the banner. Then, you just add the text and close everything out. It's pretty simple, but very effective.

On my web site, the results of the sample code look like the graphic at left.

As you can see, it looks like a normal banner in every respect. The only thing you have to be careful about is that the text you use on the banner actually fits on it.

After the complicated table shown previously, I'll bet you were glad to see an easy one!

7.15 Using Tables to Add Text to Blank Buttons

 uch like adding text to banners, adding text to blank buttons using tables is easy. But there are some additional tricks you can use to enhance your buttons. The really nice thing about using tables to add text to buttons is that you can use the same blank button over and over. If you have a page with 10 button links, and all the buttons are 3K in file size, that's 30K of data that has to download before all the link buttons show. Using just one blank button, only 3K has to download and all the buttons are there! It's an extremely effective way to speed up your web page.

With a little Cascading Style Sheets coding, you can even make the button text change color as your visitor's cursor passes over the text. I call this the Mighty Mouseover button technique. Why? Because I made it up, so I get to name it what I want. Hoorah for me!

Take a look at the code for a sample button table:

CODE EXAMPLE

```
<table cellpadding="0" cellspacing="0" border="0">
<tr>
<td width="188" height="44" background="images/blank_buttons.jpg" align="center" valign="middle">
<a href="index.html">Home Page</a>
</td>
</tr>
</table>
```

As with the banner table, the cellpadding, cellspacing, and border values are all set to zero. The blank button is used as the table **data cell** background instead of the table background, and the alignment values are set to center the text vertically and horizontally on the button.

So far, so good. Besides the background, it's just like the table used to place text on a blank banner except that the text is a link and we didn't increase the font size. The other thing to note is that, occasionally, you may have to code the size of the table data cell a pixel or two smaller than the actual button size to get it to look right.

By adding a little CSS code to the <HEAD> section of the document, you can have the link text change colors when the cursor is

127

resting on it. To create the Mighty Mouseover effect, add this code to the HEAD section of the page:

CODE EXAMPLE

```
<style type="text/css">
<!--
a:link {color: #000080; text-decoration: none;}
a:visited {color: #946c6b;}
a:active {color: #fee333;}
a:hover {color: #ff0000;}
-->
</style>
```

Cascading Style Sheets (CSS) are explained more thoroughly in Chapter 11: Cascading Style Sheets, but briefly:

- A:link sets the link color; the second part of the tag removes the underline from the link.
- A:visited sets the visited link color.
- A:active sets the active link color (shows that the link is connecting to the linked file).
- A:hover sets the hover color when a cursor is on the link text.

If you use this information in the head section, you could re-move the link, alink, and vlink attributes and values from the body tag—as far as Internet Explorer is concerned. You might want to leave them in for Netscape. Netscape's support of CSS tags has been spotty in previous versions, although the current version offers very good support.

For each link button, you need to repeat each small table. You'll change only the link text and the URL of the page the button links to. If you use them as left border style navigation buttons, then these mini-tables will be placed inside a larger table like the one shown in section 7.9 of this chapter.

Following is the code for a table with nested tables (tables within tables) that creates two buttons.

CODE EXAMPLE

```
<table width="100%">
<tr>
<td width="140">
<table cellpadding="0" cellspacing="0" border="0">
<tr>
<td width="140" height="44" background="images/blank_button.jpg" align="center"
valign="middle">
<a href="index.html">Home Page</a>
</td></tr></table>
<br>
<table cellpadding="0" cellspacing="0" border="0">
<tr>
<td width="140" height="44" background="images/blank_button.jpg" align="center"
valign="middle">
<a href="advertise.html">Advertise</a>
</td></tr></table>
</td><td>

You continue with your main page content here . . .
```

This code will create two button links in the left column—one to the home page and one to the advertising page. Three tables were opened and two were closed. The two tables containing our buttons were closed, but the first table, the master table, was left open and a new table data cell started for the main content area of the page. You place your main content there, then close the master table.

One other note: If you make a button's link text too long, it will either force the table cell to open wider and cause the button to start repeating or it will force the text onto a second line. Neither option is good, so make sure the link text fits on one line on one button.

7.16 Using Mighty Mouseover Buttons Horizontally

B rowsers never place tables side-by-side, even if there is room for them. Therefore, to use the Mighty Mouseover button technique in a horizontal navigation bar, you need to place all the buttons inside a single row control table. A control table allows the buttons to be placed side by side—otherwise the buttons will be stacked on top of each other because they are each in a separate table. A quick two link horizontal navigation bar using the Mighty Mouseover technique would look like the following example.

CODE EXAMPLE

```
<table width="200" cellspacing="0" cellpadding="0" border="0">
<tr>
<td width="100" height="30" background="images/blank_button.jpg" align="center" valign="middle">
<a href="index.html">Home Page</a>
</td>
<td width="100" height="30" background="images/blank_button.jpg" align="center" valign="middle">
<a href="advertise.html">Advertise</a>
</td></tr></table>
```

You may notice that this code is almost the same as the left border style code. The difference is, we used separate tables for each button in the left border example to keep our master table a simple two-column table rather than having one column span the many rows required for each button otherwise. Where we used a break tag in the left border table to drop one button under the other, we simply canceled one table data cell and opened another to place the buttons side-by-side. This technique can be used with or without a master table controlling the rest of the page layout.

7.17 Using Tables to Create Picture Frames

 ou can use tables to create a variety of picture frames without having to know beans about graphics creation.

The example on the left is the original picture of me. *Easy* ladies, I'm a happily married man.

On the right is the framed version of the same photo. I created the frame using tables and a background image, but you could use a background color instead of an image.

Here's how the frame was created:

CODE EXAMPLE

```
<table border="4" cellpadding="0" cellspacing="0" width="225" height="272">
<tr><td>
<table cellpadding="0" cellspacing="0" background="images/texture3.jpg" width="221" height="268">
<tr><td align="center" valign="middle">
<table border="2" cellpadding="0" cellspacing="0" width="180" height="208">
<tr><td background="me.jpg" width="180" height="208">
 
</td></tr></table>
</td></tr></table>
</td></tr></table>
```

To create this particular picture frame, I created two tables inside a third table. All three tables are single cell tables of one row, one column each. The first table sets the overall size of the frame and the outer border width. Notice that I set the border to four. This is the outer table, or master table, for the whole enchilada.

The second table adds the textured background image to the table, which is set in the table tag. Since the border of the outer master table is set to four pixels, I made this table four pixels smaller than the master table. The second table also includes the align and valign attributes and values in the table data tag so that the next table (which contains my picture) will be centered within

131

the frame. This is the table that creates the green texture between the outer edge of the master table and the outer edge of my picture.

The third table is set to the size of the picture, and it uses the picture as the background of the table data cell. This table also has a small border to create the inner frame. Since there is no actual content in this cell, I used a no break space tag to force the cell open to the coded dimensions, allowing the background image of the cell to show me in all my otherworldly glory.

Finally, we have opened three tables without closing any, so to finish it off, we close all three tables. Few people know this trick, so you are among the privileged elite. Now run out and count your lucky stars.

7.18 Border Colors

Table borders can have colors, too. Shazam, the world gets better every day! Internet Explorer and newer versions of Netscape allow a light border color and a dark border color. Combining light and dark border colors can give borders a nice three-dimensional look. Look how nice this can look:

ASCII Character Chart

Ascii #	Makes	HTML	Ascii #	Makes	HTML
0 - 8	unused		105	i	i
9	tab			106	j	j

10	line feed	
	107	k	k

This table on my site uses only a gradient background image; the rest of the color is done with coding.

To see this entire table, you'll find it at:

www.boogiejack.com/ascii-chart.html

To add border colors, use the opening table tag. Of course, you need to have a border width set in the table tag for any border colors to show. For example:

```
<table border="3" bordercolor="#D96C00"
bordercolorlight="#FBCA57" bordercolordark="#9B4E00">
```

That's all pretty straightforward. You've seen enough code now that you should be able to understand it without further explanation, and I'm just the guy to test that theory on you. (Insert Snidely Whiplash diabolical laugh here.)

7.19 Using Table Headers

A fter the complicated tables you've seen in this chapter, you'll find the proper use of table headers to be a breeze. Whoosh, feel that cool wind now.

In the table on the right, the months May, June, and July are all table headers. The names Bob, Ann, Joe, and Sue are also table headers. Headers are basically used to identify rows and columns in a table.

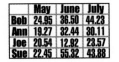

	May	June	July
Bob	24.95	36.50	44.23
Ann	19.27	32.44	30.11
Joe	20.54	12.92	23.57
Sue	22.45	55.32	43.88

If the example table contained a list of employee long-distance phone charges, you and I can see that Sue rang up $55.32 in long-distance charges for her employer in June. We can follow the "Sue" table header across and the "June" table down visually to get the data we need. A blind person cannot do this. If you use table headers, the blind person's screen reader can make that association for the person. Without the table headers, a blind person would have to mentally count and remember each row and column to figure out Sue's charges. That's not so easy to do, even for geniuses like you and me.

Most webmasters just use table data cells in place of headers and include the text in bold to set them apart. Text is automatically bolded if you use table headers. Let's look at how that table of phone charges is coded. I'll leave out the width attributes to make it easier to digest. Remember, you don't necessarily have to include width attributes; the table will expand as much as needed without them. However, if you want all the columns and rows to be even in dimensions, you will probably need to include width attributes.

CODE EXAMPLE

```
<table>
<tr>
<td> </td>
<th>May</th>
<th>June</th>
<th>July</th>
</tr><tr>
<th>Bob</th>
<td>24.95</td>
<td>36.50</td>
<td>44.23</td>
</tr><tr>
<th>Ann</th>
<td>19.27</td>
<td>32.44</td>
<td>30.11</td>
</tr><tr>
<th>Joe</th>
<td>20.54</td>
<td>12.92</td>
<td>23.57</td>
</tr><tr>
<th>Sue</th>
<td>22.45</td>
<td>55.32</td>
<td>43.88</td>
</td></tr></table>
```

If you study the code, you can see that <th> tags are used in place of <td> tags. The only difference they make in the display of the table is that the text in table header (<th>) cells is bolded by the browser.

Table headers should be used along the top row and/or down the left side of a table as needed for row and/or column identification.

Because the first cell of the table is a blank cell, I used a * * tag to hold that cell open. If I hadn't used it, it would look as if someone took a square bite out of the table in some browsers.

As with all tables, this one is coded left to right, top to bottom.

If you notice Sue's recent long-distance charges, I'm sure you agree she's been spending too much time on the phone lately. Watch it Sue, the boss is monitoring your phone activity closely!

7.20 Considerations

 hen building pages with tables, considerations include:

- Screen readers for the visually impaired read from left to right, top to bottom. Make sure your tables are understandable that way.

- Tables can make it seem as if a page loads slower because some browsers do not render the table until all the content within them is downloaded. In reality, about the same amount of data has to be downloaded, so it takes about the same amount of time. It seems to take longer because nothing appears right away. When using tables, it's wise to use several smaller tables rather than one big table whenever possible. Smaller tables load faster and give your visitors something to look at after the first table loads. While they're starting to look at the content, the subsequent tables are downloading.

- Screen resolutions should be taken into consideration when determining the width of a table. The most common screen resolution is 800×600 pixels, although the trend is heading toward higher screen resolutions. In theory, this means the viewing screen is capable of displaying a page that is 800 pixels wide and 600 pixels high without scrolling. In reality, the browser takes some of those pixels for scroll bars and tool bars.

- On my site, which serves about 800,000 visitors a month, about 60 percent of my visitors use the 800×600 resolution. About 9 percent are at 640×480 and about 22 percent are at 1024×768. The rest are at even higher resolutions or nonstandard resolutions. For tables, there is a nice option that works well in most settings: If you place the content in a 640-pixel wide table (or even slightly smaller), then center the table on the page, your site will look like it's designed just for each viewer's resolution at all but the highest resolutions. This is what I did until advertiser requirements called for a wider page. Then, like a rat, I sold out!

7.21 Online References

n online table tutorial with seven sample table layouts:

www.boogiejack.com/howx014.html

A list of table tags:

www.boogiejack.com/howx015.html

Online tutorial with an example of adding text to banners:

www.boogiejack.com/howx013.html

Online tutorial with working examples of the Mighty Mouseover buttons:

www.boogiejack.com/howx021.html

Just how fancy can a table be? Take a look at this one:

www.boogiejack.com/ascii-chart.html

Picture frames tutorials with other examples:

www.boogiejack.com/howx023.html

www.boogiejack.com/howx024.html

Blank banners, buttons, and other graphics:

www.boogiejack.com/free_graphics.html

7.22 Chapter Quiz

1. Tables are a grid consisting of vertical _____ and horizontal _____.

2. Each block of a table that holds content is called a _____.

3. True or False: A font color coded outside a table will not affect the text inside the table.

4. You have a two-column table and want the content in each column to start at the top of the columns. What is the attribute and value you would add to each table data tag to accomplish this?

5. What attribute and value would you add to a table tag to create a cushion of 12 pixels within each table cell?

7.22 Chapter Quiz (continued)

6. What attribute and value would you add to a table tag to create a cushion of 20 pixels between each table cell?

7. You have a left border background coded into a page with a two-column table. The left cell of the table is used just to keep the page's content off the border. What tag would you use to hold that cell open?

8. You want to make a table with two cells in one row, and you want the first cell to have a background color of #FF1234. In the second cell, you want to use a background image. The image is located in a folder called "images" in the root directory and the background is "TableBG.jpg." Write the code for that table with no other attributes. Indicate where the content goes with the word "Content."

9. What attribute and value do you add to a table data cell to cause the cell to span two rows?

10. When using tables to create link buttons, what kind of code is placed in the <HEAD> section of an HTML document to create the hover color change?

11. What is the most common screen resolution (at the time of this writing)?

12. What's the difference between a teacher and an engineer?

7.23 Chapter Exercises

Exercise Option 1 – Practice Site

pen your index page.

- If you're using a left border background, add the table to keep the content off the border.
- If you're using buttons in the left column for navigation, make sure they are coded into it.
- If you're using blank buttons, code the links onto them using tables. Add the CSS tags to the head section if you want a hover color.
- Optional: If you want to create two or three columns of text on your index page, or use tables in any other way, feel free to do so. The idea of this exercise is to start using tables to lay out a page in an attractive and efficient way.

Now, for those of you who don't have to do at least two of the first three items listed above, don't think you're skating off that easy. You get to create a new page and code the following table on it. It might be good for everyone to try to recreate the table using only this chapter as a reference—after all, you want to learn don't you?

- Hint 1: The border is set to a value of two.
- Hint 2: The grid is made up of 100 pixel units.
- Hint 3: Remember to work your way through it from left to right and top to bottom, starting in the upper-left corner.

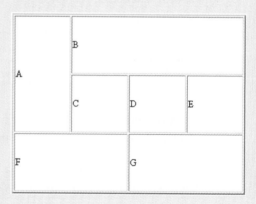

7.23 Chapter Exercises (continued)

Exercise 2 – Independent Exercise

C reate a new page and name it anything but index.html. Create the table from Exercise Option 1, except make the table data cell grid 150 pixels instead of 100. Place the following content into each cell as indicated:

Cell A: Create a link to your index page from the previous chapter exercises, and add links in a vertical fashion to the other pages you've made for your practice site.

Cell B: Create a brief message to show "what's in it for them" to encourage people to explore your site.

Cells C, D, and E: Create three lists, one in each cell. Each should have a text label in bold type, followed by a list of three things. The list items can be anything from your favorite colors to your family members' names. I suggest you do not make a list of why your socks talk to you as that will usually cause people to suspect your sanity. Obviously with cells this small, the lists should be short.

Cell F: Use this cell to say something nice about someone in your class, or if that makes you uncomfortable, say something nice about anyone you choose.

Cell G: Use this cell as you wish, just put some content in it. I had to give you a little freedom here so you wouldn't think I was some kind of dictatorial monster.

Boo, and other scary monster noises!

Using Frames

8.1 Chapter Introduction

W eb pages display one page at a time—unless you use frames. Using frames allows you to display more than one web page at a time, although they may appear to be just one page. Frames divide a browser window into sections, with each section consisting of a different HTML document. In one respect, frames are similar to tables in that you can divide a page into a grid of rows and columns. The difference is that with tables, the page is divided into cells. With frames, the browser window is divided into sections displaying more than one HTML document in the same window, and it may load other HTML documents into any frame without affecting the other frames.

Why use frames? That's a good question, especially since a lot of people detest framed sites. Most sites that use them would really be better off without them. Frames often serve little purpose other than to show that the webmaster knows how to code frames. Since many people do not like frames, be sure you have a good reason for using them or risk losing visitors due to their anti-frame bias. One valid reason might be to display thumbnail images in a small frame, while the full-size images open in the main window. Many sites use frames to create a permanent navigation system in one frame, with each link opening in the main window.

If you do decide to use frames, I strongly recommend a non-framed index page that offers visitors the option of choosing frames or standard navigation. This strategy will appease those who dislike frames and it yields better search engine placement.

Some search engines do a very poor job of indexing sites in which the index page is a frameset. The frameset page is merely a brief set of instructions telling the browser which pages to initially display and where to display them. Since no real content exists in the frameset, some search engines will give your page a lousy rating. Previously, some search engines couldn't or wouldn't index a site if the index page incorporated a frameset, and a few may still be that way.

141

8.2 An Example of Frames

To get started making a framed site, first you need a plan—a plan based on need. You have to know how you're going to divide the browser window before you can write the frameset page. For our example, we'll make a page that divides the browser into three sections. It will have a small column on the left for navigation, a larger space in the middle for content, and a small column on the right for grins and giggles.

In the framed site I made for this chapter, I made the background in the left frame light blue, the center frame blue-gray, and the right frame green.

I left the frame borders and everything else at the default settings, but as you'll soon see, there are several options available for changing these.

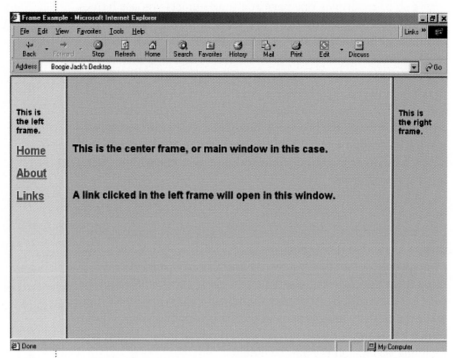

The web page you see in the graphic above actually consists of four HTML documents: one HTML document for the content of each frame and one HTML document for the frameset page, which tells the browser how to display the other three.

When activated, the links in the left frame open as new content in the center frame. This is accomplished with the target tag (addressed in section 8.9). But before we get into targeting links, we'll take a look at the frameset code I created for this example.

8.3 The Frameset

T he frameset is the HTML document that controls the initial layout of the framed pages. If you want your site to open in frames, the frameset can be your index page. Or, you can name the frameset file anything you want. Whatever you name it (except for index.html) is the name you link to from another page to open the frames.

Here's the frameset code from the example:

CODE EXAMPLE

```
<!DOCTYPE HTML PUBLIC "-//W3C//DTD HTML 4.0 Frameset//EN"
    "http://www.w3.org/TR/REC-html40/frameset.dtd">
<html>
<head>
<title>Frame Example</title>
</head>
<frameset cols="100,*,100">
<frame src="left.html">
<frame src="intro.html" name="main">
<frame src="right.html">
</frameset>
</html>
```

Believe it or not, that's it for the basic necessities of a frameset. As you can see, other than the opening DOCTYPE declaration, it starts off just like an HTML document—since it is an HTML document—with the opening HTML, head, and title tags. But, that's where the similarities end.

The opening DOCTYPE is something we haven't used yet. This element is used to declare what language (and level) a document uses, and optionally what document type definition (DTD) the browser should use when handling it. Some people believe a DOCTYPE should be used on all HTML pages. I don't teach that, at least not to beginners. For the average person, using DOCTYPE can cause more problems than not using it. I do recommend using the DOCTYPE declaration for framesets though. In Appendix I: Troubleshooting Chart, you'll find information on using DOCTYPES in all pages if you want to do that. The DOCTYPE above is for framesets *only*, so don't use it on standard HTML pages.

143

The title of the frameset page is the only title that will display in the browser's title bar, but you should still use a title on all your pages. Some folks will open the pages without frames. Plus, you need to consider the search engines that can index framed sites—they still need the page titles.

There is no body tag on the frameset page. People don't view this page on the Web unless they look at the source code, so a body tag isn't necessary. Instead, we use the frameset commands. Let's look at each one:

```
<frameset cols="100,*,100">
```

The first part establishes that it's a frameset. The "cols" attribute tells the browser that this page will display in vertical columns. If you want to create horizontal frames, you'd substitute "rows" in place of "cols."

The attribute values (100,*,100) tell the browser what size to make the frames. There are three ways to express the frame sizes: as a percentage of the page, fixed widths (in pixels, as shown in my example), or as a combination of fixed widths or percentages and a variable (as shown here).

In the code I've written, the first column and last column are hard coded to be 100 pixels wide. The center column, represented by the asterisk, is the variable that tells the browser to use the remaining available space for this column.

Due to varying screen resolutions, any time you specify a fixed pixel width in one of the frames, it's smart to code one frame with the variable so it adjusts to the remaining space.

To use percentages, we might code it to look like this:

```
<frameset cols="15%,70%,15%">
```

Using only percentages can be hazardous. If you're designing your site using a high-resolution screen, someone with a lower-resolution screen might see things quite differently than you do. Links may be cut off by the frame, which would force visitors to scroll sideways to see them. When using frames, you have the option to disallow scrollbars. If you disallowed scroll bars under the above conditions, visitors with lower-resolution screens may not be able to access the links.

The frameset command establishes the size for each frame, separated by commas. In the frameset command above, the first frame will be 15 percent of the width of the viewable space. The next frame will be 70 percent, and the last frame 15 percent again.

Specifying percentages that don't add up to 100 percent can create all kinds of unpredictable display problems. It may even cause a panic amongst mathematicians, causing them to need psychotherapy. Then you'll be sorry.

I'm not going too fast for you, am I? Just in case, I'll type slower.

8.4 The Frame Source

Following the frameset command is the frame tag and source. The frame source is a link to the web page that will display in that frame. The number of cols or rows you specify in the frameset is the number of frame tags you'll need. They are listed in the same progressive order as the sizes in the frameset command. This means the page source you list in the first frame tag will be displayed in the first frame, the page source named in the second frame tag will be displayed in the second frame, and so on for however many frames you build. An example of the frame tag and source looks like this:

```
<frame src="left.html">
```

Notice how I cleverly named the page "left.html" since it will display in the left frame. Stick with me, kid, and you'll learn to be clever, too. Remember, once we name "left.html" to open in the left frame of the browser, we have to actually create the HTML document and name it that.

Remember, you should first plan what you want the framed page to look like. Make the frameset first, and then make the pages for each individual frame. Doing it the other way around can force you to deviate from what you really wanted to do.

In the original frameset example we're working with, the left frame is coded to be 100 pixels wide. So, in creating the page for the left frame, you're making a 100-pixel wide document to be displayed in the left frame. If you create a page wider than 100 pixels, you'll end up with a horizontal scroll bar in a very small frame—and that's a bad idea. With a very few exceptions, horizontal scroll bars are almost always a bad idea.

Next, we come to our center frame:

```
<frame src="intro.html" name="main">
```

Notice this is like the other frame source, except that it has a **name="main"** attribute and value. This is the largest of the three

145

frames, and it's the frame we want to open most of our other HTML documents in. By naming the main window "main," we can use a target attribute with our links so they will open in this frame (more on that in a bit, really). You can name the other frame sources too, if you're going to have other pages open in them. I wouldn't get too clever with that though—if you start having pages flying open everywhere, you're liable to confuse visitors and make it hard for them to get around your site.

The third frame tag is like the first one, so I won't repeat the discussion on that. The last thing to do is close the frameset and HTML tags.

8.5 Frame Borders

 useful attribute for the frameset tag is the border attribute. As you might guess, you code it similar to a table border:

```
<frameset cols="100,*,100" border="5">
```

You can set the border width to any number, including zero if you don't want a border. Most professional sites that use frames set the border to zero because it is a cleaner look and better use of space.

Older Internet Explorer browsers didn't recognize the border attribute, and instead used a "frameborder=..." attribute, with the attribute value as either yes or no. Few of those browsers are in use these days, so you can just use the border attribute.

8.6 Margins

You can set the margins for both sides of a frame and the top and bottom of a frame. These are set in the <frame> tag along with the source.

```
<frame src="left.html" marginwidth="5" marginheight="5">
```

The marginwidth regulates the amount of space, in pixels, between the edges of the frame and the content on both sides of the frame. The marginheight regulates the amount of space above and below the content.

You may want to use a small margin in small frames, but give a nice cushion of space in the main frame. Remember, white space is important to the aesthetics of professional design.

8.7 Scrolling

Y ou can set frames to display scroll bars, hide scroll bars, or make scroll bars automatically appear when necessary. This is also set in the <frame> tag:

```
<frame src="left.html" scrolling="auto">
```

In the example code, I set the scrolling to auto, which is recommended. Some browsers do work automatically if you leave out the scrolling attribute and value, but to be safe, it's best to code this into the frame tag.

By changing the value from "auto" to "yes," the frames will always have scroll bars whether they need them or not. Changing the value to "no" means the frames will never have a scroll bar whether they need them or not.

8.8 Resizing

B y default, visitors can resize frames by placing the cursor at the border of the frame until it turns into a grabber arrow, then dragging it to a new location. If you don't want visitors to resize a frame, you can simply add the following to the frame tag:

```
<frame src="left.html" noresize>
```

Notice the lack of attribute, value, and quotation marks.

8.9 Linking within Frames

L inking within frames requires using a target attribute in the link tag. Without it, the link will not open in the intended frame; instead, it will either open in the entire browser window or inside the frame where the link is placed. Adding the target attribute is easy—but then, so is everything else once you understand how it works. To add a target attribute to a link tag:

```
<a href="about.html" target="main">About Us</a>
```

147

As a reminder, take a look at the original frame tags for the example site:

```
<frame src="left.html">
<frame src="intro.html" name="main">
<frame src="right.html">
```

Remember, we named the center frame "main." By using the target attribute and setting the value to "main" in the link, the link will open in "main" frame. I used the word "main" because it represents the main area of our frames. That's easy to remember and work with, but we could have named it anything. You could have named it "screaming blue fizzbot" (or "fusspot," as my spell checker wanted to change fizzbot to). Whatever you want will work, but using useful names can help you remember them. Any link can open in any frame, as long as that frame has a name—but what's a fusspot?

In addition to the named frame, other target values are intended especially for use with frames:

target="_blank"—Opens a new browser and loads the link into it.
target="_self"—Loads the link into the same frame the link is in.
target="_top"—Loads the link in the entire browser window, replacing the frames.

NOTE

These three target values are preceded by an underscore (_). If the underscore is not present, unpredictable results may occur. Most likely, the links will open in a new window.

8.10 Nesting Frames

N esting frames can get a little tricky. As you can see from the graphic on the next page, I added a center frame to the top of the main page frame, in between the two side frames.

To code the additional frame, because it's a row and not a column, I used an additional frameset tag to establish rows.

The temptation is to code the frameset, add the row, then close the frameset. It doesn't quite work that way—look at the code example on the next page to see why.

I set the two frameset tags apart to make the code easier to understand, but it isn't necessary to do that. The first frameset tag is part of the original frameset page. The second frameset tag is the new tag we added to make the top frame. As you can see, we added two rows to achieve the one extra frame. This is because by adding one row at the top, where it says "The Frame Game," we ended up with two rows. The main window becomes the second row, so it has to be coded into the frameset tag as the second row. Notice, too, that we set the first row to 75 pixels and used the asterisk to set the variable for the second (main) frame to fill the rest of the page.

The tricky part of using both rows and columns in your frameset page is to remember to code the extra row or column when you divide a frame.

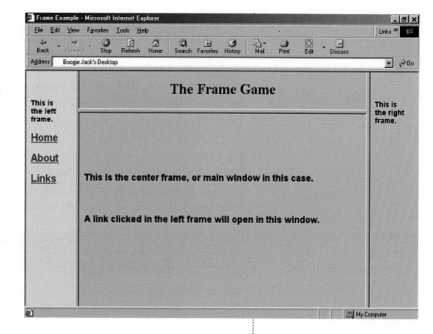

CODE EXAMPLE

```
<!DOCTYPE HTML PUBLIC "-//W3C//DTD HTML 4.0 Frameset//EN"
    "http://www.w3.org/TR/REC-html40/frameset.dtd">
<html>
<head>
<title>Frame Example</title>
</head>
<frameset cols="100,*,100" border="5">
<frame src="left.html">

<frameset rows="75,*" border="5">
<frame src="top.html" scrolling="no">
<frame src="intro.html" name="main">
</frameset>

<frame src="intro.html" name="main">
<frame src="right.html">
</frameset>
</html>
```

8.11 The No Frames Option

S ome browsers cannot view frames or may have frames turned off, so you need to include a no frames option in the frameset page. The <noframes> tag doesn't have any affect on browsers that can read frames, but for browsers that can't, the no frames tag kicks in and shows a hidden page. The noframes tag also gives search engines some content so they can index a page, even if it's not exactly what you want. Something is better than nothing, unless you're talking about warts.

Going back to our original code for the framed site example, take a look at where you modify it to include a no frames option.

CODE EXAMPLE

```
<!DOCTYPE HTML PUBLIC "-//W3C//DTD HTML 4.0 Frameset//EN"
     "http://www.w3.org/TR/REC-html40/frameset.dtd">
<html>
<head>
<title>Frame Example</title>
</head>
<frameset cols="100,*,100">
<frame src="left.html">
<frame src="intro.html" name="main">
<frame src="right.html">
</frameset>
<noframes>
<body>
Write the HTML code here for the page you want to show those using browsers without frames
support. This is a hidden page to most people, but will provide content to search engines and
non-frames capable browsers.
</body>
</noframes>
</html>
```

As you can see, this is pretty straightforward. You just add a <noframes> tag after you cancel the last (or only) frameset. Then, code a regular HTML page after the body tag. Finally, cancel the body, noframes, and HTML tags.

Rather than build a whole duplication of your main page in the noframes area, many framed sites use something like this:

```
<noframes>
<body>
```

You're viewing this page because your browser doesn't support frames. We invite you to view our site <a href="main.html"> without frames</a>.

```
</noframes>
</body>
</html>
```

This allows visitors to enter your site on the page that would normally load in the main frame, except that it opens in the full window. That means you have to do one more thing so they can navigate your site (see the next section).

> **NOTE**
>
> Using the noframes tag as shown, however, will not help much in getting your site indexed by search engines that have trouble with framed sites since the example doesn't give the search engine any real content to index.

8.12 Linking for Low-tech Browsers

To make links work for guests using browsers that don't support frames, you need to include all the links on any pages that load in the main window. Generally, these would be text links at the bottom of each page. However, since guests using browsers that do support frames may also use those links, they should all be coded as targeted links. If the links are not targeted links, they could break out of the frames the first time a visitor clicks one. Usually, an untargeted link loads in the same frame, but "usually" doesn't mean always. To be sure, include the target as follows:

```
<a href="somepage.html" target="_self">Some Link</a>
```

By including the target attribute and the value of self, the pages will load correctly for both types of visitors.

8.13 Considerations

1. Don't play games with frames and make sure you have a good reason for using them. In other words, don't make a framed site just because you can. Frames work best when using one frame for site navigation.

2. When using frames, don't forget the target attribute. Each untargeted link in a framed page could open in unpredictable

ways, causing confusion for visitors and making navigation difficult. It also makes you look unprofessional and just plain sloppy. You're not really *that* sloppy, are you?

3. When using a link to your home page on a framed site, be sure to use the link to your main page with a target of main, or a link to your frameset page with the target of top. I've seen many sites in which the webmaster links to a frameset page and includes a target to the main frame. This results in loading the original frameset within the existing frameset. It's like looking into a hall of mirrors, and it does not cast a good reflection on the site.

4. Never link to another site that uses frames with the intention of having it load within your frameset. This can create frames within frames, which creates a hyper-mess! If you frame another site's content in a way that makes it look like your own content, that's an illegal use of someone else's content that may result in legal action by the copyright holder.

8.14 Inline Frames

An inline frame is the remaining frame type to cover. An inline frame allows you to create a window in an HTML document that is capable of displaying a separate HTML document—basically, a web page within a web page. The result is a frame without a frameset, rather like a "hole" in the page that you fill with another document.

You create inline frames using the <iframe> tag. The iframe tag uses a src (source) attribute to specify the URL of the content to be displayed inside the frame.

Browsers treat inline frames as embedded objects that can be placed in text flows (the way images can). Accordingly, the iframe tag can accept align, height, and width attributes just like an image tag. This lets you determine the size of the frame's window and how it relates to the text surrounding the frame. Since inline frames can be named, you can use a link with a target attribute to change the content inside the frame. Inline frames also support scroll bars, allowing you to create a small window within a larger document. That can be pretty awkward and will be unwelcome if your implementation forces visitors to scroll both vertically and horizontally.

The iframe tag has one major difference when compared to the standard frame tag: it uses a closing </iframe> tag.

Unfortunately, not all browsers support inline frames, so you have to add a little trick for non-compliant browsers. Compliant browsers will create the desired inline frame, ignoring any content between the <iframe> and </iframe> tags. Non-compliant browsers will ignore the <iframe> and </iframe> tags, and instead display the content between the tags. To handle this, it's best to place a standard link between the two tags that goes to the information intended for the iframe. Let's have a quick peek at some incomplete code to better see how this works.

CODE EXAMPLE

```
<iframe src="mypage.html">
<a href="mypage.html">My Page</a>
</iframe>
```

In this example, compliant browsers display a frame on the page containing the contents of "mypage.html." Non-compliant browsers display a link to the same content that's displayed in the frame. Easy stuff!

As I said though, that's an incomplete iframe because we didn't set the size. Now that you're cruising at iframe speed, lets create a proper iframe:

CODE EXAMPLE

```
<iframe src="mypage.html" width="300" height="200" align="right">
<a href="mypage.html">My Page</a>
</iframe>
```

As you can see, I added the desired width and height to the iframe and aligned it to the right. Aligning the small iframe to the right forces the text to flow nicely around it on the left. Remember, you have to set rules for text or it sometimes misbehaves.

Let's say we want a link to load a different page inside the iframe. We need to add a name to the iframe to be able to do that. Here's how:

CODE EXAMPLE

```
<iframe src="mypage.html" width="300" height="200" align="right" name="#foofingoofer">
<a href="mypage.html">My Page</a>
</iframe>
```

I added the name **"#foofingoofer"** to the iframe tag. A hash mark (#), which precedes the name of the iframe and is used in the link target, prevents the link from opening in a new window. Before we add a link to the content that will be displayed in the iframe, let's see an example of the iframe I created just for you:

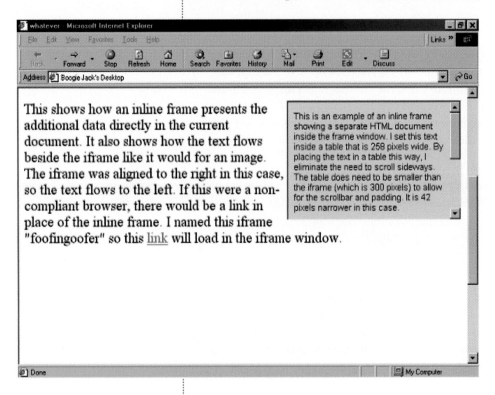

Did you notice the link in the text outside the iframe? I coded that link as follows:

```
<a href="myotherpage.html" target="#foofingoofer">
link</a>
```

As stated, the hash mark is used in the iframe name and again in the link target to prevent the content from opening in a new window. The file "myotherpage.html" will load in the iframe window when the clink is licked . . . uh, when the link is clicked.

The nice thing about this structure is that the entire page doesn't reload, just the file in the iframe window. If you use the iframe optimally—just to display text—the new page will load almost instantly and maximize your visitors' experience. Those darn visitors, they really like having their experience maximized you know.

Here is the same page after clicking the link:

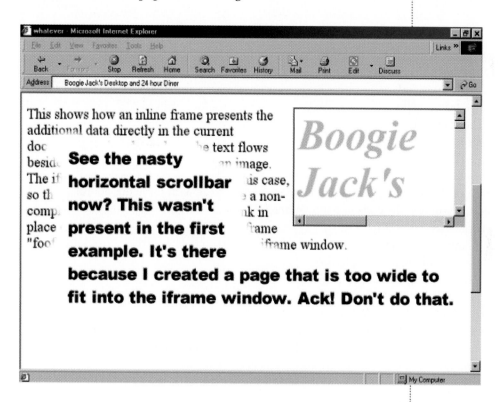

8.15 Chapter Quiz

1. True or False: Whenever possible, you should build sites using frames.

2. True or False: Search engines always rank framed sites higher than non-framed sites because they assume the webmaster of a framed site is more knowledgeable.

3. The page that tells a browser how to display the frames and which HTML documents to display is called:
   a. The framestand
   b. The frame-maker
   c. The frameset
   d. A rutabaga

4. Which of the following codes will create a framed page with three horizontal frames (assuming the code not shown here is correct as well).
   a. <frameset cols="75,*,75>
   b. <frameset rows="75,*,75">
   c. <framestand rows="75,*,75>
   d. <frame-maker cols="75,*,75">

5. You have a framed site with one frame used as a navigation tool. You want a page saved as "pictures.html" to load into another frame named "center." The link text is "Pictures." How would you code that link?

6. Write the code for a frame source of "navigation.html" with a cushion of five pixels on all four sides of the frame.

8.15 Chapter Quiz (continued)

7. You've just created a web site with a company logo in the top frame. The logo is on an HTML document called "top.html." Scroll bars display in the frame, even though there is no other content and the logo displays in its entirety. Write the code for the frame source to disallow scroll bars.

8. Starting with the frame source from question 7, add the code that prevents frames from being resized.

9. You have a link on your main page to a page called "resume.html." You want the resume page to open in the same frame as the page the link is on. The text for the link is "My Resume." Write the link code.

10. Why do you need to be careful about the width of a page that will load into an iframe window?

11. Why should you never load another site's content into a frame on your site in a way that makes it look like your content?

12. Six-year-old Josh made up a joke and I'm asking you the same thing he asked me. Why did, um, why, why did the man put his, um, why did he put his dog in the bathtub?

8.16 Chapter Exercises

Exercise Option 1 – Practice Site

H ey, guess what? You have the pleasure of making a framed site! Since I don't recommend using frames, you don't get to use them on your project web site. This is going to be a throwaway site. What an evil dictator I am. Your framed site should look similar to the one in the following graphic. The basic information you need is:

1. The top and left frames are set to 100 pixels.

2. The borders are set to 5 pixels.

3. The large frame is named "main."

4. The HTML documents to display are "top.html" for the top frame, "left.html" for the left frame, and "intro.html" for the large frame.

5. There is no need to include <noframes> information for this exercise, just the bare

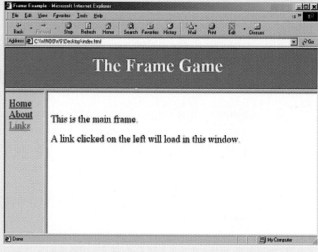

necessities and the borders. Of course, you also need to create the HTML documents to fill the frames. The links in the left frame can be dummy links.

You should be able to recreate this framed site using the information from this chapter. If you can't, you'll probably get a low grade and be scarred for life. Sorry about that. Really.

Exercise Option 2 – Independent Exercise

U sing the framed site from the previous exercise, remove the dummy links and add links to all your practice site pages in the left frame so they open in the main frame.

Create a new page that loads into the top frame from a link in the intro.html page that first loads in the main page area. This means you'll have to add a frame name to the top frame in your frame source, instead of just naming the main frame.

Creating Forms

9.1 Chapter Introduction

U ntil now, this book has focused on how to present your information to others. Forms, on the other hand, are a way of obtaining information from your visitors. Forms can include fields that visitors' can type in or have check boxes, selection lists, and other multiple-choice options. Through the use of forms, you can ask for suggestions and receive feedback, take opinion polls, take orders, and obtain other information.

Input fields in forms have a "type" value and they should have a "name" value (although they will function without a name). The type value specifies the type of input field you want. The name value provides the name of the field containing the response—so you can easily interpret the responses. For example, you may have a survey in which visitors select various colors for your new web site design. Without using the name value, your survey results might read:

> white
>
> black
>
> blue
>
> green

> Using name values, the same results could read:
>
> background color: white
>
> text color: black
>
> link color: blue
>
> vlink color: green

The name values serve as a reminder to what information you were asking for. The more information you request, the more important using name values becomes. A visitor might also skip a question or field, throwing all the answers off. By using name values, you'll always know what information they are responding to.

Forms can be processed by plain email or by CGI scripts. CGI (Common Gateway Interface) scripts are small software programs on your web hosts' server. Due to the variety of script options and the highly technical nature of scripts, this chapter covers only the plain email method of form processing. If you choose to use CGI email processing, first find out what your web host provides or search for your own script. Then, learn to work with the specific script you'll be using.

9.2 Beginning a Form

F orms are enclosed between the **<form>** and **</form>** tags. You can set up a form without them, but the information cannot be processed until you enclose a form within the tags.

The <form> tag must include an action method attribute and a method value. The method is almost always "post." The other method, "get," is mainly used when the form submission is to retrieve data rather than submit data. An example of the "get" method is when a search engine takes a search query and retrieves relevant links from its database. Unless instructed otherwise, always use the post method.

To code the first part of the form tag:

```
<form method="post">
```

A form must also have an action attribute. The action attribute specifies either the address to mail the form to, or the address of the script to process the form. To add an action attribute and value to the form tag, add the following:

```
<form method="post" action="mailto:you@your_isp.com">
```

Of course, you will need to change "you@your_isp.com" to the email address you want the form data sent to. You can send form results to more than one email address by including a second address after the first, separated by a semicolon:

```
<form method="post" action="mailto:you@your_isp.com;
me@myisp.com">
```

While the above will process a form submission and send an email to you, the results may be unreadable. In fact, the file may have so many gibberish characters you'll decide it isn't worth your time to decipher it. By adding:

```
enctype="text/plain"
```

. . . to the form tag, you will be able to read what arrives in your email inbox. If you're using the email action method, here's the best way to start a form:

```
<form method="post" action="mailto:you@your_isp.com"
enctype="text/plain">
```

9.3 Text Box, Input Type

ext boxes are boxes on a web page form that users can type text into. There are two types of text boxes: the input type and the textarea type. Input text boxes allow users to enter information into a single line text box, meaning it is only one line high on a web page, but as long as you like. Usually, the input type of text box is used for information such as a visitor's name, email address, and other information that requires only one line of text. To add an input text box:

```
<input type="text" name="Name" size="40">
```

The name="Name" part might look a little confusing. The name value (the part inside the quotation marks) can be anything you like; in this case it's a request for the visitor's name. If a visitor's name is John Doe, the form would be emailed to you with "Name=John Doe" in the message. Actually, it might not be quite that neat—but more on that later.

The size attribute of text boxes is something you'll have to play with to achieve the results you want. Basically, a 40-size text box translates into a text box that can hold approximately 40 characters before the text starts scrolling out of sight as a user continues typing.

You can also insert your own text messages into input text boxes. For example, if you were asking for a visitor's web page address, you might code the http:// part of the web address into the text box to save them that much trouble. To add text to be automatically included in an input text box, we add a value attribute. Like this:

```
<input type="text" name="URL" size="40" value="http://">
```

The text you enter for the value (the part between the quotation marks) is what will show up inside the text box on the web page. Note that there is no </input> tag—this is one of the few HTML tags that does not require a cancel tag.

You can limit the number of characters that can be entered into an input text box. Search engines often use this to limit the number of characters a web site owner can submit for a web site description or other required field. To add a limit to a text box, add the following attribute and value:

```
<input type="text" name="Name" size="40" maxlength="40">
```

The maxlength value can be set to any number you want; it doesn't have to be equal to the text box size as shown in this example. In this example, a person could type 40 characters, including spaces, into the text box before it stops accepting text.

9.4 Text Box, Textarea Type

Since one line isn't always enough for a text input field, HTML offers the textarea box type. A textarea box, often used to capture comments, gives visitors more space to type. To add a textarea text box:

```
<textarea name="Comments" cols="30" rows="4">
```

Similar to frames, a textarea tag uses columns and rows to define the size, only the column width is measured by the number of characters that will fit into the text box without scrolling out of view, the rows are roughly equal to the space an equal number of lines of text would occupy.

A textarea text box requires a cancel command. You can also include text in a textarea text box, which visitors can erase by backspacing or by highlighting it and pressing Backspace (Windows) or Delete (Windows and Mac OS). If you want to include a text message inside the box, place the text between the opening and cancel textarea tags:

```
<textarea name="Comments" cols="30" rows="4">
```

Thank you for your feedback!

```
</textarea>
```

In the example code, "Thank you for your feedback!" is visible inside the text area when the form page loads.

9.5 Radio Buttons

R adio buttons allow visitors to select a single choice from a list of options. If a user selects one choice, and then selects a second choice, the first option is deselected automatically.

The graphic to the right shows radio buttons in use on a web page. When a page loads, the radio buttons can all be deselected or one can be preselected. In this case, the preselected option is the color blue. In a question such as, "Do you want to be added to our mailing list?" the "Yes" option may be automatically selected. This adds names to the mailing list faster than requiring users to click the "Yes" option because many users will overlook the question. In my opinion, that's a cheesy way to build subscribers. Many users will be unhappy about being added to a mailing list that way, causing you to lose the good will you're trying to build.

The code for the sample series of radio buttons looks like this:

⊙ Blue
○ Red
○ Green

```
CODE EXAMPLE

<input type="radio" value="blue" name="favorite color" checked>Blue
<br>
<input type="radio" value="red" name="favorite color">Red
<br>
<input type="radio" value="green" name="favorite color">Green
```

With radio buttons, the "value" for the selected option is submitted with the form. In this example, the question asks users what their favorite color is. If the user selects the color blue, your email form result would include "favorite color=blue" when a user submits the form. As long as the value for the name attribute (name= "favorite color") is the same in all the answer options for this question, the user can select only one color choice.

Notice the input code for the color blue. The end of the tag includes "checked" to automatically select blue when users load the page. The checked option also works on check boxes, discussed in the next section.

9.6 Check Boxes

C heck boxes work just like radio buttons except they allow users to select multiple options from a list.

163

☑ Dog
☐ Cat
☑ Bird

The graphic to the left shows what a series of check boxes looks like. In this case, the user selected a dog and a bird to indicate the kinds of pets he owns. Frankly, I think he has a cat, too, but is holding back on us for fear of seeming obsessive.

Here's the code for those check boxes:

CODE EXAMPLE

```
<input type="checkbox" value="dog" name="pets">Dog
<br>
<input type="checkbox" value="cat" name="pets">Cat
<br>
<input type="checkbox" value="bird" name="pets">Bird
```

As with the radio buttons, you'll notice I inserted a break tag between the check boxes. Without the break tags, the check boxes are strung together on the same line. The boxes would still work, but with the break tags it looks neater and is easier for visitors to understand at a glance. Unlike radio buttons, check boxes allow for multiple selections.

9.7 Selection Lists

S election lists, in the form of drop-down lists (aka pop-up menus) or scrolling lists, can be limited to a single choice or allow for multiple choices.

This graphic to the left shows a drop-down list, which is the default list if you don't set a size in the <select> tag or don't include the "multiple" attribute. Users click the downward pointing arrow to open drop-down lists and then make selections.

The code for this drop-down list looks like this:

CODE EXAMPLE

```
<select name="TV">
<option>Gilligan's Island
<option>The X-Files
<option>Popeye Cartoons
</select>
```

To add more choices to the selection menu, simply add more <option> tags to the list. Some webmasters use a </option> tag after each option entry, but this is an optional tag—no pun intended. I do not include the </option> tags in my code.

By default, drop-down lists display the first option in the selection window when the web page loads. You can specify which option you want to display by adding a selected attribute to the option tag.

<option selected>Popeye Cartoons

Any option can be the selected option, regardless of where the option is located in the list. Since this attribute has only one value, you don't need to specify a value with the attribute. You can also include directions for the user such as "Please Select" or you can include a heading as an option. For example:

<option selected>Favorite TV Show

The selection lists shown previously allow users to make only one selection. To allow users to make more than one selection from a list, add the multiple attribute to the <select> tag like this:

<select name="TV" multiple>

The "multiple" attribute also has only one value, so you don't need to specify a value with the attribute.

This graphic to the right shows what happens to a selection list when you add the "multiple" attribute to it. It expands from a drop-down list into a window that shows the options.

On Windows, users press the Control key as they click to select multiple options. On Mac OS, users press the Command key (aka Apple key) as they click to select noncontiguous options. Windows and Mac users can select a range of continuous options by pressing the Shift key while selecting the first and last option.

If you have very many choices, displaying them all in a single window may be a poor choice.

By adding a size attribute and value to the <select> tag, you can specify the size of the window. The addition of a scroll bar, as shown at right, allows users to see all the selection options. The scroll bar displays automatically if the list of options is longer than the size coded for the selection list.

165

The code below shows how to create a scrollable selection list:

CODE EXAMPLE

```
<select name="TV" size="2" multiple>
<option>Gilligan's Island
<option>The X-Files
<option>Popeye Cartoons
</select>
```

As you can see, this is the exact same code the drop-down style selection list used, except the size and multiple attributes are added to the <select> tag.

9.8 Hidden Fields

HTML provides a few hidden—and quite useful—fields you can use with forms. Unfortunately, they don't work with the mailto method. The mailto method of form submission simply uses your guests' default email program to send the form submission to the address specified in the form code. Most hidden fields require your web host to have a form processing script on the server—as most professional hosting services do. These scripts will have names such as formmail.cgi, sendmail.cgi, or another name, and will be found in your CGI bin.

Since there are a variety of form processing scripts and different ways hosts can set them up, it's beyond the scope of this book to go into much detail about them. The code used to point to a form processing script will look something like this:

```
<form method="post" action="http://www.yoursite.com/
cgi-bin/FormMail.cgi">
```

Consult with your web host to find out about the script processing they offer and for the correct path to the script. Many web hosts offer this information in their FAQ file. Most hosts offer FAQ pages (answers to Frequently Asked Questions) to help new hosting clients find the information they need.

If your web host does offer a script processing form, then the following hidden fields can be quite useful.

- This code will fill in the subject line of the email you receive from a processed form:

```
<input type="hidden" name="subject" value=
"Feedback from Web Site">
```

A form with that field would send an email to you with the subject line of "Feedback from Web Site." You might use this information to sort your email to easily find the mail most important to you.

- This code sends visitors to another page after they click the send button, often back to your main page or to a thank-you page.

```
<input type="hidden" name="redirect"
value="http://www.boogiejack.com">
```

In this example, users are sent back to my index page after sending their information to me.

- This code shows how to specify required fields, which must be completed before the form can be submitted:

```
<input type="hidden" name ="required" value ="email,
name">
```

If visitors don't fill out the required fields, they receive an error page notifying them to fill out the required fields. The required fields use the same name as the name you specified in the input tag as follows:

```
<input type="text" name="Name:" size="40">
```

9.9 The Submit Button

M ost forms require a submit button. Forms can be used to trick browsers into other actions, but if you're setting up a form to obtain information from visitors, the submit button is mandatory.

```
<input type="submit" value="Shoot It To Me!">
```

This creates a gray button with the words "Shoot It To Me!" on the form. You can change the text on the button by changing the words in the value attribute. There is no cancel tag for a submit button.

NOTE

Here's a lesson in careful coding. In the previous two code examples, using the text box and the hidden required input field won't work because the name values are case sensitive. Notice that in the hidden input field, the required form fields are not capitalized, but the text box name value is capitalized. This form could not be processed because the values do not match. Since you probably wouldn't have another text box calling for the visitor's name a second time, the script would never be able to process the form because the required field couldn't be fulfilled.

9.10 Custom Submit Button

I n addition to the standard button, you can use a graphic button to create a custom submit button. The graphic replaces the standard submit button and can jazz up a form a bit. Don't get too cute with it though—you might confuse visitors who expect to see the standard submit button but see a picture of a mailman instead. To use a graphic to create a custom submit button:

```
<input type="image" src="images/yourbutton.jpg"
name="Submit Button">
```

The type is identified as an image, the source (src) is the path to the image and the image name and extension, and the name is the text you want on the button as "alt text" when someone hovers their cursor over the image. You can also use any other image attributes and values normally associated with an image tag, such as width, height, border, and align.

9.11 The Reset Button

W hile the submit button is required, the reset button is optional. The reset button simply clears the form. If you don't include it, visitors will have to backspace or delete information they've already entered to get rid of it, or they may need to reload the page to clear some form elements. The longer a form is, the greater the need to provide a reset button. The reset button code looks like this:

```
<input type="reset" value="Whoops!" name="reset">
```

This creates a standard gray button with the text of "Whoops!" You can insert whatever text you want on the button for the value attribute.

9.12 Custom Reset Button

Y ou can also use an image for a reset button, but no actual code exists for this. The best you can do is create a graphic link with a URL pointing to the same page the form is on. Basically, this code reloads the page just as clicking the refresh/reload button on a browser does:

```
<a href="formpage.html"><img src="images/reset.
jpg"></a>
```

9.13 Tidying Up Forms

F orms can quickly become unsightly messes if you don't take measures to tidy them up. Combining most of the examples from this chapter, I created this nice and tidy form.

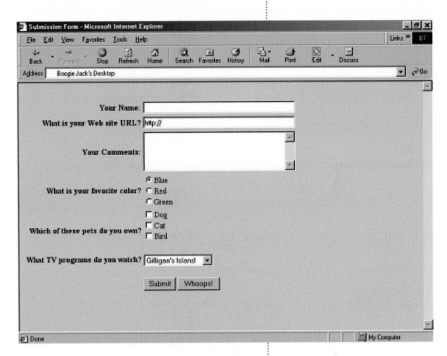

I used a two-column table to create this well-organized form. The questions and comments are all in the left column, with the cell contents aligned to the right. The right column is left at the default left alignment.

The alignment created an invisible vertical line between the text messages and the form input fields.

Here's the complete code I used to create the form:

CODE EXAMPLE

```
<form method="post" action="mailto:you@you.com" enctype="text/plain">
<table border="0"><tr><td align="right">
<b>Your Name:</b>
</td><td>
<input type="text" name="Name" size="40">
</td></tr><tr><td align="right">
<b>What is your Web site URL?</b>
</td><td>
```

CODE EXAMPLE (Continued)

```
<input type="text" name="URL" size="40" value="http://">
</td></tr><tr><td align="right">
<b>Your Comments:</b>
</td><td>
<textarea name="Comments" cols="30" rows="4"></textarea>
</td></tr><tr><td align="right">
<b>What is your favorite color?</b>
</td><td>
<input type="radio" value="blue" name="Favorite Color" checked>Blue
<br>
<input type="radio" value="red" name="Favorite Color">Red
<br>
<input type="radio" value="green" name="Favorite Color">Green
</td></tr><tr><td align="right">
<b>Which of these pets do you own?</b>
</td><td>
<input type="checkbox" value="dog" name="Pets">Dog
<br>
<input type="checkbox" value="cat" name="Pets">Cat
<br>
<input type="checkbox" value="bird" name="Pets">Bird
<p>
</td></tr><tr><td align="right" valign="top">
<b>What TV programs do you watch?</b>
</td><td>
<select name="TV">
<option>Gilligan's Island
<option>The X-Files
<option>Popeye Cartoons
</select>
<p>
<input type="submit" value="Submit" name="submit">
<input type="reset" value="Reset" name="reset">
</td></tr></table>
</form>
```

As you can see, the code is far more complex than the form appears on a web page, but that is always the case with HTML. Since you've completed the chapter on tables, you should be able to understand how the table organized the form. If not, please review the chapter on tables.

9.14 Chapter Quiz

1. Name the two form methods.

2. Which form method is most commonly used?

3. You have the code for a text box that allows visitors to submit their web site addresses: `<input type="text" name="URL" size="40">`. Add the code so `http://` is automatically placed in the text box when the page loads.

4. True or False: This is the correct code for creating a textarea:

   `<textarea name="Comments" columns="30" rows="4">`

5. True or False: A radio button allows form users to select multiple options from a list.

6. Write the code for a drop-down selection list that includes the following options: Red, Blue, and Green.

7. A drop-down selection list is changed to a scrolling selection list by adding one of two attributes to the `<select>` tag. What are they?

9.14 Chapter Quiz (continued)

8. Write the code to add a submit button to a form. The button should have the word "Send" on it.

9. True or False: A form reset button is optional.

10. You can make forms neater by using:
    a. Frames
    b. Tables
    c. Spreadsheets
    d. Hairspray

11. Write the code to create a custom submit button on a form, using an image named RedButton.jpg that is in the same directory as the form page.

12. My sister Sue didn't want me to make a joke question about her, but here it is anyway. (Hi Suzy-Q!) Why is it that my sister Sue will only stay in a hotel if she knows the owner?

9.15 Chapter Exercises

Exercise Option 1 – Practice Site

O K, it's time to make the media kit page for your web site. The page should include advertising information, a brief privacy policy, and your contact information. Combine the lessons from Chapter 7: Using Tables and from this chapter to create a contact form with the following fields:

1. A text box for visitors' names.
2. A text box for their email addresses.
3. A drop-down subject selection list that asks why they are contacting you. This might include items such as feedback, suggestions, sales inquiry, broken link report, advertising inquiry, etc.
4. A text area for visitors' comments.
5. A submit button.
6. A reset button.

Be sure to include the meta tags, background image, navigation system, and other relevant page elements. You should have a complete form and complete page when you're finished.

Exercise Option 2 – Independent Exercise

C reate two forms on your new media kit page, one for casual visitors and one for advertising inquiries. Each form should clearly designate who should be using which form, and each should have a drop-down selection list relative to its purpose. Use an image submit button for the form for casual visitors. For the advertisers' contact form, include text boxes for the visitor's name, email address, phone number, and company name along with a textarea box for the company's mailing address. This form should also include a textarea box for comments, a submit button, a reset button, and a series of radio buttons for the advertiser to select a price range indicating the company's advertising budget.

Adding Sound and Video

10.1 Chapter Introduction

T his chapter shows you how to add sound and video to your web pages. Because Internet Explorer and Netscape provide different levels of support for HTML and implement features in different ways, this chapter covers methods that work for both browsers. Most of the code that works only in one or the other is left out.

At one time, the use of Internet Explorer and Netscape was about even. This required webmasters to code in two different ways and check pages in both browsers. At the time of this writing, Internet Explorer is dominant. However, Netscape was dominant in the past and it could make a comeback.

Some webmasters quit coding extras for Netscape users because they have determined the market share isn't significant enough to justify the extra work. If things change, those webmasters will have a lot of redesigning to do. I personally think it's best to design for both browsers.

10.2 A Word of Caution

B e wary of the file size of sounds and movies you use on your web site. Sound and movie files are often very large and therefore slow to download; make sure they are worth the wait for visitors.

You should offer visitors the option of listening to sound files rather than forcing it on them. The exception might be a very short, quick, unusual sound used to grab attention as a page loads. You shouldn't force sound files on visitors because:

1. Your musical taste seems good to you, but your visitors may not like it.

2. Some people surf from work or other public places. Shhh . . . they might not want your sound files to give them away.

3. Some surfers already have music or other media playing. If you force your sounds on them, they will often hear both sounds playing at the same time. This is as appealing as a blind date who has no class and is proud of it!

4. Some people surf with their speakers off or don't have a sound card. Why should they have to wait for your sounds to download when they can't hear them?

5. If your surfers tend to go back and forth between your index page and other pages, listening to the same song or sound every time gets old—fast.

6. If you're building a professional site and want to be taken seriously, auto-play sounds are generally considered unprofessional and can only hurt your image.

All this should be reason enough not to force sound files on people. This doesn't mean you should never use them—but the evidence in favor of making sound files optional is overwhelming.

10.3 Adding a Sound File

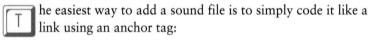 he easiest way to add a sound file is to simply code it like a link using an anchor tag:

```
<a href="sounds/mysound.wav">Click here for my
sound</a>
```

When a user clicks the link, it opens the browser plug-in associated with that type of sound file. A plug-in is a browser support program, independent of the browser itself, and may open in a separate window. Sound plug-ins usually have controls similar to a VCR that let the user start and stop the file, skip forward and backward, and control the volume.

Depending on the user's system, one of several different programs may open to play the sound. Two commonly associated programs are Windows Media Player and QuickTime. Both Windows Media Player and QuickTime are available for Mac OS and Windows. Users who don't have one of the necessary plug-ins are alerted, and in some cases prompted to download the needed program. These days, most users have the required software installed.

Another method for adding sound files is to use an <embed> tag. Embedding the sound either plays the music or sound with no visible controls for the user or it embeds the controls into the web page. The basic code to embed a sound file is:

```
<embed src="sounds/sample.wav" height="40" width="144"
align="bottom">
```

An <embed> tag does not need a cancel tag. The numeric values in this code control the height and width of the Windows Media Player; if QuickTime launches, the values are ignored. A lot of sources will tell you to set the height to 60 pixels instead of the 40 that I show. If you do that, you don't need the align="bottom" attribute and value. I set it to 40 pixels because I think it looks better. Compare the two screen captures, which show 40 pixels and 60 pixels in height, and you be the judge.

40 Pixels Tall Windows
Media Player

60 Pixels Tall Windows
Media Player

At 40 pixels with bottom alignment, the Windows Media Player graphic is cut off (which is good because it gets scrunched). You can make the window larger to fit the logo, but most people don't want to give up that much space for simple sound files.

The optimal width for the Windows Media Player is 144 pixels. If you make it narrower, the controls are cut off. If you make it wider, it's just taking up extra space. I should point out that some of the controls, including the volume control and mute button, are cut off with a width of 144 pixels. If you want to include those, then just leave the width out of the code. Visitors always have the stop button instead of mute, and can control the volume via their computer hardware or sound card software.

For short sound files, in which users won't need to skip ahead, you can reduce the width to just 70 pixels. This will give you a start button, pause button, and stop button. Personally, I like this option best.

With the code I showed in the example, the sound will automatically play once. You can set the sound to play more than once in Internet Explorer by adding a playcount attribute.

```
<embed src="sounds/sample.wav" height="40" width="144"
align="bottom" playcount="2">
```

Internet Explorer would repeat this sound twice, while Netscape would only play it once. Netscape used to have a loop tag that would do the same thing, but now it only allows a true or false attribute. False means it will play once, true means it plays forever (a very bad choice). I find it best to code it for Internet Explorer if you want it to play more than once, and forget about repeating it at all in Netscape. It doesn't handle the loop tag in the same way from version to version, so results can be unpredictable. Let it play once and forget it. Visitors can restart the sound if they want to hear it again.

You can also hide the controls from the visitor so they only hear the sound file:

```
<embed src="sounds/sample.wav" height="40" width="144"
align="bottom" hidden="true">
```

The hidden="true" attribute and value hides the player from viewers. Hidden used to be the default value, but now visible is the default value. You might want to always specify in your code whether it is hidden or visible. Then, if it changes again, you won't have to change your code . . . maybe.

If you do choose to have the control panel hidden, you should always add the sound file near the end of the HTML code. Browsers start at the top of the page and work their way down. If you code a sound file at the top, browsers start downloading it first. Since your visitors may have nothing to look at while the sound is download-ing, it will make your page seem much slower. The larger the sound file, the slower it will seem. Some people will not wait long at all. If you code the sound file at the end of your page, visitors can view content while the sound file is downloading.

One other useful attribute that works with both browsers is the autostart.

```
<embed src="sounds/sample.wav" height="40" width="144"
align="bottom" autostart="false">
```

Adding autostart="false" prevents a sound from playing auto-matically. The other value, true, is the default value. Again, I recom-mend setting autostart to false so visitors can have the option of hearing the sound or not.

Ideally, you should provide the player at the minimum size with an option for visitors to hear the sound. The last code example I provided is the best way to insert a sound file into your page.

10.4 Adding a Video File

A dding a video file is the same as adding a sound file. The only differences are that you reference a video clip as the source and have to adjust the size for optimum quality. And, as with sound files, you can add video files with a direct link, using an anchor tag that requires a plug-in to be opened. A sample video clip tag looks like this:

```
<embed src="video/myvid.avi" height="300" width="300"
autostart="false">
```

If you have trouble finding an ideal size for the player, you can leave out the width and height attributes and let the browser play the video at the size the clip was saved at. Often, though, you can increase the size somewhat to provide a better view with little loss of quality. Conversely, you can specify the video at a smaller size and sometimes improve the image quality. The autostart="false" attribute loads the first image of the video clip into the player, but won't play until the user clicks the play button. You can either remove the autostart tag or set it to true to have it play automatically.

10.5 Code for Dumb Browsers

Y ou can actually combine the two methods I've shown for playing sound and videos by adding a <noembed> tag. This allows browsers that don't understand the embed tag to display the link to download the file. In this case, use a cancel tag with the <embed> tag.

Here's how it's done:

CODE EXAMPLE

```
<embed src="sounds/sample.wav" height="40" width="144" align="bottom"
autostart="false">
<noembed>
<a href="sounds/sample.wav">Click here for a sample sound.</a>
</noembed>
</embed>
```

This is simply a matter of creating an anchor tag link to the sound file, and sandwiching it between the <noembed> tag and the cancel tag. Then, cancel the embed tag to avoid any browser quirks. A dumb browser will see only the link, while a modern browser will see the sound or video controls.

10.6 Legal Issues

There is a very good chance that many, if not most, of the music sound files you find on the Internet are illegal. I'm not a legal expert and probably won't be mistaken for one, but record companies usually require license fees for reproducing their copyrighted music.

Many sites that offer free sound files just gather them from the web and actually have no legal right to them. Use your best judgment when using sound files from various sources—or, to be safe, create your own. Creating your own doesn't mean you can convert someone else's copyrighted material into a format for the web and call it your own. That would be converting, not creating. Creating is to make something unique from your own resources and talents.

I do have original sound files on my web site that you can use. Unfortunately there are no songs, just goofy sound effects. You may use them for the chapter exercise or find other files on your own.

I won't include references to sound sites. I have no way of ascertaining if sites are offering legal sound files, and I don't want to be construed as condoning illegal files or endorsing web sites with illegal files. My sound files are located at:

www.boogiejack.com/sounds.html

If you're using this book in school, I wish I could be in your classroom when all the goofy sound effects I created are being played. I'm sure there would be some entertaining moments.

> **NOTE**
>
> Note that, unless you're running a site focused on sound files, if you use any illegal files, chances are that nobody will say anything unless your site becomes popular. I'm still not condoning illegal files mind you, but I don't want everyone that already has a web site to panic.

10.7 Chapter Quiz

1. True or False: Giving surfers the option to listen to or skip a sound file is a bad idea because they might turn it off.

2. True or False: You can use an anchor tag to create a link to a sound file.

3. Most webmasters set the Windows Media Player sound control panel to 60 pixels in height (I like it set at 40 pixels) and _____ pixels in width.

4. What is the other popular sound/video player used by Mac OS and Windows?

5. When setting the Windows Media Player to 40 pixels tall, you should align it to the:
   a. Top
   b. Bottom
   c. Middle
   d. Center

6. If you choose to hide the Windows Media Player, you should always code the sound file:
   a. Near the top of the page
   b. Near the end of the page
   c. In the middle of the page
   d. On another page

10.7 Chapter Quiz (continued)

7. What attribute and value do you add to prevent a sound or movie clip from starting automatically?

8. You can add an anchor tag link to your sound and video files, which only dumb browsers will see, by placing it between what two tags?

9. True or False: It's safe to use any sound files you find on the web as long as the web site makes them available to the general public.

10. If you code a video file so the video is played at a smaller size than it was saved at, it may result in:
    a. Slightly improved video quality
    b. A loss of video quality
    c. The video not working due to false formatting
    d. A nasty foot odor

11. True or false: On most professional sites (business sites), having a sound file play when the page loads is a great idea because it can stimulate the senses and excite people into a buying mood.

12. A man tried to squeeze silicon around his drafty window, but it wouldn't come out of the tube. He thought he'd heat it in the microwave to make it more pliable, but the tube exploded and caught fire, ruining his microwave oven. What does this prove?

10.8 Chapter Exercises

Exercise Option 1 – Practice Site

Y ou might think because this is such a short chapter you'll have an easy chapter exercise. Not so—I didn't become ruler of the universe by taking it easy on folks.

Your assignment for this chapter is to create your "about" page. This is a page about the webmaster or fictitious company behind the web site. You might include things such as a mission statement, staff qualifications, photos of the main staff, duties, personal or company accomplishments and accolades, etc.

To tie it in with the chapter, include a sound file of your choice to set the mood.

This should be another finished page, so remember to code all your meta tags and page elements into it—and make sure they all work.

Exercise Option 2 – Independent Exercise

C reate a new page and code at least 10 sounds into it, each having its own player. Use tables to keep them neat, with each sound/video player inside its own table cell.

Reminder: You are free to search the web for sound files of your choice, but if you have trouble, you'll find sound effects on my site at this address:

www.boogiejack.com/sounds.html

Cascading Style Sheets

Chapter Eleven

11.1 Chapter Introduction

W│ hat are Cascading Style Sheets (CSS)? Using my fine command of techno-babble, CSS is a cross-platform, standards-based programming language designed to facilitate page layout and display capabilities. Got it? Shall we try a definition in plain English now?

In 1996, when CSS was first introduced, the state of HTML was a mess. HTML was never meant to be a presentation language, but it had evolved into one out of necessity. Various browsers displayed the same HTML code differently—or sometimes not at all. Some browsers did not recognize all HTML elements and each browser seemed to have at least some proprietary code that would only work with it. Programming web pages to look good in all browsers was a difficult and time-consuming chore under these confusing and frustrating conditions.

Furthering the problem of layout control, many tricks used to gain control by design-minded webmasters in one browser would render far differently in another due to various browser inconsistencies, quirks, and bugs. CSS is a programming language designed as a companion to HTML to bridge these problems and give designers much more control over page presentation.

With CSS, you can control page-formatting functions such as space, color, positioning, and other stylistic factors. CSS also brings new features to page design that were not possible with just HTML, and it continues to evolve into an ever more useful language. Having previewed a few new features of the next generation of CSS, I can say with confidence that I think HTML programmers are in for some nice surprises.

This chapter will show you the most common, useful, and widely supported cascading style sheet commands. While it does cover many style sheet uses, it cannot cover them all. Entire books exist on CSS, so you can see that every detail simply can't be covered in one chapter. You will, however, learn enough to understand it and will know how to put it to use. You may even be able to determine for yourself some of the uses that aren't covered here.

CSS is used to program the "styles" HTML elements are presented with. These styles are called rules. In a sense, using CSS, you create your own page presentation rules, within the bounds of the language, of course.

Any HTML element is a potential selector for CSS. A selector is simply an HTML element that has a style assigned to it. For example:

```
h3 {font-family: Arial;}
```

We'll explain the style syntax shortly, for now try to grasp how a style rule is applied to an HTML element. In the above example, h3 is the HTML element, which is a size 3 heading tag. The rule we created is that the heading is displayed in the Arial font. In the above style rule, each time you use the h3 heading tag (`<h3>`) on a page with this style, it will be rendered in the Arial font. This is the basic idea of CSS—it lets you create the rules for how HTML elements are presented.

An HTML element can have multiple styles assigned to it through the use of different classes. A class is simply an HTML element with an assigned style that has been given a name. The style is then applied to that HTML element when the class is invoked where the element is used. The same element without the class invoked is rendered in the default style rather than the class style. For example, if we had this code in our style sheet:

```
h3 {font-family: Arial;}
h3.style2 {font-family: Verdana;}
```

In the above example, we created two different styles for the h3 heading. The h3 heading would be rendered in the Arial font when it's coded like this:

```
<h3>Popeye was a Vegetarian</h3>
```

But, the h3 heading would be displayed in the Verdana font if it were coded like this:

```
<h3 class="style2">Olive Oyl was a Greaser</h3>
```

Oyl . . . Greaser . . . I made a Foghorn Leghorn joke. By adding the .style2 to the h3 heading in our style sheet rules, we created a class for it, which is invoked by adding class="style2" to the h3 tag in the page code. To create a class, you simply add a period and a name to the HTML element in the style sheet rules. The name, in this case, was "style2," but we could have named it anything, even Flooblegoober. The name isn't important as far as CSS is concerned, but I find it helpful to use meaningful names. For example, if I wanted to create a class that made the heading text red, I'd probably name the style rule "red" instead of style2. That way, it's easy to remember the class name as you continue to code pages and you don't have to go back and keep checking on the names.

11.2 The Three Main Flavors of CSS

$\boxed{S}$ tyle sheets come in three main flavors: linked, embedded, and inline. They all do essentially the same thing, but are put in to use in different ways. Embedded styles are coded into the HEAD section of the page, inline styles are built into standard HTML tags, and linked styles are called from a remote file.

Linked Style Sheets

A linked style sheet is a separate file that resides on a server. All the formatting commands are placed in this style sheet, and linked (to) within the HEAD section of an HTML document. With one simple link on each page, the layout for the page is controlled from this linked style sheet. You can change every page on your web site that is linked to this style sheet by changing the code in the style sheet. With linked style sheets, you don't have to repeat all the style sheet code on each page. This makes it much more useful and convenient than using the HTML attribute and value counterpart to specify display properties such as colors, font sizes, etc.

Embedded Style Sheets

Of course, at times you may wish to use a slightly different style for one or more elements on a page than what is coded into the linked style sheet. By using an embedded style in the HEAD section of the document, you can override the linked style. For example, on one page you might want the font to be slightly larger than on the other pages, but leave all other style elements the same. You can code an embedded font style into that page and the browser will use it rather than the style in the linked style sheet (which is still used for the rest of the formatting).

Inline Style Sheets

Using the same scenario from the previous paragraph, you might also have text that you want formatted differently from the embedded style. Inline style tags are used in this case. An inline style overrides the embedded style, which overrides the linked style.

As you might have gathered by now, styles define formatting such as page margins, font properties, borders, and many other things. In other words, styles define how HTML elements should be displayed. By definition, it sounds as if you have to learn more code to do the same things, but style sheets can save you a lot of work and allow you to do things you can't do with just HTML.

One thing to be aware of—cascading style sheets do not act on text inside a table. As you already learned, standard HTML commands outside a table also do not affect the content inside a table. In fact, no commands I know of outside a table affect the content inside a table. Even commands within a table cell don't carry over to the next table cell. But you can set style sheets for the tables themselves, so you have extra control over a layout with that as a feature.

11.3 Style Sheet Syntax and Examples

The style sheet syntax (the official structure of the code) consists of three parts, much like an HTML element with its attribute and value. The syntax is:

```
selector {property: value;}
```

The selector identifies the HTML element you want to set the style for, such as the body, paragraph, font, or other elements. The property in CSS is like an HTML attribute for the selector you want to define, just like an attribute in a standard HTML tag defines what part of the HTML command you want to modify. For example, if you chose to define an H2-size HTML heading tag, h2 would be the selector, the property might be the color, and the value would be the actual color, such as blue. You can also use hexadecimal color codes in addition to named colors. The curly braces are used to enclose the property and value, and the property is separated from the value by a colon. The semicolon just before the last curly bracket is the terminator. Technically, the semicolon isn't required for single property rules. It is used to separate one property and value from another if you are setting multiple rules to one selector. I like to use them all the time to be consistent. That's a good habit to form—trust me on that.

An example style tag:

h2 {color: #583C59;}

Here's how that tag breaks
down to the individual parts:

h2 {color: #583C59;}
selector   property   value

With the above style, you've created a *rule* that will govern the color of each H2 heading that is used (unless you override the style). To change the color as we've done here using HTML, would require us to sandwich a font tag with a color change in between our H2 opening and closing tags.

You can also change many other properties for the same HTML element in one step. Example:

h2 {color: #583C59; font-family: Arial; text-decoration: underline;}

In the above tag, we've specified the color, the font face, and like a king, we've ruled that all H2 headings should be underlined. That's what you are doing when you use CSS—you are creating the rules that a browser will use to display the page, as long as you use legal code. With this rule set, all H2 headings will be displayed as shown above, without needing to program the rules into each H2 HTML tag.

As you can see, when setting more than one property and value for a selector, each property and value is separated from the next by a semicolon.

Let's look at another style example:

body {color: #abc123;}

In this example, the body is the selector, the color is the property, and the hex code of #abc123 is the value. When the body is the selector, the color property sets the color of the font used on the web page, not the background color of the web page itself as you may have guessed.

If a value is more than one word, such as with various font names, then you add quotes around the value:

body {font-family: "Comic Sans";}

If you remember from Chapter 4: Formatting Text, you know that when you specify a font, you should name alternate fonts in case your first choice isn't active on a visitor's computer. Additional values are separated by commas, just as they are in HTML:

body {font-family: Arial, Garamond, Verdana;}

189

Notice that I didn't use quotation marks in this code. Because each value is only one word, quotation marks aren't necessary.

If you want to specify more than one property for a selector, use a semicolon to separate each property and value from the other properties and values:

```
body {font-family: Arial, Garamond; color: black;}
```

To make things easier to read, you can code CSS in a variety of ways. The previous code and the following three examples produce exactly the same results.

Example 1

```
body {font-family: Arial, Garamond;
     color: black;}
```

Example 2

```
body
{font-family: Arial, Garamond;
color: black;}
```

Example 3

```
body
{
font-family: Arial, Garamond;
color: black;
}
```

You can group styles if you want all the selectors to have the same values. For example, you might want some of the headings to use the same color. To do that, separate the selectors with commas:

```
h1, h2, h3 {color: red;}
```

This causes the largest three heading sizes to display in red text.

Suppose you want some <h3> size headings in blue and some in red. With style sheets, you can create "classes" of styles. Creating a style class means you can define as many styles as you like for any page element, such as headings:

```
h3.blue {color: blue;}
h3.red {color: red;}
```

Where it says h3.blue, the "blue" can be any word. It's best to use names that are meaningful. With the above heading tags, an h3 size heading will display in either blue or red text, depending on which class is assigned to the tag in the code. To put the class we created to work, code a heading tag that designates the class like this:

```
<h3 class="blue">This would be in blue text.</h3>
<h3 class="red">This would be in red text.</h3>
```

By adding a period and a name to the h3 tag, you create a class for that tag. As shown in the previous code, when you use an h3 tag, you simply specify which class you want a tag to have and the heading tag will be formatted as you specify. If you do not specify a class, then the default HTML style is used.

11.4 Embedded Styles

E mbedded style tags are placed in the <head> section of a document. An embedded style applied to an HTML tag affects that tag throughout the document, unless you use an inline tag to override it. Any HTML tag without a defined style uses the HTML default setting for that tag.

You've already seen a few embedded style tags. That's what we used in the tables chapter to place link text on blank buttons. To refresh your memory, here is a small, embedded style tag:

CODE EXAMPLE

```
<style type="text/css">
<!--
body {font-family: Arial, Garamond; color: black; font-size: 12px;
      background: white;}
-->
</style>
```

You'll notice that all the style properties are enclosed between the open and closing style tags. This entire code should be placed in the <head> section of the HTML document. When using embedded styles like this, you should place the actual styles inside HTML comment tags.

```
<!-- This is an HTML comment. -->
```

HTML comment tags are not visible on web pages no matter where they are placed in the code. The reason for using comment

> **NOTE**
>
> In Appendix B you'll find a reference chart showing the most commonly used selectors and the possible properties and values.

191

tags around styles is that some older browsers may display the style code on the page if they are not commented out. A comment tag starts with a left arrow bracket, an exclamation mark, two dashes, and a space—then place the comment, or in this case, the style code. The comment tag ends with a space, two dashes, and a right arrow bracket. Be sure to include the space before and after the content enclosed in the comment tags or it will cause problems in some browsers.

11.5 Inline Styles

Inline style tags are styles added to HTML tags. You can use inline style tags anywhere in the body of a document.

```
<p style="background: aliceblue;">
```

An inline style tag, similar to a standard HTML tag, has an attribute and value. In the above example using an HTML paragraph tag, I added the style selector. Then, similar to the attribute and value of an HTML tag, the style property and value are added with an equals sign and enclosed in quotation marks. In this example, the paragraph will have the background color of alice blue. With HTML alone, for text to have a background color that is different from the web page background, you had to place the text inside a table. Not so with CSS code. Plus, with CSS code, you can even have a background color for an individual word:

```
<font style="background: yellow">guaranteed</font>
```

If you were formatting a sales pitch and wanted to emphasize a single word or phrase, the code above would produce an effect much like a highlight marker on a sheet of paper. The background behind the word "guaranteed" would be highlighted in yellow.

11.6 Linked Styles

Linked style sheets are extremely powerful. All the style properties are saved in a single file, which is separate from your HTML documents. By placing one link in the <head> section of an HTML document to the style sheet file, the whole page is formatted according to the linked style sheet specifications. If you want the same styles on every page, this single linked style sheet can control your entire web site. If you want to change the formatting of your web site, you only need to change the single style sheet and your whole web site will reflect the changes. When used properly, that's a powerful tool!

You can create a linked style sheet file in any text editor, but it should not contain HTML tags—only style sheet coding. You can save the style sheet file with any name you want, but you must use **.css** for the file extension (file type). For example, you might save a style sheet as:

coolstyle.css

You create a link to the style sheet in the `<head>` section of an HTML document like this:

`<link rel="stylesheet" href="coolstyle.css" type="text/css">`

There is no closing tag for the link. This causes the browser to use whatever styles you coded into the linked style sheet throughout the document, unless you use an embedded style or inline style to override it. Remember, an embedded style overrides a linked style, and an inline style overrides both embedded and linked styles. It may be easier to remember that whichever style is designated last is the overriding style.

As mentioned, the style sheet file you link to has no HTML code in it and it has no opening or closing style tags. Browsers simply recognize style sheet files by the reference made in the link and the .css file extension.

A linked style sheet might look like this:

CODE EXAMPLE

```
body {font-family: Arial, Verdana;
      color: black;
      font-size: 12px;
      background: white;
      margin: 0,150;}
h1 {font-family: "Brush Script, Lucida Handwriting";
     color: red;
     font-size: 24px;}
p {margin: 6px;}
```

As you can see, the linked style sheet is a plain text file. To use it for a site, we would save it with any name, being sure to use the .css extension. This is all the file would contain—no HTML codes.

193

Many more selectors and properties can go into a linked style sheet, and usually would, but this gives you an idea how one looks. As this chapter progresses, you'll learn more selectors, properties, and values that can be used.

11.7 Style Sheet Body Properties

A s you will see, cascading style sheets take document formatting to another level. You can program many formatting functions into one file, but style sheets let you do things not possible with HTML alone.

First, we'll look at some of the body elements. You can set both the background color and background image in the style sheet's body property:

body {background: transparent;}

Yes, you read that right—you can set the background to be transparent (although I don't know why you'd do that in the body tag). The transparent background value is more useful in tables and table cells.

In addition to specifying a transparent background, you can use any legal color name or hex value. You can also code an image for the background:

body {background: url(images/bg.gif);}

Where the word "url" replaced the color value, you add the path to the image, the image file name, and the image file type extension, all within parentheses.

You can also set the background image to be "fixed," meaning it will remain stationary rather than scrolling with the page. Example:

body   {background: url(images/bg.gif);
          background-attachment: fixed;}

The other attachment option is "scroll," but there really isn't a need to code that, as it is the default value.

Next, you can set the font for the body text. This can be a generic "family" name, as shown here:

body   {background: url(images/bg.gif);
          background-attachment: fixed;
          font-family: serif;}

The other generic names you can use are: sans-serif, cursive, fantasy, and monospace. Serif fonts, such as Times Roman, are characterized by small extenders on the characters that help lead your eyes across a line; serif fonts are generally used for body text. Sans-serif fonts, such as Arial, have no extenders and are generally used for headings. You can also name specific fonts such as Arial, Garamond, etc., for body text, but the computer used to view the page must have the font available for the page to render in that font. That's why it's best to stick with the few basic fonts that are always available on most computers.

You can also specify a font style, with a value of: normal, italic, or oblique.

```
body  {background-color: blue;
       background-attachment: fixed;
       font-family: serif;
       font-style: normal;}
```

You can set the style sheet's font size in one of two ways. Style sheets do not have the HTML size limit of 7, so you can specify any practical size (in a numerical value) you like with style sheet tags. The numbers roughly correspond to the traditional point sizes used in text editors and graphics programs. For this, you can code a number:

```
body  {background-color: blue;
       background-attachment: fixed;
       font-family: serif;
       font-style: normal;
       font-size: 14px;}
```

You can use other size values as well. I prefer using pixels as shown in the code above, which partially reflects my graphics background and familiarity with pixel measurements, but I also think using pixel size gives you the greatest control. The other units of measure you can use are:

Named Sizes

xx-small, x-small, small, medium, large, x-large, xx-large

Named sizes, as you can see, give you no more control than the old HTML font sizes of 1 through 7, so you gain little from using them. Fonts will also be rendered differently from computer to computer using named sizes. Furthermore, this unit of measure doesn't seem to work in all browsers.

195

Ems

Ems are actually a unit of measure for print. You can specify a font size using ems by substituting em in place of px, as in:

body {font-size: 1.5em;}

Some designers prefer using em measurements—usually those that came from the print media environment.

Points

Point sizes also come from the print design world. To code a point size, substitute pt in place of px, as in:

body {font-size: 1.5pt;}

Points are mainly included in the CSS spec so a second style sheet can be prepared for printouts.

Percentage

Fonts can be coded in percentages. A font set to 100 percent will display in the default size. A larger percentage will render the font that much larger than the default size and vice versa for a smaller percentage. For example:

body {font-size: 150%;}

As you can imagine, you have less absolute control when using percentages. The best measurement to use, in my opinion, is pixels. It's not only the most precise, but it is a unit of measure specific to computer display. Pixels also offer the most uniformity between the Windows and Mac OS platforms. You can use other units of measure (centimeters, millimeters, inches), but they are seldom used and I don't recommend them. I think once you're accustomed to using pixels as I do, nothing else will do for you.

If you use a left border image or are smart enough to plan white space into your pages, you might want to include page margins in the style sheet. A margin keeps text and other content off the colored border of the left border background. Having text overlap the border is unsightly and unprofessional. White space makes pages easier to read and keeps them from looking cluttered.

Some sites do have navigation buttons or text in the border, but text there shouldn't run into the main page area and vice versa. If you do want content of some type on the border, then don't use a margin—use a table to separate the two areas of content. Assuming you do not want content messing up your way-cool left border background, here's how to add the margin:

```
body {margin: 20px 50px 20px 160px;}
```

NOTE

If you like, these values also can be separated with a comma.

Notice the blue type. To add a margin, simply add "margin:" and the amount of space in pixels that you want for the margins. To remind you, the *px* stands for pixels, and there should be no space between the number and px. The first number represents the top margin, the second number the right margin, the third number the bottom margin, and the last number the left margin. (It runs clockwise starting at 12 o'clock, which should help you remember which value is which.)

One last thing to point out: Notice the right margin (50 pixels) in the previous code is considerably smaller than the left margin (160 pixels). This is assuming the style sheet will be used on a page with a left border background, where the white space is an equal distance from the background image border to the text, as it is from the right side of the text to the edge of the browser window.

If you don't want to set all the margins, you can individually set specific margins. To do this, you need to designate which margin to set as follows:

```
body {margin-left: 160px;}
```

To set each margin separately, use any of the following properties:

```
margin-top, margin-right, margin-bottom, and margin-left
```

Another useful item that goes in the body style rules is text alignment:

```
body {text-align: justify}
```

The other values are left, center, and right, with left as the default value.

Finally, many webmasters like to change the color of the scroll bars. You do this in the body style rules as follows:

```
body  {scrollbar-face-color: #864A71;
       scrollbar-shadow-color: #000000;
       scrollbar-highlight-color: #FFFFFF;
       scrollbar-track-color: #996666;
       scrollbar-arrow-color: #00FC32;}
```

As you can see, you can set the color for several items in the scrollbar area.

Let's put together an entire body style sample now, using the linked style sheet format.

CODE EXAMPLE

```
body   {background-color: blue;
        background-attachment: fixed;
        margin: 20px, 50px, 20px, 160px;
        font-family: serif;
        font-style: normal;
        font-size: 14px;
        text-align: justify;
        scrollbar-face-color: #864A71;
        scrollbar-shadow-color: #000000;
        scrollbar-highlight-color: #FFFFFF;
        scrollbar-track-color: #996666;
        scrollbar-arrow-color: #00FC32;}
```

That's a typical set of style rules for the body tag. Many other selectors can be added to this. A style sheet file can become quite lengthy if you choose to employ styles for many HTML elements.

11.8 Style Sheet Heading Properties

W ith style sheets, you can specify the size of each heading (h1 through h6) as well as the color, font, background color, and other properties. Adding heading styles is very similar to adding the body style. Let's build a set of heading styles:

CODE EXAMPLE

```
h1 {font-family: Arial, Verdana;
    color: navy;
    font-size: 28px;
    text-decoration: underline;}
h2 {font-family: Arial, Verdana;
    color: navy;
    font-size: 20px;}
h3 {font-family: Arial, Verdana;
    color: black;
    font-size: 14px;
    background: yellow;}
```

You can continue with style tags all the way down to the h6 heading size.

In the first set, for the h1 tag, we added a font family, made the font navy in color, set the size to 28 pixels, and underlined the headings. Anywhere you type the HTML command <h1> on the page, that heading style will be used unless you override it with other commands.

In the next series, we used the same font family and color, but we set the size to 20 pixels. Wherever you use the <h2> HTML tag on the page, this is the style it will be rendered in.

In the final heading, we did something a little different. We used the same font family—and it's a good idea to use the same font in all the headings to maintain consistency—but we set the font color to black and gave it a yellow background color. We can use this for emphasis without using a larger font. The font is set to the same size as the body text set in the body style in the previous example.

If you don't want an attribute and value for a style, simply remove them. For example, if you don't want a background color for the h3 tag, write it like this:

```
h3 {font-family: Arial, Verdana;
      color: black;
      font-size: 14px;}
```

Pretty neat, isn't it? Rather than using various attributes and values throughout the page, you can simply set the heading styles once and those are the styles the headings will be rendered in throughout the page.

You can experiment. Try one thing at a time so you know what works and what doesn't without having to sort through several items at once.

11.9 Style Sheet Link Properties

Y ou can set the same link properties in style sheets as in HTML—and then some. Two popular uses are removing the underline from links and changing link colors when a cursor is hovering over it. We'll begin with the standard link properties:

```
a:link  {font-family: Arial, Verdana;
           color: blue;
           font-size: 12;}
```

As you can see, you set the link properties as you did with the body and heading properties. As with the heading properties, you can add a background color to links also. Displaying a background color for links when the mouse is hovering over it is a popular addition.

You set the properties for active links and visited links using the same attributes and values, only in style sheets the tags have different names. See the table below to see the differences.

HTML TAG	CSS EQUIVALENT
link	a:link
alink	a:active
vlink	a:visited

As you can see, each link type in a style sheet is spelled out and coded with an "a:" in front of the link type. The "a" stands for "anchor" because some sailor made it up. OK, not really. They are anchors because they represent a specific address that connects one document to another—an anchor point so to speak.

Which brings us to the fun style sheet gizmo of creating a hover property. The hover property wasn't available using plain HTML. The hover property determines how a link is displayed when a cursor is on the link. For example:

```
a:hover {color: #FF0000; background-color: #000000;}
```

In this example, the link text turns red and the background behind the link text turns black when a cursor is on the link.

Let's take a look at the entire link setup of an example style sheet:

CODE EXAMPLE

```
a:link  {font-family: Arial, Verdana;
          color: blue;
          font-size: 12px;}
a:visited  {font-family: Arial, Verdana;
             color: gray;
             font-size: 12px;}
a:hover  {font-family: Arial, Verdana;
           color: black;
           font-size: 12px;
           font-weight: bold;}
a:active {font-family: Arial, Verdana;
           color: red;
           font-size: 12px;}
```

For the sake of demonstration, I simply used color names instead of hex codes. In the code example, the font family and font size was set the same for all states of the links. The color was set to a unique color for each, and for the hover status, I also added a rule to make the text go bold on hover.

 In the hover style, the link text will turn bold when a visitor's cursor is on the link, but you have to be a little careful where you use that effect. A link surrounded by text may cause a shift to all the text in that line, and may move a word to the next line. That can be a little disconcerting to an inexperienced user and can make your page seem a little goofy.

201

Even worse, though, if a user puts the cursor in just the right spot, it can cause the link to repeatedly activate and deactivate the hover code, and that's stoopid. Oops, I forgot I'm writing a textbook—correction: that's stupid.

An example of a smart way to use a bold hover style is when the links are all in a table where the effect won't force other content to shift.

11.10 Blockquotes

Sometimes, you'll want to set text apart from the main body for more impact. In traditional publishing, this is known as a pull quote. In HTML, you can create a pull quote with a blockquote. A blockquote is text that is indented on both sides from the imaginary vertical lines the rest of the text lines up between. With style sheets, you can add borders and other properties around blockquotes. Prior to style sheets, I used a horizontal rule on each side of the text within a blockquote to achieve a similar affect. No need for that trick anymore. Here's an example of a blockquote style:

```
blockquote  {border-style: double;
             border-color: palegreen;
             padding: 12px;}
```

The graphic below shows what the example blockquote style looks like in use.

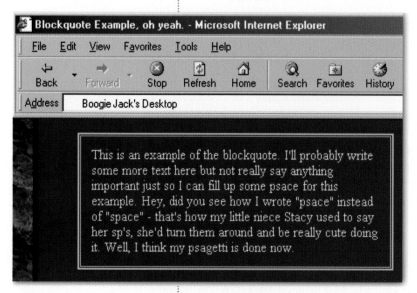

It places the text inside a box with a green, double-line border around it.

This code adds 12 pixels of padding on each side between the border and the text.

In addition to the double line, the other border styles include: dotted, dashed, solid, groove, ridge, inset, outset, and none.

If you define a blockquote style in a style sheet, you create the blockquote in the document by surrounding the text with the HTML blockquote tag:

<blockquote>

Our guarantee is simple: return our 14K gold knuckle remover for any reason within a year and we'll refund your money and send you on a three-week vacation to boot (camp)!

</blockquote>

11.11 Tables and Style Sheets

Y ou can add all the formatting options you've learned in this chapter thus far to style sheets for table and table data cells. Since we've covered that already, I'll take this opportunity to show you a simple, yet creative way you can use style sheets for tables. You could get far more creative than this, but this should spark your imagination sufficiently. If not, send me a dollar and apologize. Look at this small table:

Take a look at the style sheet code below used for the sample table at right.

Left-handed gloves	FREE!
Matching right-handed gloves	Just $99.95!
Six fingered gloves	Just $333.50!

CODE EXAMPLE

```
table {border: double;
       border-color: gray;}
td.left {background-color: gainsboro;
         font-weight: bold;
         font-family: Times New Roman;
         padding: 3px;}
td.right {background-color: #b7b774;
          font-weight: bold;
          font-family: Arial;
          padding: 3px;}
```

This is the code for the linked style sheet, which the HTML document consults to format the table when you link to it in the

203

HEAD section of a page. If you look at the table data cells on the left, you'll notice the middle row is a darker gray than the rest. The CSS code example, however, shows all the left side table data cells coded with one color. We used an inline style in that row to override the linked style when we coded the table, as you can see below.

Using HTML, all the font tags and background color tags have to be included in each and every table cell. But with style sheets, those values are extracted from the style sheet for the left and right table data cells. Again, the names "left" and "right" could be anything we want to call the class. I chose those names because they represent the left cell and the right cell. It just makes sense and is easy to remember.

Here is the HTML code for that table:

CODE EXAMPLE

```
<table><tr><td class="left">
Left-handed gloves
</td>
<td class="right">
FREE!
</td></tr>
<tr><td class="left" style="background-color: gray;">
Matching right-handed gloves
</td><td class="right">
Just $99.95!
</td></tr>
<tr><td class="left">
Six fingered gloves
</td><td class="right">
Just $333.50!
</td></tr></table>
```

The code in blue is where I used an inline style to override the background color in the linked style sheet.

In the book resources page on my site, you'll find links to software programs that make using CSS easier. Many other programs and resources are included as well. You'll find this page to be a very handy reference that you'll use often. The web address for this page is:

www.boogiejack.com/book/resources.html

11.12 Margins

The margin properties define the space around elements. An interesting option is to use negative values to overlap content. You can set all the margins with one rule—a method called a shorthand property—or you can individually set the top, right, bottom, and left margins.

In my Inner Circle newsletter, I use overlapping content to create the illusion of a graphic where there is none. Using formatted text rather than a graphic keeps the newsletter file size small so it downloads quickly in email and doesn't use excess disk space. Here's a screen shot of the "fake image" I'm referring to:

Look at the code below to see how this was created.

At the top, it says Almost a Newsletter, which is my free plain text newsletter. Overlapping that is the text Inner Circle, which is the members-only HTML version of Almost a Newsletter. There is also a shadow behind the gold text. The whole effect makes it look like an image, but it's all just HTML and CSS. Here's how it was done:

Almost a Newsletter

Inner Circle

April 1, 2003

Tower of Savings

Total savings since April 1, 2002: Over **$2,858.00!**

Below are the money saving discounts I've arranged for you in this issue.

Hi Dennis,

Welcome to another Inner Circle issue. I've got some great savings lined up for you on terrific software you're sure to enjoy. As always these savings are only for Inner Circle members. Be sure to check out the expiring offers too, many won't be around much longer.

CODE EXAMPLE

```
h1 {font-size: 38px; font-family: Impact, Arial, Helvetica;
    font-weight: bold; color: #D2E6DB;
    text-decoration: underline;}
h2 {font-size: 30px; font-family: Impact, Arial, Helvetica;
    font-weight: bold; color: #E7D974; position: relative;
    margin-top: -57px; margin-left: 188px;}
h3 {font-size: 30px; font-family: Impact, Arial, Helvetica;
    font-weight: bold; color: black; position: relative;
    margin-top: -40px; margin-left: 189px;}
```

This code introduces a few tricks. You've seen much of this in previous examples, so I'll just cover the new things here.

First of all, in the h2 and h3 headings, I used relative positioning. This means the text is placed on the page relative to its position in the code. For the h2 heading I used a negative top margin to move the text into the position where it overlaps the h1 heading. The negative value for the top margin means the text is moved toward the top from its default position. The left margin moved the text to the right so it lined up near the end of the h1 heading.

For the h3 heading, relative positioning was again used, with the negative values adjusted so that the black text was offset from the gold text to give the illusion of a drop shadow. Also, the font size for both the h2 and h3 headings were set to the same size. This is because the black text sits just behind the gold text to give the shadow effect, so we wouldn't want the text to be different sizes.

Next, here's how that entire style is coded into the page:

CODE EXAMPLE

```
<h1>Almost a Newsletter</h1>
<h3>Inner Circle</h3>
<h2>Inner Circle</h2>
```

Pretty simple as far as the actual HTML code goes. Notice that I do have the h3 heading coded before the h2 heading. This is so the h2 heading sits on top of the h3 heading. Remember, the h3 heading was the shadow so it has to sit behind the h2 heading. To accomplish that, it had to be coded first to make the h2 heading overlap it.

Of course, using margins with negative values isn't as common as using margins with positive values. A more common use is to set the margins for a paragraph of text. For example:

`p.special {margin: 20px 40px 50px 40px;}`

With the above code, any paragraph coded with the class of "special" would have a margin of 20 pixels on the top, 40 pixels on the right, 50 pixels on the bottom, and 20 pixels on the left. These margins can be set separately, as shown in a previous example. Remember, when using the shorthand margin style instead of coding each one individually, the margins read clockwise from the top. So it's top, right, bottom, and left. Shorthand margin style refers to coding all margins using one property, rather than the individual properties.

To code the paragraph with the class of "special" we just created, we simply add the class declaration to a paragraph tag:

```
<p class="special">
```

By the way, the Inner Circle version of Almost a Newsletter features top-of-the-line software you can purchase at discount prices. This is always current version software. Vendors provide discounts to my members because I offer them a nice opportunity for mass publicity without the cost of advertising. You can learn more about becoming an Inner Circle member here:

www.boogiejack.com/AANICpreview.html

You'll also find a link to this page on the front page of my site.

As I said at the beginning, this chapter covers many basics of CSS, but there is much, much more to it. Most of us mere mortals won't use a lot beyond what is included here. If you're seriously interested in learning all you can about CSS, though, you'll find many books dedicated to CSS that cover the topic in much more depth. Using a good search engine, you can also find online CSS tutorials.

11.13 Chapter Quiz

1. Name the three ways to add styles to code.

2. Name the three parts of CSS syntax.

3. If you create a division selector with a class called "hype," what HTML code would you use to call that division style into a web page?

4. You've created a style sheet in a separate file called "bizstyle.css" that is located in a directory named "Styles." Write the code for the <head> section of the HTML page to call that style sheet into action.

5. Finish the following style sheet code to link to a web page background called "bg.jpg" in a folder called "images."
   body {background:

6. Write the code to specify a body margin of 20 pixels on the top and bottom, 30 pixels on the right, and 60 pixels on the left.

7. Say you need to group the two largest heading sizes to set their colors to blue. How in the world are you going to do that?

8. Write the code that makes a link change to red when the cursor is resting on it.

11.13 Chapter Quiz (continued)

9. Add the code to specify 12 pixels of padding for this blockquote style.

   `blockquote {border-style: double;}`

10. In CSS code, what is the terminator (semicolon) used for?

11. Select the proper order in which one type of style overrides the others, from the most important to the least important.

    a. Inline / embedded / linked
    b. Linked / embedded / inline
    c. Embedded / linked / inline
    d. Inline / linked / embedded

12. If a nerd had an absurd bird that was heard to speak a slurred word unde-terred by preferred enunciation, what would the bird's name be?

11.14 Chapter Exercises

Exercise Option 1 – Practice Site

I n this exercise, you'll format your links page with cascading style sheets. Using either embedded styles or linked styles, specify at least three different style selectors. Use at least two different properties and values for at least one of the selectors.

You might set links up in a table and add hover colors, background colors, heading properties, font properties, and more. Use whatever you want, as long as you implement at least three style selectors and two different properties and values for one of the selectors.

Once you've finished the formatting, find at least three good sites on the Internet to link to that people interested in your web site's content might find interesting. Of course, if I were grading you, you wouldn't get a high grade for sticking to the minimum requirements. High grades are reserved for those who try harder. Hey, it's just like out there in the real world—the harder you work at it, the greater the rewards. Instructors, feel free to give extra credit to students who link to my site. After all, good practices are reinforced by rewards. ☺

Exercise Option 2 – Independent Exercise

C reate a new page using a linked style sheet. Use a left border background and specify page margins so that no content is on the border part of the background. Using linked style sheets, create colored headings, create links with all custom colors including the hover color, create a class for a division tag and use it at least once, and incorporate at least three other CSS selectors with the appropriate properties and values.

For extra credit, try to find a selector with a property and value combination not demonstrated in this chapter and use it.

Search Engine Optimization

12.1 Chapter Introduction

S earch engine optimization is the art and science of coding your pages in a way that helps your site rank higher than uninformed webmasters' sites in search results for keywords and keyword phrases related to your content.

This chapter presents a general strategy designed for overall performance at all search engines that consider code and content as ranking factors. It is not tailored to specific search engines, which would be a far more in-depth study for which I'd have to charge you a billion dollars and nine cents. It is the same basic strategy I've used to maintain good rankings since 1997.

Note that search engines regularly tweak and change their ranking criteria to provide better search results and thwart webmasters from manipulating the search results with trickery. Not all search engines view everything in this chapter as important, but what they don't consider important won't hurt your ranking with them. Plus, all these techniques do help at one or more search engines.

Keep in mind, the optimization techniques in this chapter comprise only a part of the ranking criteria. Other factors, which will be explained as the chapter progresses, are equally important—and even more important than code optimization at many search engines. Still, every advantage you put to use is an advantage. If all other factors are equal, the advantages you create with search engine optimization will put your site ahead of others.

One thing for certain, the search engine game isn't what it used to be. Many search engines now charge to list your site. At the time of this writing, Google is responsible for about 70 percent of all search engine traffic, and its listings are still free. It is up to you to decide if you want to pay to have your site included by the various search engines. If you do, you especially want to optimize your code. It would be a discouraging thing to pay for a listing only to have your site end up as number 9,000 in the results for your keywords.

Chapter at a Glance

Finally, still other types of search engines feature pay-per-click. With this payment structure, you bid on keywords for your site's search engine position, and he or she who bids the most gets ranked first. When someone clicks your link at a pay-per-click search engine, you pay the amount you bid for the traffic they send to your web site. You pay up front, so the money is deducted from your reserve fund. When the fund is exhausted, your listing is too. Depending on the pay-per-click search engine and the keywords you want to bid on, acquiring traffic this way can cost from pennies to several dollars for each visitor.

12.2 How Search Engines Work

T̲o better understand how to optimize your site for search engines it is helpful to have an understanding of how search engines work, from the search engine's point of view (so to speak).

The search engine site's management wants the same thing every webmaster wants—traffic to their sites. Since their content is mainly links to other sites, their goal is to make their search engines bring up the most relevant sites to the search query and to display the best of these results first.

To accomplish this, search engines use a complex array of ranking rules called algorithms. When a search query is submitted to a search engine, sites are determined to be relevant or not relevant to the search query according to these algorithms. The algorithms rank the sites and then the engine lists the best matches first. Search engines keep their algorithms secret and change them often in order to prevent database manipulation and to provide new sites at the top of the search results on a regular basis rather than having the same sites always listed first. The struggle for high rankings is a never-ending and complicated match of wits, with the search engines setting the rules.

In the lessons that follow, you'll learn the optimization techniques I have used since 1997. While my rankings go up and down from search engine to search engine at various times and for a variety of keywords, I've generally always had a high ranking at some search engines at any given moment and decent rankings most all the time.

At one time, my site was number one on 11 of the top 14 search engines. I got a bit of a reputation as a search engine guru at the time, but the truth is, it was just the ebb and flow of the changing algorithms that put me at the top of so many engines at once.

Once I design a site, I pay very little attention to tweaking pages for ranking purposes. I've found that a good, general strategy like I advocate is effective enough in the big picture. Plus, not fretting the engines frees up valuable time for creating content and taking care of business.

12.3 An Important Difference

An important difference to understand is that search engines and directories are not the same animal. Moo. Oink. See, different animals.

Search engines use a spider to "crawl" the web sites they find (as well as submitted sites) in order to add them to their databases. As they crawl the web, they gather the information used by their algorithms to rank the sites.

Directories, on the other hand, rely on submissions from webmasters and use human beings to view your site and determine if it will be accepted. If accepted, directories often rank sites in alphanumeric order, with paid listings sometimes on top. Some search engines also place paid listings at the top, so it's not always possible to get a ranking in the top three listings or more, unless you're willing to pay for it.

Examples of search engines include:

Alta Vista: www.altavista.com

Google: www.google.com

WiseNut: www.wisenut.com

Examples of directories include:

Jayde: www.jayde.com

Open Directory Project: http://dmoz.org/

Yahoo!: www.yahoo.com

You can't optimize your site for directories as you can for search engines—other than to be sure you have plenty of quality content, a visually pleasing design, and good navigation. Those are the three main things human editors look for when deciding whether or not to list a site.

A final point to understand is that many search engines and directories mix in results from other search engines and directories with their own listings. Getting listed at, or dropped by, one engine can affect your status at other sites. That's one reason it's so important to play by the rules. If you're thinking of cheating at just one search engine to see what you can get away with, know in advance that it can affect your listing at other search engines.

12.4 What Search Engines Want from Webmasters

ver the years, self-proclaimed search engine experts have touted all kinds of methods for ranking higher at search engines. This has included many illegal tactics such as hidden text, hidden links, meta tag stuffing, double meta tags, page stuffing, cloaking, redirect pages, made-up HTML tags, bulk-quantity doorway pages, link farms, and other "secrets" of dubious quality and effectiveness.

Those techniques, and newer techniques that still amount to trickery, can result in lower rankings just for using them—even if your site is the best match to the search query. In a worst-case scenario, cheating can even result in your domain being banned. Once banned, it's hard to get back into that search engine, let alone get a good ranking with them.

So what are my secrets? It's quite simple: I know how search engines want us to behave and I always follow the rules. I do everything I legally can to optimize my pages, but always play within the rules using only legitimately recognized (search-engine approved) methods. That's what this chapter teaches.

When a search engine catches on to new trickery, your site can be dropped in rank or be banned from their database without warning, so it's best to think long term. Longevity, which comes by playing within the rules, is one of the things that can help your rankings.

So what do the search engines really want? They want to be able to help their web site visitors find what they are looking for, and they want to give them the best and most logical matches first.

The short version of what search engines want to see from webmasters:

- A simple, clean design with a focus on content.
- Easy navigation.
- Well-written, keyword-rich, benefit-orientated copy.
- Title tags, meta tags, and image alt tags that are relevant.

Deeper explanation: In a way, your web site's content is the search engine's content since their primary objective is to send people to the kinds of sites they're looking for. Therefore, search engines want sites with high-quality content above all else. They want to show the best sites available in a search return, because if their search returns are helpful to the searcher, the searcher will be more likely to use their search engine time and time again.

Search engines want no trickery whatsoever used. They want webmasters to show the search engine spiders the same content you show visitors. Things such as hidden text and links, cloaking, re-directs, and other tactics that show the search engine spiders one thing and visitors another are high-risk tricks that often result in lowered rankings or even having your site banned. Most of these are old tricks anyway—search engines caught on long ago.

Design your site so your text accurately reflects the content, products, and services you offer. Search engines penalize sites that make obvious attempts at manipulating them. There should be no tricks and no misleading verbiage designed strictly for better placement.

Once you're site is flagged for cheating, you'll have a hard time getting a top ranking again no matter how well you clean up your act. You've heard the expression, "once a cheater, always a cheater"? So have the search engine staff. If they catch you once, they may check other domains you own to see if you're spamming or cheating with them, too. If you own more than one site, you could be jeopardizing the others by cheating on one.

So there you have it, search engines want the same things surfers' want, quality content that's presented accurately and honestly—and no dirty tricks. Gosh, that isn't a great revelation is it? It shouldn't be, it's the way we should all be doing business in the first place—honestly and accurately. It is what works best in the long term with search engines and in life. Your site will never be penalized or banned for playing by the rules.

By the way, I do not consider myself a search engine expert. I've got a good idea of what works from my experience and studying what the real experts say. Many people who claim they know the "search engine secrets" have no more knowledge than I do. I suppose if you don't know the techniques I'm revealing then they are secrets, but truthfully, there are no magic bullets.

There is no trick or secret that will rocket you to the top of the search engines—unless you consider paying for a top listing a secret. There are, however, a good deal of things you can legally do better than the next person to help optimize your pages so they grade out as high as they can for the portion of the algorithms that you can effect by coding strategy. Not all of the algorithm rules can be affected by site design and coding strategies.

12.5 So Just What Are the Algorithms?

No one knows every algorithm and rule a search engine uses except the search engine programmers, and they're not talking. We do know many things about them though. Before I list some of the things we know that are currently important, let me point out that what is important today may not be as important tomorrow. As the engines change their algorithm, your site ranking can go down in three search engines and up in five others, or vice versa. That's why a general strategy such as mine seems to work so well for those who don't want to constantly study the search engines and tweak and resubmit their pages every few weeks.

Unless you're going to make an in-depth and ongoing study of each search engine—and are prepared to make changes to your site on a very regular basis and prepare separate pages for each search engine—then the general strategies I present will probably be best for you. Having said that, the following sections offer the most important search engine rules.

Link Popularity

The more links there are to your site, the higher it will rank. Page design can't do anything about this very important search engine rule—obtaining links from other sites is the only thing that can help you here.

It goes farther than that, though. The more important the sites are that link to your site—that is to say, the more links pointing to the sites that link to your site—the more important the search engines think your site is. The idea behind link popularity is that the search engines consider your site to be pre-judged by other webmasters. The more webmasters that link to your site, the better the search engines figure your site is by virtue of its link popularity.

To positively affect this portion of the algorithms, you need to get links from the most popular web sites you can. That's why exchanging links with my site is an excellent idea for most people. My site ranks in the top 1 percent of the most linked-to sites on the

Internet. That's an important link in the search engine's eyes. You'll find information about exchanging links with me here:

www.boogiejack.com/link2me.html

Themed Sites

If your site follows a theme, it will be rated higher than a site about nothing in particular. For example, if someone searches for "car care" and your site has car care articles, car accessories, links to sites related to cars, and car-related sites linking to yours, you'll have a search engine advantage over a site with a car-care article or two, stupid pet tricks, Jane's poetry, granny's recipes, and no theme-relevant links.

Keyword Density

Keywords are the words someone who wants to find a site like yours would enter into a search engine. The percentage of keywords for your site's theme that are used in your page text, as compared to the rest of the body text, is an important criteria in site ranking. This ratio of keywords to non-keywords is called keyword density.

Keyword Placement

Where you locate the keywords on your page is important too. The higher up in your content, the more they will help your ranking.

Keyword Emphasis

With the page, using keywords in bold text, increased font sizes, and heading tags is good search engine food. The search engines figures that if you place more emphasis on those words, they must be more important than other text, so they place more importance on them as well.

Keyword Coding Usage

There are other legal places to use keywords in pages besides in the visible page text. I'll show you some—you might be surprised by a few.

Keyword Naming

The names you use for certain things can give your site a nice boost. We'll go over all these items in more depth, one at a time.

217

Content

High-quality content. Quality, quality, quality. In case I haven't made it clear, we're talking quality content here. Don't worry; it isn't as hard as it sounds.

Click-through Rate

At some engines, how often searchers click the link to your site when it's displayed affects how your site ranks in the future. I have tips for that, too.

Aardvark Brain Painting

Not really, I was just checking to see if you were paying attention. You done good! ☺

12.6 Guiding Principles

Before digging into the actual optimization techniques, you'll need to know a few guiding principles and how to plot a course of action. The following steps may not apply right now if you're using this book in a classroom situation. You may not have enough of a web site built to put it to use. If that's the case, just follow along for now and remember to come back to this option when you are ready to develop a plan.

To get started on a plan, first take a good look at your web site. Which pages are the most important to you? As far as the search engines are concerned, the index page is the most important, so that has to be your top priority.

Take out a pencil and paper and write "Index" at the top. Determine what the most important theme of your site is, and then write down the next most important pages of your site that relate to the theme. You can list all your pages in this second tier if you like, but if you really think about it, you probably do have a smaller subset of pages that you care more about ranking high than others. Before you continue reading, create that second tier page list now.

Hmm, hmm. . . waiting . . . la de da . . . tapping foot . . .

Ready? Good! The index page should link directly to this second tier of web pages. Not all search engines crawl every level to find every page of a site. By linking to those pages from your index page, you ensure they will be indexed by the search engines that list more than the index page.

Secrets!

Here's one of those so-called secret tips: Some search engines will only crawl two or three levels deep on your site. By creating a site map that lists every page of your site and linking to it from your index page, you ensure that even the search engines that limit the depth their spiders crawl still find all your pages. Here's how those search engines see your site:

Top: Index page

Level One: Site Map (and any page linked-to from your index page)

Level Two: All your pages, if you have a site map on level one.

Level Three: Who Cares! You win!

There is one exception: Some search engines limit the number of pages they will index for any one domain. Therefore, you may want to list pages on the site map in order of importance to your objectives.

12.7 Setting the Theme

[N] ow, back to your index page. Since this is the most important page of your site, this is where you set the site's theme. Let's suppose the primary focus of your site is raising horses and all things horsy. You also have secondary content for those not interested in horses. The secondary content consists of passions you want to share, such as book reviews, humor, links, and poetry.

The top of your index page is the most important. This is where you set the keywords and theme for the most important part of your site—the thing you really want to be found for. So, after your logo or header graphic (if you use one), you might start off the index page with a heading tag, an introductory paragraph, a smaller heading, and a closing paragraph, all targeted at the theme. Take a look at these sections in detail.

Start with a Heading Tag

A heading tag that includes a keyword(s) or keyword phrase. A heading tag is bigger and bolder text than normal body text, so a search engine places more importance on it. Example:

```
<h2>Horses, of Course!</h2>
```

Heading sizes range from h1 to h6 with h1 being the largest text. As you learned in Chapter 11: Cascading Style Sheets, you can control the size of headings using CSS. Even if you set an h1 size heading to be only slightly larger than the normal text, search engines will still see it as an important heading.

Add an Introductory Paragraph

After the heading tag, add an introductory paragraph for visitors that describes the main theme. Include several of your top keywords and keyword phrases. Repeat your top one or two keywords several times. Include other keyword search terms as well, but make it read in sentences that make sense to visitors without being redundant. Search engines will consider excessive redundancy as a spamming attempt.

Example welcome text:

Welcome to Horses, of Course! You'll find quality information about our horse breeding program, pictures of champion horses we've raised, horse care articles, stud fees, prime mare breeding ages, foal care, horse training, rider training, equine tips, and horse-related products and services.

In this example, we've installed plenty of keywords and keyword phrases at the top of the page. In order of appearance, they are:

Horses, horse breeding, pictures of champion horses, horse care articles, stud fees, prime mare breeding ages, foal care, horse training, rider training, equine tips, horse products and services.

Not bad for just off the top of my head! It makes sense to the visitor and has plenty of keywords and keyword phrases without being redundant. We might add a second paragraph that gets more specific, using other horsy words such as tack, saddles, riding gear, chaps, stallions, geldings, etc.

Continue with a Smaller Heading

After the heading tag and introductory paragraph, you can further reinforce your theme by adding a smaller heading:

<h3>Our Horse Pages</h3>

Again, the words in heading tags are considered more important than standard body text, so be sure to include a keyword or

> **NOTE**
>
> In terms of search engines, spamming is any attempt to manipulate your search rankings by illegal means, trickery, or rule violations.

two in them. After that, you might list the links to your horse pages, ideally with a brief description of each link using keywords and keyword phrases in the link text. Include several pages of quality content to link to as well. Here's an example of how you might treat your links:

<a href="horse_photos.html">**Horse Photographs**</a>: **Enjoy these beautiful photos of our prized stallions and mares. These horses are an equine lover's dream.**

Continue this way with all the links to the horse pages. We'll cover this in more depth later, but notice the name of the page. It includes a keyword (horse) with the word photos. The words are separated by an underscore rather than run together as "horsephotos" so the words will be recognized separately by search engines.

Use a Closing Paragraph

To reinforce the theme at the top of the page code, wrap it up with a keyword-laden closing paragraph. Example:

We hope you enjoy our passion for all things equine. Horses are a great love of our life. A good horse will be as devoted to you as you are to the horse. There was good reason for the old saying, "A cowboy's best friend is his horse."

More is not necessarily better when it comes to keywords, at least after a certain point. Writing "horses" 50 times across a page will probably get you caught for trying to spam the engines. Ideally, somewhere between 3 and 20 percent of a page's text would be various keywords.

The percentage of keywords to non-keywords is called keyword density. The preferred percentage changes often and is different at each search engine. The 3 to 20 percent range is a general guideline—you can go higher if the text makes sense and isn't redundant. Later, I'll show you how to figure out keyword density, and how to figure out the approximate percentage that works best at each search engine.

List Secondary Content

Now that your theme is nice and strong, you can finally list your secondary content of book reviews, humor, links, and poetry. If they aren't necessary, skip the descriptions as they will water down your theme. The top of the index page might also include a link called Entertainment or Miscellaneous or something, which links to a complete index of all your other site sections. You can submit these secondary indexes to search engines, and since they will be well themed, you should achieve decent rankings for them as well.

Now, you've set up the all-important top of your page with a strong horse theme. So far so good. This strategy isn't the only way to create a strong theme, however, so don't be compelled to follow this exact formula. This was just an example of one way to set up a strong site theme. Use your imagination—you may come up with an even better way.

It's important to note that you shouldn't try to optimize your index page for more than one theme—multiple themes just end up weakening each other's strength. By using simple links to your alternative content, visitors will be able to get where they want to go. Then, you can write the alternative content as a secondary index optimized toward its own theme. Ultimately, each page should be search-engine optimized for the main topic of that page or site section.

The search-engine optimization of my index page emphasizes a webmasters theme, but I have several secondary index pages optimized toward other themes. For the most part, all my pages are optimized in this way. I will confess, though, that I had a little fun on a few pages—pages for which I don't care if and how they are indexed. Did you know I have a page optimized for liquid squid lips?

By now you should realize that search engine optimization consists of many simple techniques that work together to create a comprehensive strategy. This combination of techniques is greater as a whole than the sum of the parts. While you can skip any small technique that is a part of the overall strategy, it will subtract from the edge you'd gain by employing all the tactics.

Now you know your index page is the most important, and you know how to set it up with a theme. Here's the final guiding principle in optimizing a page for search engines:

KISS ME RIBITS!

In other words:

Keep It Simple So Most Engines Rank It Better In Their Standings

In other, other words, search engines adore simplicity. If you check the top sites for a variety of keywords and keyword phrases, often the simple sites are listed toward the top. The main reason for this is that the keywords and keyword phrases are near the top of the code. There's not a lot of JavaScript pushing the important things farther down in the code, there's not a lot of flash, there's not many, if any, framed sites . . . simplicity.

I know, the simple sites may not be as visually appealing. That's where you have to strike a balance between optimization and visual appeal. A little creativity can go a long way here.

12.8 A Coding Practice That Costs You Positioning

One mistake many people make in coding pages is the way they set up left-side navigation. These sites are usually set up with tables, and all the navigation and other things on the left side push the main page content with its keywords way down in the code. That's not search-engine friendly.

There is a way to code a page to avoid this problem, but still have the page look exactly the same. It's called the empty table cell trick. The idea is to use an empty table cell first, and then place your content with the valuable keywords in a second cell for search engines. Then start another row to hold the left side content. Using this technique, the left side content containing the navigation is actually below your main page content in the code.

To prevent left-side navigation code from devaluing the content that search engines look for:

CODE EXAMPLE

```
<table border="0" cellpadding="0" cellspacing="0" width="600">
<tr>
<td valign="top" align="left" width="140"></td>
<td width="10" rowspan="2"> </td>
<td valign="top" align="left" width="450" rowspan="2">
This is where your main page content goes. Because of the way tables are read, this appears first in your code so it's better for search engine optimization.
</td></tr>
<tr>
<td valign="top" align="left" width="140">
This is where your navigation and other left cell content should go.
</td></tr></table>
```

Both your navigation and the body content line up at the top just like they did in a table coded traditionally. But the main content that includes your good keywords **comes first** in the code.

Notice in the code there are two empty cells before any content. The first is your navigation space, which is coded in the second row, and the second empty cell is a gutter space between the navigation and the main content area. Both the gutter cell and the main content cell have a rowspan of two. This way, you don't have to repeat the extra gutter cell and the main content cell spans the full page. Although few webmasters use this simple technique, it reaps good results for no more effort than it takes to implement it.

12.9 Link Popularity

We covered link popularity briefly, but now we'll get into the thick of it. Link popularity is one of the most important criteria search engines use to rank sites. Link popularity means an engine counts how many sites in its database link to your site. The more sites that link to you, the more popular and important the engine calculates your site to be.

The engine also goes two steps beyond that. It also determines how many sites link to the sites that link to your site—so the more popular the sites are that link to yours, the more important the links to your site are considered to be.

In the final step, a search engine determines if the sites linking to your site are of a similar theme. Similarly themed sites linking to your site are better than non-themed sites linking to yours. That is not to say, however, that sites with different themes are unimportant, especially if those sites can offer a nice flow of traffic to your site. The last time I checked, my site was in the top 1 percent of the most linked-to sites on the Internet. Most of these sites do not have the same theme as my site, but they account for about 60 percent of my traffic and I do earn good search engine rankings. Some "experts" claim you should only link to similarly themed sites. You can follow that advice if you like, but I know what works for me, and I'll exchange links with most sites that are family friendly.

Obviously then, you should entice other webmasters to link to your site. This usually means linking back to the sites that link to you. Most people just fire off an email and ask to trade links. While that works sometimes, it isn't especially impressive and will yield fewer links than if you take a professional approach—especially if you're going to ask popular sites for a link exchange.

Believe me, webmasters of popular sites are inundated with link requests, including many automated requests. You'll be wasting your time if you think you can just email them indiscriminately and have a high percentage of success. For most webmasters, requests that even hint at being a mass mailed form fall into the "spam email" category and are swiftly deleted.

Many webmasters now know that link popularity is important and take the lazy way out. They are unwilling to learn the art of obtaining quality links and instead use software robots to go out and find sites and email addresses, and then automatically send their link requests. Smoe, no, not smoe . . . some, yes that's it, some of these programs also create a directory of sites from which they requested links.

The trouble with using this type of software is three-fold. First, the links are not always to good sites. If you offer a directory like these programs make, and it's filled with lousy sites masquerading as hand-picked sites, you're doing the visitors a disservice. They won't be impressed. So while automation is nice, you still must exercise a degree of manual control and exercise good judgment.

The second problem is that these links are often not reciprocated. The more popular the site is that receives the request, the less likely you will get a reciprocal link. When the webmaster of a popular site receives these form mail link requests, he or she knows you never visited the site and often deletes your request without a second thought.

The third problem is that some of these automated programs generate a list of dynamic pages, which are hardly useful for search engine help. Dynamic pages are generated on the fly by a software program, and are generally not well indexed by most search engines, so all the mini-directories these sites build are practically useless for search engine rankings. If you receive reciprocal links from the sites you find this way, however, they can send a nice flow of traffic to your site.

On the book resources page on my site, you'll find links to one of the better automated programs for building reciprocal links. You'll find that at:

www.boogiejack.com/book/resources.html

While automated programs are nice for building reciprocal links quickly, that's not the way to get links at quality sites. Webmasters of popular sites get far too many requests to personally handle those made by artificial means. It gives you a little perspective on why search engines don't like automated submission software. The submissions increase their workload tremendously, while those requesting the inclusion haven't even bothered to visit their search engine.

A link request that gets results has several key elements. These will seem like common sense to you, but the overwhelming majority of requests I get contain very few of these key elements.

1. **Follow instructions.** Look around the site for any link request instructions. If you don't follow the instructions, you greatly reduce your chances of getting a link from that site. On my site, I use a script to handle link requests. If you follow the instructions, your site will almost automatically be linked back to (unless it has content I don't care to be associated with or you don't enter the correct information).

2. **Be to the point.** In the subject line of your email request, get right to the point. Don't try to be cute or trick the person into reading your email.

   Subject: Link Request

   . . . will do the job. If they're interested, they'll act on it. If they're not, any tricks you use will ensure that your email is deleted without the desired response.

3. **Make it relevant.** Look the site over and find what you have in common. Mention that you think the site is great and what your visitors would enjoy about it, and then tie that in with what your site offers that would benefit the other webmaster's visitors. This shows that you've actually visited the site and have a clue about building quality traffic exchanges.

4. **Use a direct and correct address.** Look around to see if you can find the webmaster's name. Your email will be read with different eyes if you start it off with "Hi John" instead of "Hello" or "Dear Webmaster" or another impersonal salutation. For example, most people who write to me call me Jack. My name is Dennis. I don't hold it against those who call me Jack—with my web site's name, it is a logical assumption. But when someone writes to me as Dennis, it gets my attention quicker because I know they are probably a customer or a subscriber to one of my ezines.

5. **Be specific.** In the body of the letter, include the name and URL of the site you're requesting to exchange links with:

   . . . I've been looking over your site, Boogie Jack's Web Depot at www.boogiejack.com, and . . .

Believe it or not, they may not know what site you're talking about if you don't cite it specifically. I own several sites, for example, and I don't always know what site people are talking about when they write to me.

6. **Be sincere and respectful.** Don't fake like you're old friends when you've never met, and don't go overboard on the flattery. Cite the reasons you should trade links and why you like the site, but don't fake it. Insincerity can be spotted a mile away. That doesn't mean you can't flatter them at all—in fact, I recommend it if you can find something honest and positive to say. If you can, your genuine enthusiasm will make the flattery real and relevant, and help endear them to the idea of trading links.

7. **Make the first link.** Link to the site before you request a link, and give them the URL to the page where the link is.

8. **Describe your site and give the URL.** Give a brief and accurate description of your site along with the exact URL (web site address) you'd like them to link to. You might also include the web page address of any graphics you'd like them to use *if* they want to use a graphic. Not everyone does, so don't make the assumption that a webmaster will or should—even if you use a graphic for them. Also, don't attach graphics to the email; just offer a link to the graphics in case they do want to use an image.

9. **Give accurate contact information.** For the extra-professional touch, include your phone number and mailing address along with your email address. No one has ever stopped by my house or bothered to call as a result of my including this information, but it looks professional in your request.

The bottom line is that you're showing respect and professionalism if you approach link requests this way. No one wants to trade links with a site that will be here today and gone tomorrow. That's extra maintenance we don't need. If you show some class, you'll create the impression that you're a real player and not just shooting arrows into the sky to see where they stick.

If you follow these guidelines, a webmaster will know from your email request that:

- You actually visited the site.
- You took the trouble to find out his or her name.
- You wrote a sincere letter, not just a form letter you spammed the webmaster and dozens or even hundreds of other webmasters with.

227

- That you've already linked to the site.
- That you're professional and sincere, and will probably not be the type of person that causes link rot or removes the link as soon as the site links back to yours.

This will put a webmaster in about as receptive a mood as possible, all without wasting the person's time. A few links at popular sites can be a nice traffic boost—and a nice search engine boost—so they're worth the trouble.

12.10 The Lazy Way to Get Reciprocal Links

A nother great way to get reciprocal links is to invite your site visitors to exchange links with you. This would be a lot of work if it weren't automated. I offer a CGI script for free if you have your own domain and CGI bin access.

Each day I receive several emails that someone new has linked to my site. I just go to my control panel, send my little robot to double-check, and either approve or disapprove the link request. Here's how it works.

1. It uses a template to create a STATIC web page that search engines can index. Each time you update your links, it makes a new static page from the template and replaces the old static page with it. It's more search engine friendly than all other scripts of its kind. A static page is one that resides on the server, rather than a dynamic page that is only temporarily generated when a link is clicked.

2. People come to you to exchange links; you don't have to go out seeking them. This reduces the time needed to gain reciprocal links. Of course, you still want to go out and obtain links from popular sites, high-quality sites, and sites with relevant content. Reciprocal links can go on a separate link page so you can label them for what they are, reciprocal links. Reciprocal links is another name for Pot Luck. ☺

    The quality links are better links as far as the search engines are concerned, but it's hard to find fault with the sheer number of links you'll get using my script. In addition to increasing your site's link popularity, you will get traffic from the sites linking to yours.

3. You have total control. You approve or reject each request. You can also ban sites and create a profanity filter so no one can use

nasty language in their links. You work everything from a handy control panel.

4. It comes with a robot to check for reciprocal links, so you don't have to surf and hunt for them. The maintenance of keeping a reciprocal links page is reduced to just minutes a week.

5. It's free, but it does carry two small text ads—one for my site and one for my partner's—that take up very little room. We will be coming out with a pro version that does not carry ads and will have many more features. When we release the pro version, you can upgrade to it without losing your current links, although the pro version will not be free.

To read more details and generate a script for your domain, visit:

http://www.boogiejack.com/linkdetails.html

If you want to trade links with me, add my link to your site and submit your site here:

http://www.boogiejack.com/cgi-bin/mrlsf.cgi

That will put your site in queue. I add the links about every seven to 10 days. If you need information on how to link to my site or want to use a graphic for the link, you'll find that here:

http://www.boogiejack.com/link2me.html

When you submit your site, you need to submit the full address including the "http://" part. Just entering www.site.com will not work. Also, if you use frames, you have to submit the actual page the link is on and not the address to the frameset. Example:

http://www.your site.com

. . . won't work if that's the URL to your frameset.
Links are good for you!

12.11 Cool Secret!

Here's a neat little way to find good sites—sites you know get a decent amount of traffic—to trade links with. This is especially useful if your site is new, because without an established presence with decent traffic, you'll be somewhat limited in the sites you'll find willing to exchange links with yours. Using this method of locating sites, you'll know just how much traffic the sites get when you request link exchanges with them.

A free page tracking service called Extreme Tracking makes its page stats available to the public. The trouble is, they don't list them anywhere for you to conveniently click and view. Alta Vista to the rescue! If you go to Alta Vista and type in:

link:extreme-dm.com/AND your_keyword

. . . make sure to include the word AND, a space, and then your keyword. Then, simply click the search button. Alta Vista will return a list of sites that link to Extreme Tracking and also contain your keyword somewhere on the page (so odds are that many of them will have relevant content).

Alta Vista will find most of these sites through the code Extreme Tracking uses to track hits for the webmaster. Click on a site, find the Extreme Tracking icon and click it, and you'll go to its stats page, where you can see how much traffic it gets. The Extreme Tracking icon is a little black square with a blue globe with white glowing edges and a Saturn type ring circling the globe. The ring has a jagged place in the front of it as if it's electrified.

Sometimes, webmasters hide the icon by reducing it to 1×1 pixels in size, or by other means, so you may have to look at the source code to find it. If it's not in the source code, they may have removed it from the page and the search engine is returning results from a page it hasn't updated recently. Find the busy sites and request a link trade. Good little trick!

12.12 Keyword Density

K eywords are the words people enter into search engines to find sites that offer what they're looking for. The ratio of keywords in the text on the visible page to non-keywords is called keyword density.

Using the "horse" theme we started with in this chapter, if you have 100 words on your index page, and five of those words are "horse" or "horses," then you have a keyword density of 5 percent for the word "horse."

In the past, search engines liked to see keyword density in the 3 to 20 percent range. If a page included only one word, such as "horse," the keyword density would be 100 percent and search engines might consider that a spamming attempt with a doorway page. Doorway pages are pages made just for search engine placement. Often, they are "stripped down" versions of an index page, but not as visually appealing. Doorway pages can be good or bad, depending how you use them. If there is quality content and information, then it's OK to use them. If it looks like an attempt to influence search engine rankings, then doorway pages can cause trouble for you.

If you write the visible text with a 3 to 20 percent keyword density ratio, you'll usually be in a good range. You don't have to figure this out on your own though—online tools will analyze keyword density for you. The analyzers differ in how they work, so use the one you like best. You'll find several listed on my site's book resources page:

www.boogiejack.com/book/resources.html

If you prefer using software on your own computer rather than working online, you'll also find a link to a good free program on the resource page. If you do a search, you'll find many other keyword density analyzers.

So, now you know how to achieve keyword density, but there's a little more to it. I showed you how to determine the keyword density for one keyword. There's something else that I call Total Density, and I'm not talking about how you perceive my intelligence!

Continuing with our ongoing example of a horse site, we used other keywords in addition to horse. For example, we also used equine. If you figure out the keyword density for all of the most important keywords, and then add up the percentages, you'll come up with the total density for all keywords on the page. The total density should 7 percent or higher.

If you look at my index page, you'll see that my keyword density for any one keyword or keyword phrase falls below the 3 percent density I recommend. If you add up the total density, however, you'll see it's quite high, and that, plus the strong webmasters theme and other factors help make up the difference. As stated before, these search-engine optimization techniques are all guidelines and not hard and fast rules. Remember, there are no hard and fast rules because the rules change often! One exception—spam is spam and search engines will not change their anti-spam policies. Any attempt to artificially or illegally manipulate their databases is considered spam.

Other points about keywords to remember:

1. The higher up on the page the keywords are, the more importance the search engine will place on them. Search engines just

love the first paragraph of visible text, so don't waste it on fluff.

2. Headings, bold text, and increased font sizes are considered more important by search engines than normal body text. If you use keywords between heading tags, make some keywords bold, and/or increase the font size for keywords and keyword phrases, the search engine gives them added importance.

3. Most search engines use "word stemming," so photo, photos, photograph, and photographs are all considered to be the same keyword. The important point is to use their plural forms when you can. If you have horses on your page and someone searches for horse, you'll have a match with horse because of word stemming. If someone searches for horses, you'll have an exact match, which is a better match than having only part of the word. Obviously, it would be better to use both forms so you get an exact match either way, but you'll find situations when you need to be selective, so that's when you go with the plural if possible.

12.13 Keyword Coding Usage

S everal places in the actual code—the stuff your visitors don't see unless they view your source code—can help your site achieve higher rankings. These are:

- Title Tag
- Meta Tags
- Image Alt Tags
- Link Titles
- Comment Tags
- CSS Class Names
- Form Names and Values
- Domain Name

Ready to get into the details? Let's go!

Title

The page title is extremely important, but it isn't the first thing you put on your page—remember, we're talking code now. Your page title is in the HEAD section of the code:

```
<html>
<head>
<title>Your Page Title Goes Here</title>
```

You should include your top keyword or keyword phrase in the title. The text in the title will show up in the top of the browser (called the title bar) and as the link text at some search engines. Therefore, it should make sense and not just be a keyword cramming exercise (but if you can fit an extra keyword or two and have it make sense feel free to go for it). Don't put in too many words or even too many keywords, however, as they will only serve to water down the whole thing. The page title on my index page at the time of this writing is:

Boogie Jack's Free Graphics & HTML Tutorials

Free graphics and HTML tutorials are the two main things I want my site to be found for at this point in time, so that's the title I use. If you're in an extremely competitive field and aren't well known, you might need to leave out everything except the keywords. I used the "Boogie Jack" part in the title because the name is recognized and respected by many, and also because if you don't know me, it's an intriguing name that is more inviting to click on than just keywords.

The title tag should be the first thing in the HEAD section. You should use a unique title for each page of your site.

Meta Tags

The two main meta tags are the keywords meta tag and the description meta tag. These are also placed in the HEAD section of the code, just below the TITLE tag. Here is an example of the two meta tags for our horse site:

```
<meta name="description" content ="Horses, Of Course! is
packed with horse photographs, horse training and horse care
tips, riding tips, and also features saddles, bridles, and other
equine tack and western gear.">
```

```
<meta name="keywords" content ="horses, horse saddles,
horse care and training, western gear, equine photos, hoarse
pictures">
```

The first meta tag, the description tag, is the text that will show up in some search engines as the description of your web site. Take great care to craft a description that uses as many keywords and keyword phrases as possible, but still reads like a normal sentence. It is also the text that may sway a searcher to click your link, so you want it to sound inviting without sounding like hype. If it sounds like hype, that not only turns off the searcher, but it can result in your site being penalized at search engines, and not listed at all in some directories.

I didn't take a lot of time to craft the description above, but think of your description as a classified ad. It has to grab the readers' attention and convince them your site is the one they want to see. The key is to make it sound interesting and inviting, using your keywords, without sounding like an advertisement. Words written in all capital letters, excessive exclamation points, and exaggerated claims are ad-like qualities that will do more damage than good.

The second meta tag, the keywords meta tag, is completely hidden. You don't have to make it read like a sentence—if you do, it's a waste of words that will only dilute the power of your keywords. Simply write out the keywords and keyword phrases, separating them with commas, and you're done.

Some important things to know about the keywords meta tag:

1. Never repeat any keyword more than three times or it's considered spamming. Remember the word-stemming lesson? Photo is the same as photograph, so you can't list:

   photo developing, photo paper, photographic backgrounds, photography equipment

   . . . because you've used a form of photo four times and three times is the maximum repetition allowed. You can run them together though, because remember, this doesn't have to read like a sentence. You could get the same results with:

   photo developing paper backgrounds, photography equipment

   Now we've only used photo twice. A search engine will assemble a keyword phrase for you from left to right for any words in between the commas. So with the adjustment made:

   photo

   photo developing

   photo paper

   photo backgrounds

   photography equipment

   . . . would all be keyword search matches.

2. Too many keywords simply water each other down. It's the pollution of dilution! Stick with your best keywords and keyword phrases, and don't try to shove in every keyword under the sun.

3. Use your most important keyword and keyword phrases first. The farther from the beginning they are, the less weight they are given.

4. You may have noticed in the sample keywords meta tag that I used a misspelled keyword: hoarse pictures. Have you ever typed a keyword into a search engine and spelled it wrong, but didn't notice it until you'd clicked the search button? Isn't it funny how the engine brought up the kind of sites you were looking for anyway! That's because the webmaster either accidentally or intentionally also misspelled the word somewhere on his page or in his code.

   Not everyone can spell well, and some words are commonly misspelled. If there is a commonly misspelled keyword in your set of keywords, include it at the end of the keywords meta tag. When a searcher misspells it, you'll have an exact match and probably the #1 listing.

   Remember, the misspelled keywords go last in your meta tag. I wouldn't use more than one or two, three at the very most.

5. Never use keywords that are irrelevant to your content. Some webmasters try to trick people into visiting their sites by putting irrelevant, but often searched for, keywords such as sex or mp3 into their keyword meta tags. Not only will such tricks get your site banned, but the resulting traffic won't be happy that they were duped. Very often, these very same people report your site to the search engines for spamming.

Two more meta tags that you can place in the head section give you an opportunity to legally add keywords to your code. These go right under the description and the keywords meta tags. They are:

```
<meta name="owner" content="Horses, of Course! Inc.">
<meta name="author" content="Horses, of Course! Inc.">
```

If you use a keyword in your business name, then listing the owner tag may help a tiny bit. Likewise, you can use the business name in the author meta tag. Another option is to give yourself a keyworded nickname. If you use a nickname, be sure to use single quote marks inside the double quote marks to prevent the nickname from messing up the author tag. For example:

```
<meta name="author" content ="Joe 'Horse' Johnson">
```

Use unique keyword and description meta tags on each page of your site. Each page should be optimized for its content. The reason for this is that search engines often list interior site pages before the home page because the interior pages are more tightly focused. Optimizing each page for its unique content gives your site that many more chances to be found through search engines.

Image Alt Tag

Image alt tags, short for alternative text, were included in HTML as a way to describe images for blind people (screen readers read the alt tags aloud) and for folks who turn off images in their browsers or use text-only browsers.

The alt tags also represent a legal way to add keywords to your code. An image tag with alt text added looks like this:

```
<img src="logo.gif" alt="Horses, Of Course! logo, an image of a horse running through the meadow with her colt.">
```

In this alt tag, we legally added horses, horse, and colt to our legal keyword usage. That's three extra keywords; I could have gobbed it up more, but you get the point.

For best performance, use alt tags on ALL your images.

Link Titles

Most people don't know there is such a thing as a link title, but it represents another legal way to add quality keywords to the code. It also adds pop-up balloon descriptions of the page you're linking to for most visitors. Add a link title like this:

```
<a href="page.html" title="Visit this page for beautiful photos of mares and their colts, wild stallions running free, rodeo bronco riders, herding horses, race horses, and other horse photos.">
```

In the previous example, we added several more keywords in a legal way to this link. Repeating this tactic on all your links gives you tons of legal keyword additions. You don't have to make it read like a sentence. We could have simply wrote the title text like this:

"photos of mares, colts, stallions, bronco riders, herding horses, race horses, and more"

Whichever way you prefer is fine. One thing to caution you about: if you make the link title too long it will disappear before folks have time to finish reading it. The pop-up balloon only lasts a few seconds, so test it to see if you can read it before it disappears. To test this, hover your cursor over the link to read it.

Comment Tags

Comment tags let you add comments to code that don't show up on the page. Comments serve as a way to remind yourself of something or to mark sections of a page. A comment tag looks like this:

```
<!-- Put your comment here -->
```

There must be a space between the opening and closing dashes and the comment itself. In the eyes of search engines, comments tags can be both legal and illegal—it depends how you use them. On the illegal front, webmasters have tried using comments to "stuff" pages. For example, they might repeat their top keyword 50 to 100 times or more between comment tags. This old trick will get your site banned. You can, however, legally use a comment tag in the following ways:

```
<!-- Beginning of horse photo gallery -->
```

```
<!-- Start of horse related links section -->
```

```
<!-- Horse tack and gear below -->
```

```
<!-- Begin table of horse hands to feet conversion chart -->
```

Using comment tags as webmaster reminders in this way is perfectly fine. The handy markers make it easy to scroll through code and find sections you want to edit, plus you are simultaneously adding legal keywords.

CSS Class Names

In CSS, you can create individual styles for page elements. The name you give these styles is called into action using a class attribute. For example, say you create a style sheet for tables that specifies a blue background color, white text, and the Arial font with a font size of 12 pixels. Instead of coding all that into a table, you simply call that style into action with a class tag.

```
<table class="horses">
```

As you can see, we added a legal keyword to our table code by simply naming the table class with a keyword. This is one place where there is little you can legally do to add hidden keywords to the code, so it's a pretty slick trick, Rick.

Granted, I've never seen this trick in use before. In fact, I recently made it up. It would be legal, though, it can't hurt, and it may help. So it's a technique you may want to try when you design new pages or redesign old ones.

Form Names and Values

Here's another technique that is seldom used, yet gives you the opportunity to add more legal keywords. Many form elements have a name and value attribute, and you can use keywords there.

A form itself can have a name. Names are usually used in conjunction with some JavaScript so the JavaScript knows which form to effect. But JavaScript doesn't have to be involved—you can simply give any form a name.

```
<form name="horses">
```

Other form elements can have names and values as well. Another example:

```
<input type="radio" name="horse breed" value="palomino horse">
```

The name labels the output, and the value indicates which radio button was selected. In the previous example, the user might have been answering the question, "What is your favorite breed of horse?" Your email response form would come with the questions answered something like this:

```
horse breed = palomino horse
```

. . . if that was the option your visitor selected.

If the question is relevant to the answers as in the example above, it's fairly easy to understand the form that is mailed to you. If you ask questions that are irrelevant to the names and values you give the form fields, reading your form results would be difficult.

You can also implement a sort of private decipher code, such as making "horse" always mean yes and "pony" always mean no. This way you can add keywords to form fields where they would usually not be available, yet still produce clear results. If you do that, I advise you to make a master list of each word substitution so you'll know what the results mean.

Domain Name

A keyword in the domain name is not as important as it used to be, but if you can find a domain name available with a good keyword in it, it will still help some. If your site is about horses, and you find a domain name with the word horses in it (such as wildhorses.com which may be taken by now), then you can receive a small boost in search engine rankings. The problem is, it can be very difficult to find an available domain name with your chosen keyword.

12.14 Keyword Naming

T he names you give pages, graphics, sound files, link text, and directories are other good ways to add legal keywords to your pages.

If you have a page with horse grooming tips, don't name it like this:

tips.html

grooming.html

page4.html

As far as search engine ranking help, the first two examples could be anything from tips to growing watermelons in an igloo to grooming your hairy big toe. They are meaningless when it comes to search engine rankings. The third example is even worse. While the first two are at least about the extremely broad topics of tips and grooming, page4 seems to be about next to nothing. A better way to name your pages is:

horse_grooming_tips.html

Use the underscore to separate words. Using spaces in page names is actually illegal in HTML and will cause broken links in some browsers. As you can see, the point is to name your pages with relevant keywords instead of with short, convenient, yet meaningless names.

The same strategy applies to naming graphics:

horses_running.jpg
stallion.jpg

And your sound files:

horse_whinny.wav

The way you code the text in links is important as well:

<a href="horses.html">Show Horses</a>

"Show Horses" is better link text for search engine food than Picture Gallery, which could be pictures of your collection of belly button lint. It also gives visitors a more descriptive and enticing link, so it may increase traffic to that page. Of course, I should tell you that I think you're really weird for keeping a collection of belly button lint.

The directory names you use are also important places to use keyword names. If you keep your images in a folder called images, why not call it horse_images instead? Some search engines like that.

To conclude this part, let's write an image link using all the tricks:

<a href="horse_pictures.html" title="Beautiful photos of mares and their colts, wild stallions running free, rodeo bronco riders, herding horses, race horses, and other horse photos.">

<img src="horse_images/horse_photo_gallery.gif" alt=
"Gallery of wild horses, stallions prancing, mares and their colts, rodeo broncos"></a>

If you're not using an image for a link, replace the image with appropriate link text that includes keywords. In the previous example, we added many keywords and keyword phrases via the page name, link title, image directory, image name, and image alt text. To add even more keywords, you can add to each link a visible description of the page it links to.

Shazam—all those keywords for just one link! Now imagine how many more keywords you can legally add to your pages when you use these techniques on all your links, images, and the other places I've shown you. That's search engine optimization at full throttle.

12.15 Web Site Content

C reating quality web site content is work, but it pays huge dividends. Quality content is the single most important item you can work on. All the code optimizing, link requesting, and everything else do little good if your web site content is weak. With directories such as Yahoo!, the content often makes the difference in whether or not your site is listed.

I've seen far too many sites where the webmasters obviously spent a great deal of time and effort on site design and graphics, but did not work half as hard on the content. When people come to your site, they may notice the nice design and graphics at first, but they're not going to sit and stare at it. If your content doesn't hold them, they won't be on your site for long.

When it comes to search engines, quality content may partly be defined as expert use of keywords for the sake of ranking purposes. Make no mistake though—quality content is your key to success.

Quality content is helpful, informative, educational, entertaining, useful, or otherwise interesting and worth your visitor's time. Most people create a page and call it done. Sometimes that's all you need. But to consistently create top-quality content, you must learn to be your own constructive critic.

Write your content, step away for a few days, put your ego in your back pocket, and go back to find everything wrong with it that you can—then make it better. I usually rework my written content several times before I'm satisfied with it. When you stop finding ways to make improvements, it's ready.

The difference between average content and high-quality content is usually a matter of effort, not talent. To be better than average, thus enabling you to enjoy more success than the average webmaster, you can't settle for half an effort. That's what the average person does, and that's what makes them average. You do want better for yourself, don't you? Remember this:

Doing no more than average is what keeps the average down.

Remember, what you settle for is what you'll receive. If you settle for mediocrity you'll have average success, which is to say your web site will be more of a hobby than a successful business. Of course, if all you want from it is a hobby, then enjoy creating it as you like. You really don't need a lot of visitors or high search engine rankings for that. If you seek success, whatever success means to you, then quality is the key.

241

". . . do not try to shortchange the Muse. It cannot be done.
You can't fake quality any more than you can fake a good meal."
– William Seward Burroughs

12.16 Getting More Clicks from Search Engine Visitors

ome search engines adjust your site's ranking according to the number of times someone actually clicks your link when they display it. If searchers click through to your site, you gain a bonus point, so to speak. Conversely, if it's displayed many times and no one clicks through to your site, you can lose ground. This is because there is no reason to display your site high in the rankings if no one is going to click the link to it. It makes sense when you think about it from their point of view.

Some search engines use the text in your description meta tag for their description of your site. That's why it's so important that you do what most webmasters don't do—take the time to write a keyword-laden description that screams to the searcher, "Click me, click me now!"

Your site description shouldn't read like a bunch of hype though—search engines are not interested in having site descriptions that look like spam ads in the top of their search results. A good description will include keywords, be informative, entice without hype, and be written in properly constructed sentences. Don't use a lot of exclamation points or capital letters to make your point. If you resort to that, you haven't worked on your description enough. You're painting a picture with words for the eyes of the person conducting the search, so you need to paint a picture of something they want to see.

Think of a good description as an ad that doesn't look like an ad, because that's just what it should be. An effective description will:

- Arouse curiosity and attract attention.
- Spell out a strong benefit.
- Answer every surfer's question of "What's in it for me?"
- Target the right audience.

Several powerful words and phrases are used time and time again in advertisements. They keep popping up because they act like human magnets that instantly attract consumers who are interested in the topic to want more information. The four most important magnetic words and phrases are:

- Free
- How To
- You
- Easy

Using one or more of these magnetic words or phrases, along with the main benefit of visiting your site, can create a compelling reason to click your link. Some further points to consider that will make searchers more likely to click your link:

- Use words that create mental images—for example, "trophy bass" is more appealing to a fisher than plain old "bass."
- The description should appeal to a feeling or sensation— love, hate, fear, desire, curiosity, etc.
- Use present tense, not past or future tense. It adds impact and immediacy and makes your words more believable.
- Use verbs that are powerful and exciting. If you are selling stereos, "Surround your senses in amazing sound!" is more exciting than "High Quality Sound."
- Eliminate all unnecessary words. It's a description, not the whole web page. Capture the essence in one to three sentences.
- Don't try to be too clever. Make the benefit of visiting your page—not your imagination—the focus. Simplicity entices while complexity overwhelms.
- Remember, sell the sizzle—and your benefits are the sizzle. The benefits are the elements that provide the answers and solve the problems. Why? People predominately act on their emotions. Benefits help bring out emotions.

12.17 Twenty-two Causes of Trouble with Search Engines

Y our site can run afoul of search engine rules in many ways. In no particular order, here are the 22 most common things webmasters do that can cause problems:

1. Using illegal HTML attributes and values. For example, adding a title attribute and value to tags that don't allow for them, such as paragraph tags. Sample illegal tag:

`<p title="free graphics">`

243

2. Using double sets of meta tags to double your keywords or adding an extra title tag will win you a trip to cyber-purgatory.

3. Using ANY keyword more than three times in your keywords meta tag. This is known as keyword spamming. This warning includes word stemming, too. For example, if you had the following keywords in your keywords meta tag:

photography, photo paper, photo albums, telephoto lens

. . . you could be in trouble for spamming with the word photo, even though they are all about different subjects.

4. Using small text, such as a size 1 font. Search engines know text that small isn't intended for people to read, but instead is usually used to stuff many keywords into a small area.

5. Using text that is the same color as the web page's background color. Hidden text will get you in trouble. Most people know not to do this anymore. What many don't realize, though, is that if you use a table with a different color background than the page background, and use a text color inside the table that is the nearly the same or the same color as the web page background color, you can be busted for hidden text. Even though all the text is readable because you set a different table background color, many search engines don't consider the table background color—they just see that the text in the table is the same color as the web page background color—and boom, they penalize the site.

6. Using popular keywords such as "sex" or "mp3" in meta tags when the site has nothing to do with those subjects is called keyword stuffing and is illegal.

7. Using too many keywords, while not illegal, does still cause trouble because too many keywords dilutes them all. I wouldn't use more than 20 to 30 keywords and keyword phrases or none will be worth any more than a comb is worth to a fish. The fewer keywords you use, the stronger each will be. If you can stick to your top five to 10 keywords and keyword phrases, you'll be in better shape than if you use 10 to 20.

8. Another issue that isn't illegal but still causes trouble is pages that are too long. Not only does this overwhelm visitors, but the search engine spider can time out before it completes the page, thus not indexing it fully. It is also unlikely that you can maintain a good keyword density on extremely long pages. If

your page is more than four or five vertical screen lengths and mostly text, consider breaking up the content into two or more pages.

9. Gateway pages, doorway pages, bridge pages, ghost pages, whatever you want to call them, are largely frowned upon by search engines and they are cracking down on them. If you use a gateway page, don't just put up a redirect page or one keyword page. Gateway pages must now have relevant content on them, and enough relevant content to make the page useful for more than the purpose of search engine placement.

   Also, keep the number of gateway pages you use to a minimum. If you have a 10-page site and 25 doorways, it's pretty obvious that it is a spam attempt.

   Gateway pages that instantly redirect to another page is automatically considered spam. While there are legitimate uses for redirect pages, such as using one to redirect visitors to your home page or another page when you remove a page from your site, you should provide an explanation on the page and a link for browsers that don't support automatic redirects (delay the redirect at least 10 seconds).

10. Link farms are really bad news. Link farms are where you sign up to place a link page on your site. This link page has all the links of everyone else who signs up for it, and everyone else who signed up for it displays the exact same link page. Your link pages must be unique to your site, not a page generated from a central source that is exactly the same as hundreds of other link pages. If caught participating in link farms, your site will be banned.

11. Cloaking will get you banned immediately. Most of you probably don't have to worry about this on your own, but you could be spammed by email from someone wanting to sell you the service so I'm mentioning it.

   Cloaking is when a software program on your server detects the IP address of a link request, and if it's a known search engine spider address, it serves the search engine a search-engine optimized page. But if it's not a known search engine spider IP address, then it serves the visitor a more attractive but less-optimized page. This is something that webmasters can get away with for a while, but if caught the domain will be banned and your other domains may be as well.

12. Similar to inventing attributes for legal HTML tags, some people have invented their own HTML tags and attributes to stuff more keywords into their code. For example:

`<hotel title="Montana hotel accommodations" zone="Helena">`

There is no such tag as "hotel" and no such attribute as "zone." Using these tactics will get you in trouble with the search engines.

13. Hidden links are another old trick that can cause you misery. Hidden links are links in which you code an image link, with the image being a small transparent GIF that visitors can't see. You can also create a hidden link by not putting any link text between the opening and closing link tag for text links. The exception to this is when you use anchor tags to link to parts of the same page.

14. Submitting multiple versions of the same page or nearly the same page (changing only the page name or making only minor wording changes on it), is just another spam sandwich to the search engines. Search engines don't say, "mmm . . . tasty!" to spam sandwiches, they say bye-bye to your ranking, or even your listing.

15. Check with each search engine to see how many pages you're allowed to submit each day and follow the rules. Your IP address is recorded when you submit, and you will be caught if you cheat. Never submit the same page more than once a day, and it's much better to wait a few weeks before resubmitting. Search engines have a long list of sites submitted in front of yours, so resubmitting too soon is often viewed as a spam attempt. This problem isn't nearly as significant as it used to be since many search engines now charge for submission, but respect the free search engines or we'll all pay the price.

16. Submitting pages that contain keyword-filled "sentences" that do not read like proper sentences is bad too. Some search engine's algorithms are sophisticated enough to determine if you are using complete sentences. So, placing sentences such as:

Horses ponies mares stallions saddles.

. . . could get you in trouble, even if it's on your visible page because it's an obvious attempt to manipulate search results.

17. Going overboard with too many keywords on a page is also an obvious spam attempt. For example, if your page contains 300 words and the keyword phrase "web design" is repeated 50 times, it's obvious you are trying to spam search engines. And, many webmasters don't realize that the detection methods are automated—the spiders can calculate the ratios faster than you can.

18. Creating a title such as "Sport's Sporty Sports" (unless that's your registered business name) or "freeware, freeware, freeware, freeware" is spam. Plus, it's so visually unappealing that very few people will click on your link even if you do get away with it for a while.

19. Page swapping is when you submit a highly optimized page for search engines. Then, after the page is indexed, you upload a replacement page with the same name—except now the page is designed for human appeal.

    No-no, Nanette.

20. Repeating dozens of transparent GIFs to stuff with extra alt tags is another no-no.

21. Using a host that also hosts adult sites and/or documented spammers can result in your site being banned. Adult sites are notorious for abusing search-engine policies. Some search engines retaliate against adult site-hosting companies by blocking those sites' underlying IP addresses. If your site is with the same host, your site may share that banned IP address.

    Adult sites are also bandwidth hogs, so your site can easily become very slow or unreachable at times. Before selecting a hosting company, always check to see if they host adult sites. If your current host does, I highly recommend changing hosts.

22. Using automated submission software, which submits your site to search engines without you visiting them, is not a good idea. While automatic submission is very handy, the practice is banned at all the big search engines.

    You must submit to the important search engines and directories by hand, one at a time. It's a tedious process—but it is necessary. I do use submission software to submit to the thousands of small search engines and directories. They're not important individually, but the power is in the numbers. Occasional hits from thousands of sites do add up to significant traffic. Most small search engines aren't sophisticated enough to detect automated submissions, and many don't expressly prohibit the practice.

12.18 Closing Tips

 few final thoughts on search-engine optimization:

- The first thing most people want to do when they finish a web site (or even before it's finished) is to submit it to search engines so the site can begin receiving traffic. This can be a big mistake! Some search engines won't list your site if no other sites are already linking to it—so going through the submission process is a waste of time at this point.

  What you should do before submitting your site to search engines is seek reciprocal links. Reciprocal linking is when you agree to link to a site in exchange for that site linking to yours.

- If you're thinking of using illegal (spamming) tricks to obtain high search engine rankings, consider this: At least one search engine company, and probably more, have employees that do nothing but see which sites come up in their top listings for various keywords and keyword phrases. The employees then surf to those sites to see if they are using illegal methods to obtain the high ranking. They explore your source code, check your content, and check to see if the pages you submitted are the pages you show visitors.

- When you request a reciprocal link and the other site doesn't link back to yours, the temptation is to remove their link. That may not be in your best interest! If you're linking to relevant content sites, the link will still help your web site's search engine placement because it reinforces your site theme, even if the sites don't link back.

  Think of your outgoing links as valuable content you're providing for your visitors. People visit search engines to find sites. If you have an excellent links directory of your own, people will find value in that. I've got sites bookmarked simply for their links directory and I know I'm not the only one who does that.

  People may come back to your site, or bookmark your site, just because of your links. When they return again and again, they begin to trust you and will more readily buy your products, subscribe to your ezine, or do whatever it is you are trying to accomplish. View your outgoing links as another area of quality content you provide to visitors. Once you put a link on a links directory, keep it there unless you have a good reason for going to the trouble of removing it. It blesses you twice by reinforcing the theme and providing quality link content. If a site links back, you're thrice blessed, and "two out of three ain't bad," as the saying goes.

- Make sure ALL your links work. Broken links probably won't cause listing or ranking problems in search engines, other than their inability to index the pages the broken links lead to, but they CAN prevent you from being listed in most directories. Surfers don't like broken links, and surfers are human. The humans that determine your fate in directories don't like broken links either!

- When your link text, link title, and link page all contain keywords, and the search engine finds those same keywords used again in the page title, meta tags, and visible text near the top of the page being linked to, you'll get a boost in relevancy.

- One search engine recently cracked down on cheaters and deleted more than 25 MILLION pages from its database. And remember, the higher you rank, the more likely that your competitors are reviewing your site to see how you got the good ranking. They want to know so they can adopt your legal techniques and possibly report you for spamming techniques so their site can move one step closer to the top.

- Some folks think they can get away with cheating because they use illegal tactics and enjoy good search engine rankings. What they don't realize is that their site may be ranked higher if the illegal actions were cleaned up. It's possible they are already being penalized, and when they've finally pushed it over the limits, their domain will be banned.

   Sometimes, a web site will slip through the cracks. But these are exceptions to the rule. Don't be misguided by a lucky webmaster who is temporarily getting away with cheating—they too will be caught eventually. By practicing ethical search-engine optimization strategies, you can achieve a good ranking without resorting to cheating, and you'll sleep better at night not worrying about having your site banned.

> **NOTE**
>
> Speaking of broken links, here's a bonus tip. When you click a link, your browser sends a data packet to the server that hosts the linked file. Sometimes these data packets get lost or caught in a traffic bottleneck and your link request times out before the file is retrieved. I've discovered that, as often as not, reloading the page loads the file. So, not all that appears to be a broken link is a broken link. Always check two or three times. Unfortunately, there's no way to prevent these problems.

249

- You may see search engine advice on the web that contradicts what you see here (for example, someone suggesting the use of hidden text). Remember, a lot of old advice is still floating around out there and a lot "experts" are not experts at all.

  Most webmasters either don't know much about search-engine optimization, or are too hurried or too lazy to implement all the possible techniques across the important pages of their sites.

  You can have the edge if you are willing to do the work. With all other things being equal, optimization will put your site over the top.

12.19 Chapter Quiz

1. In your own words, explain what a search engine algorithm is.

2. True or False: Your web site's status at one search engine is not affected by other search engines.

3. Choose the most accurate statement about link popularity:
   a. The number of times searchers click your link at a search engine determines link popularity
   b. The number of links pointing to your web site determines the link popularity
   c. The number of relevant keywords on your site is your site's link popularity
   d. The more popular your link is, the more parties you get invited to

4. Your site theme refers to:
   a. The complementary color scheme of your web site
   b. The song you use as your theme song
   c. The central or unifying theme of your content
   d. The thematic derivative value of your ranking vs. your keyword execution in relation to the substrata persistence factor

12.19 Chapter Quiz (continued)

5. As far as search engines are concerned, what page of your site is the most important?

6. In my list of important search engine rules, which of the following does not belong:
   a. Keyword density
   b. Content
   c. Click-through rate
   d. High-quality graphics

7. Which of the following statements is most true:
   a. Adding emphasis to text, such as using headings or bold text, has no value with search engines because with CSS you can remove the emphasis generally applied by HTML.
   b. Adding emphasis to text, such as using headings or bold text to keywords, can result in a little boost for the emphasized words.
   c. Adding emphasis to text can cause a search engine to lower your site ranking because it could be a spamming attempt.
   d. Adding emphasis to text is the leading cause of UFO reports.

8. Which of the following statements about making a link request is true:
   a. Many people are bogged down with email. Use a clever subject line to get their attention and make your request stand out from their other emails.
   b. Forget hunting for link request instructions—it will just slow you down and keep you from getting as many links as you would otherwise.
   c. Never link to the site you're requesting a link from first. They might not link back, and since it was your idea, they should have to link first to show their willingness to reciprocate.
   d. Include the name and URL of the site you're requesting to exchange links within the body of the email letter.

9. In reference to keyword coding usage, which of the following is NOT a legal place to use keywords:
   a. Link titles
   b. Image titles
   c. Comment tags
   d. CSS class names

12.19 Chapter Quiz (continued)

10. When naming a file using more than one keyword, which is the best way to do it:
    a. RedPlanet.jpg
    b. Red-planet.jpg
    c. Red_Planet.jpg
    d. Red Planet.jpg

11. An effective description meta tag will help your site gain click-throughs from search engines. I listed four things that help make a good description. Name two of them.

12. Once, I was called to testify about an accident I witnessed. During a break in the case, the judge started reciting poetry. When a reporter asked him why he was doing that, what was his answer?

12.20 Chapter Exercises

Exercise Option I – Practice Site

pen the index page of your practice site and optimize it for search engines using the techniques discussed in this chapter. For extra credit, optimize your entire practice site.

Exercise Option 2 – Independent Exercise

Create a new page, fully coded and optimized on any of the following topics:

- Famous quotations
- Recipes and kitchen tips
- Gardening tips
- A fan page for any person, team, band, or sport
- A topic assigned by the instructor

This gives the instructor an opportunity to compare student's efforts.

Creating Image Maps

13

13.1 Chapter Introduction

I n Chapter 6: Creating Links, you learned to create a link from an image. With an image map, you can code two or more links into one image by using pixel coordinates. In other words, different parts of the image can be linked to different pages or files.

You can use image maps in many ways. For example, you might have a map of your county with each town linked to a page or sub-site about that town. On the personal side, it might be a group picture of your family with a link from each family member going to a page about or by that family member.

There are two types of image maps: client-side and server-side. Server-side image maps are very outdated, so we won't be covering them here. You will learn to make client-side image maps and happy days are here again, they're not very difficult. The hardest part is figuring out the pixel coordinates of each area within the image that you want to make into a link. You can use a graphics program to find the pixel coordinates, but if you don't have one, I can show you a nifty trick for finding them using only a browser.

13.2 What Are Image Coordinates?

I mage coordinates are reference points on an image that specify the boundaries for the hot spots that you want to link to other pages or files. When you use a graphic button for a link, the entire graphic works like an image map with the entire button included in the coordinates. With an image map, your code has to tell the browser which parts of the image link to which files. These reference points are called coordinates, and they represent a mapped location within the image.

You can map out three types of shapes with coordinates: rectangular, circular, and polygonal. In this chapter, you'll learn how to determine the coordinates for each type and how to code an image map. We'll take a look at the coordinates for a rectangular shape first.

Each coordinate has two measurements. The first measurement is the distance in pixels measured from the left edge of the image toward the opposite edge. The second measurement is the distance in pixels measured from the top edge of the graphic toward the bottom edge, thus forming a single coordinate. Look at the graphic below for a visual reference.

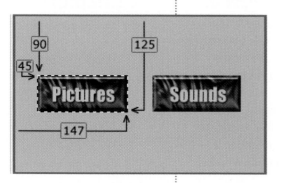

Rather than seeing this graphic as two buttons, imagine it as one image. The red line represents the outer edges of the image.

The dashed lines represent the area of the graphic we want to link to a pictures page. If you look at the upper left corner of the box with dashed lines, you can see that the coordinates for this corner are 45 and 90, in that order. That is the first coordinate, which represents the starting point for the hot spot. The hot spot is the part of the image that will be a live link.

As you can see, the lower right coordinates are 147 and 125. This example creates a rectangular region that is the hot spot. For a rectangular shaped area, you only need the upper left coordinates and lower right coordinates.

13.3 Finding the Coordinates

To determine the coordinates for an image's hot spots, you can use a graphics program or a browser. With a graphics program such as Corel Photopaint or Paint Shop Pro, you can open an image and move the cursor around to display the cursor's coordinates in the lower left corner of the program's window. In Adobe Photoshop, the coordinates display in the Info pane, which you can open by choosing Window > Show Info.

Using the program's masking tool or marquee tool, you draw the hot area and get the coordinates as you go. That way, you can be sure the area you've mapped is exactly what you want. A masking tool (sometimes called a marquee tool) creates the dashed lines shown in the graphic in Section 13.2 above. In a graphics program, the dashed lines move like marquee lights (sometimes called "marching ants").

Since not everyone reading this book will have a graphics program, I'll go straight to using a browser to gain the coordinates for an image. The principle is the same, so the steps carry over to those with a graphics program. With a graphics program, however, you don't have to place the image on a web page and you can easily see the area you've mapped out. With a browser, you're guessing a little bit about the exact placement of the hot spot.

To learn the coordinates of an image area with a browser, first place the image on a web page and make it a link. The link doesn't have to lead anywhere, but it's necessary to have the coordinates show up. The image also needs a special code as shown:

```
<a href="whatever">
<img src="imagemap.jpg" ismap>
</a>
```

As you can see, the link doesn't even have to be properly coded —there just needs to be something there. Inside the image tag, you need to add "ismap," as shown in blue text. This allows the browser to display the cursor coordinates in the status bar of the browser, as shown in the next graphic. If your image doesn't have obvious edges, you may want to include a border as you plot your image coordinates. It isn't necessary, but it can be a useful visual reference.

This graphic shows how to find the coordinates for the upper-left corner of the hot area. The cursor point is 99 pixels from the left side of the image, and 9 pixels from the top of the image. That is the starting point of our hot area. Next, for a rec-tangular hot area, we need to find the coordinates for the opposite corner. This

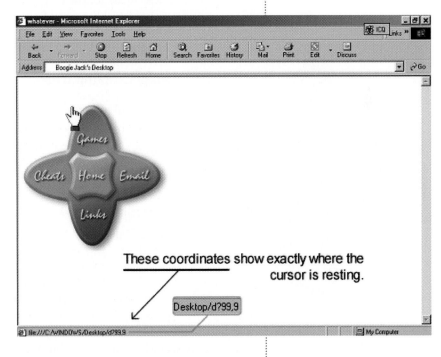

is just a matter of moving the cursor to the opposite corner of the hot area. To create a hot area of the entire Games tab of our graphic, the coordinates for the opposite corner are 180,85. Once we know the coordinates of the hot areas for our Games link, we can code that portion of the image map.

13.4 Coding the Image Map

T he code to start an image map begins with a simple map declaration. The map should also have a name:

```
<map name="gadget">
```

The map name can be anything. The name is also used in the actual image source tag to tell the browser which map instructions to use for that image.

After the map declaration, you can start adding the area tags. The area tag consists of the shape, the pixel coordinates, and the link. Area tags tell the browser which areas of the map are the hot spots.

In most cases, you'll use only one shape per image map. However, we'll use all three in this example so you can see how each type is coded. Look at the following graphic. I've marked off the hot spot areas with dashed lines and listed the coordinates for each area.

Map Coordinates

Rectangular Areas

Games, top left: **99,9** / bottom right: **180,85**

Cheats, top left: **9,92** / bottom right: **89,174**

Links, top left: **87,184** / bottom right: **178,262**

Circular Area

Home: **133, 133, 30**

Polygonal Area

Email: **187,96 / 175,135 / 189,171 / 259,148 / 258,120**

For the polygon, I started at the top left coordinate and worked counterclockwise to establish all five coordinate points. It doesn't matter which direction you go. Most people would go clockwise, but I'm a rebel without caws, he crowed.

Ready to get down to business? Good! We'll open the map declaration, and then add the first three rectangular hot spots.

CODE EXAMPLE

```
<map name="gadget">
<area shape="rect" coords="99,9,   180,85" href="games.html">
<area shape="rect" coords="9,92,   89,174" href="cheats.html">
<area shape="rect" coords="87,184,   128,262" href="links.html">
```

The area tag tells the browser this is a hot spot. The shape attribute and value tell the browser what kind of shape the hot spot is (in this case "rect," which is short for rectangular). The coords tell the browser the coordinates of the hot spot. And the href tells the browser what file the hot spot links to. Wowsers, this is really easy!

You don't have to separate the pairs of coordinates with extra spaces—I just did that to make it easy for you to understand how the pairs of coordinates work together. The browser parses the coordinates by pairing two consecutive numerical units at a time to pinpoint each hot spot reference point. You do, however, need to separate each of the coordinates with a comma.

Next, we add the circular coordinate in the center of the image, like this:

```
<area shape="circle" coords="133,133,30" href="index.html">
```

Again, the area tag tells the browser this is a hot spot, but this time the shape attribute tells the browser the hot spot is a circle. The first two coordinates represent the center of the circle. The third coordinate is the radius of the circle. In this case, the center of the circle is 133 pixels from the left, 133 pixels from the top, and it extends 30 pixels in any direction. These are all the coordinates you need for circles. Circles are even easier than rectangles.

The final area to code is the polygonal shape for the email link.

```
<area shape="poly" coords="187,96,175,135,189,171,259,
148,258,120" href="mailto:you@yourisp.com">
```

A polygon is a closed shape bounded by three or more line segments. A polygon can take on a variety of odd shapes to accommodate your image needs, and it can have many, many sides. Each side of a polygon is a straight line, and no line should cross another line or everyone named Polly will be gone just when you need them most. That's the rule . . . really.

The last thing to do is close the map tag. The tag now looks like this:

CODE EXAMPLE

```
<map name="gadget">
<area shape="rect" coords="99,9,180,85" href="games.html">
<area shape="rect" coords="9,92,89,174" href="cheats.html">
<area shape="rect" coords="87,184,128,262" href="links.html">
<area shape="circle" coords="133,133,30" href="index.html">
<area shape="poly" coords="187,96,175,135,189,171,259,148,258,120" href="mailto:you@
yourisp.com">
</map>
```

Now you have the complete code for this image map. The last thing to do is add the image map to a page.

13.5 Adding the Image Attributes

N ow that you have the image map plotted, you need to add the image to a page. To do this, you use a regular image source tag, with two new references added to it.

```
<img src="images/mymap.jpg" border="0" usemap="#gadget"
ismap>
```

If you recall, when we first opened the image map tag, we named the map "gadget." With the usemap attribute, you identify the map by the name we gave it earlier. This ties the image map graphic to the image map code so they function together.

The **ismap** attribute isn't technically necessary for the map to work, but it can be a good idea to use it. With the ismap attribute in the image source tag, you can add a link to the image tag for older browsers that can't read client-side image maps. For browsers that can read image maps, the image map will function as it should; but for browsers that can't read image maps, the entire image works as a link. Since you won't know which section someone with an older browser would want to go to, the ismap link should take them to an alternate style menu from which they can choose a section of your site to visit.

The only drawback to using the ismap attribute to link the entire image for older browsers is that some people look at the status bar in the bottom of their browsers to see the name of the page a link goes to. In this case, the page will not show the individual links for each section of the map, but will instead show the link you coded for older browsers. The image map still works, and it takes people to the right pages, but they won't be able to tell ahead of time that the image links to different pages.

Instead of using the ismap attribute, you could simply offer text link alternatives for older browsers. Text links also help newbies navigate web sites since they may not understand how image maps work. Some search engines have trouble with image maps too, so including text links assures that search engines will be able to crawl your web site to catalog it.

> **NOTE**
>
> Newbies is a term that refers to anyone who is new to using the Internet and doesn't yet understand many aspects of it.

13.6 Where to Place the Code

Obviously, you place the image source <img src...> tag where you want the image to appear on a web page, but you may be wondering where to place the actual image map code you just learned to write. Should it be above the image tag or below it?

It really doesn't matter. There are two schools of thought on this. One option is to place the map code immediately above or below the image source link, where both are handy for editing because they are together. That makes sense, but so does the other option, which I prefer.

My preference is to put map codes at the very end of the page. I think it's crucial to have your key content as close to the top as possible, where search engines place more importance, than to have a lot of jive code that won't help you rank higher in search results. The map will still work fine, with no noticeable difference in performance. Plus, you know the map code is at the end so it isn't hard to find if you do need to edit it. In my way of thinking, the benefit of a higher search engine position far outweighs the inconvenience of not having the image source link and map placed next to each other in the code.

13.7 An Image Map Alternative

As an alternative to image maps, you can take the graphic you would use for the image map, dice it into individual graphics, and save all the pieces as separate files. You can then put the pieces back together on your web page so the individual images look like one piece.

Obviously, this takes some graphics experience. This isn't a graphics book, so I'll point you to an easy way to dice the graphics. Software programs are available to do this for you, and they give you the code you need to make it work. One such program, which just happens to be freeware, is Shoestring PictureDicer for Windows. You can find a link to it on my book resources page at:

www.boogiejack.com/book/resources.html

Diced images can give your web page the illusion of loading faster because the smaller sections pop in faster. In reality, the total image size may be larger and it may actually take a little longer to load. Another advantage of diced images is that, with several smaller image files, you can use more image alt text tags, which may help with search engine placement.

A disadvantage of diced images is that it usually takes more code, and it is usually necessary to place the diced images inside a table, which adds still more code and can slow the page down a bit.

Should you decide to use the dicing method, be sure not to put any line breaks or spaces between the image tags. If you do, the edges of the images will be separated and will not look like one image. Also, if you use a table to put the graphic back together, you need to set the table border, cellspacing, and cellpadding all to zero or the individual pieces of your image will be separated by spaces.

Some webmasters do recommend using diced images whenever possible to avoid incompatibility problems with older browsers. If you include text links on your pages as an alternative (which I always recommend doing) you don't have to worry about that. Besides, there just aren't enough browsers in use anymore that can't read a client-side image map to worry about it. If we always design for the lowest common denominator, the Internet would still be text only, and that's graphically unappealing.

In the final analysis, it's your choice whether to create real image maps or fake them with diced images. You may find occasions for both, as both have their advantages.

13.8 Chapter Quiz

1. In an image map, coordinates are:
   a. The overall dimensions of the image
   b. The ability of an image to serve as a software program that redirects users to specific files on the web
   c. Specific points on an image that set the boundaries for a hot spot that can be linked to other pages or files
   d. Images that are optimized to fit in with the color scheme of the page they reside on

2. Each image coordinate has two measurements. In order, they are:
   a. The distance in from the left edge and the distance down from the top edge
   b. The distance down from the top edge and the distance in from the left edge
   c. The distance in from the right edge and the distance up from the bottom edge
   d. The distance from my desk to the refrigerator

3. For a rectangular map area, you program the coordinates for:
   a. All four corners
   b. The upper left and bottom right corners
   c. The distance from the center to each corner, then add the center point
   d. The upper left and upper right corners, then add the height of the rectangle

4. What are the three shapes you can map?

13.8 Chapter Quiz (continued)

5. To use a browser to find the map coordinates you need, first place the image in an HTML document and create a link around it. You must then add _____ to the image tag.

6. A map tag should have a name attribute and value because:
   a. Without it, the browser could mistake the code for an old style server-side image map
   b. A map tag should not have a name attribute and value
   c. It is used in the image tag to tell the browser which map code to use for that image
   d. Maps tags get depressed when they don't have a name

7. What type of map shape uses a center point and radius for coordinates?

8. We have plotted an image map and named it "Flooberham." Finish this image source code to use the map.

   ```
   <img src="images/map.jpg" border="0" width="480" height="40"
   ```

9. An alternative to using image maps is to use diced images. If you use diced images, make sure you don't have any line breaks or spaces between the image tags because:
   a. It will cause each link to go to the first link coded
   b. It will cause a new browser window to open for each link
   c. It will break the chain and no links will work
   d. It will create a gap between the image parts

13.8 Chapter Quiz (continued)

10. You can place the image map code near the image map to keep them together for easy editing. I prefer another location. Where and why?

11. Server-side image maps are very outdated. Name the more popular, widely used kind of image maps.

12. Old ghosts never die, they just fade away. Old dogs never die, they just "flea" the scene. Old astronauts never die, they just _____. (Finish the sentence.)

13.9 Chapter Exercises

Exercise Option 1 – Practice Site

C reate a new page for your practice site. It will contain an image map. Make the image map link to all the pages of your practice site. You can use any image you want to. Since many students may not be skilled in creating graphics, the image map doesn't have to be relevant to the pages you're linking to—or even to your site itself. Just start with an image you like and create a two-column table listing what part of the image is the hot spot in the left column, and which page that part of the map links to. Be sure to use table headers (<td>) at the top of the table to label your columns.

Exercise Option 2 – Independent Exercise

I n this exercise, you get to make another throwaway web page. Your assignment is to create a page with an image map—gee, I'll bet you didn't see that coming, did you?

Again, using any image you like, plot the coordinates for all three types of map area shapes, then link them to different files. Your pages should be relevant to the image. For example, if you grab an image of your favorite band off the web, you might make each band member's head link to a page about him or her. Oh my yes, you do have to make a small page about each of the members too. Can't let you off too easy.

A word of advice, don't throw away the web page until you've been graded on it. The dog ate my homework doesn't work very well for computer assignments.

Code Bits and Pieces

14.1 Chapter Introduction

This chapter offers many bits and pieces of HTML and JavaScript code that are handy to have on hand. Some fall under the heading of tricks, but most are just clever or convenient ways to accomplish certain effects.

14.2 Drop Caps

To add a little visual spice to web pages, you can place drop caps at the beginning of paragraphs. A drop cap, short for dropped (in) capital letter, can give pages a fancier appearance. In HTML, drop caps are actually images added to the text—in which case you need to remember to remove the first letter of the paragraph so the letter isn't repeated. (Then, if you spell check the document, be sure to ignore any errors resulting from the missing letter.)

The idea comes from traditional publishing, where it's been done for years to lead readers' eyes into the text. Normally, drop caps are used on the first paragraph of a page or section. If you use them on every paragraph, especially several very short ones in a row, the page can look cluttered.

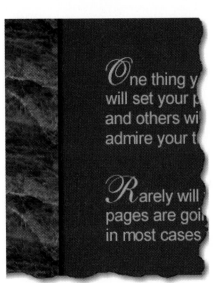

In the graphic at left, take a look at drop caps in action. You don't see many web pages fancied up in that way, but it's very easy to do.

Besides adding a drop cap, I did two other things to create a neater page.

First, I put the text inside a table to control the width and allow ample "white" space.

Secondly, to ensure the page looks right in the major browsers, I added an align attribute to the cap image.

The drop cap code looks like this:

```
<img src="dropcap.gif" align="bottom">text starts here . . .
```

I intentionally left off the image height and width attributes in this example to make the code less cluttered. You should include them when you use a drop cap.

You'll find a complete set of drop cap images on my web site at:

http://www.boogiejack.com/dropcap.html

Check my huge, free graphics section as well. By the time this book is published, more sets of drop caps may be available.

Now, with CSS, you can also program drop caps into your code without using images, although they won't be as fancy. To add drop caps to the beginning of each paragraph using CSS, add this to the HEAD section of your page.

CODE EXAMPLE

```
<style type="text/css">
p:first-letter {color: #ff0000;
        font-size: 24px;
        font-family: cursive;
        font-weight: bold;}
</style>
```

In the previous example, the first letter of the first line of each new paragraph will be red, 24 pixels tall, cursive, and bold. Where I specified cursive, you can also specify: serif, sans-serif, mono-space, fantasy, or specific fonts by name (Garamond, Verdana, Arial, etc.). See sections 4.2–4.4 of Chapter 4: Formatting Text for more information.

14.3 Pop-up Window

 ometimes, it's helpful to present bits of information in a small pop-up window. This gives guests quick access to the information, without leaving the page then being forced to use the back button.

To accomplish this, you use a two-part code. The first part determines the size and functions of the pop-up window, and links it to the information you want to present in it. The second part calls the pop-up script, and contains the actual content.

CODE EXAMPLE - PART ONE

```
<script language="JavaScript">
<!--
function popjack()
{
window.open('xyz.html','popjack','toolbar=no,location=no, directories=no,status=
no,menubar=no,resizable=yes,copyhistory=no,scrollbars=yes,width=400,height=300');
}
//-->
</script>
```

In the previous code example, the two lines in blue type should all be on one long line; if it's not, the script won't work. It's OK if the line wraps in your text editor, but do not type hard returns.

Where it says "xyz.html" is where you place the link to the information you want to present in the pop-up window, which is a separate HTML page.

You can change some of the options for the pop-up window. Any "no" options can be changed to "yes" and vice versa. You can change the size of the window to suit your needs. The second part of the code is below. It shows you how to code a link so that it opens in the pop-up window.

CODE EXAMPLE - PART TWO

```
<a href="JavaScript: popjack()" onMouseOver="window.status='Status Bar Message';
  return true" onMouseOut="window.status="; return true">Link Text Here</a>.
```

You can change the text in the "Status Bar Message" part, which displays in the browser's status bar when a user rests the cursor on the link text, to suit your needs. If you do change the message, and you need to include apostrophes, single quotation marks, or double quotation marks in the text, you need to preface them with a backslash. For example, if you want the status bar message to read, "You won't believe this!" code it like this:

'You won\'t believe this!'

The single and double quotation marks have another meaning in JavaScript. The backslash tells the browser to print the next character rather than interpret it. The message itself must be enclosed in single quotation marks in the code.

Although the information in the pop-up window is another HTML page, you won't want to present a full page of information this way. The pop-up window is ideal for presenting a small bit of text data or a single picture. If you need to present a full page, use the target="_blank" attribute and value in the link.

If you have trouble getting this code to work, visit the tutorial on my web site, which allows you to simply copy and paste code. You'll find it at:

http://www.boogiejack.com/howx005.html

I like to include close buttons on these pop-up windows as well. If you'd like to add one to your pop-up windows, just add the following code to the pop-up HTML page:

```
<form>
<input type="button" value='Close Window'onClick=
'self.close()'>
</form>
```

14.4 Break Out of Frames

|S| ometimes, other web sites link to a page on your site and display it within their frames. Most people find this practice to be rude and undesirable. This presents legal questions as well, as sites have tried to present the linked information as their own content.

To prevent this, you can add code to help visitors break out of frames. The first two methods are automatic; the last and most reliable method is to offer a link for users to click. The reason the first two methods are less reliable is because they depend on JavaScript, so visitors with JavaScript turned off, or who are using browsers incapable of parsing JavaScript, will not be able to break out of frames. Not many visitors use browsers that can't parse JavaScript anymore, so while I say the methods are less reliable, the numbers affected are minimal.

Method 1 (Less Reliable)

CODE EXAMPLE

```
<script language="JavaScript">
<!--
if (top.location != location) top.location.href = location.href;
-->
</script>
```

Method 2 (Better)

CODE EXAMPLE

```
<script language="JavaScript">
<!--
setTimeout ("changePage()", 3000);
function changePage() {if (self.parent.frames.length != 0)
self.parent.location="http://www.yoururl.whatever";}
-->
</script>
```

Method 3 (Most Reliable)

CODE EXAMPLE

```
Trapped in a Frame?
<a href="http://www.your_url.com" target="_top">Click Here to Escape</a>
```

14.5 Email Tricks

ave you ever seen those email links that pop up with the subject already filled in? Here's how it's done:

```
<a href="mailto:dork@dorkville.com?subject=I'm a Geek">
Email Me</a>
```

It's the basic mail link, but with a question mark and subject= whatever added to the end of your address.

Well now, that's pretty easy isn't it? If you emailed someone from a link on the example page shown, the message would pop up with "I'm a Geek" as the subject, and they'd have to take your word for it.

You can change the word "subject" in the code to "body" and have a message automatically placed in the body of the email letter.

You can also specify the subject and the body of the message at the same time.

I don't know why you'd want to, but it can be done like this:

```
<a href="mailto:ratboy@thedump.com?subject=Rats&
body=need love too">Rat Lover</a>
```

That opens a letter with the subject of "Rats" and "need love too" in the body. But wait! We're not finished with email tricks yet! You can also send an email to multiple recipients:

```
<a href="mailto:me@here.net?cc=you@there.com&
bcc=joe@wherever.net">E-Mail</a>
```

In the previous example, one copy goes to "me," one copy to "you," and a blind carbon copy to "Joe." I didn't want to leave Joe out—he doesn't have very many friends.

14.6 Back Buttons and Links

hen you need a back button, you can, of course, use a direct URL. I'm referring to an image link that is hard-coded to a specific page, like this:

```
<a href="index.html"><img src="images/backbutton.jpg">
</a>
```

> **NOTE**
>
> There should be no line breaks in the code. The line breaks were necessary in print, but these mail links should all be on one line. It's okay if the text wraps to the next line in your text editor, but there should be no hard breaks in the code.

Or a back text link:

```
<a href="index.html">Back</a>
```

The trouble with using direct URLs with back buttons or back links is that you don't know which page someone came from to arrive at where they are (the page containing the button). You can assume he or she made a logical progression through your site, but that often isn't the case. The user may not have even seen your home page yet. He or she may have clicked a link from a search engine or another site that went to a page somewhere deep within your site. (This inability to control how people arrive at a page is why you should have a "home" link on every page.)

Back Button: Form Type

You can use a simple form method that takes visitors back to the page they came from using their own browser's history. It's easy, and it goes like this:

```
<form><input type="button" value="Back"
onClick="history.go(-1);return true;"></form>
```

This code takes users back to wherever they came from, even if it wasn't one of your own pages. It's a standard looking gray button, like you'd see on any submit form, that simply says "Back." In the code, where it says, "Back," that's the text that displays on the button. You can change it to anything you want, like "back to where you came from you wascally wabbit," but the longer the text, the longer the button will be.

Nudge nudge, wink wink: Here's a dirty little trick if you're feeling mischievous. Change the "-1" to "-3" in the code. That will send them three pages back and make them wonder what happened. You wouldn't really do that would you?

Back Button: Text Type

Since the gray form buttons aren't very attractive, you might prefer to use a text link to take a user back one page. I use that on many of my pages. Here's how to create a back text link:

```
<a href="#" onClick="history.go (-1);return true;">Back</a>
```

Back Button: Image Type

You can also use an image for a back button that uses the browser's history.

```
<form><input type="image" src="images/backbutton.jpg"
value="Back" onClick="history.go(-1);return true;"> </form>
```

Simply change the source (src) value to reflect the path to the image and the image name and file type. Currently, image back buttons don't work in Netscape.

14.7 Refresh Button or Link

Y ou can create your own refresh button or text link for web pages. This is useful for web-cam pages, dynamic scripts such as random story generators, slide shows, or anything you can think of that requires users to refresh pages. If you update your site often, you might offer the refresh button/link to make sure users are not viewing an old page from their cache.

The code is a very simple JavaScript, and you can replace the image with a text message such as "Click to Reload" or whatever. Here's the code:

CODE EXAMPLE

```
<a href="javascript:document.location.reload();"
onMouseOver="window.status='Refresh'; return true"
onMouseOut="window.status='ah...that was good'">
<img src="images/refresh.jpg" width="130" height="46" border="0">
</a>
```

This code also shows the word "Refresh" in the status bar when the cursor is resting over the refresh link. When you move the mouse away from the refresh link, the status bar message changes to "ah...that was good." You can change those messages—just don't include any apostrophes, single quotation marks, or double quotation marks in the message unless you preface them with backslashes. For example, if you want the status bar message to read, "You won't believe this!" you'd code:

```
'You won\'t believe this!'
```

The single and double quotation marks have another meaning in JavaScript. The backslash tells the browser to print the next character rather than interpret it. The message itself must be enclosed in single quotation marks in the code.

As long as you don't link directly to it, you can use my demonstration image and you won't have to change the code at all. You find it here:

http://www.boogiejack.com/howx016.html

14.8 JavaScript Drop-down Link Menu

A JavaScript drop-down menu lets you place a lot of links in a compact area.

These scripts proved popular, but too difficult to copy from the book, so you can copy and paste the code from these locations:

Go-button menu: http://www.boogiejack.com/howx017.html

Automatic menu: http://www.boogiejack.com/howx033.html

This graphic shows the Go-button menu. Visitors select a link and click the Go button to visit the selected page. The automatic menu looks just like this, minus the Go button. When a visitor selects a link from the automatic menu they are taken to the selected page automatically.

14.9 Redirect Page

A utomatically redirecting visitors from one page to another isn't something you want to do every day. Use it only when necessary because it tends to tick people off when abused.

Places to use a redirect page include:

- When you remove a page or change a page name, replace it with a redirect page so visitors don't get 404-errors. Even if you remove all the links to that page on your site, there may still be links to it from other sites and search engines.

- When you create something dynamic such as a virtual tour of images in which one image is shown for a set amount of time, and then the next image automatically loads.

- When you change your web site location, such as moving from one host to another. Leaving behind a redirect page takes visitors directly to your new site.

- A survey results page.

- A thank-you page that displays after an order is submitted or a form is completed.

- When you just want to mess with people's heads. Oops, bad idea.

273

Of course, there are many other reasons to use a redirect page. To create a redirect page, just paste this into the HEAD section of an HTML document:

```
<meta http-equiv="Refresh" content="20;
URL=http://www.boogiejack.com">
```

In this example, most users are sent to my web site after 20 seconds. Older browsers don't support the redirect tag, so some users are not sent to your new site. It's wise to include a link to the new page for both the browser challenged and for those who are too impatient to wait 20 seconds.

Notice the content attribute—there seems to be a double quotation mark missing after 20 and another missing before the http. The code you see is correct though; the time delay and the URL are both values of the content attribute. With this special tag, a semicolon separates the two values.

Change the amount of time to fit your purpose, and change the URL to the page you want to send them to. If you're redirecting them to a page on the same site, you don't have to include the full URL, and it will work faster if you don't. Just put in the page name and extension as long as it's in the same directory.

14.10 Show Location

H ere's a simple script that shows visitors which page of your site they are on. It's most often used as a supplement to the normal navigational tools. Just enter the script below wherever you want it to appear on a page:

CODE EXAMPLE

```
<script language="JavaScript">
<!--
document.write("This page is:  " + document.location);
-->
</script>
```

If this were on the front page of my site, it would display as:

This page is: http://www.boogiejack.com

Of course, you can change the wording before the document location to whatever suits you. Just don't use an apostrophe or any special characters or it will break the script.

If you need to use an apostrophe in the text, preface it with a backslash, as that tells the browser to display the character rather than interpret it. Here's an example of that, using just the one line from the code that is editable:

```
document.write("You\'re here:  " + document.location);
```

You can also add text after the document location. Example:

```
document.write("You\'re here:  " + document.location +
", friend.");
```

Now, are you ready for a pop quiz? You must pass this pop quiz before moving on. Here's your pop quiz:

Which brand of pop is known as Dr. Pepper?

a. Orange Crush

b. Coca-Cola

c. Dr. Pepper

If you said "c. Dr. Pepper," you may go to the next tip. If you said anything else, go stand in the corner until Monday and think about it.

14.11 Alert Box

This very simple script pops up an alert box when your page loads. You can put any text message you want in the alert box—it can be a welcome message, call attention to a new page, or just tell someone his or her Aunt Fred wears army boots.

```
onLoad="alert('Put Your Way Cool Message Here')"
```

Simply add that little JavaScript snippet to the body tag of your web page.

The text in the 'Put Your Way Cool Message Here' area is what displays in the alert box. Two things to note: The single quotation marks before and after the message must remain in the code. Since the single quotation mark means something else in JavaScript,

275

words such as "can't" and "don't" require special treatment or they will cause errors. Simply place a backslash in front of the single quote to tell the browser to display that character rather than interpret it. So using the word "can't" in the alert box is written like this:

```
onLoad="alert('Never say you can\'t do it.')"
```

You can also have the alert message display when someone leaves your page. To do that, just change "onLoad" to "onUnLoad" and you can kiss them good-bye.

That's all there is to it. Now go alert someone, you rascal, you.

14.12 Preformatted Text

H ere's a quick and easy tip for forcing text to display exactly as you write it (without the extra spaces closed and line breaks removed, etc.). This is especially handy when you're creating forms to print, or perhaps have a poem or haiku you want to display in a certain way. Because preformatted text uses a monospace font, there may be some parts you will have to play with to get them to look right.

Use the <pre> tag to render text as you type it rather than in HTML fashion. It can get a little tricky if, for example, you have fill-in-the-blank lines that should all be the same length (that may require you to make some adjustments). For example:

```
<pre>
Your Name: _____
  Address: _____
     City: _____
    State: _____   ZIP Code: _____
</pre>
```

The pre tag forces the text to display on the page with the same indents as you typed, and it preserves the extra spaces between the State line and the ZIP Code.

14.13 Changing Cursors

Y ou probably know what happens when you place your cursor on a link. The cursor turns into a hand. I'll bet a nickel and a stick of Black Jack gum that you didn't know you could pick what that cursor turns into. The cursor options include:

Hand: The default, so there's no need to code it.

Wait: The hourglass symbol.

Help: A question mark by an arrow.

Crosshair: A large plus sign (just like it sounds).

Text: The vertical bar you get when your cursor is on text.

Move: The four-way mover pointer thingy, common in most graphic and page layout programs.

Then there's the resize cursor, which has eight options. I think it's misnamed, as it's really an arrow, and the options are the directions it can point. The options are:

n-resize: Arrow points straight up.

s-resize: Arrow points straight down.

e-resize: Arrow points straight right.

w-resize: Arrow points straight left.

ne-resize: Arrow points toward 1 o'clock.

nw-resize: Arrow points toward 11 o'clock.

sw-resize: Arrow points toward 7 o'clock.

se-resize: Arrow points toward 5 o'clock.

So how does it work? Easy:

```
<a href="link.html" style="cursor: ne-resize">Link</a>
```

As you can see, you simply add the style tag and "cursor: type" to a regular link. Some of the options might confuse guests, but the help cursor can be very useful when used correctly, and the arrows (resize) or crosshair can be OK. The rest look like monkey business to me—maybe you can think a good use for them.

14.14 The   Tag

A h, the handy little no break space command: ** **. Where would we be without it? Probably living in some palace somewhere with servants to peel grapes for us and . . . Oh, I got a little distracted there, 'scuse me.

This little command can make life a bit easier at times. Places you might want to use it include:

- To prevent the browser from breaking phrases into the next line at inappropriate places. For example, in 1 1/2 miles, you wouldn't want your line to break at 1
1/2 miles (like this) because it's hard to understand and looks goofy.

    So you write 1 1/2 miles to keep it together.

- To insert extra spaces. For example, to indent the beginning of a paragraph or add space between graphics:

        Start of the paragraph . . .

    <img src="img1.jpg">   <img src="img2.jpg">

There are other uses for the no break space tag, so be creative. Just remember the tag when you need a little extra space or don't want something broken apart. Don't forget the semicolon at the end of the tag. The correct tag is: ** **

14.15 Page Transition Effects

H ave you ever seen a site in which the page goes through some kind of weird effect as you enter? Perhaps the old page dissolved on your screen to reveal the new page, or the old page sort of slid out of the way? If you haven't seen that, you're probably using a browser that doesn't support it.

It's much easier to code a page transition than you might think. All you have to do is add a new meta tag to the <HEAD> section of the page as follows.

```
<meta http-equiv="Page-Enter"
content="revealTrans(Duration=5,Transition=17)">
```

That's all there is to it! In this code, the time it takes to transition is five seconds and the effect is #17. Following is a list of all available transition effects and their codes.

TRANSITION EFFECTS

0:	Shrinking Box	12:	Dissolve Screen
1:	Growing Box	13:	Horizontal Curtain Closing
2:	Shrinking Circle	14:	Horizontal Curtain Opening
3:	Growing Circle	15:	Vertical Curtain Closing
4:	Wipe Up	16:	Vertical Curtain Opening
5:	Wipe Down	17:	Left-Down Wipe
6:	Wipe Right	18:	Left-Up Wipe
7:	Wipe Left	19:	Right-Down Wipe
8:	Right Moving Stripes	20:	Right-Up Wipe
9:	Downward Moving Stripes	21:	Horizontal Bars Dissolve Screen
10:	Right Moving Boxes	22:	Vertical Bars Dissolve Screen
11:	Downward Moving Boxes	23:	Random, for the adventurous!

There you have it, magical page transitions.

14.16 Accessibility Feature for Windows

Did you know you can code pages for Windows users so the links are accessible by keystrokes rather than clucking lunks . . . I mean, clicking links? This is mostly used for disability accessibility, but can be fun to play around with. Just drop this into your page and try it:

```
<a accesskey="C" href="contest.html">Guess the Celebrity Contest</a>
```

This code lets visitors either click the link, or press the Alt and C keys, then the Enter key to activate the link. To link to a page off your site, include the full URL in the link. You can change the "C" to any letter or number. If you use keystrokes, be sure to tell guests how they work with something like:

For additional accessibility, press the Alt key while you type the bold letter in the link and then press the Enter key.

If you use a bold letter as the signal, you might code a link like this:

```
<a accesskey="G" href="goodies.html"><b>G</b>oodies</a>
```

The access key is the letter G in this case, so I made the first letter of the word Goodies in the link text bold. In this way, users who find it quicker or easier to press keys than use the mouse can activate your links with keystrokes.

14.17 Status Bar Link Message

T he status bar in the browser displays a message when a visitor rests the cursor over a link. You can customize the message with this JavaScript snippet:

CODE EXAMPLE

```
<a href="http://www.boogiejack.com"
onMouseOver="window.status='Boogie Jack is Weird!'; return true"
onMouseOut="window.status='Aw man, click the link!'; return true">
Boogie Jack's Web Depot</a>
```

Just change the message from "Boogie Jack is Weird!" to whatever you want to say. Of course, if you're linking to my site, you might want to leave it! This also reveals a new message when the cursor focus is removed from the link. In this case it reads, "Aw man, click the link!"

By now, you should know that you can change the link and link text to whatever you want.

14.18 Colored Horizontal Rule

T o create a colored horizontal rule (or line), use CSS. Just place this in the HEAD section of your page or in your linked style sheet:

```
<style type="text/css">
<!--
hr {color: red; width: 300px; height: 1;}
-->
</style>
```

Of course, because I'm so generous, I'm going to let you change the color, width, and height if you want to.

14.19 Definition Alert

A re you an egghead? Do you use words the average person doesn't understand? 'splain yourself, Lucy! Or let this JavaScript alert provide definitions of words for you.

. . . and the <a href='javascript:alert("A toadie is a yes man.");'>toadie</a> said "yes, sir!"

In this setup, clicking on the word "toadie" pops up an alert box that explains, "A toadie is a yes man."

14.20 Password Protection

T he following script password protects a page on your site. Visitors need to know the password to enter.

To prompt users for a password, paste this in the body of the transition page:

CODE EXAMPLE

```
<script language="JavaScript">
<!--
var password = prompt("Please enter your password.")
if (password == "Pick One"){
alert("Welcome!")
location = "protected.html" }
else {
location = "oops.html"
}
-->
</script>
```

> **NOTE**
>
> This script doesn't offer a high level of security. Someone will a little intelligence can easily discover how to enter your protected areas. For real password protection, you need to learn about .htaccess files, which are beyond the scope of this book. Many hosts offer easy-to-use control panels that enable you to easily password protect directories.

Where it says Pick One, insert the word you want for your password. Right now, the password in this code is Pick One. Where it says protected.html, substitute the name of the page you want to protect. Visitors who enter the correct password are forwarded to this page. Users who enter incorrect passwords are sent to the oops.html page as shown in the example.

While a password like this shouldn't be used as a substitute for true security, it isn't bad in a pinch if all you need is light security.

All someone has to do, though, is view your source code to get the password.

Lastly, if you do use this script to protect a page, you might want to use a tag to keep search engines from listing the protected page. Place this in the <HEAD> section of your protected page:

<meta name="robots" contents="noindex">

That will keep most search engines from indexing the page.

14.21 No Right-click

f you implement a password as shown in Section 14.20, anyone clever enough can get the password right from the source code. Although users can always view the source code from the browser menu, you can prevent Windows users from right-clicking on the page to view the source. This code also helps prevent Windows users from stealing your images.

CODE EXAMPLE

```
<script language="JavaScript">
<!--
function stopthief(ie) { var warning = "Right clicking not allowed.";
if (navigator.appName == 'Netscape' && ie.which == 3) {
alert(warning);
return false;
}
else
if (navigator.appName == 'Microsoft Internet Explorer' &&
event.button==2) {
alert(warning);
return false;
}
return true;
}
document.onmousedown = stopthief;
-->
</script>
```

For those few persistent enough to seek out the source code anyway, you can sort of hide the source code. Just start your page with a couple screens of blank lines, hiding the code below the visible window. That will fool a lot of people, especially if you include some nonsense code right at the top like this:

```
<protected-html; unlock-code="retrieve:secure-bin/B23";
print=doc:"B23">

<!-- HTML code for this web page is protected Guard Dog.
Access denied. -->
```

While the code is total nonsense, if you tried to view the source code and saw only that, with nothing but a white screen beneath it, wouldn't you be fooled?

You know, I don't do it often, but it is kind of fun to be sneaky once in a while.

14.22 No Copy and Paste

This little JavaScript snippet will prevent someone from highlighting part of your text and using their computer's copy function to copy it. It also prevents them from using Ctrl+A/Command+A to select all the text for copying.

Of course, since it is JavaScript, it doesn't work if the visitor has JavaScript disabled or has a browser that doesn't support JavaScript. That isn't very many users, but anyone with some experience would know a way around this trick. It will stop new users, and at least make it harder for everyone else. That may be all the discouragement visitors need to move on to easier pickins.

Just add the following code to your BODY tag:

```
onDragStart="return false" onSelectStart="return false"
```

Has anyone seen my muse?

14.23 Turn Off Internet Explorer Image Toolbar

Internet Explorer 6 and later has an image toolbar built into it. If you hover your cursor over an image, a floating image toolbar pops up that allows users to save the image, email the image to a friend, or print the image.

If you use a no-right click script to stop people from stealing your graphics, it won't stop anyone from grabbing images via the floating image toolbar. This had a lot of webmasters concerned about Internet Explorer making image theft too easy.

To their credit, Microsoft did include a way for webmasters to prevent the image toolbar from activating on their sites, but it does mean extra work. I may have been the first publisher to show webmasters how to turn this function off when I published this tip in my ezine, Almost a Newsletter. It pays to dig into the deep crevices of the Microsoft site sometimes.

By including a no right-click script, your images can be as safe as they were before the image toolbar. That's not to say there aren't still ways to steal images, because there are, but it does bring things back to the previous level of difficulty and required know-how.

To turn off the image toolbar for individual pictures, use either of these tags:

```
<img src="pic.jpg" galleryimg="no">
```

```
<img src="pic.jpg" galleryimg="false">
```

As you can see, it's an ordinary image tag with an attribute and value added to turn off the image toolbar function (shown in blue text). You should still use the other image attributes and values: border, width, height, and alt tags. I left them out in the above examples for the sake of simplicity.

To turn off the image toolbar for all pictures on a web page, add either of the following meta tags to the HEAD section of your page:

```
<meta http-equiv="imagetoolbar" content="no">
```

```
<meta http-equiv="imagetoolbar" content="false">
```

If you turn off the image toolbar functions for all pictures on a Web page, you can enable them for individual pictures by setting the "galleryimg" attribute to "yes" or "true." –For example:

```
<img src="pic.gif" galleryimg="yes">
```

```
<img src="pic.gif" galleryimg="true">
```

This method is faster than including individual tags for each image when there are one or two images you want to let people grab, but you don't want them to grab the majority of your images.

Note: You can only turn off elements that use the <img> tag; this doesn't affect other graphics tags such as <embed> or <object>.

14.24 Stop JavaScript Error Alerts

N ot all JavaScript codes are compatible with all browsers. A JavaScript that causes an error in a browser will show your visitor either an Error Alert or an little exclamation sign in the status bar, depending on how their browser is configured.

The alert can be especially disconcerting to new users who might wonder if you're trying to pull some funny business. On pages that use JavaScript, you might want to add one more little snippet of JavaScript that will prevent visitors from seeing the error message.

CODE EXAMPLE

```
<script language="JavaScript">
<!--
//from boogiejack.com
function stopError() {
return true;
}
window.onerror = stopError;
-->
</script>
```

Placing that code in the HEAD section of a page will stop the browser from showing both the alert and the status bar error symbol.

14.25 Chapter Quiz

1. To align text correctly with a drop cap image, you use an align attribute. What value is used for the align attribute?

2. Apostrophes, single quotation marks, and double quotation marks are part of the JavaScript language. To present a word such as "can't" in a message that is displayed through JavaScript, what character must be used before the apostrophe?

3. Say that you want your email link to open with a predetermined subject line. Finish the link below so that "Website Feedback" is in the subject line.

   `<a href="mailto:me@isp.com`

4. Pages that automatically forward users from one page to another are called:
   a. Autoforward pages.
   b. Progressive pages.
   c. Relocate pages.
   d. Redirect pages.

5. Preformatted text preserves spaces as you type them, rather than closing extra spaces to a single space as HTML does. What are the opening and closing tags for preformatted text?

6. In the link code below, add the style code to display the cursor as a question mark next to an arrow when it's over the link.

   `<a href="help.html">Help</a>`

7. What is the code for a no break space tag?

14.25 Chapter Quiz (continued)

8. The meta tag for a page transition effect is placed:
   a. Between the <head> and </head> tags.
   b. Inside the <body> tag.
   c. Before the opening <html> tag.
   d. Under a rock in your front yard.

9. Add the attribute and value to the following link to allow users to activate it by pressing the Alt key and the letter "A" on a PC keyboard.

   <a href="about.html">About Me</a>

10. The Internet Explorer image toolbar makes it easy to copy images—too easy, many people say. Which of the following codes stops the toolbar from displaying on ALL images on a page when placed in the HEAD section of a web page?
    a. <meta http-equiv="imagetoolbar" content="no">
    b. <meta http-equiv="imagebar" content="no">
    c. <meta http-equiv="toolbar" content="no">
    d. <meta http-equiv="IEtoolbar" content="no">

11. The purpose of the code to stop JavaScript errors is:
    a. So your JavaScript will self-correct if an error is encountered.
    b. To prevent the browser from reporting errors to the user.
    c. To prevent faulty JavaScript from crashing browsers.
    d. To help keep movie producers from drinking too much coffee and misreading the script.

12. Why does a bicycle need a kickstand?

14.26 Chapter Exercises

Exercise Option 1 – Practice Site

B y now, you should have created all the pages for your web site except the actual content pages. The content pages are the pages that contain the real subject and purpose of your site. Your assignment is to make those pages now, using at least two of the tips and tricks from this chapter.

If you're adding more than one content page, save some pages to make later. These are the last two exercises in the book, as the remaining chapters discuss site promotion, netiquette, and other topics that don't lend themselves to practice exercises. The final portions of the book include a glossary, tag index, and other reference material. To your great pleasure, I'm sure, there are more chapter quizzes.

Exercise Option 2 – Independent Exercise

I t's possible you may have gone ahead of the class—or that I have forgotten one of the exercises I wrote—and you have your content pages already written. For this exercise, add three more content pages to your practice site.

Be sure to incorporate at least one of the code bits and pieces from this chapter on each new page. Use at least one instance of inline CSS code on each new page.

Uploading Files via WS_FTP

15.1 Chapter Introduction

S ooner or later you'll want to put your web page creations on the Internet for the world to see. This is commonly called uploading your files or uploading your web site.

Options for uploading your files depend, in part, on where your site is hosted. Some hosts have online programs that allow you to upload right from your browser. These are generally free web space providers, which are fine if your web site is a hobby or a family site. Each provider has their own way of letting you upload files, and there are dozens, if not hundreds of free providers. Since there are far too many methods to cover in this book, I will focus on uploading via FTP (file transfer protocol), which almost all web host providers allow.

15.2 File Transfer Programs

O n Windows, I prefer WS_FTP LE, a freeware version of Ipswitch's WS_FTP Pro file transfer program. It's the program I've used since the first day I uploaded a web site, and I've found no reason to try another. It does exactly what I want and need, and of course, the fact that it's free is a nice bonus. You can download your own copy from:

www.ftpplanet.com/download.htm

WS_FTP is short for WinSock File Transfer Protocol. It enables you to transfer files from your computer to the remote server where your site will reside.

On Mac OS, my editor recommends Fetch, a user-friendly, very popular FTP client. Free to students and charitable non-profits, a Fetch license is only about $25 for other users. For more information:

www.fetchsoftworks.com

15.3 File Transfer Methods

here are two modes of file transfer: ASCII mode or binary mode.

- ASCII mode (pronounced ask-kee) is generally used for text files such as HTML pages. In addition, most CGI scripts must be transferred in ASCII mode. Occasionally an unusual script might need to be transferred in binary mode, but it will (or at least should) tell you of that irregularity.
- Binary mode is usually used for transferring images. In fact, images must be transferred in binary mode.

You'll upload a lot of HTML pages and images, so you won't have any trouble remembering which mode to use for those. CGI scripts aren't something you upload very often, and when you do it's often hard to remember which mode you should use. The easy way to remember is simply that both CGI and ASCII end in the letter "i" (so it's an eye for an eye, he sermonized).

You can use either mode to transfer some files. Technically, HTML pages are text and should be transferred in ASCII mode, but I always upload them in binary mode and have never had any trouble with it. There's no profound reason why I do that, I just find it easier than switching back and forth. Call it lazy. Call it Snodgrass, whatever makes you happy!

15.4 Creating Your Profile

efore you can start uploading files, you'll need some information from your web host provider. You will need to know:

- The host name and address for your server space
- The host type
- Your user ID
- Your password

Armed with this information, you are ready to create your profile within the FTP program. If you're on Mac OS, follow the instructions provided with Fetch or for your program of choice. If you're on Windows and choose to use WS_FTP LE, I'll show you how to use it here. If you select another program, follow the instructions provided with it.

To use WS_FTP LE, select it from the **Start** menu's **Programs** list. If you have a Programs toolbar or desktop shortcut, you can start it that way too.

When you first start the program, this screen displays:

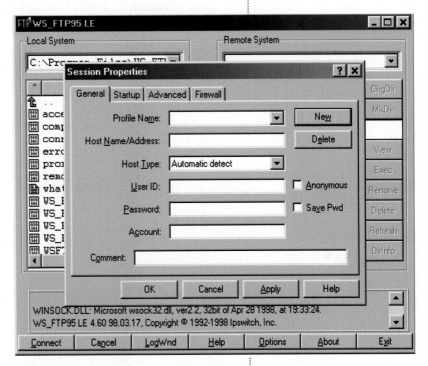

The **Session Properties** dialog box lets you create your profile.

1. **Profile Name field:** Enter the name you want to use for your site. The name doesn't mean anything to the FTP program or the server you're uploading to—it's just a name you'll recognize for your site.

2. **Host Name/Address field:** Enter the numerical address or your domain address, which is provided by your host.

3. **Host Type drop-down list:** Select the appropriate option, provided by your host, from the drop-down list. Automatic Detect is usually the preferred option.

4. **Anonymous check box:** Leave this field blank.

5. **User ID field:** Enter the User ID provided by your host. The field may or may not be case sensitive, depending on how your host's server is set up, so be sure to type your ID exactly as provided.

6. **Password field:** Enter the password you selected when you signed up or the one assigned to you by your host. This field is always case sensitive.

291

7. **Save Pwd (password) check box:** If you don't want to enter your password each time you start a session, check this.

8. **Account field:** Leave this field blank.

9. **Comments field:** This space is for a short note to yourself, for example, to differentiate between a new and old account if you move your site.

10. Click the **Apply** button, and then click the **OK** button. Your profile is saved and you should be connecting to your space on the web host's server.

15.5 Transferring Files

nce you've created your profile using the Windows program WS_FTP LE, here's how you transfer files. Connect to your web space on the remote server (your web host). You will see a dialog box similar to this:

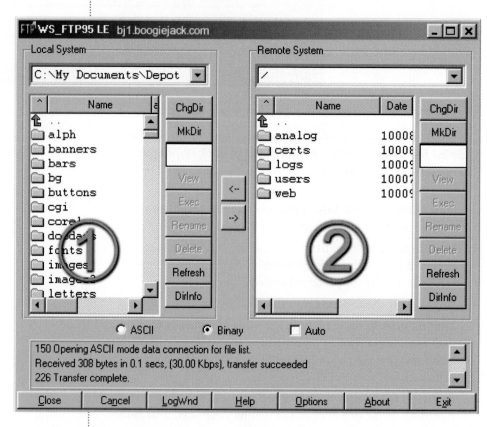

In the **Local System** area at left (labeled with a circled number 1), you'll find your own computer file system. In the **Remote System** area on the right (labeled with a circled number 2), you'll find your space on the remote server, where your web site will reside on the Internet. Servers can be set up in many ways, so what you see in the **Remote System** area will probably look different on your server.

You open folders on either computer by double-clicking them. Double-click the upward pointing arrow to move up a directory. In the **Local System** area at left where your computer displays, you'll find all your drives listed at the bottom. You may double-click them to access them as well.

For the web host provider in the example graphic on the previous page, the folder that reads "web" is the directory where you would begin building your web site. Double-click it to open it. Depending on the host, this directory might be called by another name such as "public html" or simply "public." It probably won't be called "Melvin" though.

Once you've opened the directory on the remote computer where you plan to begin building your web site, you can start uploading your HTML pages:

1. From the radio buttons under the two areas, click **ASCII** mode.
2. Locate the HTML files on your computer.
3. Click a file to select it.
4. Click the arrow between the two areas to begin the file transfer. (The arrow pointing from your computer to the server uploads files. The arrow pointing from the server to your computer downloads files.)

If you lose or accidentally delete a file on your computer, you can also download files from the web server. Just select the file on the remote server and click the arrow in between the areas that points to your computer.

> **NOTE**
>
> To upload more than one file at a time, hold down the Control key and click each additional file you want to upload. To select several files in succession, hold down the Shift key and click the first and last file. Once you have selected all the text-based files you want to upload, click the arrow that points to the remote server from your computer.

15.6 Creating a Directory

Once you've uploaded your text files, you'll need to create an image directory and upload your images. I'll show you how to do this using the Windows program WS_FTP LE. To create a directory on the remote computer, click the **MkDir** button on the right side of the remote computer's file area. The button is the second from the top; **MkDir** is short for Make Directory.

This opens a dialog box that lets you type in the name of the directory you wish to create. Type the directory name exactly as it is on your computer. By keeping the directories the same, you'll have half as much to remember—and all your files will work the same on the web as on your own computer. This allows you to test your links locally before you upload the pages. Once you've typed in the directory name, click the **OK** button.

Here's an example:

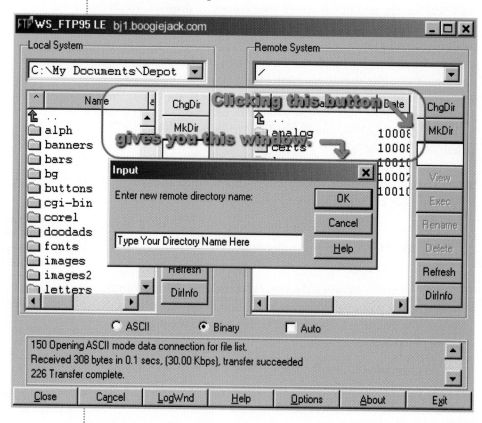

Once created, double-click the directory to open it. Then, open the same directory on your computer. Since we just created the images directory and images are binary files, select the binary mode of transfer. Finally, select the files and click the transfer arrow just as you did for the HTML text files.

Repeat this process for all the directories you need for your web site.

15.7 Tips

- If you always want to start in the same directories on both computers, you can save the locations in the dialog box. Once you've started a session and navigated to the directories you want, click the **Options** button at the bottom. Then, click the **Save Current Directories as Connection Directories** button.

- If you receive "failed data channel" errors when you try to connect, try clicking the **Advanced** tab on the **Session Properties** dialog box, then check the box for **Passive Transfers**. If you're behind a firewall or gateway, this is sometimes necessary.

- A shortcut to transferring files into the currently open directory is to double-click them. Just make sure the correct directory is open on the target computer and that the correct transfer mode is selected so the files aren't corrupted.

15.8 Chapter Quiz

1. FTP stands for:
   a. File Terminal Program
   b. Free Tasty Pickles
   c. Free Transfer Protocol
   d. File Transfer Protocol

2. What are the two modes of file transfer?

3. Before you can set up a Session Profile using WS_FTP LE and other programs, your host needs to provide you with the host name/address, the host type, a user ID, and _____.

15.8 Chapter Quiz (continued)

4. In the WS_FTP program, does the area at right show you the files and directories on your computer or those on the remote computer?

5. In WS_FTP, how do you open a folder on the remote computer?

6. What mode of file transfer should images be uploaded in?

7. In WS_FTP, what button do you click to create a folder (directory)?

8. If you want your session in WS_FTP to always begin in specific directories, you can click the Save Current Directories as Connection Directories button to set them as the default directories. Where do you find this button?

9. Failed data channel errors can often be overcome by checking what check box in the Advanced tab of the Session Properties dialog box?

10. You click a file on your computer to select it. How do you transfer that file to your web site server?

11. How do you select more than one file at a time to send to the server?

12. A wise person might be said to have common sense in an uncommon degree, but the same can be said of a fool for lack of it. What's the difference between a wise person and a fool?

Design Points

16.1 Chapter Introduction

|N| ow that you know how to build a web site from a technical standpoint, we'll look at some basic principles of good web site design. Knowing the techno-babble is only part of the puzzle. You also need an eye for color, space, and proportion as well as the ability to plan site navigation and ensure usability.

Many design and usability basics are discussed throughout the book. In this chapter, we'll pull together the ideas for handy reference and add a few new thoughts along the way. One thing to remember is that these are tried-and-true principles, but not hard-and-fast rules. While you may break these rules at any point—and may have good reasons to do so—keep in mind that the more you try to reinvent the wheel, the more you risk a digital flat tire.

Having said that, web design is still a subjective medium. What constitutes good design for one person may be very different from what the next person thinks. While design is subjective, there is a consensus on what makes good design in many areas. Some of these no-no's are because they make good sense, others are because the design techniques have been done too often, making them a broken record. You'll read about these items in the Section 16.11: Why Your Site May Exhale to a Negative Degree.

16.2 File Size

|W| hile a growing number of users have high-speed Internet access, the sad truth is that the vast majority of people still connect at 56K or less. The average Internet surfer won't wait more than 20 or 30 seconds for a page to load—or for enough of a page to load so they have something to do while it finishes. For these reasons, webmasters must take steps to ensure their pages load fast.

Your index page is the most important page as far as load time goes. Most of the time, it's the first page people see on your site.

You have to grab their attention there and then—and keep it. To do that, the rule of thumb is to keep the total file size of your index page to 40K or less. The total file size includes the HTML page itself, the graphics on the page, and any other components that need to be downloaded to complete the page. If you can keep the file size under 30K, that's even better.

Of course, there are always exceptions to the 40K rule. If your site is on a particularly fast server, you can bend the rule a bit and have a larger page. If your site is on a slow server, you should bend the rule the other way and make your index page even smaller.

Your interior pages can be a little larger in file size, but don't go overboard. If you've won over visitors on your index page and they've found something they want to see, they'll be a little more patient with subsequent pages.

Users expect some types of pages to load slower. For example, my free graphics pages have several graphics on each page, so they aren't as fast as the text pages in the HTML tutorials section. Users expect that. They know graphics take longer to download. Since they're seeking graphics, I can safely break the 40K rule with no qualms—as long as the graphics are high quality.

16.3 Optimize Those Graphics

An important part of keeping a page's total file size down is optimizing its graphics. You can use a variety of software tools to optimize images, including graphics creation tools and utilities developed specifically to optimize images. You'll find the small cost is worth the investment. Try out a few and buy the one that works best for you. You can also use free online tools to optimize images. Here is a free online service that offers Windows and Mac OS support:

Gif Cruncher: www.spinwave.com

This service offers GIF and JPG optimization free online, and offers software that you can purchase for your computer system. Most good graphics programs have tools that enable you to optimize images as you save them.

Bear in mind that optimizing images by increasing the compression rate (JPG) or reducing the number of colors (GIF) aren't the only ways to improve their load time. Reducing the overall dimensions also reduces file sizes. Graphics should complement a site, not overwhelm it. Is that huge image that takes up half the screen on the opening page really necessary? Are those bandwidth hogs—GIF animations—really necessary? Consider whether your graphics enhance anything or whether they just annoy visitors and slow down your pages. If you're honest with yourself about it, the answer may surprise you.

Unless the animation is the content, it often distracts from your real content. The visual noise from animation is tiring to the eyes, and, unless you make your own or have it custom made, it's all been seen before anyway. The last thing you want is to have your site look like the site the 12-year-old down the block just built. If you must use animation, make sure it's good, and make sure you don't loop it forever. (Looping refers to how many times the animation repeats.) You'll need a GIF animator program to limit the loops. However, before you go using animations you find on the web, make sure you read Section 18.3: Copyrights and Bandwidth in Chapter 18: Good Things to Know.

Remember, your content is more important than snazzy graphics, although graphics do help create a mood and show visitors how professional you are. Cheap-looking graphics give visitors the impression that whatever you offer is of lower quality than what your competitor with sharp, professional graphics offers. If your content is terrific and exceptional, you may be able to overcome a bad first impression, but it's better to make a good impression and reinforce it with quality content.

16.4 White Space

An important part of design is white space. Of course, white space isn't necessarily the color white—it simply refers to empty space on your page. If you run your text from edge to edge and fill up all the space with something, the page looks cluttered. While your intent may be to pack as much information as possible into the space, it actually serves to make everything harder to find. With no visual "rest stops" for the eyes, everything becomes a jumble of confusion for visitors.

Smart design has ample white space planned into it. This includes white space on each side of the page. Keep in mind that reading text on a monitor is different from reading text on paper. While a standard sheet of paper is 8.5 inches wide, monitors are often 17 or more inches wide. Because of the extra width, when you read on a monitor and come to the end of one line, it can be much harder to find the beginning of the next line. With margins of space on both sides, you not only create a cleaner and more professional look, you make it easier for visitors to read your text.

299

Vertical white space is equally important. Running on and on without paragraph breaks or breaks for headings makes a whole text passage look overwhelming. Few will read it all. By creating short paragraphs and adding plenty of headings, visitors can grab bite-size chunks and are more likely to read what you have to say, you gabby little thing, you.

Take a look at my old Software & Services index in the graphic shown below. Notice the white space on each side and the short descriptive paragraphs, which are conducive to easy reading. Everything is broken up into easy-to-digest pieces, but it still maintains a consistent flow of design and thought. I had to use an old page because, after this book is finished, my next project is to redesign my site.

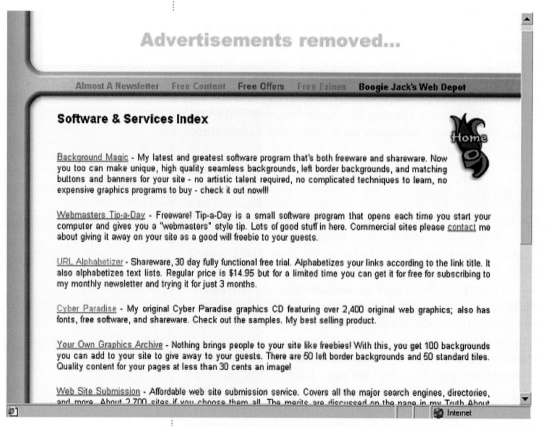

Web surfers tend to skim pages to look for the meat rather than starting at the top and reading straight through. Short bursts of words are more conducive to the way surfers view web pages and they help keep visitors from skipping over your important points.

Long paragraphs are more tiring on the eyes and are more likely to be skipped. Think about it, don't you do the same thing? I know I do.

This is crucial: Important points are usually lost in long paragraphs unless you write like a world-class author.

I'll bet you read that last sentence didn't you? It was isolated within the body of this text and prefaced with bold text, which told you immediately that it was important. If that line was buried at the end of the previous paragraph, it wouldn't have had the same impact. If you have a must-read key point to make, take steps to make sure your readers don't skip over it.

If you have an important point to make, but you can't isolate it in one sentence as I did above, then headings may be the way to go. Headings draw visitors into your message. Think of headings as newspaper or advertisement headlines. They should be short and punchy, and sell the reader on reading the next paragraph. If you can work a keyword or two into your heading, that's even better as it will help you with search engine placement.

Another way to isolate text is by treating it as a pull quote. Isolate the whole paragraph by indenting it on each side. For information about how to do this, see Section 11.10: Blockquotes in Chapter 11: Cascading Style Sheets.

16.5 About Your Text

In addition to the importance of white space, many other factors make your web site easier to read. If you deviate from the default font, take care that the fonts you specify are easy to read. Decorative fonts, handwriting fonts, grunge fonts, and many other fonts are meant only for use at large sizes for items such as banners and logos. If you use unusual fonts for the basic text font, you will lose readers. It may look cool to you, but it makes reading more difficult for visitors. Unless your message is super-compelling, they probably won't bother with it for long.

Another taboo for body text is using all capital letters. Using all capital letters on the Internet is considered the equivalent of SHOUTING in person (plus, it's hard to read text in all caps). You don't want people to think you're shouting at them; in addition to seeming rude, it will make you seem desperate for attention.

Super-size text has a similar affect. It's pushy and brash, and the mark of an amateur. It's the equivalent of the obnoxious fellow who talks louder than everyone else because he is desperate to have someone listen to him talk about himself. It won't help you win friends or customers.

Another mistake is using too many different fonts, font colors, and font sizes—commonly called the "ransom note" effect. You've probably heard the expression "too many cooks spoil the broth" before. Similarly, too many fonts, font colors, and font sizes spoil the web page. They create too much competition for the eye and serve as a distraction rather than an enhancement of your page.

If you really want to look like a rank amateur, center all your text. New webmasters, who often have no layout or design experience, think centering looks neat. Because of their inexperience, they have no concept of page layout and balance—or how to make text easy to read. They center everything and think it looks neat and balanced, but unfortunately all it shows is inexperience.

You should spell check and proofread your pages. Spell checking will catch most typos and words you thought you knew how to spell but didn't (and don't feel bad, it happens to everyone). Proofreading will catch mistakes that a spell checker won't. If I accidentally typed an "m" instead of a "p," a spell checker would be turned into a smell checker. And you don't need a smell checker to know copy like that stinks. Your spell checker won't catch that type of mistake, but hopefully your eyes will.

Unfortunately, Notepad doesn't have a spell checker. There are free online spell checkers you can find through any good search engine. If you'd like spell checking software for your computer, for Windows or Mac OS, you might try the low-cost Spell Catcher from:

www.spellcatcher.com

If you want to look up a word while you're working away, and refuse to lift your fingers from the keyboard or mouse to grab an actual hard-copy dictionary, head to Merriam-Webster Online at

www.m-w.com.

16.6 Background Images

B ackground images need to be chosen carefully, or at the very least, used carefully. On a professional site, it's not unheard of to *not* use a background image. Not using a background image is a legitimate option.

If a full-page style background (opposed to left-border style background) is used, and it's too busy, too loud, or has too many contrasts, the text on the page will be hard to read. For this style of background, it's better to use textures or patterns that don't have a lot of contrasting color or light/dark areas. The contrast should be between the text color and the background image, not within the background image. This often means choosing a text color that helps provide a contrast to the background's overall tone.

If you want to use a background that doesn't offer enough contrast for text, you can still use it. You can place text in a table centered on the page, which will allow the background to display on both sides of the table yet provide a clear and clean place for text.

I prefer left-border style backgrounds. They allow you to add color to your page yet leave the main content area clean and easy to work with. The only thing you have to be concerned with is that the text color contrasts with the main area of the background. Studies show that black text on white is the easiest to read. This stands to reason, as black text on white is the most contrast you can have. Using a background with white for the main area is often considered the most professional looking.

16.7 Color Usage

Color coordination is an important part of design. I designed a site for a company whose owners insisted on using red, green, and yellow as the color scheme. It went against my grain, but I made the best look I could with those colors. They loved it, but I would rather have sent it to the recycle bin. It looked cartoonish, and in my opinion, didn't suit their type of business. However, color choices are personal in nature—what is beautiful to one person may be hideous to another and vice versa.

Color theories abound, and professional colorists rarely agree. One person may design using analogous colors, while the next swears by complementary colors. Meanwhile the designer down the road uses triad color schemes. Since we all see colors differently, and our monitors render colors differently, I won't attempt to teach you how to color coordinate your site. That could be an insult to your color tastes. Instead, I'll pass on a few thoughts on color usage, and leave the color choices where it should be—up to you.

The ability to use color properly is a powerful design tool, turning average sites into something special. But beware: The use of too many colors can destroy the flow of a site. As with too many fonts and font sizes, too many colors create too much competition for the eyes' attention, leaving users with no intuitive way to know where to focus their attention. Controlling the color scheme, on the other hand, can create harmony and balance, and even help control your visitors' eye flow.

Picture a woman in a black dress. She has on a white pearl necklace, white gloves, and white shoes. I don't know if a woman would wear white shoes with a black dress—fashion isn't my thing. But that isn't the point. The pearl necklace stands out and makes you notice it. Then your eyes catch the white gloves, and next the white shoes. She controls the way she is seen by her color coordination. Guys, women do this to us all the time, God bless them. They have a great eye for color and excel at color coordination. That's why my wife decorates our house. Well, that and because she's the boss, at least that's what she tells me.

On a web site, you can use color to control the way your visitor views your page. If your page starts off with a paragraph of black text on a white background and then has a big heading in red letters, what do you think people will notice first? If you said the big red letters, you are correct. By using color to lead a viewer from left to right and top to bottom, you can control their eye movement and entice them to read what you want them to read first.

There's no doubt about it, color adds spice to a page and is a powerful tool when used correctly. But just like spice, a little goes a long way, and too much can ruin a good recipe.

There's a very nice online tool that will help you coordinate your color schemes. Just click a primary color on a color chart, and it gives you that color plus 15 colors that go well with it according to its built-in mathematical formula. It's called the Color Schemer, and thanks to developer Aaron Epstein, you can find this tool on my site at:

www.boogiejack.com/colormach2.html

Although the online version works on both Windows and Mac OS, it doesn't work with most versions of Netscape. However, you can purchase this software to install on your own computer. You'll find purchase details at:

www.colorschemer.com

Take a look at Color Schemer in action:

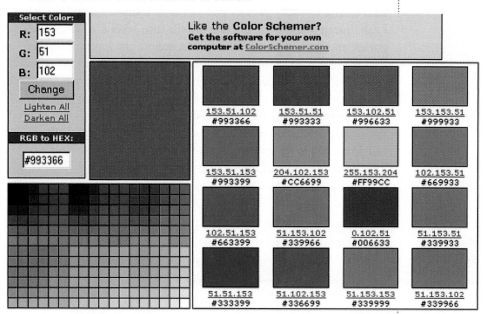

Using Color Schemer is simple. Just click any color in the lower left color samples area, and the color schemes show up in the large area at right. The RGB values and hex code for each color displays below the color swatch. To display complementary colors for any RGB color you like, type values in the R, G, and B fields in the upper left corner.

16.8 Navigation

avigation is another key element to how well received your site will be. The navigation system should be consistent throughout your site. The idea is to have your visitors become familiar with the navigation as soon as possible so they feel comfortable finding their way around. The easier it is to find your goodies, the more sections of your site visitors are likely explore—as long as the content is of sufficient quality to hold their interest.

On a small site, an intuitive navigation system is pretty easy to achieve. On a large site, it is more of a challenge. If your site is going to be 10 to 12 pages or fewer, and you know it's not going to grow, then you can simply link to every page from every page. If you know it will be bigger than that, then you should plan for the growth.

My site contains more than 500 pages. It is completely imprac-
tical to link to every page as you can with a smaller site. I use what
I call "jump stations." I divided my site into several content cate-
gories, and each category has its own index. The links on the bottom of every page of my site go only to the jump stations, my contact
page, and my home page. Through this type of navigation, users are
never more than two clicks away from what they're looking for.
The previous graphic of my Software & Services page is one of
these jump stations. I suppose I could also call them sub-indexes,
but admit it—jump station is more fun than sub-index. Here's a
look at another one of my old jump stations:

Advertisements Removed

Almost A Newsletter   Free Content   Free Offers   Free Ezines   **Boogie Jack's Web Depot**

Webmasters Resource Index

You'll find all kinds of web page building help here, with more coming if I ever get caught
up on all my work! Any volunteers for tedious paperwork chores?

Pixel River Free Graphics - Free backgrounds, left border backgrounds, wallpaper tiles, textures, button
sets, divider bars and more. Professional graphics for your web pages, enjoy.

HTML Help Center - From complete beginners tutorials to more advanced techniques, you'll find it here.
Copy and paste code, color charts, web etiquette, copyright issues and more.

Corel Tutorials - Step by step tutorials for Corel Photopaint.

Sound Effects - Not your normal midi songs, these sound effects are strange noises and fun sounds that
grab your visitors attention.

The navigation system provides advantages for me as well.
When I add a page to my site, I only need to add it to the category
index (the jump station). If it's a continuing page in a series of
pages, such as the background graphics, I add a "next" link to it
from the previous page.

Let's suppose you are building a family site. We'll assume that
it's starting off small, but will grow into a huge resource for your
family. You also plan to offer your secret family recipes to the
world, so you want it to be professional and easy to navigate, as

well as easy for you to maintain. You might plan out your site as follows:

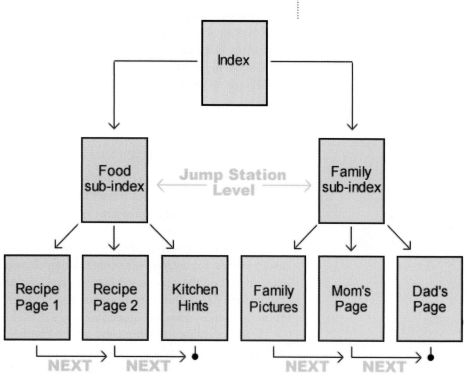

Anytime you start a new site, it's a good idea to plan out it out. You can solve problems before they occur and save yourself a lot of trouble. As you can see, it starts with the index page. At the jump station level are the family links and the food-related links. Those two jump stations serve as the sub-index pages. When you add a new page, you only have to add them to one of those two pages. The arrows at the bottom show how you might use a "next" link on each page of content.

The links on the bottom of all the pages (except the index) are merely links to the home page and two jump stations. If you want people to contact you, creating a contact link on each page is wise. Likewise, create links on every page for advertising information or other types of information that needs to be available from every page. Also, always include a link to your home page on every single page of your site.

Of course, this is the poor man's way of doing things. If you have money to burn, you can use active server pages, build a search engine, or use other sophisticated navigation tools. I don't expect many big spenders are using this book though, so I'm teaching a very effective navigation system that doesn't cost anything but the time to plan and create it. You'll also find two additional methods of implementing an easy to maintain navigation system in Chapter 18: Good Things to Know. Using remote JavaScript and SSI are extremely useful tools; I recommend you take the time to read about them.

16.9 Consistency

onsistency in the navigation structure helps people learn your site quickly, but it isn't the only area you need to be consistent in. Keeping a consistent look from page to page of a site is also highly important.

You'll rarely find a professionally designed site that changes backgrounds, fonts, colors, or other design elements from page to page. If you do that, users can begin to feel lost, and may not even know if they're still on the same site. You want visitors to feel at home as soon as possible, and consistency is the key to that.

If you're trying to earn money on the Internet, consistency is particularly vital. If you change design elements from page to page, as hobbyists who create personal home pages often do, you will be thought of in that same group. Don't take that wrong—there's nothing wrong with personal home pages; in fact, I enjoy them tremendously. However, I'm probably not going to send money to someone who appears to have no business experience and may be gone tomorrow. To make money, you need to earn trust, and that is accomplished through professional design as much as anything.

16.10 Affiliate Ads and Banner Ads

owadays, it seems everyone is trying to earn money from affiliate programs. Companies and individuals plaster several banners on a page and call it a business. I'll tell you a non-secret—they're not making any money to speak of.

No one wants to wait for pages of banners to load, especially if there's little content of merit. If I'm going to a new site and I see too many banners, I'll hit my back button because I know that 99 percent of the time there won't be anything on that site worth my attention.

To keep from chasing away visitors, limit banners to one per page. And even at that, if the banner is from an affiliate program and that's all you do, you're not likely to make much money from the banner. It does make it look like you have advertisers though, which can result in side benefits such as lending credibility to your site and having visitors think you're a professional (if you choose the programs you advertise with care).

If you really want to make money using affiliate programs, use links within the context of your content. For example, if you have a site about debt management, you might write an article about re-building credit with a secured credit card. From the article, you can link to an affiliate program for a credit card company; if your article is well researched and well written, you might create a nice income stream from it.

In short, don't shove banners and any old affiliate program down people's throats. That will just create a slow ride to nowhere for you. Affiliate programs should be related to your content, re-searched, and worked into your content. If at all possible, buy whatever it is you're trying to sell. If you're familiar with the product and can honestly generate enthusiasm about it, that enthusiasm will come through in your words and you'll have better luck with it. Never try to market a product you don't believe in—you can ruin your reputation and credibility very quickly.

16.11 Why Your Site Might Exhale to a Negative Degree*

In no particular order, my top 20 reasons people think a web site exhales to a negative degree are:

1. **Access Time:** If you make someone wait too long, they will quit waiting and go elsewhere. Enough said.

2. **Under Construction Signs:** "Under Construction" signs were cute back in 1996 when they first appeared, but now they are nothing more than an old and overused cleverness. Old clever-ness is still old, but no longer clever.

   Remember, no web site is ever finished, but each should be complete. Don't link to content that isn't ready yet. You can

---

* Use your imagination to figure out what "exhale to a negative degree" means. Hint: I originally used one word in place of that phrase, and it rhymed with "duck." My publisher thought it best to change that.

make a "coming soon" announcement if you must, but don't send them to nonexistent content or you'll be guilty of wasting their time—and that will not endear them to you or your site.

3. **Horizontal Scrolling:** Nothing annoys visitors more than having to scroll right, scroll left, scroll right, and so on, just to read a page. At the time of this writing, about 60 percent of web surfers have their computers set for an 800×600 resolution, with the rest at higher and lower resolutions. If you design your site for a higher resolution than 800×600, you're making it an annoyance to the majority of Internet users.

4. **Auto-play Music:** Many people surf the Internet at work, school, and from other public places. The last thing they want is music blaring from their computer that gives them away. Others, like yours truly, like to listen to radio stations from around the world via the Internet. Auto-play files often play at the same time as a radio station, so they interfere with my chosen listening preference. Offer a choice, or at least a control to turn the music off.

5. **Browser-crashing Code:** Be sure to check your code in at least Internet Explorer and Netscape. What may work fine on your favorite browser could crash your visitor's browser. No one will return to a page that causes his or her system to crash. Java is a major culprit in causing computer crashes. Java applets run off the memory resources of the visitor's computer. Computers with little memory muscle will crash. Even a high-octane machine will crash if it has many programs open already or encounters poorly written code (and there's plenty of that around). Always warn guests that a link contains Java so they can make an informed choice. Other than perhaps a small, well-behaved menu applet, I suggest never putting Java on your index page.

6. **Bleeding-edge Technology:** Technologies on the cutting edge can be exciting and fun, but since they often lack browser support, use them with caution. I usually stay a year or so behind the bleeding edge to keep my site enjoyable (such as it is) for the vast majority. By then, if the technology is proven worthy, it will usually have support. Keep in mind though, you don't have to use cutting-edge technology to have an effective and useful web site.

7. **Content:** Or more specifically, the lack of quality content and originality. No matter how pleasing a site is to the eyes, no matter how hard you want it to be cool, no matter what

technologies you use, content is and always will be king. Without quality, original content, your site will be lost in a sea of mediocrity.

8. **Poor Grammar, Spelling, and Punctuation:** Unless you want your site to appeal to kids and dull minds, pay particular attention to your grammar, spelling, and punctuation. Everything doesn't have to be perfect, but it should be close. Use of jargon and informal language is fine too, as long as it's understandable and used in appropriate places. However, if you're going to tell me about how you're an expert in search engine placement, I'm not going to believe you if you write: I garruntee you a top, placment. In all, the majer search enjines.

9. **Wrong Attitude:** Some folks, including many businesses, build web sites with a me-first attitude. I have a news flash for you—your visitors don't care about you. They want to know what's in it for them. They may come to care about you in time, but when they arrive on your site for the first time, you'd better show them what's in it for them or they're gone. Even worse than a wrong attitude is a bad attitude. This can be anything from a condescending superiority to outright disrespect for visitors. Hey, if you don't want visitors and aren't going to at least pretend to be cordial, why did you build a web site?

10. **Poor Design:** Low-quality graphics, amateur formatting, confusing navigation, cluttered pages, pages that are five miles long, clashing color schemes, lack of focus, broken links and images, mismatched images, too much animation, blinking text, inappropriate scrolling text, rambling text passages that never make a point, lack of paragraphs and white space, poor text contrast . . . the list goes on and on. If you don't have talent for creating a nice layout and design, find sites that do and emulate them. Notice I said emulate, not copy!

11. **JavaScript Text Scrolling:** Scrolling text has gone the way of blinking text and is considered annoying at best.

12. **Page Counters:** If you have a lot of traffic, page counters looks arrogant. If you don't, do you really want people to know that? Page counters are considered amateurish; if you really want to use one, hide it.

13. **Excessive Animation:** Animated GIF images are distracting and annoying if used too much. If you can make your own cool animations, great—but still limit the use. Otherwise, the best ones

at free archives have been overexposed, so using them makes your site look like hundreds or thousands of other sites. That's the last thing you want.

I also recommend against using free or generic "clip art" graphics. Most are rather cheesy, which is great for us Green Bay Packer football fans, but not good when it comes to your web site look.

14. **Page Fade-ins:** Having a page fade-in from one color to another seemed a bit amazing when it was first done. Since then, it's been done to death. The page transition effects built into Internet Explorer will likely fall into the overused category sooner or later as well.

15. **Frames:** Don't use frames unless you have a good reason and know what you're doing. Most framed sites are unnecessary, and many people detest frames. Besides, some search engines can't index framed sites. Why shoot yourself in the foot before you even publish your site?

16. **Yakkety-yak:** Don't spend too much time talking about yourself or your company. People are at your site to see what's in it for them—they care little about you until they find value in what you offer.

17. **Inconsistency:** Maintain a consistent look and feel throughout your whole site. Changing the look and feel from page to page makes people wonder if they've left your site. In addition, they may consider your web presence as less professional than your competitors.

18. **Lack of Updates:** Provide fresh content and updates on a regular basis. No one will keep coming back to see the same old thing. Repeat visits are vital to success.

19. **No Credibility:** The most obvious yet most important tip is to always be honest, ethical, and fair. I see far too many sites that don't seem to get it, and it's a critical issue to your online success. Word travels the online world at lightning speed. If you're a shady dealer, people will know sooner rather than later.

20. **Excessive Pop-ups:** This has fast become the most annoying thing going. Pop-up windows can serve a legitimate purpose, but if you overuse them, expect angry emails and declining traffic.

16.12 Accessibility

In response to my Guess the Celebrity contest entry form, someone typed the following comment (as a joke I assume):

"design your site for the blind — hahahaha"

What they probably didn't know is that blind people do access the Internet and do so without human help. How is this possible? They use software programs called screen readers. There are some basic design principles to follow when creating a site that is accessible to vision-impaired people, blind people, and people with other types of handicaps such as motor impairment.

1. Screen readers read from left to right. If you use tables, the information must be understandable that way.

2. Frames are a no-no. Most screen readers don't recognize when you change a frame and will not re-read that part of the screen. Of course, frames also kill your site with some search engines, so there's another reason to stay away from them.

3. Use alt text tags for all images so a screen reader can read your link buttons and other graphics.

4. Keep a high contrast between the text and background color.

5. Small link buttons are hard for motor-impaired people to click, so keep link buttons large enough to be clicked easily. Including text links in addition to buttons is a nice touch.

6. Keep a consistent layout.

7. Make sure your font size is large enough for your primary audience.

8. Finally, keep the page clean and uncluttered so it's easy to understand.

These are just the basics. If you'd like to learn more about making your web site more accessible for the handicapped, I recommend reading the World Wide Web Consortium standards at:

www.w3.org/TR/WAI-WEBCONTENT/

For a free online report of how your site stacks up in accessibility, try Bobby:

www.cast.org/bobby

313

16.13 Conclusion

A s I mentioned earlier, page layout and design are subjective. Beauty is in the eye of the beholder. The important thing to remember is to have an actual layout. Just putting up information in an unstructured way is not page design. Some general guidelines to remember are:

- Plan your site out before you start designing it.
- Divide each page, and your site, into logical sections.
- Have a consistent visual theme and site navigation throughout.
- Use colors that complement each other and provide contrast with the text.
- Use white space; don't try to crowd too much into too little space.
- Design for the major browsers and the most common screen resolution (800 × 600).
- Understated design is usually more effective than in-your-face design.

While everyone has his or her own idea of what good design is, don't minimize the importance of it. The first impression is often the last impression if you don't make a good first impression!

16.14 Chapter Quiz

1. Most Internet users connect at 56K or less. To ensure that your site loads quickly, the rule of thumb is to keep the index page's total file size to _____K or less.

2. True or False: You should use as much animation as possible because it grabs visitors' attention.

16.14 Chapter Quiz (continued)

3. True or False: White space is wasted space. You should fill all the white space with content so pages don't look barren.

4. True or False: Make important points in long paragraphs because visitors skip over short paragraphs, thinking they are unimportant.

5. Use as much color on your pages as possible because:
   a. It adds spice to pages
   b. It makes everything stand out better
   c. It prevents boredom
   d. You shouldn't use too many colors

6. You can improve navigation on large sites by using jump stations. Jump stations are:
   a. Category specific sub-index pages
   b. A site map of all the pages on your site
   c. Links programmed with an access key
   d. Gas stations where attendants jump up and down and cheer you on as you fill your tank

7. Choose the truest statement about background images:
   a. Change the background image on every page so visitors don't become bored
   b. Use the same background image on every page so your site has a consistent look and feel
   c. Use the same background image on every page so you can practice laziness and enjoy ennui
   d. Change the background image on every page so visitors know they're on a new page

16.14 Chapter Quiz (continued)

8. Choose the truest statement about banner ads:
   a. Add as many to your pages as possible so your site looks well sponsored
   b. Add as many to your pages as possible so you have a better chance of making money from affiliate programs
   c. Do not use more than one or two banner ads on your pages
   d. Bald men should rent out the tops of their heads for banner placement

9. Which statements, if any, are true in regards to screen readers:
   a. Use frames on your site so screen readers don't have to read repetitive items such as links over and over
   b. Screen readers read from left to right, top to bottom
   c. Use alternate text tags for images
   d. Screen readers are devices for detecting holes in screen windows

10. Using all capital letters in body text is:
    a. A good way to let people know your message is important
    b. Considered the equivalent of shouting in real life and should be avoided
    c. The professional way to let people know you're confident about your message
    d. A great idea because it makes the message easier to read

11. It's usually considered bad taste to wear clothing that clashes. Choose the truest statement about using colors that clash on a web site:
    a. It helps make each item stand out better so each item gets the user's attention
    b. It makes people realize yours is no ordinary web site
    c. It shows you're bold and daring, so it sets your web site apart from the competition
    d. What do you think I am, a knucklehead? You shouldn't use clashing colors on a web site

12. What web designer was so famous some birds even called out his name?

Promoting Your Site

17.1 Chapter Introduction

B uilding a web site is only half the task of establishing an Internet presence or business—promoting the site is the other half. Skipping the task of promoting your site means that few visitors will find you. There are millions of web sites, so getting folks to visit yours is no small undertaking. You should approach promoting your site as seriously as you approached building it.

Site promotion is 50 percent science, 50 percent art, and 50 percent luck. If you can add, you probably noticed that adds up to 150 percent—and that's how much effort you need to put into it! My site doesn't serve more than 800,000 pages a month because it's a great site; it serves that many because I've worked very hard to promote it (although having a nice site does help in the effort). In this chapter, you'll learn about all the things I've done to promote my site. I don't use all these techniques now that my site is well established, but all are important when you're starting out, especially if you don't have an established network of contacts.

17.2 Search Engines

S earch engines can bring you great quantities of traffic—if you place in the top 20 or 30 sites. If your site is lower than that, the traffic you receive from search engines drops off significantly. You've learned about meta tags, keywords, the title, image alt tags, and other elements that help your site rank higher. These things vary in importance from search engine to search engine, and can even vary in importance from month to month at the same search engine. Search engine creators are constantly revising their algorithms and changing the importance of this and that. You could work 12 hours a day, everyday, to figure search engines out (and some people do).

I don't devote nearly as much time to search engines as you might think. I've found that if you do the legal tricks and play within the rules, your site will usually be ranked fairly well by at least a few search engines at any given time (although your position may vary from month to month or even day to day). One month, you might have two top 10 rankings, while another month you might have eight. I submit my web site and forget it for months at a time.

Too many people spend all their time and energy focusing on search engines and overlooking all the other ways to promote their sites. Some say 90 percent of traffic comes from search engines. I suppose that's true—for those people, because that's about the only way they promote their sites.

About 40 percent of my traffic comes from search engines, 25 percent from bookmarks, and the other 35 percent are from other means. I'll discuss the other means in this chapter, since Chapter 12: Search Engine Optimization covers the search engine topic in full. I will just remind you of a few things regarding search engines first. Remember:

- Submit your site to the major search engines, by hand, one at a time.

- Make sure you follow all the rules for each search engine.

- Either buy software to submit your site to all the smaller directories and search engines you've never heard of (even to thousands of Free For All link pages if you want) or hire a service to do that for you.

Some webmasters will tell you it isn't necessary to submit your site to the small search engines that few have heard of because the traffic they offer is insignificant, but I disagree. While any one of them may be insignificant, because there are so many of them, they add up to a major traffic source when considered as a whole. For my site, it means about 10,000 to 20,000 unique visitors per month. That's a lot of traffic to ignore. If you're building a commercial site, that's a lot of sales you'll be missing if you ignore this traffic resource!

17.3 Beware of Submission Service Hype

S ubmission services may offer to submit your site on a schedule. It's a selling point. They tell you that you have to submit your site every so often for one reason or another. While I do offer a submission service, I don't offer recurring submissions because I don't believe in it.

If you resubmit your site too often or haven't made any updates since the last submission, the search engine could take that for spamming and lower your ranking or remove your listing. If you have a good position, resubmitting your site might cause your site to fall in position. Resubmitting on a timetable is a sales pitch to make you think you're getting more for your money. I often leave my site untouched on search engines for two years or more and have noticed no loss of position other than the regular fluctuations.

You'll hear, "We'll submit your site to five billion search engines!" The shear numbers are also hype. Only a dozen or so search engines and directories are vital, a few hundred are good, and the rest are Free For All (FFA) pages that will bring a trickle at best. Enough trickles from FFA pages do add up, but it's not like you're going to get thousands of hits from them. From most of them, you won't get any traffic at all because your submission will fall off the page within minutes because of automated submissions and limits on the number of listings at any one time on an FFA page. Note that FFA pages are not the same as small search engines. The traffic from small search engines can be significant, the traffic from FFA pages is not.

Nowadays, people own FFA pages so they can send email to you with their sales pitches and not get blamed for spamming you. After all, you did submit your site to them. It's called permission marketing. I still submit my site to FFA pages—because it doesn't hurt and the process is automated so it doesn't take any extra time—but I use an email account from a free email provider for the submission so I don't have to sort through the junk mail in my regular account. The free account is just a dumping ground for the volumes of junk mail. A week after submitting a site, I go to my free account and mass delete everything without even reading it. I don't give the address out for any other purpose, so I know there is nothing legitimate for me to be concerned with.

17.4 Link Trading Tips and Tricks

H ere, I share a few tips about trading links and swapping ads.

Reciprocal Links

One effective means of gaining traffic is through reciprocal links. Reciprocal linking means that you place a link to someone else's

319

site on your site, and in exchange they place a link to your site on theirs.

Ideally, you trade links with sites that have a reasonable amount of traffic and content that complements yours. You'll have to decide for yourself whether you want to trade links with competitors.

I have no fear of linking to competitors for two reasons. First, I think my content is good enough to stand on its own merit. Second, if traffic comes to me from a competitor's site, there is a very good chance it is qualified traffic. Plus, if they come to my site from a competitor's, they probably haven't found what they are looking for yet, giving me the chance to provide it.

Some webmasters don't like to trade links. They fear that links tempt visitors to leave their site. That's flawed thinking. Every visitor will leave your site sooner or later—whether they enter a new web address into the address bar, select a bookmark, use the back button, or click a link that you provide—they are going to leave at some point. If your content is good, users will leave your site later rather than sooner. If your content is bad, nothing you can do will keep them from leaving quickly. The best you can do is provide quality links for users to surf when they are ready to leave. They may think more highly of your site for that alone and come back again to check out more. Whatever excellent content your site provides is an asset, even if that content consists of links leaving your site.

I've already covered link trading in some detail in Chapter 12: Search Engine Optimization, but here's another resource for finding link trades:

www.hitbox.com/cgi-bin/page.cgi?my_ranking

> **NOTE**
>
> The link to the Hitbox directory may change. It changed from the first edition to the second edition of this book, so it could again. If so, you may have to hunt for the link, but this company has been around for a long time and providing visitor statistics to webmasters is a major part of their business, so the directory should be around somewhere.

Scroll down and find the category your site belongs in and click the link. Once in your category, you'll find all kinds of sites with similar content. Some will have competitive content and others will be complementary. The icing on the cake is that Hitbox includes a daily average of unique visitors that each site receives. That makes it pretty easy to find high-quality, high-traffic sites to try to trade links with. It only counts the pages where the Hitbox code has been placed, so it doesn't count all unique visitors. For example, I use the code only on my index page, but I have a lot of traffic to interior pages that doesn't get counted, but it will give you a good idea about any web site's traffic.

Swap Sponsor Ads

Here's another link-trading idea. Find sites that have like-minded audiences, a reasonable amount of traffic, and no paid ads. Put on your Elmer Fudd cap and hunt those wascally wabbits down. Offer to swap banner ads with them, or offer them a few dollars to post your banner if you don't want their banner on your page. They've probably never had an offer like that before and may well love the idea. Smaller sites can look like they have a real sponsor and that can enhance their image. Although users say they don't like banner ads, when you have paying sponsors some people do give you more credit as a professional. And if you don't overdo the banners, users really don't mind all that much.

This won't give you a lot of traffic—banner ads are more for branding than creating traffic. But banner ads will bring some traffic and every little bit helps. See the next section for tips on creating effective banners.

When you've exhausted these possibilities, you can use the search engines, web rings, online communities, and other resources to locate likely trade candidates.

Reciprocal Link Script

In case you skipped Chapter 12: Search Engine Optimization, I'll quickly mention a final way to obtain reciprocal links: using a CGI script is one of the easiest and most effective ways. If your host lets you use custom CGI scripts (and most hosts do if you pay for hosting) then you might want to consider Master Reciprocal Links. My good friend William Bontrager wrote this script, based on an idea of mine.

The Master Reciprocal Links script allows anyone who visits your site to add a link from your site to his or hers—pending your approval. Your approval, within the script, is based on whether they place a reciprocal link to your site on their own site. A little spider (software robot) will go out and check for the link so you don't have to physically visit their site to check it. The script includes a lot more features than that, which you can read about on my site if you're interested.

There is a free version and a professional version in the works. The free version carries an advertisement for my site and William's site at the bottom of your reciprocal links page. The professional version will be ad free and include more features.

You can generate a link script and automate reciprocal links (which requires a host that provides you with CGI access) for your own site here:

www.boogiejack.com/cgi-bin/makemrl.html

To trade links with my site, go to:

www.boogiejack.com/cgi-bin/mrlsf.cgi

17.5 Banner Tips

C reating an effective banner is part luck, part experimentation, and part smarts. An effective banner might average only a 10 percent click-through rate, or 10 or so click-throughs to your site out of every 100 times it's shown. The average rate of click-throughs is somewhere between 1 and 2 percent. Not great by any means, but it's on a par with having a link on another site. While you want to optimize your click-throughs as best you can, remember that the real power is in the numbers. The more links there are to your site, in as many places as possible, the more traffic your site will receive.

Here are a dozen down-and-dirty tips for creating effective banners:

1. Call to action. Believe it or not, a simple "Click Here" message will bring more click-throughs than the same banner without one.

2. Create urgency. "Last Chance," "Discontinued Soon," and similar phrases create an urge to NOT miss out on something.

3. Use the word "FREE!" This should be self-explanatory, but if you use the word for enticement, make sure you have something worthwhile for free. Getting people to your site under false pretenses is not the way to win friends and influence people.

4. Animated banners command attention, which can be good or bad. Excessive motion can become annoying in short order, especially if someone really wants to concentrate on something else on the page. Some banner exchanges limit the number of animation loops you can use, and I recommend limiting the loops whether it's required or not.

This plain looking banner yielded a 5.1 percent click-though ratio. The area displaying the

Boogie Jack's Web Depot All FREE!

words "All FREE" is animated. The words changed every couple seconds to "Graphics" then "Tutorials" and a few other words that appealed to webmasters.

The banner at right was not animated, and yielded a low 1.3 percent click-through ratio.

5. Bright, ugly colors work. As a graphic designer, this goes against my grain. But the fact is, some of the best looking banners I've made have had the lowest click-through ratios. Intentionally ugly banners have done fairly well.

6. Be innovative and experiment. Surfers have seen a million ads so just marching in line won't get you noticed. Strive for that "something different" feel. Originality is rewarded in nearly every aspect of the Internet.

7. Create a compelling reason to click the banner. Point out what the immediate benefit is. People want to know what's in it for them.

8. Make it believable. People will figure it out—either before or after they visit your site—but they will figure it out. Exaggerations get you absolutely nowhere.

9. If appropriate, offer a strong guarantee, and back it up. A strong guarantee wins over the indecisive.

10. Use emotional appeal. Ads work better when they appeal to emotion rather than intellect. People do things because they feel a certain way about something.

11. Mix in bold type and colored text for emphasis. For example, if you use the word "FREE" in your copy, make it stand out.

12. Use short sentences and weed out words and phrases that aren't essential. You're writing an ad, not a short story.

In addition to trading banners with other sites, you can join banner exchanges. The exchanges work on a ratio system. For example, for every two banners you display on your site, yours will be displayed once on another site. The extra banners are used by the banner exchange to promote themselves or they are sold to third parties. You'll find a searchable list of banner exchanges at:

www.bxmegalist.com

You can also go to your favorite search engine and search for "banner exchange." You'll find a ton of them—or at least 1,800 pounds worth.

17.6 Awards

Awards can bring traffic to your site, whether you receive the awards or give the awards. Literally thousands and thousands of sites offer web page awards. The only ones worth applying for are those that list the winners. The other sites are only in it to get links to their own sites. They are disparagingly referred to as "vanity" awards. All you have to do is ask for an award and you will get it from a vanity award site. In most cases, there is no judging criterion whatsoever for vanity awards.

Some sites that offer vanity awards even use autoresponders to answer your submission. An autoresponder is a software program that sends a predetermined message to anyone who sends a message to a specific email address. You apply for an award and almost immediately you get a reply stating you've won and your site is great. If you can send an email, you get a site reward. Big whoop, there's no glory in that—and no traffic to gain by receiving it.

A legitimate award site, which lists the winners permanently or for a period of time, can bring a great deal of traffic. These awards are worth applying for when you're starting out as they can help bring a large quantity of traffic to you for a short time. Read their judging criteria and apply for awards when you think your site passes muster. Things that will keep you from winning awards include "under construction" signs, broken links, broken images, lack of originality, lack of content, difficult navigation, lack of purpose, and 107 other things.

Another way to create traffic to your site is to give your own award. Before jumping into it, decide what type of sites you'd like to award and define your selection criteria.

For best results, try to find an un-exploited niche of sites. If your award is designed for a niche group, your chances of having sites accept the award and link it to your site are very good indeed. For credibility, the niche you identify should be a part of your content also. On the other hand, offering a general site award will allow more types of sites to apply, and may earn you more (but less targeted) links.

Unless you already have a popular site, you'll probably need to start small, awarding home pages, new sites, and sites in early growth stages. I haven't seen many awards for beginners, so that's an idea. You can always aim higher, but don't be surprised if established sites say thanks but don't display your award. Well-established, quality sites have received so many awards that most don't bother displaying them any more. Although they still appreciate the gesture, posting awards becomes an unproductive task after a while. These sites spend their time on more productive activities.

A new webmaster, however, would be thrilled to receive an award from you and would display it proudly. Not only do you get a link from a page you probably wouldn't have gotten, you get to make someone happy at the same time. It's really a win-win situation.

To increase the chances of having people apply for and display your award, you need to create a good-looking award graphic. If you can't design a good-looking award, find someone who can. I used to offer that service when I first started out. All you have to do is ask the right person and he or she will design it for a reasonable price. You also don't have to wait for someone to apply for your award. Seek out recipients and tell them how much you enjoyed their site. Stroke their ego a bit and offer them your award. It works.

If you offer an award, you need to list the winners on your site. If you don't, it will be perceived as a vanity award and you'll find a lot fewer people will apply for it, and fewer willing to accept it if you seek them out.

Don't forget to put up some sort of submission form or at least an email link for people to apply for your award. Once you start developing traffic to your site, you'll have a ready group at hand just hoping to win it. When you're ready to accept submissions for your award, then list the award with all the award sites you can find. Award sites, as you might guess, list sites that give awards. People seeking awards—the people you're looking for—are the people who go to award sites, so you'll have an eager audience vying for your awarding attention.

Offering awards was one of the methods I used to build up my traffic—back when my site averaged about 40 visitors a day! It helped get me started on the road to high traffic, and it can help you too.

My site offers many link graphics for others to use to link to me. A few of the more popular graphics are pseudo-award graphics. Many webmasters love them, and it's something you might want to consider. Here are a couple of my pseudo-award examples:

17.7 Signature Files

M ost email programs have a signature file feature. If yours doesn't, use a copy and paste signature until you get an email program that does. A signature file is a message attached to the end of any and every email you send. As long as you're initiating and replying to email, you might as well use a signature file to promote your site.

Signature files should be kept short. Many people use ASCII art in them, but that's not a good idea. The ASCII art looks great when you send it, but it often looks ridiculous on the receiving end. Because of different screen resolutions and email programs with different settings, the art is often just a scrambled mess when opened on another system. Scrambled eggs are OK, scrambled text isn't as appetizing.

A good signature file will include your sign-off salutation, your web site address, and a line or two about your site or business services. You might also include your position or title, your email address, or other items that help identify you and may serve to impress.

Here's an example:

All the best to you, Dennis

Owner and CEO
Boogie Jack's Web Depot
http://www.boogiejack.com

Boogie Jack's Web Depot is a webmasters' resource site featuring free professional graphics, web design tutorials, sound effects and other webmaster help. And you know, it's fun too!

Notice I get right to the "what's in it for them" part. I don't use statistics to show how popular it is and I don't list my awards, testimonials, or any other kind of "it's about me" information because they don't care about that. They want to know what's in it for them and that's what I give them. As the kicker, I let them know it's not just another boring, technical site—I tell them it's fun.

Another approach is using testimonials, another powerful advertising tool. If you have the right testimonial (that is short and to the point) you might try using it in your signature. The problem with including a testimonial in an email signature file is that you do have to keep it short. There is no room for explanations about the author of the testimonial and many recipients might think it's a company employee saying the niceties. I find it more effective to use the "what's in it for them" approach.

17.8 Usenet and Newsgroups

Site promotion isn't limited to email and the web. An often overlooked but sometimes excellent way to bring in visitors is through newsgroup postings. Newsgroups are public discussion forums sorted by topics. Messages are presented in a list called threads, which show the original message and the responses to the message. You can follow an entire conversation or just read the messages you are interested in.

To access newsgroups, you'll need a newsreader. You can use Microsoft's Outlook Express email program or the email program built into Netscape (in version 7, simply choose Mail & Newsgroups from the Windows menu; look around in the menus when using previous versions).

The messages in newsgroups are stored on news servers owned by ISPs, businesses, educational facilities, and other organizations. You can usually access newsgroups through your own ISP. Some have a small number such as 5,000 or 10,000, while others carry more than 50,000 newsgroups.

Whatever your area of expertise or interest, your ISP will probably have several newsgroups on that topic. Use your expertise to promote your site, or learn more about an area of interest so you can become an expert. Even if you don't think of yourself as an expert, you might be surprised to find that what you already know is just what a less-experienced person might be looking for—and to that person you will be an expert.

Depending on the group and the usefulness of your post, you can get anywhere from a few dozen to a few thousand new visitors over the course of two or three days. Posts do expire though, so you need to post once or twice a week to stay on top of it. There is a right way and a wrong way to go about it, of course. The wrong way will get you a box full of flames (nasty, derogatory email).

You don't want to just post a notice to come and visit your site, that's how you get flamed. Blatant advertisements are considered spam to group regulars and they don't appreciate it. Start by lurking—that is, just monitor the group for a few days to get a feel for it. Read some of the posts and watch for a group etiquette or FAQ posting that explains the protocols of the group. If you don't see one, ask by posting a message yourself.

When you're comfortable within the group, look for messages asking questions you can answer. Give a thoughtful answer and include your URL and a brief description of your site in your signature file. If it's a good answer and a popular group, you may see an almost immediate surge in traffic.

If no one is posting questions you can answer, ask an intelligent question and leave your signature file with it. Newsgroups can be an excellent way to receive help as well as gain traffic by helping others. Do realize, though, that not everyone that answers will necessarily know what they're talking about.

When posting to newsgroups, be prepared for an onslaught of spam if you don't take measures to stop it. Bulk emailers' use spiders on newsgroups to harvest email addresses. There are ways to avoid this spam trap.

Suppose your email address is abc@123.com, you could change it to:

abcREMOVE_THESE_CAPS@123.com

Most users will know to remove the "REMOVE_THESE_CAPS" part of the address if they want to contact you, while the words added to the address render it useless to bulk emailers. Not all users will know to change the address though, so you might add something like the following in your message:

To email me, remove the capital letters from the email address given. They are there to foil address-harvesting spam spiders.

You can find free and low-cost newsgroup readers at shareware sites or through a search engine. You can also access newsgroups via Outlook Express or Netscape, but I don't recommend it. For your convenience, here are two lists of newsreaders:

Windows users:

www.newsreaders.com/win/utilities.html

Mac OS users:

www.newsreaders.com/mac/utilities.html

17.9 Little-known Traffic Generator

A little known technique to generate a lot of traffic for a short time is to create special informational pages on current events. When something big makes the news, lots of people hit the search engines to learn all they can about it. Create an informational page and submit it to the search engines.

Infoseek, now called Go.com and powered by Google, used to be the best for this technique as they were the fastest to index new pages. Since few search engines add sites quickly, it's much harder to do now than it used to be. It helps to be able to anticipate news items. Google is the best bet of the large search engines. If you use auto submission software for your web site, use it to submit your topical pages, as many of the smaller search engines are able to add new URLs to their directory the fastest.

Since you'll be linking the special page to your site, make it an accurate and useful page, as it will be a reflection of you and your site.

Wondering how you can relate the event to your content? Actually, it doesn't have to. Post the information as a public service page and list yourself as sponsor. The page might be as simple as a page of links to good online news articles. You might ask, "If it's just a link page to other sites, how does that help me?"

Good question.

Some of the visitors will also visit your site. If you are a member of a banner exchange or sell your own ad space, just think how many ad displays you'll get when several thousand people come to find more information about whatever the event is.

Several years ago, a site that used this technique when Princess Diana died had more than 25,000 visitors above average in just one day! You can debate the merits of using a death to generate traffic, but you get to choose your own topics to report on. With your conscience as your guide, it's a moot point. Cool word, moot.

Moot, moot, moot.

If you're good at analyzing news events, you can make a page and submit it to all the search engines before most others do, ensuring that your page is everywhere first. As the story unfolds, just keep adding the content and links.

17.10 Ezines

One of the best promotional tools going today is ezines. Ezines, sometimes called eletters, are electronic magazines (newsletters) delivered by email or the web. Ezines offer several advantages over traditional marketing methods. By choosing which ezines to promote yourself in, you can target your audience to a great degree. The subscriber base of any reputable ezine consists of people who elect to hear from the publisher, so they are a willing audience. The cost per thousand subscribers is usually very reasonable when compared to other marketing methods.

You can also use ezines to promote your business for free! There are three ways to freely promote your site in ezines:

- By writing an ezine yourself.
- By submitting articles to established ezines.
- By trading ads spots with other ezines (if you have your own).

Writing Your Own Ezine

To be effective, your ezine should be published at least biweekly (that's every other week, not twice a week). Monthly ezines can be successful, and my biweekly ezine started out as a monthly, but they only bring a surge of traffic to your site once a month. You can get more information about subscribing to my ezine, which is geared toward beginner to intermediate level webmasters, people who like to read enlightening articles about success in life, and people who like a slightly off-the-wall sense of humor, by visiting my web site at www.boogiejack.com.

No matter how often you choose to publish, you must be sure of one thing—you must be sure you can produce the ezine on a regular schedule with quality content. Anything less than that and it's doomed to mediocrity or worse. To really stand out, strive for originality and uniqueness. Most ezines are lost in a sea of sameness.

For distribution options for your ezine, check the books resources page on my web site for a list of email list hosts. You could purchase software to run your list from your own computer, but this does present problems. The more successful your ezine, the more problems you can have. It can be very time consuming, your ISP may place limits on the amount of mail you can send, and someone could (and sooner or later probably will) forget they subscribed and accuse you of spamming them, which could result in you losing your Internet access if they complain to your ISP and your ISP sides with them.

List hosting services process your subscribe and unsubscribe requests for you, keep the customer database for you, and take care of all the little problems and technicalities associated with running an ezine. The free services are free because most insert a small advertisement. All you have to do is promote your ezine. Don't be discouraged if your subscriber base doesn't grow fast. There is a lot of competition for people's eyeballs, and most people already subscribe to several ezines. Just put out quality content and your audience will grow steadily as the word spreads.

It helps to archive your ezines on your web site so potential subscribers can read past issues. If your content is good, access to back issues sells. You should also put your subscribe invitation and instructions in prominent places, including your home page. I have my subscribe information on almost all of my pages, and my ezine grows by about 300 to 600 subscribers each month.

Submitting Articles

If you don't have time, or feel you can't produce quality ezine content on a regular schedule, then write articles whenever you can and submit them to other ezine publications. The drawback to this method is that you can't control who includes your articles or how often or when they appear. Other than not having to produce content so often, writing articles has other advantages. The articles could appear in ezines with large subscriber bases, producing a lot of targeted traffic for your site. Even if you do start your own ezine, you can, and probably should, still submit articles to other ezines to help increase your subscriber base.

Writing articles for other publications can help establish you as an expert in your field. If you write a good article that's included in a targeted ezine, it can bring a significant amount of traffic and new subscribers to you. When you submit an article to other ezines, your publicity comes in the way of a resource box (author's credits). A resource box is sort of an "about the author" blurb at the end of the article. Each ezine owner will set his or her own limit on the size the resource box can be, but it's usually in the range of five to eight lines. For example, a blurb about me in a resource box might look like this:

> Dennis Gaskill is an author, graphics and web site designer, and the creator and owner of Boogie Jack's Web Depot. Boogie Jack's Web Depot is a webmasters' resource site featuring free professional graphics, web design tutorials, sound effects and many other webmaster aids. You can visit his site to find the resources and help you need, and sign up for his free ezine for more articles like this one.
>
> www.boogiejack.com

Trading Ads

Trading ads with other publications is fairly straightforward. Most publishers will want to trade ads on a somewhat even basis. If you have 2,000 subscribers and try to trade with a publication that has 4,000 subscribers, they might trade or they might require two ads in your ezine for one in theirs. You never know until you try. Some publishers don't ask how many subscribers you have—they figure any publicity is good.

Some publishers exaggerate their subscriber base, and you can never really know if they are telling the truth. You have to take it on faith, as most won't give you access to their mailing list. That's as it should be—otherwise unethical publishers would steal the list and abuse it with spam. Most publishers assure subscribers that their names will never be bought, sold, or traded. If you want to be taken seriously, you should provide that same privacy assurance.

You can learn more about ezine publications and find free articles to supplement your own ezine at:

www.ezineuniversity.com

You can also join a mailing list exclusively for other publishers looking for ad swaps. It's a very easy way to find like-minded publishers. You'll find it at:

www.homebasedprofit.com/east

17.11 Web Rings and Alliances

W eb rings are groups of sites that join together in the common cause of cross-promotion. Rings are usually grouped together by a common theme such as graphics sites, poetry sites, women-only sites, or other common characteristics. All members display a graphic for the ring, which has links to the next site or the previous site in the ring. Each member site will also have a "List All Sites" link and a link to the ring home page so others can join.

Web rings can be a good way to generate traffic when you're just starting out, especially for personal sites. However, they may not be a good idea for business sites because it takes away from the professionalism of the site. A better idea for business sites is to create an alliance.

An alliance is an association of like-minded businesses that have similar target audiences and agree to promote each other by way of web site links or newsletter listings. Each site agrees to promote the others in the same or a similar way. Some freedom is usually given to allow for the various web site designs, but the reciprocity is roughly equal. Alliances such as these are rarely as obvious as web rings. Each site may simply place a row of buttons on their home page to the other sites involved, with no telltale label that it's a joint marketing effort.

Generally, you'll have to form your own alliances. But if you search for "web rings" on any search engine, you'll come up with several on any topic you need. You might also try:

www.webring.org

17.12 Offline Promotion

A key to success online is marketing your web site offline—in all the ways you would market a brick-and-mortar business. Wherever and whenever your company telephone number, address, and other information is printed, include your web site address. This includes:

- Letterheads
- Business cards
- Yellow Pages ads
- Newspaper display ads
- Classified ads
- Invoices
- Sales receipts
- Product packaging materials
- Direct mailings
- Business checks
- Magnetic signs on your business transportation
- The entrance to your business or a display window
- Everywhere!

Any promotional material you produce should include your web site address. The wider the use of your Internet address, the more reach it will have.

Answering Machines

How many times have you heard an answering machine message that announces the company's web address? Not many—but including it can make sales for you. Perhaps your web site will answer the question they were calling about. Or, by providing an email address or feedback/inquiry form on your site, you give customers an alternate way to contact you. If potential customers contact you this way, you have permission to market to them once in response. Since they represent a qualified lead at this point, it could be the difference between making and losing a sale.

Advertisements

We have already mentioned some forms of advertising, but other forms of advertising are equally relevant. Include your web address in any advertising you do. Other forms of advertising include:

- **Inserts and Flyers:** Promotional brochures loosely inserted into magazines and newspapers or used as handouts and stuffed into bagged purchases.

- **Joint Ventures:** Enlist the cooperation of other local merchants with web sites to print a local Internet guide. You can share the cost of printing and all can distribute it. That's a very handy reference for a consumer to have next to their computer.

- **Radio and Television Spots:** Although this is a pricier option, it is likely to reach a larger audience and can drive significant traffic to your site. If your web site is professional looking, you might get local stations to trade advertising airtime in return for promoting them on your site.

- **Press Releases:** If a newspaper picks up a story from a press release, the editors include only the information they care to. Therefore, be sure to include your web site address, emphasizing that the full story is on your web site. Newsworthy items for press releases include:
  - New launches (including a new web site)
  - New products or services
  - Business expansion
  - Employee promotions and new hires
  - Competitions
  - Industry news

Think Integration

Too many companies separate offline and online activities. They view their physical business as one entity and their web site as a separate entity. An integrated marketing approach is the most effective strategy.

Strategically placing signs for your web site in your physical store will not only generate more traffic to your web site, it shows the public you are a modern company interested in serving their needs in every way possible.

Print web cards for people to take, and place them by the cash register or other high-traffic locations. Web cards are simply business cards dedicated to your web site. If customers pick up your web card, they will likely visit your web site. The card should include your web site address and a brief, descriptive hook.

You can also use your web site to promote your physical store. Things like printable coupons, special sales, or events announced on your web site can increase walk-in traffic.

Be Creative

This section includes just a few ideas to increase your web site traffic by integrating it with your offline promotions. Be creative, you may make discoveries that will amaze you. If you make any traffic building discoveries on your own, I hope you'll share them with me by writing to me at:

Boogie Jack
P.O. Box 603
Plover, WI 54467

17.13 Chapter Quiz

1. Keyword density is:
   a. The length of your keyword phrases
   b. The ratio of keywords to non-keywords
   c. How many keywords you have in your keywords meta tag
   d. How stupid your keywords are

2. True or False: You should submit your site to search engines on a regular schedule.

17.13 Chapter Quiz (continued)

3. True or False: Link trading is a waste of time.

4. When creating a banner ad, you shouldn't use a call to action such as "Click Here" because:
   a. It's an insult to the viewer's intelligence
   b. It prevents the viewer from clicking another part of the banner
   c. It might not work and you'll look incompetent
   d. You should use a call to action

5. True or False: You should apply for as many vanity awards as you can find because they show how cool your site is.

6. A good signature file includes what three items?

7. You shouldn't blatantly promote your site in newsgroups because it will result in a box of flames. What are flames?

8. Writing articles for other ezines is a good promotional tool because:
   a. It helps establish you as an expert in your field
   b. It can bring targeted traffic to your site
   c. Both a. and b.
   d. You shouldn't waste your articles in other publications

17.13 Chapter Quiz (continued)

9. Promoting your web site offline:
   a. Is a bad idea because it divides your resources
   b. Is a sound, integrated marketing approach
   c. Is a useless idea because the target audience isn't online
   d. Is a stupid idea because nothing rhymes with silver

10. Publishing your own an ezine is an excellent way to keep in touch with others who have demonstrated an interest in your subject matter. If you write your own ezine, you should publish it at least:
    a. Every other week
    b. Every month
    c. Quarterly
    d. Whenever you eat ice cream

11. In business terms, a web card is:
    a. A system of referencing data similar to library catalog cards
    b. A business card dedicated to your web site
    c. An electronic greeting card (e-card)
    d. A snail mail postcard invitation to join your mailing list

12. If a web designer and a writer walked into a brick building, what would happen?

Good Things to Know

18.1 Chapter Introduction

T his chapter is a collection of good things to know if you want to be a webmaster. These tidbits will help you work more efficiently, help you understand acceptable behavior on the Internet, and hopefully teach you a few new things.

18.2 Netiquette

T he word netiquette is a marriage of the two words "Internet" and "etiquette." As you might have guessed, it describes proper etiquette on the Internet. The people who visit the Internet and build sites represent a melting pot of ideas, opinions, individuals, and cultures. As such, it has been likened to the days of no rules and no authorities in the Wild West. While that may be true for some, the vast majority of users quickly adapt to standards of conduct and voluntarily follow rules, both as a courtesy to others and to be respected by others. If you want to be accepted by the majority of users, and especially among the movers and shakers of the industry, you need to follow these accepted standards.

Most of these items are simple and amount to using common sense, but are often overlooked. There is no official set of rules, no central place to learn the rules, and no one authority to go by. What follows is my interpretation of the rules of Netiquette based on my experience. While these are expressed in my words, the rules are common knowledge to many.

- Don't send mass, unsolicited commercial email (UCE). This is known as spam, and is hated far and wide. Plenty of spammers exist, but they are so afraid of being known and hated as a spammer that they often use elaborate ruses to hide their true identity.

- Don't type in all CAPITAL LETTERS. It's considered the equivalent of shouting at someone face to face. It's also harder to read text in all caps because it detracts from a lifetime of word shape recognition. We're just not used to reading all capital letters, so when we encounter it, we have to slow down to read the message.

- When sending messages to people you don't know, keep it short and to the point. Many people are very busy and don't have time to read rambling, unfocused messages.

- Do not use deceptive subject titles in your email messages as an attempt to trick people into reading them. Also, don't mark messages as urgent when they are not urgent.

- When quoting others or replying to ezine publishers and other lengthy emails, edit out all but the relevant portion of the message or newsletter you're replying to.

- Never send messages to multiple recipients in a way that each recipient can see everyone the message was sent to—unless you're certain all the parties know each other. Newbies who forward false virus warnings are almost always guilty of this. The addresses could also fall into the wrong hands and someone will use them for spam. It's a breach of privacy to share contact information that has been entrusted to you among people who don't know each other.

- Never, EVER forward a virus warning unless you verify it first. About 99.9 percent of the virus warnings you receive by email are hoaxes. When you forward these bogus warnings, you only serve to perpetuate lies. Never forward chain letters either. You can lose your Internet access and your credibility if enough people complain to your ISP.

- Never assume the message you're sending will only be read by the person you intend it for. Never write anything you'd be ashamed or embarrassed to see on the evening news.

- Never send HTML email without permission. HTML email isn't compatible with all email clients so it looks like HTML source code to some. They often delete it without reading it rather than trying to decipher the message from the gibberish. Among the other reasons not to send HTML email:

  - It is slower to download. People like me who regularly receive hundreds of emails per day don't need the delays.

  - It uses more space on the recipient's computer, and many don't welcome that.

- It costs people more money to download if they pay by the hour.

- It ties up bandwidth and slows down the Internet.

  This list goes on and on . . . just trust me, never send HTML email to strangers and check with your friends first to see if it's welcome.

- Never add anyone to a mailing list without his or her permission.

- Never, EVER send file attachments with email without asking if it's OK first. The only exception to this is the vcard (virtual business card).

- Never trash someone's guest book or criticize him or her in public forums. If you have issues with someone, take it up with that person in private.

- Never blatantly advertise in newsgroups.

- Cite all quotes and references, respect copyrights.

- Many consider attaching return receipts to email messages an invasion of privacy. A return receipt means that when someone opens your message, his or her email program sends you a notification that the message was opened.

- Be careful what you write! A user can't see your facial expressions. Your token joke might easily be taken as sarcasm or insult. Remember, once your words are written and sent, the recipients can save them. Your words may come back to haunt you!

- The Golden Rule applies on the Net just like in real life. Do unto others as you would have them do unto you.

- You are not the center of the universe. When you write to someone hoping for a little of his or her time, don't expect an instant reply. People have other concerns. Be patient and respectful. One person wrote to me complaining that she asked me a question yesterday and hadn't received a reply yet. The messages were actually about 11 hours apart. The user went on to tell me how I should shut down my site if I wasn't going to reply promptly, and went on and on about her problem. The user was looking to me for help, and then became rude when she didn't get a response fast enough to suit her. Do you think I helped her? If you said no, you win a dust bunny and a pebble. Send $5 to me for shipping and handling to claim your prize.

- Don't be confrontational. There is intelligent life out there. If you're a troublemaker, I guarantee you will sooner or later be on the ugly end of a verbal butt kicking, with your only recourse being to slink away to lick your wounds.

- Share. Everyone starts out on the Internet as a newbie. Others probably helped you along the way. When the opportunity arises, give back.

- Be forgiving. Everyone makes mistakes. Don't play it up to be bigger than it is, and forgive and forget when asked.

- Keep your ego and power in check. No one likes a bully and no one likes to be lorded over. Remember, there are real people with real hearts and feelings behind all the email addresses, web sites, and all of cyberspace's places.

As you can see, netiquette primarily consists of treating your fellow men and women as you would like to be treated—with respect and dignity. When all you see in front of you is your computer, it's easy to forget there is flesh and blood on the other end of the line. Your words can often make a person's day or ruin it. I encourage everyone to be a builder and not a destroyer. Anyone can insult and degrade others—it doesn't even take brains. But it does take an ounce of courage and a pound of heart to help build up others. That's something missing in many people's lives: someone to encourage them and give them a shred of respect to hang on to. When it comes down to basics, everyone wants to be liked. You can feed that need and be an unsung hero.

18.3 Copyrights and Bandwidth

S erious legal issues surround copyright violations and stealing bandwidth from other sites. Read on for specific information that will help you stay on the straight and narrow.

Copyrights

Downloading an image from a web site is theft—unless permission is expressed beforehand, such as with an image archive. Most people who wouldn't shoplift from a store don't think twice about stealing web site content. Most do it out of ignorance, but ignorance, as you may know, is no excuse in the eyes of the law.

Many sites, such as mine, make it clear that free images are available. You may download and use those images since permission is granted beforehand. This does not mean you can do anything you want with these images, such as using them to create your own graphics archive or remaking them into a new image. The creator of the images still holds the copyrights; you are simply granted a nonexclusive license to use them in an acceptable manner. This license does not extend to other images not included in the free archives and may be revoked at any time.

The same rules apply to text. Each page has implied copyrights by virtue of being published, whether there is a copyright notice or not. You cannot legally take text any more than you can take graphics—unless you have consent from the copyright holder.

Here are five myths about Intellectual Property Copyrights:

Myth 1: If it doesn't have a copyright notice, it's free to use.

Fact: This was true at one time, but today most nations abide by the Berne copyright convention. Original works created after 1989 are copyrighted whether a notice is provided or not. This applies to web sites too. Once a web site is published (placed online) it has copyright protection, providing the content was not stolen from another in the first place.

Myth 2: If I make up my own story based on someone else's story, the new story copyrights belongs to me.

Fact: These kinds of works are called derivative works. If you write a story using settings or characters from someone else's work, you need that author's permission. The lone exception is for parody.

Myth 3: Copyright violation isn't a serious offense.

Fact: In the United States, a commercial copyright violation involving more than 10 copies or more than $2,500 is a *felony*.

Myth 4: If I don't charge for the content, it's not against the law to use it.

Fact: If you charge for it, penalties and awarded damages can be more severe. But penalties and damages can be awarded whether you charge for it or not.

Myth 5: Copyrights expire after three years.

Fact: A work that is created (fixed in tangible form for the first time) on or after January 1, 1978, is automatically protected from

343

NOTE

These five myths about Intellectual Property Copyrights are taken from my eBook titled, *eBook Farming: How to Grow Money Selling Your Words and Ideas.* More information is available at: www.ebookfarming.com.

the moment of its creation and is ordinarily given a term enduring for the author's life plus an additional 70 years after the author's death, or until the author has legally transferred the copyrights to another entity.

Final Note on Copyrights: Facts and ideas can't be copyrighted, but the way those facts and ideas are presented and the system of implementation can be. You can write about anything that you research, as long as you use your own words and style of presentation.

Bandwidth Can Be Stolen Property Too

Bandwidth occurs when something is downloaded. For example, if you have a web page that is 40K in total file size, when some clicks a link to that page, 40K of bandwidth is used from the site that hosts the page and page content. It is possible to link to files that are not on your own server—for example, you might link to an image on another web site and have it display on your site. This is bandwidth theft unless you have permission to do it. Note that this is not the same as linking to someone else's web site.

When you link to someone else's web site, you are sending a visitor to that site. However, when you link to files on someone else's site in order to have those files display on your site, the other site is using its bandwidth to furnish content to your site. Since excessive bandwidth usage can be costly, this is highly illegal. Before filters were put in place on my site, bandwidth usage caused by others linking to graphics on my server caused an excessive usage charge of $5,000 for one month!

Many free graphics sites such as mine get thousands of visitors per day. If just one-tenth of those visitors linked to just one graphic, in a short time thousands of people would be stealing bandwidth from the site.

Using my site as an example, if just one-tenth of my visitors illegally linked to graphics on my server, in one year's time more than 100,000 people would be stealing bandwidth from me. As a novice, you probably don't realize that I have to pay for that bandwidth. Not only is it money out of my pocket, but also it slows down my site tremendously for other users because my server is sending out information to thousands and thousands of other sites at the same time.

You can see why some sites shut down because of the high cost of popularity. It's just not fair for anyone to expect us, the people who provide free things for everyone's enjoyment and benefit, to pay money out of our pockets for illegal linking because someone is too lazy to learn or to be bothered with doing things the right way.

Just Be Kind

Graphic artists and designers do not deserve to lose their web sites because of this ever-increasing problem. Please be kind enough to allow those of us who give so freely to keep enjoying what we do. If not, the best graphics sites will disappear and you will have to pay for every decent graphic you use or will have to make your own. No more freebies!

You Can Easily Be Caught!

People don't realize how easily they can be caught stealing band-width. Each time a file is called from the server, it is recorded in what is called a log file. If you link to a graphic on someone else's server, it records the web site the file is called from. Therefore, if you link illegally to someone else's files, each time your page is accessed by anyone, the link is recorded on the host server.

If you've signed up with a free host, you may think you can still get away with it. Perhaps you used a fictitious name and address when you signed up and used a free email account too. That doesn't matter. Every time you send an email or create, modify, or add content to a free web site, your ISP records your IP address. Your IP address can easily be tracked to your ISP, who has logs of which account used which IP address on what dates and what times. You are **never** completely anonymous on the Internet. These are the same files the FBI uses to catch child pornographers, hackers, and other nefarious types.

What the Law Says

Log files are considered legal evidence and you can be sued for stealing bandwidth or copyrighted property. Damages can be awarded into the six-figure range, plus proven costs. *Proof of monetary loss isn't necessary for damages to be awarded.*

Many graphic artists, myself included, invisibly watermark our images so copyright protection is intact even if you use screen capture software to obtain the image. I haven't had to sue anyone, but I have had offenders' sites shut down and they've lost their ISP accounts. I'm very serious about protecting my original content, as are most quality sites. Now, bear in mind I've only done this with sites that refused to cooperate with my request to cease and desist.

In Conclusion

The long and short of it is, don't steal images or bandwidth. If you are taken to court and forced to pay damages, it can mess up your life for a long, long time. It's just as easy to do things the right way. Think about it.

18.4 Spotting a Hoax

E mail hoaxes are usually intended as pranks, but in reality, they are nuisances that make you look silly for forwarding them. They can range from warnings about nonexistent viruses to bogus rewards for forwarding the email or even cruel letters that play upon users' sympathy regarding dying or missing children.

A few commonalities will help you spot hoaxes. A hoax often uses technical sounding language, claims associations with people of authority, or mentions personal acquaintances.

For example, with technical sounding language, a hoax may say, ". . . it uses mathematical harmonics convergence to reallocate binary data fields that will destroy your hard drive through infinite loop interrupt requests."

Yeah, whatever.

Or, a hoax may claim, "This happened to my girlfriend's brother so I know it's true," or they may reference corporate officers, doctors, lawyers, and other official types. The hoax writer may even sign the letter as one of these people to make it seem official and important sounding. The writers try to make their hoaxes seem real by association.

An email that says, "pass this letter on to everyone you know," should raise a huge red flag. That's how hoaxes are spread—by well-intentioned but misguided email users. Another red flag is a message that purports to be an FCC warning or other governmental agency warning. The FCC does not issue warnings, nor do most governmental agencies.

In short, don't forward any warnings that you haven't investigated for authenticity. Here are some reputable sites where you can investigate virus warnings and chain letters:

www.symantec.com/avcenter/

www.f-secure.com/news/hoax.htm

www.virusbtn.com/

www.stiller.com/hoaxes.htm

http://hoaxbusters.ciac.org/

http://vmyths.com/

All the sites feature hoax information and the first three also cover actual viruses. These sites all verify any information they disseminate and can be trusted as authorities.

18.5 Copying and Pasting

ne of the handiest computer skills you can learn is to copy and paste. It can save you hours of typing each week. If you know how to do this, just skip this section. I'm always amazed, however, at how many users don't know how to copy and paste. I recently showed this to one person who has been using a computer longer than I have because they'd never heard of it. To copy and paste:

1. Place your cursor on one side of the text you want to copy and highlight it by pressing your left mouse button and holding it down. (On a Mac, simply hold the single mouse button down.) Continue to hold the mouse button down and drag your cursor to the end of text you want to copy. The text should be highlighted with a color now. At the end of the text you want to copy, release the mouse button. If you did it correctly, the text should remain highlighted.

2. Next, click the Edit command on any program's menu bar to display a menu. From the Edit menu, select Copy. This will copy the highlighted text to your computer's clipboard. You won't see anything happen, but it did. You can also use a keyboard shortcut to copy. On Windows, press the Ctrl and C keys at the same time to copy highlighted text. On a Mac, press the Command (aka Apple) and C keys at the same time.

3. Now that you have the text copied to the clipboard, you can paste it into any file in any program that supports text. Decide where you want the text to go in a document, place the cursor there, and then click once. The cursor should flash. (You can also copy images this way in some programs. You can paste the image into any program that supports images.)

4. To paste the text into the spot where the cursor is flashing, click the Edit command on the program's menu bar. From the Edit menu, select Paste. This will paste the clipboard contents into your document, provided the program supports the content. You can't, for example, paste an image into Notepad because Notepad doesn't support images. You can also use a keyboard shortcut to paste. On Windows, press the Ctrl and V keys at the same time to paste copied text. On a Mac, press the Command and V keys at the same time.

You will do this so often that you should make an effort to memorize the keyboard commands: Ctrl+C/Command+C for Copy and Ctrl+V/Command+V for Paste. What took a page to explain here takes only seconds to accomplish. It's a handy skill you'll use over and over.

18.6 Unsubscribing from Spammers' Mailing Lists

H ave you ever gotten spam with some sort of unsubscribe link, even though you never subscribed in the first place? Of course you have. Have you ever tried it, only to have the mail come back as undeliverable? Or worse, you get spammed even more from the same party? If you've been on the Net for a few years, you probably had all that happen and more.

When spam was in its infancy, trying to unsubscribe from a list you didn't subscribe to usually meant you had confirmed your email address as a responsive user. The spammer would then sell his or her list of confirmed addresses to other spammers as a responsive list, which was worth more money, and of course, this resulted in still more spam. Back then, there were more spammers buying and selling lists than there were spammers offering legitimate unsubscribe options—so trying to unsubscribe actually increased your inbox junk mail clutter.

Now though, you can help yourself receive less spam by trying the unsubscribe links they offer. I'm not inferring spammers have suddenly gone ethical, because some out there are still operating as shadily as ever, but the industry has tried to change its image some. Most of the time, you will be able to unsubscribe from unwanted mailing lists.

Unfortunately, with some of these "companies," you somehow often seem to be magically subscribed again at a later date, but at least you are removed for a period of time.

18.7 Converting RGB Color to Hexadecimal Code

M ost graphics programs will tell you the RGB value of a color, but many won't tell you the hex value, which is what you need for web pages. Windows 95 and later provides a way for you to find the hex value of an RGB color.

1. Click the **Start** button. Choose **Program Files**, then choose **Accessories**, then choose **Calculator**.

2. Make sure **Scientific** mode is checked in the **View** menu.

3. Across the top are seven radio buttons, a group of four and then a group of three. In the first set, click the radio button for **Dec** (decimal). In the second set, click the radio button for **Degrees**.

4. Next, follow these instructions to convert an RGB number to a hex code:

   a. Enter a value for the **Red** field (for example, 159).

   b. Click the **Hex** radio button. The number will change to 9F—the red hex value.

   c. Go back and change the radio button to **Dec**.

   d. Enter a value for the **Green** field (for example, 122).

   e. Again click the **Hex** radio button. The number will change to 7A—the green hex value.

   f. Go back and change the radio button to **Dec**.

   g. Enter a value for the **Blue** field (for example, 223).

   h. Again click the **Hex** radio button. The number will change to DF—the blue hex value.

So from the RGB color values of:
Red: 159, Green: 122, Blue: 223

We have calculated the exact hex color value of:

9F7ADF

If you're not sure what color you want, visit my color machine and play around with the controls. When you find a color you like, just look in the box for the hex code.

www.boogiejack.com/colormach.html

There is also a conversion chart in Appendix A of this book. If you're online when you need to convert an RGB color, you can use this online converter:

www.univox.com/home/support/rgb2hex.html

18.8 Creating a Good Password

In your life online, you'll need to use a password with regularity. Most people want to create a password that is easy to remember, such as their birthday, their maiden name, their middle name, their dog's name, and things like that. The trouble with that is, if it's easy to remember, it can also be easy to guess.

People also tend to use the same password for everything so they don't have to remember several different ones. There's a problem with that too. If someone learns or guesses your one password, they will have access to everything you use the password for.

It's better to use a unique password for each and every place you need one, and to make them hard to guess. Keep a list on paper of all your user names and passwords as you collect them. Each time you create a new user name and password, add it to the list immediately. I'm recommending actual hard copy here—if you keep the list on your computer, it can be accidentally deleted or become corrupt.

A good password consists of a mix of uppercase and lowercase letters, plus numbers. Some web sites and software programs also allow using extra characters (@ $ %, etc.), which makes passwords even harder to crack. Be sure to use more than the minimum number of characters required—the more characters you use, the harder it is to guess or hack.

Some people use a system to create unique passwords. A comedienne friend of mine uses a name that is easy for her to remember, but then moves each character over and up a row on the keyboard. Doing this, the name "Anthony" becomes "Qh5y9h6," which is much harder to guess than Anthony.

You can create your own system, just remember to make your passwords hard to guess and keep track of them off your computer in case of any computer problems.

18.9 Enabling Thumbnails in Windows Explorer

I f you want an easy way to view thumbnails of images, but don't want to buy or install any new software, then I have a tip for you. In some versions of Windows you have an option that's pretty nifty. Open Windows Explorer and right-click the folder in the left pane with the graphics you want to view as thumbnails, and then choose **Properties.** Check the box at the bottom that says **Enable Thumbnail View.** Click **Apply.**

Next, highlight that folder to open it. Click the **View** menu and notice that the **Thumbnails** command is added to it. Simply choose **Thumbnails from the View** menu to display thumbnails of all compatible files types, including HTML pages. If you don't see the **Thumbnails** command, close the Windows Explorer, then reopen it. You may also need to close and reopen Windows Explorer to actually see the thumbnails once you've set a folder to display them.

To add the **Thumbnails** command to the **View** menu, you need to perform these steps individually for each folder of graphics that you want to view.

18.10 Better Graphics in AOL Browsers

A OL users often write to me about poor image quality or complain that when they try to save a GIF or JPG image it turns into an .art file. This is because, by default, AOL browsers are set to display compressed images, which don't look as nice. The browser saves the images in its own format, thus the .art images resulting from GIF and JPG files. All is not lost though—you can correct this browser behavior.

Here is how to turn off AOL image compression: (I have no way to verify it, this was sent to me by an AOL user.)

1. Click **My AOL** at the top of the screen.
2. Click **Preferences.**
3. Click **WWW.**

351

4. Click **Web Graphics**.

5. Uncheck **Use Compressed Graphics**.

6. Click **Apply**.

If you return to a previously visited page, AOL will load the old compressed graphics from the cache. A browser's cache is where web pages you've visited are temporarily stored on your computer. If you revisit any of these pages before the stored pages expire, you may be viewing pages that are on your computer rather than on the site. To change that, you need to clear out your temp files while you are still in MY AOL/Preferences. To do that:

1. Click **General**.

2. Click **Delete Files**.

3. Click **Apply**.

Enjoy the web in glorious full color.

18.11 Finding a Good Web Host

F or a web site to be available on the Internet, it has to be located on a web server somewhere. However, finding a good web host for your web site can be a daunting task. A web host makes server space available to you at a price; you're basically renting space on the server. There are free hosting services, but if you're serious about having an Internet presence, I don't recommend them. Free services are fine for personal pages, but not much more than that. With a free-hosted site, your options are very limited and so is your perceived credibility. To be taken seriously, you need your own domain name and some flexibility, and that usually means paying for server space. Take a look at the options for hosting plans.

Free Non-Virtual Hosting

If you need somewhere to host a personal web site, choosing a web host is a simple task. Dozens of free hosts can give you space in a directory under their domain, such as:

www.thehost.com/somedirectory/yourname

There are a few drawbacks to this:

- Your web site address is usually long and hard to remember.
- You usually have to display advertising for the host.

> **NOTE**
>
> These instructions are subject to change because of browser changes after the book is published. If so, you may have to explore the menus to find where or how to make the changes. You can also use a search engine to find more current instructions.

- Web site extras such as CGI scripts, autoresponders, and other goodies are very limited in availability if they are available at all.

- The amount of web space dedicated to you is predetermined by the host and very limited.

- You're restricted in what you can do with the site. For example, most free hosts don't allow you to run a business or display banners if you belong to an affiliate program.

- If you move your site, all the links pointing to it will be lost.

Free Virtual Hosting

If you are on a tight budget, but want to have a web presence, then free virtual web hosting may be the solution for you. You will be able to host your web site with your own domain name such as:

http://www.yourname.com

Or it could be in a sub-domain, such as:

http://yourname.yourhost.com

Usually, with this type of site, you will have to display the host's advertising on your web site as well. If you move your site, all the links pointing to it will be lost if it's a sub-domain. If it's a true domain name that you own, however, your links will be preserved when you move your site. The amount of space dedicated to you is usually restricted and so may be the options of what you can do with your site.

Virtual Hosting

Virtual hosting means you can host your web site using a domain name of your choice from available domain names, such as:

http://www.yourname.com

Your options really open up here. To start with, you can choose the amount of web space you need from among a list of plans. You can choose from many other options as well, such as having your own CGI bin, your own domain email, autoresponders, and dozens of other enhancements. You will be hosted on a server that you share with other virtual hosting clients. You won't have to carry advertisements for the host and you will have a professional image. You can change hosts with minimal hassle and you won't lose your incoming links.

Dedicated Server Hosting

A dedicated server means that you rent the use of a whole machine. Since you are renting a machine instead of space on a shared machine, you have more control over what software is installed. The main benefit is that you're usually allowed much more data transfer. Data transfer is the amount of data the server sends out on your behalf. This is not an inexpensive option, so renting a dedicated server isn't something you will want or need to do until your site has developed a strong presence and high traffic.

Reseller Web Hosting

You can also resell web hosting for your host. Reseller plans let you act as a web hosting company—but usually don't require you to set your clients up or lease the lines. If you're reading this book, this probably isn't something you're ready to do. You need experience to be a reseller because you'll need to provide technical support to your resold accounts.

Data transfer is the amount of data that is piped out from the host on your behalf. Many hosts will claim unlimited data transfer as well, but if you pin them down, there are limits. Hosts make that claim because it's reassuring and wins new customers—and because very few of the sites they host will approach the point at which the host has to restrict your account or force you into moving your site or upgrading to more expensive plans.

This isn't something you will have to worry about unless your site becomes very popular. It's a nice problem to have though. To give you an idea, most sites use less than a gigabyte of data transfer per month. I didn't have to upgrade to a more expensive solution until I started using about 15 gigabytes of data transfer a month. Not all hosts will let you go that far—and some may let you go higher. But once you get in the 15-gigabyte neighborhood, you'll have to start looking at a higher-end solution. You may be wondering, just how much data transfer is 15 gigabytes. For me, it was when my site was serving about 700,000 page views per month. That's an awful lot of traffic.

> **NOTE**
>
> The area of data transfer is misleading to many people. Many hosts offer unlimited bandwidth, and people take that to mean data transfer. But bandwidth and data transfer are two different things in the eyes of the host. Bandwidth is the amount of data that can be piped out from the host at any given moment. It's their total data transfer capacity, but you share this capacity with everyone else on the server. When a host says you will have unlimited bandwidth, it's misleading because it only means you have as much of the bandwidth that is available after it's divided between all the sites hosted on the same server as yours—but their bandwidth is not unlimited so yours can't be either. What they should say is that they won't place any artificial restrictions on your bandwidth.

For help in locating a hosting company, you can search host-rating sites. They allow users to vote on web hosts and rank them according to user voting and a mix of other criteria. One thing to be aware of—the host is never as bad as the worst reviews or as good as the best. The worst reviews are usually submitted when someone has just had a bad experience with their host and they want revenge. The best reviews are often submitted by someone associated with the host in some way, and they are intended to drive up their rating. It's also possible that some host-rating services have gone the way of search engines and the top listings are paid placements. Take everything with a grain of salt.

The best way to find a good host is to ask web site owners you respect to recommend one. If they are satisfied with their hosts, they will probably recommend them.

Try these host-rating indexes for help in finding a host:

www.hostindex.com

www.webhostdir.com

www.ihostcafe.com

You'll also find hosts that I've had good experience with listed on the books resources page on my site at:

www.boogiejack.com/book/resources.html

If you're looking for a free web host provider, you'll find the majority of them listed at:

www.freewebspace.net/

What's the Norm?

Virtual hosting is the most common and most sensible way for a business to start out. It allows people to start a serious business or online presence at a fairly low cost. They can increase the services they purchase as their needs grow, and can move their site if need be without losing all they've worked for. A typical virtual hosting plan can range from under $10 to more than $100 per month, depending on the features you need and the host you select. The options and costs vary greatly, so do your homework or you could be paying more for less if you make a poor choice. Don't skip the research, as you'll pay for a poor choice over and over again.

To choose a hosting plan, first identify your needs. Make a list of the things that are "must haves" and another list of things that

355

would be nice to have. A host may make many options sound exciting, but will you use them? If not, there's no sense paying for them. Think about picking a host that will allow you to upgrade your hosting package as your needs grow. For example, say you pick a host based solely on cost, but know that in the future you will need a feature the host doesn't offer. It will be easier to find a host now that offers a smaller plan for your current needs plus offers the features you need later than to find a new host later and move your site.

18.12 Registering a Domain

I f you've picked out a web hosting company and a domain name, most web hosting companies will register the domain for you at no additional charge. Be sure the company lists you as the administrator (owner) of the domain. Some unscrupulous companies register themselves as the administrator, and then try to use that to prevent you from moving your site if the need arises.

There are many registrars you can use to register a domain name. Prices vary from a little under $10 per year up to $35 per year. Personally, I like using 000domains. It's easy, fast, and just $13.50 a year, plus the support has been excellent when I've needed it. You'll find them at:

www.000domains.com

Note that those are zeros, not the letter O in the web address.

Once you log onto 000domains, type the domain name you want into the **Search A Domain Name** field, select an option from the menu (.com, .net, .org, etc.), and then click the **Check Domain Name** button. If the domain name is available, you will be given the opportunity to register it on the next page. If the domain name is not available, you will be notified and can search for a new name. If you have a list of names, you can use the **Search A Group Of Domains** field to search for them all at once.

18.13 Spell Checking Documents

B efore you post pages for the world to see, spell check them! Wouldn't you rather find the errors than have someone else write to you and point them out? I would . . . and people *will* write to you and point them out.

Many text editors and HTML editors have built in spell checkers, and there are online spell checkers as well. Some check the spelling of pages that are online, while others let you copy and paste text into a field to check. At:

http://www.spellcheck.net/

. . . you can paste your text into a text field and click the **Check Text Body** button. It processes your text, shows you the words that may be misspelled, and offers suggestions. Below is a graphic showing the results of a spell check I ran on a document with a few intentionally misspelled words.

As you can see, the misspelled words are displayed in a field with an accompanying drop-down list of possible correct words. You can choose a replacement spelling from this list.

I typed in a few words and | intenshunally ▼ | spelled some wrong so ewe could see what it looks like with questionably | speld ▼ | | werds ▼ |.

| werds ▲ |
| wards |
| words |
| worlds |
| ward |
| wars |
| word |
| wardship |
| world |
| worse |
| worst ▼ |

You might also notice that I typed "ewe" instead of "you." Spell checkers can't find mistakes like that, which is why it is also necessary to proofread your pages.

You can also spell check web pages that are online. Use a good search engine to look for online spell checkers and you'll find several.

18.14 Gluing Your Visitor's Eyeballs to Your Copy

C atchy title, huh? It creates curiosity and makes you want to read this article so you can find out what it's all about. I've glued your eyeballs to this tip.

Whether you have a business or personal web site, the one thing both have in common is the need for page copy that is compelling enough to make visitors want to read it. Would you

357

like to know HOW to keep your visitors reading your message from one paragraph to the next?

You just witnessed one way—ask a question! This simple but effective writing trick can be used from one paragraph to another, or from page to page. Of course, there are other techniques to writing good copy, and that's what this tip is about. Would you like to see 10 great tips for writing bang-up copy?

1. To glue your visitor's eyeballs to your copy, lead them from paragraph to paragraph or page to page by asking questions, then answering them in the next paragraph or at the beginning of the next page. Of course, it isn't practical to do that with each paragraph, but the idea is to continually engage their minds to keep their interest. Build anticipation and they'll read with appreciation!

2. Good writing flows smoothly. Each sentence, paragraph, and page should have a natural rhythm that makes reading an easy progression of ideas rather than a chore to follow.

3. Good writing is focused. Don't stray far from the objective of the copy. Causing the reader to jump back and forth between nonrelated ideas can make visitors feel lost in your words. If they're lost in your words, you've lost them.

4. Good writing is simple and tight. Eliminate unnecessary words. Using language to excess may make you feel more serious as a writer, but readers best understand simplicity. Use casual conversation as your guide.

5. Practice. The more you write, the better you'll become at it. Use descriptive wording to create mental pictures. Use action words to create excitement. Write to bring out emotions to make readers personally involved with what you're saying. Be honest to be credible.

6. Remember the basics. Capitalize what should be capitalized. Use commas sparingly because they break up the natural flow of text. Keep paragraphs short and brisk to leave plenty of white space. Use a spell checker.

7. Don't write anything that you wouldn't say to someone's face. It's easy to be bold and forceful in print, but is that really you? Be your higher self and be true to who you are—that will bring out the best in you.

Add visual magnetism to your text.

---

8. Make use of pull quotes, headings, and subheadings to add visual appeal to your copy. With interesting, provocative, or curiosity-provoking text set apart from the copy, readers are more inclined to read your messages.

9. When you've finished writing your text, rewrite it. You'd be surprised how much better copy can become with a rewrite or two. For example, my Life's Little Goodies columns usually receive three or four rewrites before I conclude the Law of Diminishing Returns* applies.

10. Read it out loud. While writing, it's easy to miss the overall tone of the message, especially if you're not in a good mood when you write. Reading aloud also helps locate passages where the text doesn't flow smoothly, where you've made mistakes, and where more clarification is needed.

18.15 Installing CGI Scripts and CHMOD

This tutorial is intended for those with little or no experience installing CGI scripts. It only covers installing ready-made scripts you can find at free script resources; it does not cover customizing scripts for your own purpose.

What is a CGI Script?

CGI is an acronym for Common Gateway Interface. It's not a programming language, as many novices believe, it's actually a small, uncompiled software program that provides a way for a web server to communicate with a browser in ways not possible with HTML alone. Most CGI scripts are written in a programming language called Perl. Although other languages can be used to create CGI scripts, Perl is by far the most common, so this tutorial will focus on Perl scripts.

A Perl script is actually a common text file written in the Perl language and saved with a .cgi extension (or .pl extension for some

---

* The Law of Diminishing Returns is when you reach the point where the improvements you make to the copy no longer justify the time it takes to find and make them.

scripts). CGI scripts are server-side scripts, which means the scripts are executed on the server with only the output of the script shown in the browser. This is the opposite of most JavaScripts, which are usually scripts contained within an HTML page and executed client-side, by the viewer's computer.

Requirements

1. Before looking for scripts, first check to see if your web host supports them and that you have permission to use them. Some don't allow them; especially free hosts. If you've seen a folder called cgi-bin or cgibin when you uploaded your HTML files, then you are most likely allowed to use them.

   With some hosts, you may have to request that they create a CGI directory for you as it's not always included by default (even with hosts that allow and support them). A few hosts may even want to test and approve any scripts before allowing you to use them.

2. You also need a text editor to edit the script (Notepad, Textpad, etc. on a PC, or SimpleText on a Mac). You won't have to edit much, if anything, but you will need a text editor and not a word processor. A word processor may add formatting to the saved file, which will break the script. Whatever you use, you must be able to save the file as plain text. (Some word processors will add formatting if the file doesn't have a .txt extension, which in this case, the extension will be .cgi.)

3. You'll also need an FTP program. I use WS FTP, which comes in a free Lite version and a commercial Pro version. Either will work fine. CGI scripts should be uploaded in ASCII mode.

4. A little bit of common sense and perseverance helps since CGI can be frustrating, especially if you're new to it.

Configuration

The first thing you need to know is the path on your server to the Perl interpreter. If you have cgi-bin already in place, there's a good chance there's a script already in there. View the script to see the correct path to Perl. It will be the first line. Usually, you can also find the path in the FAQ pages, setup message, or support documents provided by your web host.

The most common error that webmasters new to installing CGI scripts make is having the path to Perl incorrect. The first line will look something like this:

#!/usr/bin/perl ... or ... #!/usr/local/bin/perl

This may or may not have to be changed. The path has to be the correct one for your server or it won't work. About half the time, the script you download will have the right path already there when you check; but when you don't check, somehow Murphy's Law always seems to apply.

Check for More ...

While you've got the script open to check the path to Perl, look at the top of the script for comments regarding any other variables that need to be configured. Often there are none, but occasionally you'll find one or more. Read the comments to see what to do. Comments in Perl are lines that start with the hash mark/pound sign (#).

This is a comment in a Perl script.

Comments often read across multiple lines.

Each line that starts with # is a comment ...

except the first line, which is the path to Perl.

Occasionally, the path to your site must be specified somewhere in the script, and you'll find directions on this in the comments. The path is not the same thing as the web address (URL). My URL is http://www.boogiejack.com, but the path to my site ON THE SERVER is like this:

/mmt/web/users/boogiejack/www

The above example probably won't work on your server, even if you change the domain name portion from mine to yours. The paths are different at almost every host. If you use WS FTP, you'll be able to see the complete path in the window above the server-side files when you connect. Otherwise, check your web host's support, FAQ, or setup pages.

Installation

Once you've configured the script for your server, it's time to upload it. When uploading CGI scripts you must upload them in ASCII mode. Remember the memory trick? ASCII and CGI both end in the letter "i" so that's the mode to upload a CGI script. The other option is binary mode, which is used for images and other types of binary files.

Most hosts only allow CGI scripts to be executed from the cgi-bin, so you should upload the script to that directory. After uploading the script, you still aren't finished. You must set the correct file permissions for the script and any other directories and files the script uses.

Understanding File Permissions

UNIX servers allow you to set different levels of access to a file for different groups of people. In terms of file access, there are three groups and three different permission types each group can receive. You don't really have to understand this part to set permissions if you know what permissions the script should have, but I'll show you anyway. Feel free to skip down to "Setting Permissions" if you're in a hurry.

The groups are:

- **User:** The "user" group consists only of the owner of the file (your hosting account).
- **Group:** The "group" group (Tricky English, huh? Pay attention!) consists of the other users on the server—you can usually remove their permissions entirely if you think it is necessary.
- **Other:** The "other" group consists of everyone else—most importantly, the web server falls into the "other" category.

The permissions are:

- **Read:** The "read" permission allows a user or program the ability to read the data in a file.
- **Write:** The "write" permission allows a user or program the ability to write new data into a file, and to remove data from it.
- **Execute:** The "execute" permission allows a user or program the ability to execute a file, if it is a program or a script.

Setting Permissions

Permissions are set with a UNIX command called CHMOD. Don't worry, you don't have to know UNIX commands as this can be accomplished quite easily with your FTP client. You'll have to check with the place you got the script from or with any help files or comments within the script to see what permissions are needed. Most scripts require a permission of 755. If the script your using doesn't indicate it, try 755.

To set file permissions using WS FTP, left-click the script to highlight it, then right-click on the highlighted file and a drop-down list will open. Choose chmod (UNIX) from the drop-down list. At right is a screen capture of the dialog box for setting file permissions.

Some FTP programs and older versions of WS FTP (and perhaps WS_FTP LE) do not show the actual file permission number on the permissions screen.

I'll show you how to figure out file permissions shortly, but first . . .

Here's a handy chart of the most commonly used CHMOD settings.

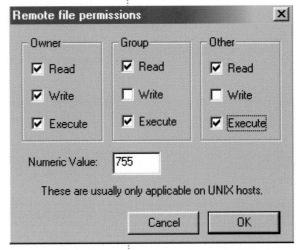

LEGEND: r = read w = write x = execute				
Permission #	Owner	Group	Other	What it means...
777	r w x	r w x	r w x	Writable Directory
755	r w x	r x	r x	Standard (non-writable) directory/executable file
666	r w	r w	r w	Writable File
644	r w x	r	r	Readable File

Obviously, many other combinations exist, although they are rarely used. It's not too hard to figure out the settings when you run into an oddball script. Each group and permission has an assigned number. To get the correct permission number (CHMOD setting), just add up the combinations.

Permission Assignments:

400   read by owner
040   **read by group**
004   read by anybody (other)
200   write by owner
020   **write by group**
002   write by anybody
100   execute by owner
010   **execute by group**
001   execute by anybody

Here's an exercise for you. You have a script that calls for the following permissions:

Owner: read, write, execute
Group: read, write
Other: read, execute

Before looking at the chart below for the answer, see if you can add up the correct numbers according to the permission assignments and come up with the correct CHMOD setting number.

This chart to the left shows the answer worked out in living color for you.

You peeked at the answer without trying to work it out for yourself didn't you? Tsk, tsk . . . how are you going to learn that way?

As you can see, if you add up the subtotals in the right-hand column in this table, you get a file permission of 765. The numbers in each column were taken from the permission assignments shown previously.

	Read	Write	Execute	Totals
Owner	400	200	100	700
Group	040	020	000	060
Other	004	000	001	005
File Permission (CHMOD) #:				765

Troubleshooting

If you're reading this tutorial, you're likely inexperienced at installing CGI—and the bad news is that many things can go wrong. To compound the problem, the thing that is wrong isn't likely to be obvious to you. Here are the three most common errors and possible causes:

- **403 Permission Denied:** Error 403 is as much of a sure thing as you'll find. You get this error when you forget to change the file permissions of the script or you change them to the wrong setting.

- **404 File Not Found:** The actual file (the script) was not found. This is the same error you get for broken links. You simply entered the link incorrectly somewhere.

- **500 Internal Server Error:** You don't want this one! Don't do it!! It will blow up the entire Internet!!!

The last one is the most common error, and also the worst one to try to correct. It's most likely an error in the script itself. Read the documentation for the script very carefully and make sure you followed each step correctly. Go back through all the configuration and installation steps and try to find out what is incorrectly configured. Of course, this assumes you have a good script to begin with. It could also be a programming error by the script author; although that isn't common, it does happen. Most authors will test their scripts thoroughly before releasing them to the public.

If you have access to the log files on your server, find one called **error_log** and check the end of that file—assuming you can check it right after you discover your script doesn't work. When a script fails to execute, errors are logged in that file and you will find recent script errors listed there. It may give you a clue as to what is wrong.

There might be something peculiar to your web host as well, so read all your host's documentation. If you can't find anything there, you might check with your host's support services. As a last resort, you could contact the script author. Be sure you've gone through all the other means of troubleshooting first before contacting the script author, especially if it's a free script. The author may help you for free, or he or she may ask for a fee for the service.

Finally, make sure your script works before linking to it for public access/use. If you serve up a broken script, it causes the clock on the users computer to skip ahead four years. People really don't like aging that fast.

Whew! That was a humdinger, wasn't it? Yeah, you loved it though.

You'll find a complete listing of server errors in the appendices.

18.16 Stopping Directory Snooping

S uppose you have a directory named "Software" where you keep the programs you sell for paying customers to download. Hang on if you don't have a commercial site, this tip does apply to you too.

If you don't have an index page in that directory, the entire contents of that directory may be open to the public. If someone bought one program and noticed it was downloaded from the Software directory, and then wanted to see what else you have, he or she could type this URL into the browser:

http://www.yoursite.com/Software/

If you don't have an index page in that directory, many servers will return a list of everything in the directory, including subdirectories. The person would have access to any directory on your server and they could download anything they wanted at that point.

Even if you don't have a commercial site, you still have directories that are vulnerable. Perhaps you have a secret family page, a private journal, or other things you don't want to be publicly available.

The solution is to put an index.html page in all your directories. On the index page you could have a "You've been busted!" notice. You might use a script that identifies their IP addresses and tell them they've been logged so you can scare them a little. You could also put up a "Restricted Access" notice. Or, you could do what I do: Place a redirect page there so that if someone tries to gain access to your directories, they'll get shuttled to your home page instead. In some directories, I shuttle them off to my ebookfarming.com site. Let them try to figure that one out.

18.17 Disabling Smart Tags

M icrosoft has developed a technology they call Smart Tags. What they do is add links to Microsoft sites and partner sites in places on your site where you never intended for links to be. If you wrote an article about repairing broken windows, it is possible that the word "windows" could be turned into a link to one of Microsoft's pages featuring one of their Windows Operating Systems.

You can prevent Smart Tags from appearing on your pages. Just add the following meta tag to the <head> section of your pages and Smart Tags will not appear on them.

```
<meta name="MSSmartTagsPreventParsing" content="TRUE">
```

18.18 Server Side Includes

S erver Side Includes, or SSI for short, offers a marvelous way to add site navigation or other elements to several pages of your site via one file. For example, all my site navigation is printed into each web page on my site via SSI. If I were to add a new site section, I'd only have to change my one navigation.ssi file to have that change reflected on all 500+ pages of my site.

To use SSI, your web host has to have the server enabled for SSI. Many hosts enable it automatically, so you can test it for yourself without their help. If it doesn't work, then request that the host enable SSI.

For SSI to work, most hosts have it set up so that you must name your HTML pages with a .shtml extension instead .html or .htm. They can, however, enable your server so that all pages, regardless of the page extension, can run SSI. This is what I prefer.

To include SSI on a page, place the following at the place on your page where you want the SSI file to appear.

```
<!--#include file="ssi_files/navigation.ssi"-->
```

This example references a file named "navigation.ssi," which is located in the folder (directory) called "ssi_files." Of course, you have to use the correct path and file name for the file you want to add via SSI or it won't work.

That's all there is to adding a navigation system to your page using SSI, as long as your web site is SSI enabled (and if necessary for your server, your page is named with a .shtml extension).

The only thing left to do is create the actual navigation.ssi file you are referencing. This file simply contains whatever code you would actually place on the page if you weren't using SSI. For example, for links to show up like this:

Home Page | Contact Me

Create your navigation.ssi file with only this in it:

```
<div align="center">
<a href="index.html">Home Page</a> |
<a href="contact.html">Contact Me</a>
</div>
```

> **NOTE**
>
> Some text editors will automatically add a .txt extension to a file when you try to save it as "something.ssi," leaving you with "something.ssi.txt" instead. To prevent the .txt from being added, place the file name and extension in quotation marks when you save it. For example, "something.ssi" will be saved as you wanted, without the .txt extension.

If those are the only links you want in a navigation system, that's all you need to include. Just save the file with a .ssi extension, such as "navigation.ssi," and you're finished.

You can use any standard HTML code in an SSI file that you use on a web page. Just don't start it off with the <HTML> declaration and go through the TITLE, HEAD, BODY routine. You only add the code that you want to place at that spot on the page you're inserting the file into.

18.19 Chapter Quiz

1. Netiquette is mostly common sense and courtesy toward others. Which of the following are true:
   a. You should forward all virus warnings to everyone you know just in case they are true.
   b. Never send file attachments without checking with the recipient to see if it's OK first.
   c. The Golden Rule applies on the Net just as it does in real life.
   d. You should attach return receipts to your email to show the recipient that you really care.

2. True or False: You can take anything you want from a web page if no copyright notice is posted.

3. True or False: It's safe to link to graphics on other people's web sites because there's no way they can catch you.

18.19 Chapter Quiz (continued)

4. The FCC:
   a. Is the only trusted source that emails virus warnings.
   b. Is one of many government agencies that emails virus warnings.
   c. Never emails virus warnings.
   d. Has never heard of the Internet.

5. What are the keyboard shortcuts for Copy and for Paste?

6. Which of the following, if any, are generally true about unsubscribing to spammers' mailing lists?
   a. You should act on unsubscribe requests to be removed from their mailing list.
   b. You shouldn't respond to spammers' unsubscribe requests.
   c. You should send unsubscribe requests to the National Clearinghouse of Email Marketers.
   d. You should order whatever they are offering so they will leave you alone.

7. Which of the following, if any, are true about creating passwords?
   a. You should use the same password for all your accounts to avoid confusion.
   b. You should use a word that is easy to remember.
   c. You should use a mixture of numbers and uppercase and lowercase letters.
   d. You should keep your password list in a file off your computer in case of accidental deletion or computer problems such as hard-drive failure.

18.19 Chapter Quiz (continued)

8. True or False: AOL browsers, by default, save GIF and JPG images as .art files. You can change this browser behavior.

9. What is the most commonly used type of hosting plan that a new Internet business starts out with?

10. What does the acronym CGI stand for?

11. How can you stop people from "directory snooping" on your web site?

12. If you bought a gallon of polka dot water, a digital aroma, and a melon-flavored tractor tire, what would you be?

Appendices

Introduction

This section features several handy reference charts that you'll refer to often. There is so much to know that it's hard to remember it all. You'll find yourself referring to these charts again and again as I still do.

Owners of the first edition of this book will notice the Resources section pointing to useful web sites and tools is no longer included. It's online now, where you can simply click a link to go to the resource that interests you. This makes it easier for you to use and allows me to edit the listings. I ran into a problem after the first edition when an adult web site purchased the domain name of a resource I listed. Obviously, this was not a good situation, and one I can avoid by keeping the resources list online. You'll find it here:

http://www.boogiejack.com/book/resources.html

HTML Chart

Comment Tags

HTML Tag	Attributes	What It Does
<!— ... —>		Creates a hidden comment.
<comment> ... </comment>		Creates a hidden comment.

Basic Structure Elements

Note that some HTML tags in this chart are deprecated elements. They are still supported by browsers, but the World Wide Web Consortium recommends you use Cascading Style Sheet alternatives for them. They are included here because they are still legal HTML elements, and may still serve you well. For a list of deprecated and forbidden elements, see Appendix G.

> **NOTE**
>
> Comment tags are used to hide JavaScript from older browsers or to mark sections within an HTML document for easier editing. Comments do not show up on web pages—they are visible only in the source code. A sample:
>
> <!-- This marks the start of my master table -->
>
> The text wouldn't show up on the web page, but it helps you locate items in the code. You must include a space after the first set of two dashes and before the second set of two dashes.

HTML Tag	Attributes	What It Does
<html> ... </html>		Begins an HTML document and encloses the entire page.
<head> ... </head>		Encloses the head section of an HTML document.
<title> ... </title>		Encloses the title of the HTML document and is placed within the <head> section.

HTML Tag	Attributes	What It Does
<body> ... </body>		Encloses the body of an HTML document. The content of the body, minus the HTML code, is what you see on a page.
	background="..."	The URL of the image to tile as the web page background.
	bgcolor="..."	Sets the background color of the page.
	text="..."	Sets the text color of the page.
	link="..."	Sets the link color of the page.
	alink="..."	Sets the active link color of the page.
	vlink="..."	Sets the visited link color of the page.
	bgproperties="..."	The value of "fixed" keeps the web page background from scrolling. This doesn't work in all browsers.
	topmargin="..."	Sets the top margin of the page, measured in pixels. (IE)
	leftmargin="..."	Sets the left margin of the page, measured in pixels. (IE)
	rightmargin="..."	Sets the right margin of the page, measured in pixels. (IE)
	bottommargin="..."	Sets the bottom margin of the page, measured in pixels. (IE)
	marginwidth="..."	Sets the left and right margin of the page, measured in pixels. (Netscape)
	marginheight="..."	Sets the top and bottom margin of the page, measured in pixels. (Netscape)

HTML Tag	Attributes	What It Does
<base>		Optional tag used in the <head> section to list the document URL.
	href="..."	The full URL of the page.
<meta>		Used to indicate information about the document.
	name="..."	Defines the type of meta tag it is. Example: keywords.
	content="..."	The content for the named type.

Heading Elements

HTML Tag	Attributes	What It Does
<h1> ... </h1>		1st level heading (largest).
<h2> ... </h2>		2nd level heading.
<h3> ... </h3>		3rd level heading.
<h4> ... </h4>		4th level heading.
<h5> ... </h5>		5th level heading.
<h6> ... </h6>		6th level heading (smallest).

Formatting Elements

HTML Tag	Attributes	What It Does
<em> ... </em>		Adds emphasis (usually italics).
<strong> ... </strong>		Strong emphasis (usually bold).
<cite> ... </cite>		Citation (usually italics).
<b> ... </b>		Bold text.
<i> ... </i>		Italic text.
<tt> ... </tt>		Typewriter text (monospace).

HTML Tag	Attributes	What It Does
<pre> ... </pre>		Preformatted text.
<big> ... </big>		Text is slightly bigger than normal.
<small> ... </small>		Text is slightly smaller than normal.
_{...}		Subscript (lower than normal).
^{...}		Superscript (higher than normal).
<strike> ... </strike>		Line through the text.
<blockquote> ... </blockquote>		Indents text on both side margins.
<address> ... </address>		Used for signatures to create a line break on both sides.
<center> ... </center>		Centers the content.
<font> ... </font>		Changes the font attributes.
	size="..."	Controls font size from 1–7, with 1 being the smallest.
	color="..."	Changes the font color.
	face="..."	Changes the font typeface.
<basefont> ... </basefont>		Sets the default font size.
	size="..."	Values are from 1–7.
<p> ... </p>		Paragraph. Creates a double line break. A cancel tag is optional.
	align="..."	Aligns the paragraph. Values are left, right, center, and justify. (Justify is an unofficial value, but it works in most browsers.)
 		Break. Creates a single line break. No cancel tag is used.

HTML Tag	Attributes	What It Does
	clear="..."	Causes text to stop flowing around images. Values are left, right, and all.
<nobr> ... </nobr>		Causes text not to wrap to the next line. May cause page to scroll sideways.
		Creates a non-breaking space.
<hr>		Horizontal rule (line). No cancel tag is used.
	size="..."	The vertical thickness of the rule, as measured in pixels.
	width="..."	The horizontal width of the rule, as measured in pixels or a percentage of the page or table cell that encloses it.
	color="..."	The color of the rule. (IE)
	align="..."	Aligns the rule left, right, or center.
	noshade	Makes the rule a solid line instead of two-tone bevel.

Link Elements

HTML Tag	Attributes	What It Does
<a> ... </a>		With "href," creates a link to another file; or with "name," creates an anchor point on a page that can be linked to.
	href="..."	Hypertext reference, the URL of the file to be retrieved.
	name="..."	The name of an anchor point.

HTML Tag	Attributes	What It Does
	urn="…"	Uniform Resource Number. The numerical address of a file. Seldom used.
	title="…"	The name or title of the linked file.
	target="…"	The frame name or window the link should appear in.

List Elements

HTML Tag	Attributes	What It Does
<ol> … </ol>		Ordered list.
	type="…"	Defines the list labels, values are A, a, I, i, and 1.
	start="…"	The label value to start the list.
<ul> … </ul>		Unordered (bulleted) list.
	type="…"	The style of bullet to use; values are circle, disk, and square.
<menu> … </menu>		Menu list. Not often used.
<dir> … </dir>		Directory list. Not often used.
<li>		A list item for ordered lists, unordered lists, menu lists, and directory lists. No cancel tag is used.
<dl> … </dl>		Definition list.
	compact	Creates list with less white space.
<dt>		Definition term, used with definition lists. No cancel tag is used.
<dd>		Definition of the definition term, used with definition lists. No cancel tag is used.

377

Form Elements

HTML Tag	Attributes	What It Does
<form> ... </form>		Begins an input form.
	action="..."	The URL of the script to process the form, or the mailto reference.
	method="..."	How the form is processed. Values are get or post.
	name="..."	Name of the form, used in JavaScript references.
<input> ... </input>		An input device for a form.
	type="..."	Input type. Values are checkbox, radio, text, submit, reset, hidden password, or image.
	name="..."	Labels output in a processed form.
	value="..."	The default value for a text field or hidden field; for a checkbox or radio button, the value to be submitted with the form; for reset or submit buttons, the text that should appear on the button.
	src="..."	If using an image, the path and file name to the image.
	size="..."	The size of a text box, as measured in characters.
	align="..."	If using images, works like an image align tag.
	maxlength="..."	The maximum amount of characters allowed in a text box.
	checked	Causes a checkbox or radio button to be checked by default when the page loads.

HTML Tag	Attributes	What It Does
<textarea> ... </textarea>		A multi-line text input box. Text can be placed in the box by default by placing it between opening and closing tags.
	rows="..."	Controls the height of the text box.
	cols="..."	Controls the width of the text box.
	name="..."	Labels output in a processed form.
	wrap	Controls text wrapping. Values are physical, virtual, and off.
<select> ... </select>		Creates a drop-down list or scrolling menu of items.
	size="..."	Number of items to display in a scrolling list. If size is not indicated it becomes a drop-down list.
	name="..."	Labels output in a processed form.
	multiple	Allows more than one selection from the list to be made.
<option>		Lists an item within the <select> tags. No cancel tag needed.
	value="..."	Value to submit when form is processed.
	selected	Makes one item the default selection when a page loads. Can only be used with one option per <select> list.

Table Elements

HTML Tag	Attributes	What It Does
<table> ... </table>		Creates a table of rows and columns.
	cellpadding="..."	The space between the edge of a table cell and the cell contents, measured in pixels.
	cellspacing="..."	The space between the table cells, measured in pixels.
	width="..."	The width of a table, measured in pixels or page percentage.
	border="..."	The width of the table border, measured in pixels.
	align="..."	Horizontal alignment of the table. Values are left, right, and center.
	valign="..."	Vertical alignment of content within the table. Values are top and bottom.
	bgcolor="..."	The background color of all cells that do not have their own color or background image specified.
	background="..."	The URL of a background image to tile in all the cells that do not have their own background color or image specified.
	bordercolor="..."	The border color if the border attribute is used.
	bordercolorlight="..."	Color for the light shade in 3-D look borders. (IE)
	bordercolordark="..."	Color for the dark shade in 3-D look borders. (IE)

HTML Tag	Attributes	What It Does
	frame="..."	Controls external table borders. Values are: above (top border), below (bottom border), hsides (horizontal sides, top and bottom borders), lhs (left hand side), rhs (right hand side), vsides (vertical sides, left and right borders), box (all sides), and void (no borders).
	rules="..."	Controls internal table borders. Values are none, all, basic, cols, and rows.
<caption> ... </caption>		Sets a caption for the table.
	align="..."	Sets the horizontal alignment. Values are left, center, right, and justified.
<tr> ... </tr>		Starts a table row. Can contain headings and data (<th> and <td>).
	align="..."	Sets the horizontal alignment for this row. Values are left, center, right, and justified.
	valign="..."	Sets the vertical alignment for this row. Values are top, middle, bottom, and baseline.
	bgcolor="..."	The background color of all cells in that row that do not have their own color or background image specified.
	background="..."	The URL of a background image to tile in all the cells in that row that do not have their own background color or image specified.

HTML Tag	Attributes	What It Does
	bordercolor="…"	The border color in that row if the border attribute is used.
	bordercolorlight="…"	Color in that row for the light shade in 3-D look borders. (IE)
	bordercolordark="…"	Color for that row for the dark shade in 3-D look borders. (IE)
<th> … </th>		Sets a table heading cell. Text is rendered in bold.
	align="…"	Sets the horizontal alignment for the cell. Values are left, center, right, and justify.
	valign="…"	Sets the vertical alignment for the cell. Values are top, middle, bottom, and baseline.
	rowspan="…"	Sets the number of rows the cell will span.
	colspan="…"	Sets the number of columns the cell will span.
	width="…"	Sets the width of this cell column. Measured in pixels or page percentage.
	bgcolor="…"	The background color of this cell.
	background="…"	The URL of a background image to tile in this cell.
	bordercolor="…"	The border color if the border attribute is used.
	bordercolorlight="…"	Color for the light shade in 3-D look borders. (IE)
	bordercolordark="…"	Color for the dark shade in 3-D look borders. (IE)
	nowrap	Prevents text from wrapping to the next line.

HTML Tag	Attributes	What It Does
\<td\> ... \</td\>		Sets a table data cell.
	align="..."	Sets the horizontal alignment for this cell. Values are left, center, right, and justified.
	valign="..."	Sets the vertical alignment for this cell. Values are top, middle, bottom, and baseline.
	rowspan="..."	Sets the number of rows the cell will span.
	colspan="..."	Sets the number of columns the cell will span.
	width="..."	Sets the width of this cell. Measured in pixels or page percentage.
	bgcolor="..."	The background color of this cell.
	background="..."	The URL of a background image to tile in this cell.
	bordercolor="..."	The border color if the border attribute is used.
	bordercolorlight="..."	Color for the light shade in 3-D look borders. (IE)
	bordercolordark="..."	Color for the dark shade in 3-D look borders. (IE)
	nowrap	Prevents text from wrapping to the next line.

Frame Elements

HTML Tag	Attributes	What It Does
<frameset> ... </frameset>		Divides a browser into areas that can each display separate HTML pages.
	rows="..."	Causes the window to be divided horizontally into rows.
	cols="..."	Causes the window to be divided vertically into columns.
	border="..."	Size of the frame border. Set to 0 (zero) for Netscape for no border.
	frameborder="..."	Turns frameborder off for IE. Values are yes and no.
<frame>		Sets a single frame of a frameset. No cancel tag is used.
	src="..."	The URL of the page to be displayed in this frame.
	name="..."	A name used to target pages to be loaded into this frame.
	marginwidth="..."	The space (padding) between the left and right side of the frame and the frame's content.
	marginheight="..."	The space (padding) between the top and bottom of the frame and the frame's content.
	scrolling="..."	Sets whether a frame has scrollbars. Values are yes, no, and, auto.
	noresize	Prevents visitors from resizing the frames.
<noframes> ... </noframes>		Provides an alternative document to browsers that do not support frames.

Image Elements

HTML Tag	Attributes	What It Does
<img>		Places an image into a document. No cancel tag is used.
	src="..."	The URL to the image.
	width="..."	The width of the image, measured in pixels.
	height="..."	The height of the image, measured in pixels.
	align="..."	The alignment of the image. If set to left or right, text will flow beside the image. All other values (top, middle, bottom) determine vertical alignment with other content on the same line.
	alt="..."	Alternative for browsers that do not support graphics or have graphics turned off.
	border="..."	Creates a border as measured in pixels around the image. If the image is a link, it's common to set the border to 0 (zero).
	ismap	Declaration for an image map.
	usemap="..."	The name of the map to use for an image map. Used with map and area tags.
	vspace="..."	Sets the space (padding) above and below an image.
	hspace="..."	Sets the space (padding) on both sides of an image.
	lowsrc="..."	The URL to a smaller image to be loaded before the larger image loads.

HTML Tag	Attributes	What It Does
<map> ... </map>		Contains the image map coordinates. Must have at least one <area> tag, referenced by the usemap attribute in an image tag.
<area>		Defines the coordinates of each clickable link in an image map. No cancel tag is used.
	shape="..."	Defines the shape of the clickable area. Values are rect, circle, and poly.
	coords="..."	The coordinates of the clickable area for an image map link.
	href="..."	The URL that should be activated when the defined coordinates are clicked.

T he CSS chart is organized differently from the HTML chart because of the structural differences between the programming languages. This chart begins with the properties, rather than the selectors, because the selectors can be any HTML element for the most part. Obviously, there are some exceptions, but if you use common sense you should be able to apply the CSS properties you want to HTML elements. Showing every possible combination here is not feasible.

Keep in mind, while modern browsers offer excellent CSS support, the older the browser in use, the fewer CSS properties it will support.

Background and Color Properties

Property	background
Description	A shorthand style for setting all the background properties in one declaration. See individual properties below for values.
Possible Values	background-attachment background-color background-image background-position background-repeat
Example	body {background: #00ff00 url("images/stucco.jpg") no-repeat fixed top left}

> **NOTE**
>
> A shorthand property lets you set more than one property for an HTML element. The first property listed in the chart below is the background property. With it, you can set the background-color, background-attachment, background-image, background-position, and background-repeat all in the same declaration rather than listing them one at a time. When you use a shorthand property, do not use the semicolon terminator between each item or it will not work. Use the semicolon terminator between pairs of properties and values only when you list them as individual properties.

387

Property	background-color
Description	Sets the background color of an element. Note that RGB values range from 0–255 each, for red, green, and blue.
Possible Values	color (in Hex or RGB values, or a named color) transparent
Example	p {background-color: #dd32f7;} h1 {background-color: rgb(102,55,107);} div {background-color: honeydew;} table {background-color: transparent;}

Property	background-image
Description	Sets an image as the background of an element. Depending on the value for background-repeat (if used), the image may tile full page or along a vertical or horizontal axis. It may also be set to not repeat and be placed anywhere on the page.
Possible Values	URL none
Example	body {background-image: url(images/ocean.jpg);} h3 {background-image: none;}

Property	background-position
Description	Sets the starting position of a background image to begin tiling or its position on the page if no-repeat is set.
Possible Values	percentage length {20,50} top, center, or bottom (vertically) left, center, or right (horizontally)
Example	body {background-position: center center;}

Property	background-repeat
Description	Sets whether or not a background repeats, and if so, how it repeats. In the example below, the background is coded to repeat across the top of the page, which creates a top border background pattern.
Possible Values	repeat (background fills the area of the element selected) repeat-x (background repeats on a horizontal axis) repeat-y (background repeats on a vertical axis) no-repeat (background does not repeat)
Example	body {background-image: url(wood.jpg); background-repeat:repeat-x}

Border Properties

Property	border
Description	A shorthand property for setting all the border properties the same for all four borders. Each border can have different settings by coding each border separately.
Possible Values	border-width border-style border-color
Example	p {border: 2px dotted red;}

Property	border-bottom
Description	Another shorthand property for defining the border-width, border-style, and border-color in one declaration for the bottom border of an element.
Possible Values	border-width border-style border-color
Example	div {border-bottom: 1px dashed blue;}

Property	border-bottom-width
Description	Sets the width (thickness) of the bottom border.
Possible Values	thin medium thick length
Example	ol {border-bottom-width: .25in;}

NOTE

In the previous examples for the border-bottom, you change border-bottom to border-left, border-right, or border-top to set the individual properties for each of those borders.

Property	border-color
Description	Sets the colors of the borders. If one color value is entered, all four borders will be the same color. If two color values are entered, the top and bottom will be the first color, and the left and right sides will be the second color. If three color values are entered, the top will be the first color, the two sides will be the second color, and the bottom will be the third color. If four color values are entered, the colors start with the top border and rotate clockwise. **You must also set a border-style to use the border-color property.**
Possible Values	color (in Hex or RGB values, or a named color)
Example	h4 {border-color: #dda343; border-style: solid;}

Property	border-style
Description	Sets the border style for all four borders. **You must also set a border-color to use the border-style property.**
Possible Values	none dotted dashed solid double groove ridge inset outset
Example	p {border-style: groove; border-color: purple;}

Font Properties

Property	font
Description	A shorthand style for setting all the font properties in one declaration. See individual properties below for values. **Note that when setting this shorthand style, font-weight must come first and font-style must come before font-size.**
Possible Values	font-family font-size font-style font-variant font-weight
Example	p {font: bold oblique 16pt Arial, sans-serif;}

Property	font-family
Description	Used to declare a specific font, a generic font family, or both. Since the font declared will only be displayed if it is available on the viewer's system, I encourage you to also declare a generic family when declaring a specific font.
Possible Values	specific font (Arial, Garamond, Verdana, etc.)
	serif
	sans-serif
	cursive
	fantasy
	monospace
Example	div {font-family: Souvenir, serif;}

Property	font-size
Description	Sets the font size in either an absolute size, relative size, length value, or percentage value. Note that you often will not see a difference between some sizes, such as xx-small and x-small, or 11 pixels and 12 pixels. **Do not put a space between a numeric value and the unit of measurement.**
Possible Values	px (pixels)
	pt (points)
	em (em-quad)
	percentage
	xx-small
	x-small
	small
	medium (named)
	large
	x-large
	xx-large
Example	p {font-size: 12px;}

Property	font-style
Description	Sets the font to italic, oblique, or normal.
Possible Values	italic oblique normal
Example	b {font-style: italic;}

Property	font-variant
Description	Sets text to small caps or normal.
Possible Values	normal small-caps
Example	h2 {font-variant: small-caps;}

Property	font-weight
Description	Sets the weight of a font. In the numeric values, 400 is equal to a normal font and 700 is equal to bold text.
Possible Values	lighter normal bold bolder 100 200 300 400 500 600 700 800 900
Example	p {font-weight: 500;}

List Properties

Property	list-style
Description	A shorthand property for declaring all list values at once.
Possible Values	list-style-type list-style-position list-style-image
Example	ul {list-style: circle url(images/bluebullet.gif) outer;}

Property	list-style-image
Description	Sets an image for the list item bullet.
Possible Values	url none
Example	ul {list-style-image: url(redcheck.gif);}

Property	list-style-position
Description	Used to declare the position of the bullet or number in ordered and unordered lists. Inside sets the bullet even with the vertical line of the left side of the text; outside sets the bullet outside the vertical line of the text.
Possible Values	inside outside
Example	ol {list-style-position: inside;}

Property	list-style-type
Description	Used to set the numbering system or bullet type.
Possible Values	none disc circle square decimal (number) lower-alpha (alphabet) upper-alpha lower-roman (Roman numerals) upper-roman
Example	ol {list-style-type: upper-alpha;} ul {list-style-type: square;}

NOTE

The following section deals with margins and padding. In CSS, margins are defined as the space around elements and padding is defined as the space between the element edges and the element content. In other words, margins are outside an element and padding is inside an element.

Margin and Padding Properties

Property	margin
Description	Sets the size of all the margins (margin-top, margin-right, margin-bottom, and margin-left) of an element at once.
Possible Values	length percentage auto
Example	p {margin: 12px;} (sets all margins at once) p {margin: 10px 6px 10 px 6px;} (sets margins clockwise from top)

Property	margin-bottom
Description	Sets the bottom margin of an element.
Possible Values	length percentage auto
Example	h1 {margin-bottom: 6px;}

Property	margin-left
Description	Sets the left margin of an element.
Possible Values	length percentage auto
Example	img {margin-left: 3px;}

Property	margin-right
Description	Sets the right margin of an element.
Possible Values	length percentage auto
Example	p {margin-right: auto;}

Property	margin-top
Description	Sets the top margin of an element.
Possible Values	length percentage auto
Example	img {margin-top: 2%;}

Property	padding
Description	Sets the size of the padding for all the borders (padding-top, padding-right, padding-bottom, and padding-left).
Possible Values	length percentage
Example	td {padding: 5px;} td {padding: 3em 5em;} (sets top/bottom and left/right) td {padding: 3px 5px 7px 3px;} (sets padding clockwise from top)

Property	padding-bottom
Description	Sets the padding size on the bottom of an element.
Possible Values	length percentage
Example	ol {padding-bottom: 1.5em;}

Property	padding-left
Description	Sets the padding size on the left side of an element.
Possible Values	length percentage
Example	td {padding-left: 2%;}

Property	padding-right
Description	Sets the padding size on the right side of an element.
Possible Values	length percentage
Example	p {padding-right: 12px;}

Property	padding-top
Description	Sets the padding size on the top of an element.
Possible Values	length
	percentage
Example	ol {padding-top: 12px:}

Text Properties

Property	letter-spacing
Description	Sets the white space in between characters within words. Negative values cause the words to condense; positive values cause the words to expand.
Possible Values	length
	normal
Example	p {letter-spacing: -2px;}

Property	line-height
Description	Sets the space between lines. Technically, this doesn't apply only to text, but since it's mainly used with text it's included here. Altering the line-height will create whatever space you specify between other elements as well.
Possible Values	normal
	length
	number
	percentage
Example	p {line-height: 18px;}

Property	text-align
Description	Sets the text alignment.
Possible Values	center
	justify
	left
	right
Example	p {text-align: justify;}

Property	text-decoration
Description	Sets effects on text.
Possible Values	none
	line-through
	overline
	underline
Example	h2 {text-decoration: none;}
	h1 {text-decoration: underline overline;}

Property	text-indent
Description	Indents the first line of text.
Possible Values	length
	percentage
Example	p {text-indent: 15px;}

Property	text-transform
Description	Changes the case of the text.
Possible Values	none capitalize (capitalizes the first letter in every word) lowercase (prints all letters in lowercase) uppercase (prints all letters in uppercase)
Example	h4 {text-transform: capitalize;}

Property	white-space
Description	Sets how white space is handled. Normal is how browsers handle non-CSS pages, nowrap prevents a line from breaking, and pre is like the HTML element of <pre> in which extra spaces and carriage returns are preserved.
Possible Values	normal nowrap pre
Example	td {white-space: pre;}

Property	word-spacing
Description	Increase or decrease the space in between words.
Possible Values	normal length
Example	p {word-spacing: .3em;}

Pseudo-class Properties and Miscellaneous

Property	:active
Description	Sets the style for links when they are clicked. Does not apply to named anchors.
Possible Values	n/a
Example	a:active {color: red; text-decoration: none;}

Property	:first-letter
Description	Sets a style for the first letter of an element, such as a paragraph.
Possible Values	n/a
Example	p:first-letter {color: green; font-size: 24px;}

Property	:first-line
Description	Sets a style for the first line of an element, such as a paragraph.
Possible Values	n/a
Example	p:firstline {font-weight: bold;}

Property	!important
Description	Sets the style declaration as important. Important declarations outweigh all others in the cascade order.
Possible Values	n/a
Example	b {color: red !important;}

Property	:hover
Description	Sets the style for a link when the cursor is resting on it. If using the a:hover pseudo-class property, it must follow a:link and a:visited and be before a:active in the definition for all properties to work correctly.
Possible Values	n/a
Example (Shown in the correct order to work properly.)	a:link {color: blue;} a:visited {color: black;} **a:hover {color: red; background: black;}** a:active {color: yellow;}

Property	:link
Description	Sets the style for links. Does not apply to named anchors.
Possible Values	n/a
Example	a:link {color: blue; text-decoration: none;}

Property	clear
Description	Defines the sides of an element that should not have floating elements placed on it. Floating content will be moved down until it clears the element where clear is declared.
Possible Values	none left right both
Example	p {clear: both;}

Property	color
Description	Sets the foreground color of an element. Sets the text color in body, paragraph, division, and other similar selectors.
Possible Values	color (in Hex or RGB values, or a named color)
Example	b {color: #44dc59;}

Property	float
Description	Used to declare the float direction of an element. Commonly used to flow text around images, but can be used to float tables and other elements.
Possible Values	none left right
Example	img {float: right;}

Property	height
Description	Used to set the height of an element. Can be applied to any block level element, although browser support is spotty for some elements. The example below shows declaring the height for an image class named "button." This could be used for your button navigation, rather than setting the height in the <img> tag. You can set the width this way, too.
Possible Values	auto length
Example	img.button {height: 140px;}

Property	vertical-align
Description	Used to set the vertical alignment of an element to the baseline.
Possible Values	baseline bottom length middle sub super text-bottom text-top percentage
Example	img {vertical-align: text-bottom;}

Property	width
Description	Used to set the width of an element. Can be applied to any block level element, although browser support is spotty for some elements.
Possible Values	auto length percentage
Example	p {width: 400px;}

Y ou can access the extra characters within a font that are not found on the keyboard in a number of ways. To place them in an HTML document, you can use the HTML codes shown in the following chart.

You can access the extra characters not found on your keyboard in a number of ways. To place them in your HTML document you can use the HTML codes shown in the following chart.

ASCII #	Makes	HTML	ASCII #	Makes	HTML	ASCII #	Makes	HTML
0–8	Unused		46	.	.	63	?	?
9	Tab			47	/	/	64	@	@

10	Line Feed	
	48	0	0	65	A	A

11–31	Unused		49	1	1	66	B	B
32	Space	 	50	2	2	67	C	C
33	!	!	51	3	3	68	D	D
34	"	"	52	4	4	69	E	E
35	#	#	53	5	5	70	F	F
36	$	$	54	6	6	71	G	G
37	%	%	55	7	7	72	H	H
38	&	&	56	8	8	73	I	I
39	'	'	57	9	9	74	J	J
40	(	(	58	:	:	75	K	K
41	)	)	59	;	;	76	L	L
43	+	+	60	<	<	77	M	M
44	,	,	61	=	=	78	N	N
45	-	-	62	>	>	79	O	O

ASCII #	Makes	HTML	ASCII #	Makes	HTML	ASCII #	Makes	HTML
80	P	P	109	m	m	163	£	£
81	Q	Q	110	n	n	164	¤	¤
82	R	R	111	o	o	165	¥	¥
83	S	S	112	p	p	166	¦	¦
84	T	T	113	q	q	167	§	§
85	U	U	114	r	r	168	¨	¨
86	V	V	115	s	s	169	©	©
87	W	W	116	t	t	170	ª	ª
88	X	X	117	u	u	171	«	«
89	Y	Y	118	v	v	172	¬	¬
90	Z	Z	119	w	w	173	–	­
91	[	[	120	x	x	174	®	®
92	\	\	121	y	y	175	¯	¯
93	]	]	122	z	z	176	°	°
94	^	^	123	{	{	177	±	±
95	_	_	124	|	|	178	²	²
96	`	`	125	}	}	179	³	³
97	a	a	126	~	~	180	´	´
98	b	b	128	€	€	181	µ	µ
99	c	c	153	™	™	182	¶	¶
100	d	d	154	š	š	183	·	·
101	e	e	155	›	›	184	¸	¸
102	f	f	156	œ	œ	185	¹	¹
103	g	g	157	Unused		186	º	º
104	h	h	158	ž	ž	187	»	»
105	I	i	159	Ÿ	Ÿ	188	¼	¼
106	j	j	160	Unused		189	½	½
107	k	k	161	¡	¡	190	¾	¾
108	l	l	162	¢	¢	191	¿	¿

ASCII #	Makes	HTML	ASCII #	Makes	HTML	ASCII #	Makes	HTML
192	À	À	214	Ö	Ö	236	ì	ì
193	Á	¾	215	2	×	237	í	í
194	Â	Â	216	Ø	Ø	238	î	î
195	Ã	Ã	217	Ù	Ù	239	ï	ï
196	Ä	Ä	218	Ú	Ú	240	∂	ð
197	Å	Å	219	Û	Û	241	ñ	ñ
198	Æ	Æ	220	Ü	Ü	242	ò	ò
199	Ç	Ç	221	Ý	Ý	243	ó	ó
200	È	È	222	Þ	Þ	244	ô	ô
201	É	É	223	ß	ß	245	õ	õ
202	Ê	Ê	224	à	à	246	ö	ö
203	Ë	Ë	225	á	á	247	÷	÷
204	Ì	Ì	226	â	â	248	ø	ø
205	Í	Í	227	ã	ã	249	ù	ù
206	Î	Î	228	ä	ä	250	ú	ú
207	Ï	Ï	229	å	å	251	û	û
208	Ð	Ð	230	æ	æ	252	ü	ü
209	Ñ	Ñ	231	ç	ç	253	ý	ý
210	Ò	Ò	232	è	è	254	þ	þ
211	Ó	Ó	233	é	é	255	ÿ	ÿ
212	Ô	Ô	234	ê	ê			
213	Õ	Õ	235	ë	ë			

Note: 127, and 129–152 are unused.

Supplement: Entering Special Characters

In addition to entering special characters with codes, you can copy them into documents from character map utilities that come with your operating system and you can type them directly into documents.

Windows

On Windows, to type special characters directly into a document, press and hold the Alt key on the keyboard, and then using the number pad, type the ASCII number listed in the chart. The number pad consists of the numbers on the right side of the keyboard, not the numbers above the alphabet keys. If that doesn't work on your system, try pressing and holding the Alt key and adding a 0 (zero) in front of the ASCII number. For example, if you wanted to type a copyright symbol, the ASCII number is 169. You might have to type 0169 instead. After you've typed the number, release the Alt key.

Most Windows machines have a Character Map utility, which offers another method for entering characters. To open the Character Map utility:

1. Click the **Start** button.
2. Point to **Programs**.
3. Point to **Accessories**.
4. Point to **System Tools**.
5. Click **Character Map**.

Once the Character Map utility is open, you can click and hold on a small character to preview a larger example. You can move any character to the **Characters to Copy** field by double-clicking it or by highlighting it and clicking the **Select** button. Once you have selected the characters you want, click the **Copy** button. The selected characters will now be on the Windows clipboard to paste into another program.

Macintosh

On a Macintosh, use the free Key Caps utility. (In Mac OS 9 or Classic mode, select **Key Caps** from the **Apple** menu. In Mac OS X, open the Applications folder, and then open the Utilities folder and double-click the Key Caps icon; if you use it often, drag it to the dock.) A small keyboard displays, showing all the standard characters on a keyboard. Press any modifier key—Option, Control, or Shift—or any combination such as Option+Shift to see the various characters available. For example, if you press the Option key, an entire new set of characters displays. Click on a character to place it in the field at the top of the **Key Caps** dialog box. You can copy and paste characters from this field into any document.

With Key Caps, you can work backward to figure out the keyboard command for a special character. For example, if you press the Option key and see that the R key now displays the registered copyright symbol ®, then you know that Option+R creates ®. This can be kind of a hassle, so most Key Caps users copy and paste special characters.

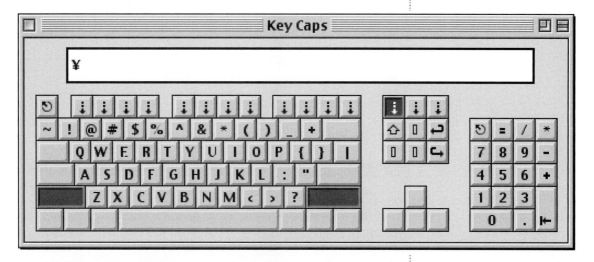

If you use a lot of special characters, you might want to buy a copy of PopChar Pro, a popular utility for locating special characters available for Mac OS 9 and Mac OS X. PopChar Pro displays a tiny icon in the menu bar at all times. Click on the icon to see a font's entire character map, drag to the character you want, and click. Presto—the character is popped into the document. You can download a time-bombed trial version. When the time is up, and you find you can't live without it, order a serial number for $29. Most Macintosh publishing professionals swear by PopChar Pro, which you can find at:

http://www.macility.com/

> **NOTE**
>
> Key Caps actually shows you the characters available in the font selected in its Fonts menu. Fonts do not all have exactly the same special characters available.

Browser-safe (216) Color Chart

B ecause colors displayed on a monitor use the RGB (red, green, blue) color model and colors that are printed on paper use the CMYK (cyan, magenta, yellow, and black—the four process ink colors) color model, the colors shown here may not appear the same as you will see them on your monitor. Some RGB colors cannot be recreated in the CMYK color model so the closest color that *can* be created is substituted.

#000000	#000033	#000066	#000099	#0000CC	#0000FF
#003300	#003333	#003366	#003399	#0033CC	#0033FF
#006600	#006633	#006666	#006699	#0066CC	#0066FF
#009900	#009933	#009966	#009999	#0099CC	#0099FF
#00CC00	#00CC33	#00CC66	#00CC99	#00CCCC	#00CCFF
#00FF00	#00FF33	#00FF66	#00FF99	#00FFCC	#00FFFF

#330000	#330033	#330066	#330099	#3300CC	#3300FF
#333300	#333333	#333366	#333399	#3333CC	#3333FF
#336600	#336633	#336666	#336699	#3366CC	#3366FF
#339900	#339933	#339966	#339999	#3399CC	#3399FF
#33CC00	#33CC33	#33CC66	#33CC99	#33CCCC	#33CCFF
#33FF00	#33FF33	#33FF66	#33FF99	#33FFCC	#33FFFF

#660000	#660033	#660066	#660099	#6600CC	#6600FF
#663300	#663333	#663366	#663399	#6633CC	#6633FF
#666600	#666633	#666666	#666699	#6666CC	#6666FF
#669900	#669933	#669966	#669999	#6699CC	#6699FF
#66CC00	#66CC33	#66CC66	#66CC99	#66CCCC	#66CCFF
#66FF00	#66FF33	#66FF66	#66FF99	#66FFCC	#66FFFF

411

#990000	#990033	#990066	#990099	#9900CC	#9900FF
#993300	#993333	#993366	#993399	#9933CC	#9933FF
#996600	#996633	#996666	#996699	#9966CC	#9966FF
#999900	#999933	#999966	#999999	#9999CC	#9999FF
#99CC00	#99CC33	#99CC66	#99CC99	#99CCCC	#99CCFF
#99FF00	#99FF33	#99FF66	#99FF99	#99FFCC	#99FFFF

#CC0000	#CC0033	#CC0066	#CC0099	#CC00CC	#CC00FF
#CC3300	#CC3333	#CC3366	#CC3399	#CC33CC	#CC33FF
#CC6600	#CC6633	#CC6666	#CC6699	#CC66CC	#CC66FF
#CC9900	#CC9933	#CC9966	#CC9999	#CC99CC	#CC99FF
#CCCC00	#CCCC33	#CCCC66	#CCCC99	#CCCCCC	#CCCCFF
#CCFF00	#CCFF33	#CCFF66	#CCFF99	#CCFFCC	#CCFFFF

#FF0000	#FF0033	#FF0066	#FF0099	#FF00CC	#FF00FF
#FF3300	#FF3333	#FF3366	#FF3399	#FF33CC	#FF33FF
#FF6600	#FF6633	#FF6666	#FF6699	#FF66CC	#FF66FF
#FF9900	#FF9933	#FF9966	#FF9999	#FF99CC	#FF99FF
#FFCC00	#FFCC33	#FFCC66	#FFCC99	#FFCCCC	#FFCCFF
#FFFF00	#FFFF33	#FFFF66	#FFFF99	#FFFFCC	#FFFFFF

As you can see, the browser-safe colors are any combination of 00, 33, 66, 99, CC, and FF. Here are the grayscale colors again, grouped together for your convenience this time.

#000000	#333333	#666666	#999999	#CCCCCC	#FFFFFF

413

Named Colors Chart

Y ou can use the following named colors in place of hexadecimal color codes. Note that the colors here approximate the colors you will see on-screen, but are not exact representations due to print and individual computer aberrations.

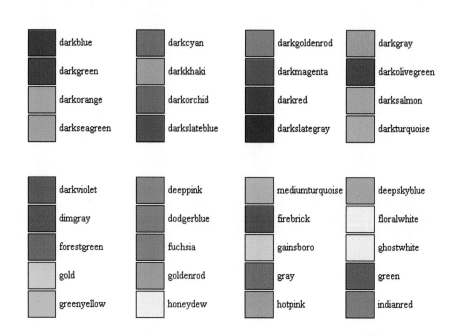

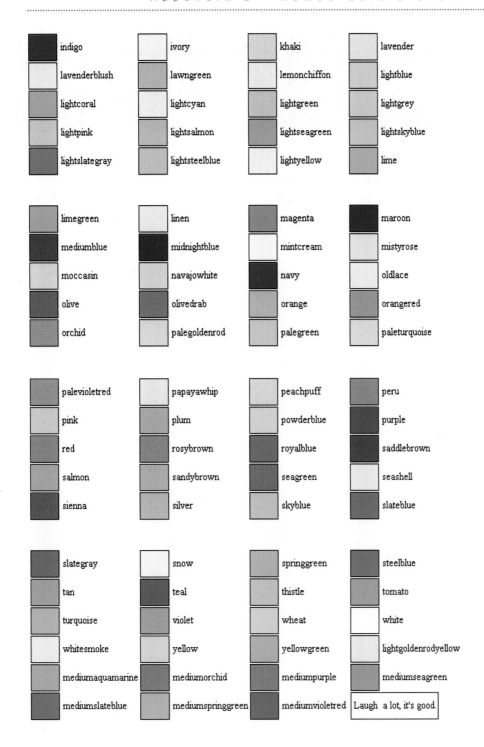

indigo	ivory	khaki	lavender
lavenderblush	lawngreen	lemonchiffon	lightblue
lightcoral	lightcyan	lightgreen	lightgrey
lightpink	lightsalmon	lightseagreen	lightskyblue
lightslategray	lightsteelblue	lightyellow	lime

limegreen	linen	magenta	maroon
mediumblue	midnightblue	mintcream	mistyrose
moccasin	navajowhite	navy	oldlace
olive	olivedrab	orange	orangered
orchid	palegoldenrod	palegreen	paleturquoise

palevioletred	papayawhip	peachpuff	peru
pink	plum	powderblue	purple
red	rosybrown	royalblue	saddlebrown
salmon	sandybrown	seagreen	seashell
sienna	silver	skyblue	slateblue

slategray	snow	springgreen	steelblue
tan	teal	thistle	tomato
turquoise	violet	wheat	white
whitesmoke	yellow	yellowgreen	lightgoldenrodyellow
mediumaquamarine	mediumorchid	mediumpurple	mediumseagreen
mediumslateblue	mediumspringgreen	mediumvioletred	Laugh a lot, it's good.

RGB to Hexadecimal Conversion Chart

This chart will help you convert RGB (red, green, blue) numbers into hexadecimal codes. Just look up the RGB number in the left column; the number next to it in the right column is the hexadecimal equivalent. When you convert all three RGB numbers you'll have the 6-digit hexadecimal number.

RGB	Hex	RGB	Hex	RGB	Hex	RGB	Hex	RGB	Hex	RGB	Hex	RGB	Hex	RGB	Hex
0	00	32	20	64	40	96	60	128	80	160	A0	192	C0	224	E0
1	01	33	21	65	41	97	61	129	81	161	A1	193	C1	225	E1
2	02	34	22	66	42	98	62	130	82	162	A2	194	C2	226	E2
3	03	35	23	67	43	99	63	131	83	163	A3	195	C3	227	E3
4	04	36	24	68	44	100	64	132	84	164	A4	196	C4	228	E4
5	05	37	25	69	45	101	65	133	85	165	A5	197	C5	229	E5
6	06	38	26	70	46	102	66	134	86	166	A6	198	C6	230	E6
7	07	39	27	71	47	103	67	135	87	167	A7	199	C7	231	E7
8	08	40	28	72	48	104	68	136	88	168	A8	200	C8	232	E8
9	09	41	29	73	49	105	69	137	89	169	A9	201	C9	233	E9
10	0A	42	2A	74	4A	106	6A	138	8A	170	AA	202	CA	234	EA
11	0B	43	2B	75	4B	107	6B	139	8B	171	AB	203	CB	235	EB
12	0C	44	2C	76	4C	108	6C	140	8C	172	AC	204	CC	236	EC
13	0D	45	2D	77	4D	109	6D	141	8D	173	AD	205	CD	237	ED
14	0E	46	2E	78	4E	110	6E	142	8E	174	AE	206	CE	238	EE
15	0F	47	2F	79	4F	111	6F	143	8F	175	AF	207	CF	239	EF
16	10	48	30	80	50	112	70	144	90	176	B0	208	D0	240	F0
17	11	49	31	81	51	113	71	145	91	177	B1	209	D1	241	F1
18	12	50	32	82	52	114	72	146	92	178	B2	210	D2	242	F2
19	13	51	33	83	53	115	73	147	93	179	B3	211	D3	243	F3
20	14	52	34	84	54	116	74	148	94	180	B4	212	D4	244	F4
21	15	53	35	85	55	117	75	149	95	181	B5	213	D5	245	F5
22	16	54	36	86	56	118	76	150	96	182	B6	214	D6	246	F6
23	17	55	37	87	57	119	77	151	97	183	B7	215	D7	247	F7
24	18	56	38	88	58	120	78	152	98	184	B8	216	D8	248	F8
25	19	57	39	89	59	121	79	153	99	185	B9	217	D9	249	F9
26	1A	58	3A	90	5A	122	7A	154	9A	186	BA	218	DA	250	FA
27	1B	59	3B	91	5B	123	7B	155	9B	187	BB	219	DB	251	FB
28	1C	60	3C	92	5C	124	7C	156	9C	188	BC	220	DC	252	FC
29	1D	61	3D	93	5D	125	7D	157	9D	189	BD	221	DD	253	FD
30	1E	62	3E	94	5E	126	7E	158	9E	190	BE	222	DE	254	FE
31	1F	63	3F	95	5F	127	7F	159	9F	191	BF	223	DF	255	FF

Deprecated and Forbidden HTML Chart

In the following chart, the Closing Forbidden column lists tags for which it is illegal to use a closing tag. These tags have only an opening tag, no closing tag. Deprecated tags are still legal HTML and still have browser support. The World Wide Web Consortium suggests using Cascading Style Sheets instead of deprecated HTML tags, but until they are ruled obsolete, they are still a valid option—although perhaps not the wisest option in the long term.

Opening Tag	Concerns	Deprecated	Closing Forbidden
APPLET	Java applet	✓	
AREA	Image map area		✓
BASE	Document URI		✓
BASEFONT	Base font size	✓	✓
BR	Forced line break		✓
CENTER	Alignment	✓	
COL	Table column		✓
DIR	Directory list	✓	
FONT	Local font change	✓	
FRAME	Subwindow		✓
HR	Horizontal rule		✓
IMG	Embedded image		✓
INPUT	Form control		✓
ISINDEX	Single line prompt	✓	✓
LINK	Media-independent link		✓
MENU	Menu list	✓	
META	Meta-information		✓
PARAM	Named property value		✓
S	Strike-through text	✓	
STRIKE	Strike-through text	✓	

Web Server Error Code Chart

When you click a link, you are sending a data packet to a server somewhere. These data packets can be routed through several different servers and data stream pipelines before they reach the host server.

Sometimes, when you click a link and receive an error message such as the famous "404 - Page Not Found" error, it can be because the data packet you sent was lost or caught in a traffic bottleneck and timed out. Often, reloading the page will retrieve the page you were seeking.

Here are the various server error codes:

Error Code	Error	Explanation
Error 400	Bad Request	The request could not be understood by the server due to incorrect syntax.
Error 401	Unauthorized	The server has determined that you are not authorized to view the page requested. This can be because of coding errors or intentional restrictions.
Error 402	Payment Required	This message means a charging specification has not been met. A suitable ChargeTo header must be implemented before access is granted.
Error 403	Forbidden	The request is for something forbidden, which is not the same as needing authorization. This status code is often used as a catchall error message used when no other response is applicable. It can also indicate that you're trying to access a part of the server that the host has disallowed access to. If this happens on your web site, try CHMOD-ing the file permissions to "read" for all users.

Error Code	Error	Explanation
Error 404	Not Found	The server can't find a match for your request. If this happens on your site, make sure the web address (URL) has proper text case, spelling, punctuation, file extension, and file paths correctly coded. Be sure you are using the forward slash (/) and not the backward slash (\). If this is on someone else's site, try simply reloading the page. Your data packet (link request) may have been lost or it may have timed out due to heavy Internet traffic or a slow server response.
Error 405	Method Not Allowed	The method specified is not allowed for the resource identified by the request.
Error 406	Not Acceptable	The resource identified by the request is incapable of generating a response according to the accept headers sent in the request.
Error 407	Proxy Authentication Required	Similar to the 401 error (Unauthorized), this indicates that the user must first authenticate with the proxy server.
Error 408	Request Timeout	The user did not produce a request within the time limit the server is programmed to wait.
Error 409	Conflict	The request could not be completed due to a conflict. This error is used in situations when it is anticipated the user may be able to resolve the conflict and resubmit the request.
Error 410	Gone	This is a web maintenance message used to notify the webmaster of the site containing the link that the resource is intentionally unavailable. The site owner of the resource attempted wants remote links to that resource removed.
Error 411	Length Required	The server refuses to accept the request without a defined content length.
Error 412	Precondition Failed	The precondition mandated was not met. This allows servers to prevent the requested method from being applied to a resource other than the one intended.

Error Code	Error	Explanation
Error 413	Request Entity Too Large	This is a server refusal to process a request because the request entity is larger than the server will process. The server may close the connection to prevent the client from continuing the request. This also helps prevent unauthorized resource usage.
Error 414	Request-URI Too Long	The server refuses the request because the Request-URI is longer than the server can interpret.
Error 415	Unsupported Media Type	The request is in a format not supported by the server.
Error 500	Internal Server Error	The request could not be processed due to an internal server error. The server encountered an unexpected condition that prevented it from completing the request.
Error 501	Not Implemented	The server doesn't support the function requested. This is the standard response when the server doesn't recognize or understand the request or it isn't capable of supporting the request.
Error 502	Bad Gateway	The server encountered an invalid response from the upstream server it accessed in attempting to fulfill the request. In this case, the server is acting only as a gateway or proxy server.
Error 503	Service Unavailable	The server is currently unable to handle the request due to a temporary overloading or maintenance of the server. This implies it's a temporary condition and service will be restored to normal after a period of time.
Error 504	Gateway Timeout	The server did not receive a timely response from the upstream server it attempted to access to complete the request. In this case, the server is acting only as a gateway or proxy server.
Error 505	HTTP Version Not Supported	The server does not support the HTTP protocol version used in the request. The response may contain a description of why it is not supported and which protocols that server supports.

Troubleshooting Chart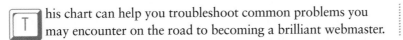

Appendix

T his chart can help you troubleshoot common problems you may encounter on the road to becoming a brilliant webmaster.

Problem	Possible Solutions
Broken images.	Check that the capitalization (uppercase/lowercase pattern) is correct. Image names and the image path to your server are case sensitive.
	Check the file path; many times people have the image coded to a location on their own computer rather than on the server.
	Be sure you uploaded the images in binary mode.
	Check your typing, as misspellings do break your code. Be sure you didn't type something like "igm src" instead of "img src."
	Check that you have referenced the right image extension. Many times people will type .gif or .jpg as the extension when the image is actually saved as the other type.
	Check that you're using a universally supported image type, which is either JPG or GIF.
Unexpected layout.	Check your code. Unexpected results are often caused by a simple code error such as leaving out one end of the quotation marks (") in an HTML tag.
Page doesn't display or only displays to a certain point and is then blank.	Check for any unclosed tables. Internet Explorer forgives you for forgetting to close table tags, but Netscape does not. Any open table in a page viewed with Netscape will cause the content not to display from the beginning of the open table on. If your page is a framed page, make sure you closed the framesets.
Code is showing up on the page.	If it's a left arrow bracket (<) or right arrow bracket (>), chances are you typed in two brackets at the beginning

Problem	Possible Solutions
	or end of a tag. For example, <<font...> would cause one < to show up on the page.
	If the whole page is showing up as code, make sure you saved the page as .html and that your program didn't add a .txt extension on the end.
	Check that you started the page with the <html> declaration and ended it with the </html> tag.
There's an extra table cell off to the side of my table.	Somewhere in your code you have an extra and unnecessary table cell or you have spanned too many columns with one or more cells.
My brakes squeak.	This is a built in warning device. When you hear that, your brake linings probably need replaced.
There's a blue "tick" after one of my links.	You either have a space at the end of the linked text or image (before the </a> tag) or you have a hard return in the link.
I made changes on my website but they're not showing up.	Your browser or ISP may be caching the page. Click the reload or refresh button on your browser. It's sometimes necessary to reload a page three or four times to get the new page. If this fails, try emptying your browser history folder and retrying. If that fails, check with your ISP to see if they are serving cached pages instead of fresh pages.
My pages are loading in the wrong frame.	Check your target tags and frame names. They must correspond exactly, and each link should include a target.
A table is sandwiched between paragraphs of text instead of the text wrapping around the table.	Include an align="left" or align="right" attribute and value to the <table> tag. It works like an image align attribute and value. To clear the wrapping, use a <br clear="right"> (or "left" or "all") tag where you want the text to stop wrapping. To move into the future, use Cascading Style Sheet coding to align tables.
The links to my favorite sites aren't working.	Check that you have used the full web address of the site rather than a relative path, which would point to your own web site.

Problem	Possible Solutions
	Check that the site is up and running—sites often go down for a few minutes or an information packet can become lost or time out. Try reloading the page.
	Check your syntax and that you've included the quotation marks around the addresses.
My link points to the wrong site!	You've probably forgotten to close a previous link on the page. Check to be sure the </a> tag is included after each link.
All my text looks like a link.	You've forgotten to close a link. Look at the point in the code where the link begins to find the place to cancel the link tag.
All my text after a list remains indented.	You've left a list tag open.
I used a lot of CSS on my page and it looks great in Internet Explorer, but crummy in Netscape.	Older versions of Netscape did not support CSS well, be sure you're using a modern version. For Netscape 4, if you're still using a version that old, you need to go into the browser preferences and check the boxes for CSS and for JavaScript in order for styles to work at all.
People are complaining that my site is too slow.	Well they've certainly got a lot of nerve! Check that your images are optimized and are not too large, that your page isn't too long, and that you've included image size tags and proper code.
	If your page is 40K or under including the graphics, then it's definitely not your page. It could be that your server is bogged down or you chose a host with substandard equipment and poor performance.
	Other possibilities include: a lot of Internet traffic at the time they visited, the visitors ISP is suffering from too many users, they have a bad/slow connection.
	If you're lucky, your site could be slow because you have a ton of visitors.
My CGI script isn't working.	Check for the correct path to Perl at the beginning of the script.
	Make sure you uploaded it in ASCII mode.

Problem	Possible Solutions
	Make sure the correct file permissions are set.
My site is down. What should I do?	First, make sure your site is actually down and that it's not something at your end.
	Check other sites to see if you can access them. If not, the trouble is with your computer or your ISP. If you can't access other sites, contact your ISP.
	If you can access other sites, wait 10 or 15 minutes and try your site again. Often, little problems occur that seem to self-correct in a short time. If you still can't access your site, contact your web hosting company.
I linked to graphics on another site and they're not working.	Good! You should never link to graphics on another site. That's stealing bandwidth and is illegal. Why should someone else have to pay for your web site's bandwidth? You were lucky if all they did was disallow the link. They could have taken you to court, reported you to your web host provider (causing you to lose your site), reported you to your ISP (causing you to lose your Internet access), or uploaded another image—a nasty image—in place of the one you linked to and made you look like a pervert or an idiot. Never link to any types of file on someone else's site unless they give you permission to do so.
The first link on my index page is to my Brain Café. I thought it would be my most popular section, but hardly anyone clicks the link to check it out.	It could be that they don't understand what's at the other end of the link. Brain Café? What does it mean? Cutesy names should include a descriptive caption so your visitors understand rather than have to guess at what the content is. There are so many choices of where to go and what to do on the Internet that not many people are willing to play guessing games. Most want to know what to expect before they get there.
Whenever I get into the shower the phone rings.	This is called the law of attraction. You're attracted to the shower just before the phone rings because you're a little ringy-dingy. ☺

The most common cause of page malfunctions is simply typing mistakes. Check and recheck your code, or use an HTML validator to look for errors on pages. If you use a validator, some may require a !DOCTYPE tag at the beginning of your document. This tag tells the browser which version of HTML to validate your page against. The !DOCTYPE tag is only necessary for a validator; I haven't seen one browser that it makes a difference to, but the World Wide Web Consortium recommends them and your instructor may require them as well. I don't use them because, well, I'm a real wild and crazy guy.

You'll find many validators online and some that you can install on your computer. If you want to try the toughest of them all, go to:

http://validator.w3.org/

Don't be discouraged if it finds a ton of errors—it will. I've not seen many pages that pass without several warnings, but most of them only matter to W3C, the organization that writes the standards. Browsers are much more tolerant.

Otherwise, a more user-friendly test, along with a spell checker, link checker, and more is at:

http://www2.imagiware.com/RxHTML/htdocs/single.html

To add a !DOCTYPE declaration at the beginning of your page (before the opening HTML tag), add one of the following choices, depending on which HTML version you want your page graded against:

HTML 2.0

The HTML 2.0 specification does not include tables. If you have included tables in the document, you should use the HTML 3.2 DTD or later. You can use any of the following:

<!DOCTYPE HTML PUBLIC "-//IETF//DTD HTML 2.0//EN">
This refers to the W3C's HTML 2.0 DTD.

<!DOCTYPE HTML PUBLIC "-//IETF//DTD HTML 2.0 Level 2//EN">
Same as above, basically.

<!DOCTYPE HTML PUBLIC "-//IETF//DTD HTML 2.0 Level 1//EN">
This refers to the HTML 2.0 DTD, level 1; no form elements are permitted in an HTML document of this type.

<!DOCTYPE HTML PUBLIC "-//IETF//DTD HTML 2.0 Strict//EN">
This refers to the strict HTML 2.0 DTD, a more structurally rigid version of HTML 2.0.

<!DOCTYPE HTML PUBLIC "-//IETF//DTD HTML 2.0 Strict Level 1//EN">

As above, this refers to a more strict HTML, this time with the same restrictions on forms as the HTML 2.0 Level 1 doctype.

HTML 3.2

Any one of the following is acceptable for HTML 3.2:

```
<!DOCTYPE HTML PUBLIC "-//W3C//DTD HTML 3.2 Draft 19960821//EN">
<!DOCTYPE HTML PUBLIC "-//W3C//DTD HTML 3.2 Draft//EN">
<!DOCTYPE HTML PUBLIC "-//W3C//DTD HTML 3.2 Final//EN">
<!DOCTYPE HTML PUBLIC "-//W3C//DTD HTML 3.2//EN">
```

HTML 4.0

You can use any of the following for HTML 4.0:

```
<!DOCTYPE HTML PUBLIC "-//W3C//DTD HTML 4.0 Transitional//EN"
"http://www.w3.org/TR/REC-html40/loose.dtd">
```

Graded by the transitional 4.0 HTML standards.
If you've built a site using frames, then add:

```
<!DOCTYPE HTML PUBLIC "-//W3C//DTD HTML 4.0 Frameset//EN"
"http://www.w3.org/TR/REC-html40/frameset.dtd">
```

HTML 4.01

The HTML 4.01 Strict DTD includes all elements and attributes that have not been deprecated or do not appear in frameset documents. For documents that use this DTD, use this document type declaration:

```
<!DOCTYPE HTML PUBLIC "-//W3C//DTD HTML 4.01//EN"
"http://www.w3.org/TR/html4/strict.dtd">
```

The HTML 4.01 Transitional DTD includes everything in the strict DTD plus deprecated elements and attributes (most of which concern visual presentation). For documents that use this DTD, use this document type declaration:

```
<!DOCTYPE HTML PUBLIC "-//W3C//DTD HTML 4.01 Transitional//EN"
"http://www.w3.org/TR/html4/loose.dtd">
```

The HTML 4.01 Frameset DTD includes everything in the transitional DTD plus frames. For documents that use this DTD, use this document type declaration:

```
<!DOCTYPE HTML PUBLIC "-//W3C//DTD HTML 4.01 Frameset//EN"
"http://www.w3.org/TR/html4/frameset.dtd">
```

Glossary

This glossary defines common terms you'll encounter while designing web sites. It does not include HTML and CSS terms, which are defined in Appendix A and Appendix B, respectively, as well as throughout the book.

Absolute Address: The full address of a file. The address is the physical location of the file on a computer. See also, *Relative Address*.

Access Provider: An Internet service provider (ISP) that provides local access to the Internet.

Adware: Software that is free to the user, but supported by advertisers.

Anchor: A named point (anchor) on a web page that specifies where a link will go. All links use the anchor tag.

Animated GIF: A series of images shown one after another to simulate animation.

Announcement List: A mailing list that restricts who may send messages to the list of subscribers.

AOL: America Online, a large national ISP.

ASCII: American Standard Code for Information Interchange. The lowest common denominator method for transferring information with almost universal support.

ASP: (1) Active Server Pages: A form of programming available only on servers that run the Windows NT operating system. (2) Application Service Provider: A company that creates business software applications, and then makes the applications available on a subscription basis to other businesses.

Attachment: A file attached to an email message that can be sent to any other email account. Attachments can be any type of file—including text, graphics, fonts, programs, compressed files, etc.

Attribute: Describes an aspect of an HTML tag that is modified with a value.

Autoresponder (or Infobot): A type of email account that automatically responds to requests for information with a prewritten message. See also, *Smart Autoresponder*.

Bandwidth: The amount of data you can send through a connection. Usually measured in kilobits per second (Kbps).

Baud: A measurement of how fast data flows through your modem or router.

Binary File: A file that is not in ASCII text format, such as an image or a program.

Bit: A single binary piece of information, consisting of a 1 or 0 (zero).

Bookmark (or Favorite): A feature included in browsers such as Netscape and Microsoft Internet Explorer that allows you to save addresses of your favorite web sites and quickly access pages of interest.

Browser: See *Web Browser*.

Bulletin Board: An electronic message center that usually serves a specific interest group. You access a bulletin board through the Internet, and then read or post messages to relate to others who frequent the specific board. Bulletin boards are often topical in nature.

Byte: One word of binary information (eight bits long).

Cache: A location on your computer that stores recently visited web pages so they can be accessed faster. When returning to a recently visited web site, you may be viewing a page from your computer's cache rather than fresh content, depending on how you configure your browser.

Cascading Style Sheets: See *CSS*.

CGI: Common Gateway Interface. A scripting language that allows HTML pages to interact with programming applications.

Chat Room: An area on the Internet where people can communicate in real time. As users type their messages, they appear on-screen along with messages from other visitors to the chat room.

Client-side Image Map: An image that is divided into clickable regions; each region can be linked to a different file.

Compression: A technology used to make files smaller so they transmit faster over the Internet and take up less

427

hard drive space. To use a compressed file, you must expand it. Compressed files are often called zipped or stuffed files.

Compuserve: A large national ISP.

CPM: Cost per thousand impressions. A pricing method usually used for pricing banners. (For example, a $5 CPM means that $5 is paid for every 1,000 displays of a banner on a web site.) CPM is also used for mailing lists—one impression usually equals one email address the mailing is sent to.

CSS: Cascading Style Sheets. A web page formatting language that gives greater control and more flexibility in page design than is possible only with HTML, including the ability to use a single file as a central control mechanism over the layout of an entire web site.

Cyberspace: A sweeping term used to refer to anything on the Internet.

Dedicated Server: A computer that runs only one type of server software and is usually configured according to the user's specifications. Dedicated servers are typically used for web sites that have high traffic, and need many resources and much processing power.

Demoware: Programs you can download and use for evaluation. Often, some features are disabled until you actually pay for the program. Demoware is sometimes disparagingly called crippleware.

Digital: Electronic information that uses on/off sequences to convey information.

Discussion List: A moderated or unmoderated mailing list that allows any member to send messages to the other members (subscribers).

DNS: Domain Name Server. A method of indexing the Internet based on site names. DNS is sometimes referred to as domain name system.

DNS Aliasing: The Internet relies on Domain Name Servers (DNS's) to translate domain names into IP addresses. Every web hosting company must have a domain name server.

Domain Name: The name that defines your presence online. A domain name is much like a trademark or a license. It allows people to find a web site by name instead of by number (IP address). Domain names must be unique—only one of each name can exist in the world. Domain names can be 67 characters long, including the ".com" at the end, but not including the "http://www" at the beginning.

Downloading: The process of copying files from the Internet onto a computer or removable media (floppy

disk, zip disk, iPod, etc.) using a variety of methods. See *Web Browser*, *FTP*, and *Telnet*.

DSL: A technology that utilizes unused frequencies on copper telephone lines to transmit data at high speeds.

E-commerce: Short for electronic commerce, it means to conduct business online.

Email: Short for electronic mail, email is a method for sending messages along with attachments such as letters, sales notices, brochures, pictures, and countless other things over the Internet.

Email Alias: Sometimes called a forwarding account, this type of account forwards email sent to the alias account to another account.

Email POP Account: See *POP*.

Encryption: A process of scrambling information so it is unusable to all but the intended users.

FAQ: Frequently Asked Questions. An easy-to-read list of common questions and answers about a web site, individual, company, or specific topic.

Firewall: Software or hardware that creates a protective barrier between an individual user's computer or a company's internal network and the rest of the Internet.

Flame: A fiery (read angry) complaint sent via email. Often generated when sending unsolicited email or posting commercial ads to noncommercial areas of the Internet.

Form: A web page that has input fields for a user to submit information.

Frames: A feature that divides a web page into separate windows, each of which can be scrolled independently. Many search engines cannot index framed sites well.

FreeBSD: An operating system that is a version of UNIX. FreeBSD runs on Intel microprocessors and powers the servers of the web's largest sites.

Freeware: Software that is free.

FrontPage: A Microsoft Office program for web site creation and management that lets users easily manipulate and publish web pages with no knowledge of HTML codes.

FTP: File Transfer Protocol. A means of uploading files to the Internet or downloading files to your computer.

GIF: Graphics Interchange Format. A common image format that allows up to 256 colors. GIF images work best for text, sharp lines, and large areas of continuous color. GIF images support transparency and can be displayed in rapid succession to simulate animation.

Helper Application: An application that is launched to view files that browsers can't parse (such as videos).

Hit: A request from a browser to a server. A web page with 14 images will count 15 hits, one for the main page and 14 for the images (one per image). Hits are often confused with other measurements, such as page views or users.

Host: A company that provides server disk space to other companies and individuals so their web sites are available on the Internet.

HTML (HyperText Markup Language): The simple programming language that allows formatted pages to display on the World Wide Web via a web browser.

Hyperlinks: See *HyperText Links*.

HyperText Links: A method of embedding a URL into an object, such as a segment of text or an image. When this object is clicked, the browser activates the embedded URL to retrieve the linked file.

ICANN: The Internet Corporation for Assigned Names and Numbers. An organization recognized by the U.S. government in November 1999 to administer the Internet's core technical functions and foster competition among domain name registrars.

IDE: Integrated Drive Electronics. A standard connector for connecting computer peripherals.

Internet: The catchall word used to describe the massive worldwide network of computers. The word "Internet" literally means, "network of networks." In itself, the Internet is comprised of thousands of smaller regional networks scattered throughout the globe. There are currently an estimated 580 million Internet users worldwide (Nielsen/Netratings), with a projected 945 million users by 2005 (Computer Industry Almanac).

InterNIC: Internet Network Information Center. InterNIC began as a cooperative effort between the U.S. government and Network Solutions, Inc. They were initially responsible for registering and maintaining the com, net, and org top-level domain names on the World Wide Web.

Internet Service Provider: See *ISP*.

Intranet: A private network of computers in which access from the outside is restricted.

IP Address: Internet Protocol Address. The numerical addresses that relate to a specific domain name, which may identify one or more IP addresses. The format of an IP address is a 32-bit numeric address written as four sets of numbers separated by periods. Each number can be from zero to 255. For example, 204.17.42.69 could be an IP address.

IRC: Internet Relay Chat. A massive network of text-based chat channels (rooms) and their users all across the world.

ISDN: Integrated Digital Services Network. A type of phone line that can handle both analog and digital data and is used for higher speed Internet access. If you have ISDN, you can use the same line for talking on the phone and accessing the Internet simultaneously.

ISP: Internet Service Provider. An Internet service provider that provides local access to the Internet and may provide hosting services as well. Also known as a local dial-up provider or access provider.

Java: A general programming language developed by Sun Microsystems in response to problems encountered with the C++ language. Suited for use on the web, Java is intended to produce simple, cross-platform, high-performance, multi-threaded, dynamic programs.

JavaScript: A movie script about the coffee industry . . . just kidding. A popular client-side, interpreted scripting language used to bring additional functionality and interactivity to web pages.

JPEG: Joint Photographic Experts Group. A common image compression format capable of including more than 16 million unique colors. JPEG images, recognizable by the file name extension .jpg, are best suited for textures, photographs, and gradients.

JSP: Java Server Pages. A scripting language similar to ASP and PHP, JSP allows the use of Java on the server side to produce dynamic web pages.

Kbps: Kilobits per second. The transfer rate of information from one point to the next.

Kilo: 1,000—unless you're referring to computers, when it sometimes refers to 1,024 bytes of binary data.

Mac: An Apple Macintosh computer such as an iMac, an eMac, a G4, a G5, or a PowerBook.

Mbps: Megabits per second. Equal to 1,000 Kbps.

Modem: Modulator/demodulator. A device to convert digital signals to analog for transfer over phone lines.

MRA: Multiple-recipient alias. An email alias account that forwards mail to multiple email addresses.

MSQL: Mini Structured Query Language. A lightweight database engine designed to provide fast access to stored data with low-memory requirements.

Multimedia: Content in the form of images, sound, video, or animation.

Navigation: A system of links used to access web pages and other files on the Internet.

Network: Two or more computers connected so they can communicate with each other.

Netiquette: The art of employing common courtesy while using the Internet, email, newsgroups, and other

429

resources. Although the rules are informal, when you break them, some people get quite upset.

Newbie: A somewhat affectionate term for someone new to the Internet. It generally takes a while to learn Netiquette and find your way around the World Wide Web.

Newsgroup: An individual newsgroup within a Usenet group.

NT: A Windows operating system designed to act as a server in network settings.

Operating System: An operating system (OS) is what runs your computer. Most computer users have most likely heard of Windows, DOS, or Macintosh. These are operating systems that are normally used on private individual computers. A computer that is used as a web server must also have an operating system. The two most common operating systems used on web servers are UNIX and NT.

Opt-in List: Email addresses of people who have agreed to receive email messages, usually ezines or announcement lists.

Ordered List: An indented list of items prefaced with a number or letter.

Pageview: The display of a web page on a browser. Counting the total pageviews offers a good measure of web site popularity.

Password: A secret code that allows a user to access a restricted area.

PC: Personal Computer. A general term for IBM-compatible computers running the Windows operating system.

PDF: Refers to Adobe Acrobat files. These files are cross-platform (Windows and Macintosh) and are useful for routing documents for feedback, electronic publishing, and prepress.

PERL: Popular Extraction and Report Language. Designed for processing text, this popular programming language is also used for creating interactive web sites.

Pixel: An individual dot of color in an image or on a computer screen.

Plug-in: A program that is not part of the original software (in this case, browsers such as Netscape, Internet Explorer, Opera, etc.). For example, Macromedia's Flash/Shockwave, Real Audio, and a number of other companies have plug-ins to make web sites more interactive. Also refers to components added to software programs such as Corel Photopaint and Adobe Photoshop that extend a program's capabilities.

POP: Post Office Protocol. An email account for sending and receiving email. When email is sent to a POP account, the mail is stored on the server until the user logs in with their email software and downloads it. (Same as Email POP and POP account.)

POP Account: See *POP*.

Protocol: Specific rules governing how data is exchanged between two electronic devices.

Public Domain: Works in the public domain are available to the public at no charge because their copyrights, trademarks, or patents have expired or somehow been nullified. This may include information on government sites. This does not include information that is publicly visible on private or commercial web sites. Just because it's there, does not mean you may copy it for your own site or publications without permission from the copyright holder.

RAM: Random Access Memory. The most common type of memory used by computers and other devices. The "random" part means that any byte of memory can be accessed without touching the preceding bytes. RAM is commonly known as the amount of memory that is available to programs.

RealAudio/RealVideo: RealMedia technology that allows you to stream audio and video from your site.

Registrar: A company or organization that registers domain names. Previously, Network Solutions was the only domain name registrar, but competition for registrars opened up in November 1999. Now, dozens of registrars exist globally. ICANN is the new governing body for registrars.

Relative Address: An Internet address defining the path to a file within a domain (rather than using the full Internet address). For example, a link to a page within your own site can use a relative address rather than an absolute address.

Remove List: A file containing the email addresses of those who have asked to be removed from a mailing list.

Resolution: The number of pixels per inch that an image is saved with or that a monitor can display.

Router: On the Internet, a router is a mechanical device or software that determines the network path a data packet should be sent to reach its destination.

SCSI: Small Computer Systems Interface. Used for connecting peripherals to your computer via a standard hardware interface.

Search Engine: A web site providing searchable index of content on the web. Search engines are consistently ranked among the most popular sites on the Internet because they help people find what they are looking for.

Secure Server: A web site that uses encryption technology to protect information being transferred over the Internet.

Servlet: Server Side Java that replaces CGI and allows access to Java functionality from both client-side and server-side web applications.

Servlet Container: A program that plugs into your web server and allows it to serve Servlet and JSP (Java Server Page) technologies. These are small programs that provide similar functionality to Microsoft's Active Server Page.

Shareware: Software that you may download and use at no initial charge. If you like the software and want to keep using it, some form of payment is usually required. Shareware is sometimes referred to as nagware, as it often prompts you to register if you keep using it.

Sig File: Short for Signature File. Contact information and marketing materials in a brief format at the end of an email message. Sig files are the only accepted way to advertise within newsgroup posts.

Sit File: A compressed file usually produced with Aladdin's StuffIt Standard, which is available for both Macintosh and Windows. Most versions of StuffIt Expander, included with StuffIt Standard, can unstuff both .zip and .sit files.

Smart Autoresponder: Smart autoresponders are similar to standard autoresponders, but they can send multiple emails at varying intervals of time, from one hour apart to many days apart.

SMTP: The server address of the account through which you send email.

Spam: The practice of sending massive amounts of email promotions or advertisements (and scams) to people who have not asked for it. Also refers to the messages received as such. Spam email lists are often created by harvesting email addresses from discussion boards, newsgroups, chat rooms, IRC, and web pages. Spam is universally hated by almost everyone except the spammer.

SSL: Secure Sockets Layer. SSL protects transmissions over the World Wide Web from spectators by encrypting the data while it is transmitted. SSL works through a certificate that authenticates the domain. With this certificate, secure transmissions on the server are "certified" and valid. Many web sites use this protocol to obtain confidential user information, such as credit card numbers. Web pages that require an SSL connection start with (**https:**) instead of (**http:**).

Storefront: To sell your products on the web, you must build an electronic storefront where users can browse your products, put desired products into an electronic shopping cart, and check out to pay for the items in the cart.

Streaming: This technology promises quick access to media content without waiting for files to download. Downloading requires files to be sent to the user's computer in their entirety before they can be played. Streaming sends files to the user's computer in such a way that they can begin viewing or listening to the file after an initial buffer is set. Downloaded files remain on the user's computer until deleted by the user; when a streaming file ends, no data is left behind on the user's machine.

Sub-domain: Anything that appears before your master domain in the URL, such as http://www.yourchoice.masterdomain.com.

Surfer: Slang for a person browsing the web.

Surfing: The act of browsing the web.

Table: A formatting method for arranging web page content into orderly rows and columns.

Tag: The term for an HTML command; also known as an element.

TCP/IP: Transmission Control Protocol/Internet Protocol. The set of protocols that allows the web, Telnet, FTP, email, and other services to function between computers using varied networks and operating systems.

Telnet: A program commonly used to remotely control web servers. The Telnet program runs on your computer and connects your computer to a server on the Internet. You can enter commands through Telnet to be executed as if you were entering them directly on the server console. Telnet requires a valid user name and password.

Templates: A web page format designed to accept information from someone by simply typing or pasting content into it. It enables a less-skilled (or non-skilled) web site owner or newsletter operator to post regular updates without having to do any programming and without the danger of messing up the site's code.

Tracking Code: The means by which you keep track of the response generated by marketing messages. Often expressed as a department number, operator code, extension, or specific email box.

Undeliverables: Email addresses that return to you when the person at the other end has closed their account, has a full email box, or provided you with a faulty address.

UCE: Unsolicited Commercial Email. Informally referred to as spam.

Unique User: One user identity. When talking about the number of unique users to a web site over a specific time frame, this counts each user as one visitor, no matter how many times he or she may return. A web site that has the same 1,000 users returning every day will have 30,000 user sessions in a month, but only 1,000 unique users for that month. This statistic is a good measure of site popularity.

Unordered List: An indented list of items prefaced with bullets.

UNIX: A popular multi-user, multi-tasking operating system developed at Bell Labs in the early 1970s. Due to its portability, flexibility, and power, UNIX has become the leading operating system for Internet server workstations.

Uploading: Taking files from your computer or disk and sending them to the Internet. Generally, this is done through FTP or a template provided by your host. You need to upload files to put your site's pages onto the Internet. Many sites also offer online templates or forms to let you simply paste in the information and put it in their pages.

Upstream Provider: A larger, faster Internet provider that gives connectivity to local or smaller ISPs.

URL: Uniform Resource Locator (sometimes referred to as Universal Resource Locator). This is the address at which you can find a specific web site or file.

Usenet: A collection of newsgroups, and the system to index and access them.

User Session: A person visiting a web site over a short period of time. Usually, a user session is considered ended if there is no activity from that user for 30 or so minutes.

USP: Unique Selling Proposition. The reasons a consumer should use your products rather than a competitor's products.

Virtual Server: A web server that shares computer resources among many clients (hosted sites) on a single machine. Virtual web servers provide low-cost web hosting services because instead of requiring a separate computer for each server, dozens of virtual servers can reside on the same computer.

Visitors: The people who come to your web site.

Web Browser: A software program that allows your computer, once connected to the Internet, to retrieve documents from web servers around the world,

translate the HTML code in the documents, and display the information on your screen.

Web Designer: A person who creates web sites. Web designers may use web-authoring software, an HTML editor, or a simple text editor to create the actual pages, or they may design the overall look and let a webmaster do the actual coding. Web designers are usually proficient with web graphics and images.

Web Developer: The person who develops the interface between the front and back end of a web site. Although web developers may be web designers as well, they typically have more database, CGI, and engineering experience.

Webmaster: A very broad term generally meaning anyone who builds web sites. The scope of webmaster duties vary greatly. For a small company, the webmaster may design and build the site, market it, and handle all Internet related activity. For a large company, it could have as little meaning as the person that answers email inquiries.

Webmaster Service Provider: A company in the business of providing webmaster services to clients on a contract basis.

Web Page: Any one particular page that is accessed via the World Wide Web. Web pages comprise a web site, and are distinct from other pages by their URLs (web addresses).

Web Server: A computer on the World Wide Web (connected to the Internet backbone) that stores HTML documents that can be retrieved via a web browser. An Internet backbone is a larger transmission line that carries data gathered from smaller lines, such as a local phone line or cable, that interconnect with it.

Web Site: A location on the World Wide Web. Each web site contains a home page, which is the first document or page that users see when they enter the site. The site might also contain additional documents, files, or web pages, which are sometimes called "child pages."

WWW: See *World Wide Web*.

World Wide Web: Also known as simply the web, this is the graphical, fastest growing part of the Internet. It is sometimes disparagingly referred to as the World Wide Wait because of slow Internet connections, slow servers, or slow web sites.

Zip File: A compressed file format. A zip file may contain one or more files, which are compressed to save space or allow for faster transmission to others. Zip files are generally for Windows operating systems.

Index